TRUE

GENIUS

Reach **Sport**

TRUE
G E N I U S

The games, the goals, the glory. The complete untold story.

BY WAYNE BARTON

Reach Sport

www.reachsport.com

Published in Great Britain and Ireland in 2021 by
Reach Sport, a Reach PLC business,
5 St Paul's Square, Liverpool, L3 9SJ.

www.reachsport.com
@Reach_Sport

Reach Sport is a part of Reach PLC.
One Canada Square, Canary Wharf, London, E15 5AP.

Hardback ISBN: 9781914197000
eBook ISBN: 9781914197017

Photographic acknowledgements:
Reach PLC, PA Images.

Design and production by Reach Sport.
Edited by Chris Brereton and Simon Monk.
Additional production: Nick Moreton.

Printed and bound by CPI Group (UK) Ltd,
Croydon, CR0 4YY.

CONTENTS

Acknowledgements

It just so happened that I started to write these acknowledgements on November 25, 2020. Fifteen years to the day after George passed away. George's death was the first real emotional footballing experience I shared with my new girlfriend of the time. She later became my wife. On November 25, 2015, my father-in-law passed away. It is a day of some significance to me. A day of reflection and a day of nostalgia. The truth is, it's just an excuse to indulge in that feeling which is present all year round. It does, however, place a certain poignance and perspective when considering both the gratitude I have for the people who assisted me with writing this book and also the emotional way they often spoke about George.

The very first interviews I did were with Brian Greenhoff and Harry Gregg, both of whom have since passed too. I only wish I could thank them again for their time and assistance. When I decided I would go ahead with writing the book, my first thought was to track down as many of his youth-team colleagues as possible. I am so grateful for how many of them were keen to just speak about the footballer they all adored.

John Fitzpatrick, Eddie Harrop, Jimmy Rimmer, Alan Wardle, Willie Anderson and Jimmy Ryan were all so helpful and so enthusiastic. Then there were those who played with him at a more senior level. David Gaskell, Pat Crerand, Alex Stepney, Carlo Sartori, Willie Morgan, Nick Murphy, Sammy

McIlroy, Ian Storey-Moore, Lou Macari, Rodney Marsh, Tony Gale, and Ray Hudson.

Those who managed him – Wilf McGuinness and Tommy Docherty. Those who nearly did – Gordon Jago, Ron Atkinson and Clive Toye. Those who played against him, and were often victims of his – Graham Williams, Mike England, Alan Hudson, Ron Harris and Antonio Simões. They all helped to paint a picture of George with their wonderful recollections.

I have to thank the following people for their assistance in the above interviews: Billy Anderson, Paul Murphy, Stephen Murphy, Fabio da Silva, John Stepney, David Rimmer, Claire Harris, Ricardo Maia, Danny Woodvine, Jonathan McEvoy, Paul Banks, Chris Barnett and Geoff Snape. A huge thank you to Martin Edwards and John Roberts, and a special thank you is also owed to Marcela Mora y Araujo.

I'm grateful to Gordon Hill and Paul Parker, who shared their own stories. Paul, for instance, remembered staying at the Midland Hotel soon after signing for Manchester United. George was a regular patron and was very polite and welcoming to the new player. It just goes to show that everyone had a story about him, from the beginning to the end of his career.

In the time that passed from the moment I started writing these acknowledgements to the publication of the book, two of the above men passed away – John Fitzpatrick and Tommy Docherty. John had asked me to send him a copy of the book when it was done because he wanted to read a pure celebration of George told through the tributes of other colleagues. He was so proud to speak about George that some of his comments to me were used in his funeral service; recognition of the bond they shared. To say that was an honour and an emotional experience for me is an understatement to say the least.

It was also a tremendous privilege to know Tommy Docherty. I worked with Tommy over the last eight years of his life and I grew tremendously fond of him. When I discovered the truth about George's exit, my first port of call was to contact Tommy's family, as I knew he wasn't well, and discuss how he might respond, considering the truth of George's exit had never been revealed. I initiated that cautiously, thinking I should give him the right of reply, but also with the knowledge that we'd had these very conversations, and Tommy said his version of events quite clearly. There was little point in creating conflict. Indeed, I've spent so much time trying to ensure Tommy's spell as manager is perceived more generously. I still believe it should be. It was a complicated time.

I have been dependent on the assistance of a great number of people. I can't thank George's family enough for getting behind the book – but I will try. Barbara and Norman, it has meant a tremendous amount that you supported my quest to do as George wished in wanting to be remembered for his football. I know it is a cause you believe passionately in and I hope this book is a true representation of that. Ian, I am so grateful for your support, and for giving me the encouragement to continue in the knowledge I was being faithful to the memory of your brother. Calum, I am appreciative – beyond how these mere words convey – that you were enthusiastic about my desire to portray your father in a positive light.

To Chris Dangerfield and Lindy. Thank you for taking the time to be so open and honest with me for this book. To Paul Collier and Phil Hughes – I'm so appreciative of your support for this work, and I hope it reflects the George you knew.

To the team at Reach Sport. Paul Dove, your support in this project has been very much appreciated. Claire Brown, you're a diamond, and I appreciate everything you do. Chris Brereton – every writer needs an editor. I'm thankful that you were mine for this book. Thanks also to Simon Monk for all your hard work in editing and honing the finished product and Lee Ashun for the artistic endeavours.

Thanks to Barney Chilton, Eifion Evans, Ben McManus, Ben Greenwood, Mark Foster, Bob Bolton, Barry Shmeizer, Luke Smalley, Des McKibbin, Steven Slack, K Stand Kev, Anthony Hetherington, Matthew Smallwood, Alan Monger, Ben Thornley, Bjarte Valen, Deiniol Graham, Jimmy Williams, Kevin Pilkington, Matthew Galea, Nipun Chopra, Stel Stylianou, Roy Cavanagh, Tony Park, Steve Hobin, Stan Chow, Matt Beadle, Ben Price (and your own little George), Sean Smyth, Andrew Keighley, Chris Culkin, Ben Allen, Richard Cann, Colin Blackadder, Danny Bradley, Phil Marsh, Steve Whittle, Matthew Battle, Jon Wilson, Les Richardson and Mark Foster. Thank you for all of your help, support, assistance and enthusiasm. For some of you I know George was your hero. I hope this book reflects the man you idolised.

To Paddy Barclay – I am forever indebted to you for your support, mentorship and friendship. To be able to call on you is a true privilege, and one I'm fully conscious of. Likewise Rob Smyth, Simon Mullock, Ian Herbert, Danny Taylor and James Robson, whose professional eyes, guidance, kindness and generosity have been so gratefully received.

Thanks to all at BT Sport for helping to bring this version of George's story to life in a different way. To Tom Boswell, a good friend and great director; thanks to Mark Sharman, Theo Lee Ray, Jake Löfdahl, Jenny Chiapponi, and Sally Brown.

Thanks to Dan Burdett, who gave me the belief that I could and should write this book. Thanks also to Kim and

Alex Burdett. Thanks to Steve and Gem – Steve, your lifts were crucial for some of those interviews! Thanks to Helen Yates-Shute (Mozza). Big thanks to Oyvind Enger. Thanks to Tony Bil. To Charlie Baker and family. Thanks to Hayley, Elfyn and Gruff Roberts. Thanks so much Mike Pieri – a real friend and comrade.

Dave Murphy, saying thank you barely seems to cover it. Your friendship, your guidance, your generosity, your common sense in my moments of struggle. I am so grateful to you, and also to Caroline and the kids for keeping you sane so that you can do the same for me!

Finally my family. Steven Marrable, your support means a great deal. The same goes for Lisa, the best mother-in-law, and all my in-laws. A big thanks to Glen Barton. To my mum, whose eternal support is something I'm grateful to carry with me. My nephews. Freddy, who, during the writing of this book, learned how to drop the shoulder and scored a goal where he ran past the entire opposition. And Noah, who has learned to kick the ball powerfully with both feet. May you always find football as enjoyable as you make it for us watching you.

And my beautiful wife – your support and belief are always the most crucial elements in giving me the confidence to write, but more than ever on this book. Again, it is fitting that I write this one week after our tenth wedding anniversary – on our first, 'paper', you reignited my lifelong ambition to write. Now look what you've done! Your encouragement to always find a solution and contentment to allow me to work any hour of the day has been the most important factor in making this book what it is. I love you – and I'm so thankful and grateful for your presence in my life.

Wayne Barton, 2021

OUR GEORGE

O ur George was a funny, kind, shy and intelligent boy. Then he belonged to the world, and he came to be perceived as something quite different. Sometimes the perception was quite different to the truth.

The reason for that: he was extraordinarily gifted as a footballer. That gift took him to Manchester United. On the biggest platform in world football he did things that were unexpected. It propelled him to stardom, and a level of which that took him – and all of us – some time to get used to. If we ever did.

It was surreal to watch as he became the most famous person in the country. To see these moments of brilliance unfold before your eyes, to know that is your brother, and to know life will never be the same again. It was sometimes difficult to reconcile the idea that our brother was the best player in the world with the fact that he was just George. He was just the same whenever we saw him, always ready to help where he could. He had the biggest heart.

It is no secret George had his troubles. It was played out

in the newspapers and has been recounted like a soap opera. That was not the life he wished for. He simply wished that the public, the supporters, would remember him for his football.

Since he passed away, we have been dedicated to fulfilling his wish. We are delighted that this book has been written with the focus concentrated on just that. George's great footballing love was Manchester United. Those were the best days of his life. His magic ability with a football earned adulation and adoration from the support – a feeling we know was returned.

He was always someone who would take and accept responsibility at times when things did not go right. Some 15 years after he has passed, it is reassuring and heartwarming – with a tinge of bittersweet melancholy – to finally have it irrefutably put on record that George was not responsible for his departure from Old Trafford. In his perfect world, he would have remained there for all of his career. Of course, he didn't.

His time after United has often been dismissed as an anti-climax. We are happy that Wayne has taken the time to shine a different perspective on this period; to show that wherever George went, he left some very fond memories, both as a player and as a person.

Once he belonged to the world he became all things to all people. That is what happens with such a level of fame. The memories of watching him play football and score great goals became like a movie or a song; the soundtracks to transport you back to a period of your own life. What a gift to give to the world. And, when his football career was over, he was still the same George to us.

It is so wonderful to hear and read stories from George's peers throughout his career. To read about how his imaginative formative years developed into planned moments of excellence, and how, despite the issues he sometimes had with the game, he never fell out of love with it. To hear new stories and old ones recounted through the view of those he played with and against. But more than that, it is wonderful to know that wherever George went in football, whichever dressing room he spent his time in, they all spoke of the person we knew him to be. Funny. Shy. Generous. Intelligent. Our George.

The Best family, 2021

A BELFAST BOY

The journey towards realising your potential depends on so many individual elements coming together. Some of these elements include ambition, education, experience, intelligence, opportunity, luck, circumstance. Personality. Humility and respect. A willingness to work hard, a capability to recover from a setback or adversity, a certain bravery.

Each of these factors play an integral part of the process and most of them are the responsibility of the individual. Some – such as opportunity, luck, circumstance, education – are influenced just as heavily by external factors. Perhaps the strongest of all begins with opportunity and circumstance.

What was Vincent van Gogh without a paintbrush?

Lennon without a guitar?

Scorsese without a camera?

Most young boys who become footballers – and this is certainly true of George Best, the subject of this book – are given a football to play with before they are even consciously aware of their desire to play with it. Environment plays a part. The Cregagh estate in the southeastern area of Belfast is not (and was not, in the 1950s) an affluent region in which potential can obviously be identified and placed in an environment where it is given the opportunity to flourish. Indeed, it can quite easily be missed, and very nearly was, in the case of George Best.

So it is somewhat ironic that as a bright young boy, he was the only child in his class to pass his eleven-plus exam and be granted entry into Grosvenor High Protestant School. It was difficult for George to settle, as he had to catch two buses to this new school, and their official sport was rugby.

In less than two months, he said his dislike for the school became "pathological" and he would play truant so he could play football in the afternoon. When he was finally caught, he was given an option – he could go into a lower form or leave the school and join a secondary school closer to home. George took the first option initially but by lunchtime on the first day, had decided against it, feeling that the other boys still "regarded themselves as superior beings".

Lisnasharragh Secondary School was approximately a mile away from the doorstep of the Best family home on Burren Way. The first question George remembered being asked there was: "Can you play football?"

On a bright Wednesday in late May, 1946, George Best was born to Dickie and Ann Best. They had been married for two months when Ann – a former hockey player of national distinction – discovered she was pregnant. Dickie worked at an iron turner's lathe, but was also an amateur footballer for the first 10 years of George's life. Sport was in the blood, even if sporting privilege was not quite.

Dickie's father, James, treated his grandson to his first ever football match when he took him to see Glentoran play at the Oval. George was hooked, and began a scrapbook with local newspaper reports of Glentoran's games. When he was seven, he was captivated by English champions Wolverhampton Wanderers on the black and white television of his neighbour – and when the commentators referenced the gold shirts Wolves were wearing, George dreamed of how such a shirt might look in his own hands. Wolves were playing against Honved of Hungary in an exhibition game broadcast on the BBC before the European Cup even existed.

Given the opportunity at his new secondary school with all of his close friends, George enjoyed playing for the school team, though they did not play organised games in any meaningful competitive fashion. Then, the local youth club - Cregagh Boys' Club – added football to their activity list and George and his friends were the first to sign up. The youth club team was being run by a man by the name of Hugh 'Bud' McFarlane, who was reserve team trainer for Glentoran, and the pitch was right at the end of the street where Best lived.

McFarlane immediately saw George had potential and took a special interest. George turned up to an early game with a boot on his left foot and a plimsoll on his right, because McFarlane had advised him to practise his weaker left side in the prior week. George avoided using his right foot in the match, and scored 12 goals in a resounding win.

In subsequent weeks the boy was so enthusiastic that he would play two full matches in the same morning if the club had a different game with another age group. His coach was impressed enough to start writing to Irish League clubs and notify them of this prodigious talent. He had initially tried to convince his own team, George's boyhood club, to take a chance, but Glentoran felt he was too small. Time and again scouts would turn up and feel this tiny adolescent would be too vulnerable, even in the rigours of the part-time leagues, and they projected that even when he had fully developed into all that he could be, it would still not be enough.

There was one local man who had a more discerning eye, capable of seeing beyond the physical limitations of a child to give an almost unfailingly accurate judgement of their potential. Yet even he required some convincing. Bob Bishop was almost the opposite picture of the traditional football scout who would trawl touchlines in a hat and big coat, distinguishable by his very attempt to appear incognito.

In fact, Bishop, in his sportswear, could well have passed for a coach himself, and often did, as he spent much of his time training youngsters at Boyland Youth Club, which had a reputation as the country's premier facility from which English clubs would pluck the prime talent. Bishop and McFarlane knew each other well, and so the former was suitably convinced to take George on one of his training camps at a cottage called The Manse in the seaside village of Helen's Bay, County Down.

Bishop concurred that the player had talent but was erring; inclined to agree with the verdict of those other scouts. "He was 5ft 3in and 7st 7lb when he was well soaked," Bishop once said. "In fact, he was no Goliath. I said to myself, 'I'll get the sack if I send this fellow over'. But, anyway, when I had seen him on the field he was bursting with ability."

Bishop's concerns were seemingly vindicated when George narrowly missed the cut for selection for the Northern Ireland schoolboys' team, despite George feeling he had impressed in the trial match. Good – but not quite good enough. And more fuel to the flames of internal insecurity for the boy who was well aware of the reservations held about him.

Even the stars needed some intervention to align. McFarlane, sensing that the opportunity was drifting away with George only a couple of weeks away from turning 15, proposed they create a scenario in which the boy could prove himself. It was to be George, in his under-16 team, against Bishop's Boyland under-18s. It would be a testing ground to see how the boy – underdeveloped for his age – would deal with older lads, some of whom were now built like men. He was a revelation, scoring two of his team's four goals in a comprehensive win. More impressive than that was the way he dealt with the physical attention of those older boys.

Bishop now was not just convinced, he was bowled over and converted to McFarlane's way of thinking. His primary allegiance as a scout was to Manchester United – he had been hired as the head scout in Northern Ireland in 1960, on the basis that he shared an insatiable and perhaps even consuming love for football in the same way that Jimmy Murphy and Joe Armstrong, those legendary talent spotters at Old Trafford, did. Murphy and Armstrong left little to chance in their recruitment of a player and they knew Bishop was just as meticulous.

It was at this moment in the spring of 1961 that Bishop contacted Armstrong with a telegram that included the famous message: "I think I have found you a genius."

Still, for all his nous, Bishop could be as thankful to McFarlane as Matt Busby was to him. Bishop arranged for George to go on a two-week trial at Old Trafford in June 1961, with a Boyland's defender, Eric McMordie, who had been very impressed with Best in that friendly game. "George became one of the first to go to United who didn't play for Boyland," McMordie told the *Belfast Telegraph* in 2019. "Bob's eye for talent was unequalled – he was a very special man. But a match between us and Cregagh Boys, who George played for, was set up.

"I've never seen a player with so many bruises on his body as George. He was picked on not just because he was wee but because he was so talented. But he fought back and that's what made George the great player he was."

George came home from school one day early in the following week, still sore with the bruises from the weekend's game, to find Bishop in his living room, talking to his parents.

"How would you like to join Manchester United?" Bishop asked him.

"I'm going to play for Manchester United!" the youngster screamed to his disbelieving friends who were already playing football on the green at the end of the road. But the excitement quickly gave way to anxiety. There were a few weeks before George was due to travel to Manchester.

First of all, there was victory in the Castlereagh under-15 league and cup competitions for Cregagh Boys' Club, and team captain George Best could be seen beaming with a smile on the page of the same *Belfast Telegraph* he had previously cut up for a scrapbook. Now, being passed silverware from Jimmy Murdough, the captain of Glentoran, George could start a book of his own personal memories. Then, there was his 15th birthday on May 22, and four weeks later, another clipping for him from the local newspaper that told all the area that he would be going to Manchester for a trial.

Reality dawned for this quiet, introverted boy who was being sent on a boat from Belfast to Manchester, dressed by his mother in his first pair of long trousers. Nothing nor nobody was familiar – not even Eric McMordie, the boy who George knew nothing of other than he'd probably been one of the many Boyland lads to leave a mark on his frail body. This diminutive boy was heading to the foreign land of Manchester where he seemed more likely to fit in on the canvas of a LS Lowry painting than the pitch of Old Trafford.

He was unsettled by arriving in Liverpool with nobody to greet them; by asking the taxi driver who picked them up in Manchester to take them to Old Trafford and then being embarrassed when the driver replied, "Which one?"; by consequently arriving late for training when they first went to the cricket ground and feeling he'd upset Joe Armstrong, who was at the football ground waiting; by being too embarrassed to speak up to tell Armstrong he'd already had breakfast, and therefore eating another when the plate carrying a full English was put in front of him; and finally, by seeing the supposed Manchester United junior players who exacerbated his own insecurities about his physical size ("We looked like a pair of raggle-taggle scrubbers," Best recalled).

After they had spent most of the afternoon kicking a ball to each other, John Aston, coach of the youth team, took the boys to their digs – a council house in Chorlton, where a lady by the name of Mrs Fullaway would house out-of-town boys who came to stay for differing periods of time while they were playing for Manchester United.

From there, Mrs Fullaway's teenage son Steve offered to take the pair out for a walk alongside the canal, where George and Eric were fearful of speaking because they felt their Belfast accent might be too strong for their new Manchester friend to understand. The unfamiliarity of eating a home-cooked meal in front of a lady who wasn't their mother and boys they had only just met was enough to round off a day to forget for George Best and Eric McMordie. Both overwhelmed, they

talked each other into the only common ground they knew –
returning to Belfast at the earliest convenience.

George was so anxious he cajoled Eric into telling Joe
Armstrong the following morning that they were homesick
and wanted to go home immediately. Armstrong had an ace up
his sleeve in the shape of two players, Harry Gregg and Jimmy
Nicholson. Gregg needed little introduction. The world's
costliest goalkeeper, the man named best goalkeeper at the
World Cup in 1958, and the indomitable hero of the Munich
Air Disaster earlier that year when he had walked back into
the wreckage of a burning plane to rescue survivors and pull as
many bodies to safety as possible. Nicholson, meanwhile, was
the perfect example for these boys – in the United first team at
17 and in the Northern Ireland side soon after.

It was not enough. Instead of being inspired, George was
intimidated by the colossal frame of Gregg, and that evening
the two young boys were on their way back to Belfast.

The Ulster Prince docked at dawn and now George was back
in his home comforts, catching the bus back to the Cregagh
estate. He dwelled upon the inevitable confrontation with his
dad, who would be up early as usual. The truth was, Dickie and
Ann had been reluctant for George to leave and the previous
evening Ann had cried herself to sleep in her husband's arms.

Once home, George could tell his father was upset. He
tried to talk himself into the prospect of a career in printing,
which would hopefully compensate for some of Dickie's disappointment, as he had lined George up with a job just in case.

After breakfast, Dickie left the house and walked to the
telephone box at the end of the street to make a reverse charges
phone call to United so he could speak to Joe Armstrong and
get the story. Joe – a wily old hand who was well-versed in

homesickness of teens who weren't local – joked that boys still normally stayed longer than a day before going, but stressed that George would be welcome back if he wanted to come of his own volition.

Considering Best had not kicked a ball in Manchester with anyone other than McMordie, and considering neither Matt Busby nor Jimmy Murphy had laid eyes on him, this was a representation of the tremendous trust United – as a system – had for their scouting network.

Dickie knew he had some power, but had to figure out the optimum way to deploy it. He allowed George to wallow in his worst fears, and gave his son the opportunity to raise the subject, as he knew a phone call had been made. When he did, Dickie told George that the club were disappointed and didn't want him back.

In that single moment of having his dream taken away from him, the father could see the hurt in his son's eyes. That mixture of regret and also a momentary feeling of self-pity, the affirmation that the youngster had been right to harbour these deep-rooted insecurities. He felt too small. He was too small. And, worse still, there was confirmation that even his talent, the one thing he had that could compensate, in fact did not.

After giving him a few moments to dwell, Dickie revealed the truth. Again, though, a half-truth. United would be willing to see him again, but he would have to wait until Christmas. This time the father laid it on a little thick – Matt Busby had heard great things and was sure he would become a great footballer. George was elated and said he didn't want to wait – he wanted to go straight back. Soon after, the 15-year-old was getting his sea legs back on board the Ulster Prince.

ON THE SHOULDERS OF GIANTS

T he date of March 26, 1958 might seem an odd place to start when chronicling George Best's journey at Manchester United. But the FA Cup semi-final replay between United and Fulham has a certain significance that has hitherto gone unrecognised.

United won 5-3 on the day. They qualified for the FA Cup final. United have won many FA Cup semi-finals and they would be favourites to beat Fulham but in 1958, it was not as clear cut as it might have been in any other year due mainly, of course, to the devastating impact of the Munich Air Disaster.

It was indeed just a matter of weeks after the tragedy which cost 23 people – eight of whom were Manchester United players – their lives, and two further players their careers. I will assume some familiarity on part of the reader with the events surrounding the disaster – but as a summary to bring us up to speed, United manager Sir Matt Busby was convalescing, and his assistant Jimmy Murphy was controlling first-team affairs. And a grand job he was doing. Despite losing so many players, Murphy had embarked on a fateful journey for both himself and the club by deciding he would remain as true as he could to the philosophy he and Busby both shared and worked upon for the many years preceding Munich. That meant minimal supplementation from players outside the club.

A couple of experienced professionals had come in – they were needed. But Murphy went to the youth team, to lads he knew, and hoped that raw emotion would compensate for the education they were missing by skipping valuable reserve games and moving straight to the senior side.

One of those players was Alex Dawson. Dawson, a striker, scored a hat-trick in that 5-3 win. That was his job and he did it expertly. He was a player of immense promise. His three goals in three first-team appearances in the closing weeks of the previous season had shown that. He was also a player who needed some time to adapt to the rigours of the professional game, as was reflected in the fact he had made just one single appearance in the 1957/58 campaign prior to the disaster. He scored in the first game after it, against Sheffield Wednesday. In all, he scored 10 goals in 17 games after the crash, a very respectable return, with the highlight coming at Arsenal's former ground Highbury in that semi-final.

Replace respectable with impressive and you have a description for Dawson's career record. Fifty-four goals in 93 games gives him a tally and a ratio which would be the envy of many. But it's the latter number – 93 games – which gives us cause to stop and consider. Those 93 came over a spell of four-and-a-half years, and, whilst his rate of scoring never diminished to signify a drop in form, he never bettered the feeling of scoring a hat-trick in an FA Cup semi-final. Now there's nothing wrong with that, you might say. And you could well be right – after all, no United player has done it since.

The point is that Dawson – and many other young players at Manchester United at this time – had limitless potential. Their destiny was to score goals in cup finals. To win trophies. Certainly in England. Maybe even Europe too. If they had been able to develop at their natural rate, perhaps they would have done. The emotional and physical pressure of representing the club in those days is unquantifiable but must not be underestimated. You are not awarded medals for appearances, which is a shame, because Dawson – and those young men who stepped into the breach with him – certainly deserved something more. Something tangible. Anything would have been better than the curtailed career that the beautiful – but sometimes, utterly, utterly cruel – game provided them. They gave everything they had, but maybe the cruellest blow of all was that they could never really be themselves.

Munich claimed the careers of more than 10 men. These are just a few. Alex Dawson. Tommy Heron. Bobby Harrop. Mark Pearson. Kenny Morgans. Freddie Goodwin. Young players who coped so wonderfully and admirably in the short term to carry the club through its darkest days, but paid the price with a career much shorter than had been tipped. None of these players were part of United's next great triumph when they won the FA Cup in 1963.

"I don't think you could ever fully judge how good a player could be until they were given that chance in the first team," says former United midfielder Carlo Sartori, who was at the club in the Sixties. "There were some who were great at

youth-team level who struggled against the senior professionals in the Central League. There were some who were
even brilliant at Central League level but for whatever reason
couldn't handle the step up to first-team football. There's an
extra percentage you have to add along the way. There were
some players who just froze, for want of a better word. They
did brilliantly coming in and dealing with the pressure but
they were thrown in too soon, sooner than was intended."

When Busby was well enough to continue his job, the
urgency for United to compete for trophies meant there was a
readjusting of the philosophy. The holistic approach of supple-
menting a home-grown team with a world-class player here
and there had effectively been flipped by the time of the 1963
FA Cup final. Bobby Charlton and Bill Foulkes – Munich
survivors – were in the team, as was David Gaskell (though
Harry Gregg was normally first choice, the reasons for his
absence from the final were disputed). Three players developed
by the club was fairly admirable but other teams had followed
the trend – even Leicester, their opponents on that day, had
more home-grown players in their team than the famous
Manchester United.

Jimmy Murphy had pledged to give Busby one more FA
Youth Cup winning team. He had already provided five
before the disaster. And those were teams that included the
likes of Charlton, so were obviously brimming with talent.
But even within those parameters, some players are just even
more excellent than others. United struck lucky with Duncan
Edwards, a player of such outstanding talent that opposition
teams complained he should no longer play against players
his own age. According to Charlton, Edwards was "the only
player who made me feel inferior". Edwards was a bulldozer.

A tank. A man whose size was not defined or regarded by feet and inches; rather, an aura if you were on his side and a feeling of intimidation if you were not. He could beat you with skill and with strength. He knew he could. He knew he was better than players with ten years' experience on him. He played with that belief. He was one of the few players in football history where the phrase 'generational talent' is in fact a colossal understatement. Not even death could defeat him, because his legend has grown ever since.

It was inconceivable that British football could have another talent as mercurial as Edwards. It went against all conventional logic. It certainly couldn't happen at Manchester United. Too much had changed. It was harder now. Even if a player had the raw talent, there would have to be a concession for the weight of expectation that would be carried on those shoulders as soon as they graduated into the first team. Murphy could build a team to win the Youth Cup but finding another Edwards was another matter.

* * *

It is important to mention the burden. It is important to remember the likes of Alex Dawson just as much as it is to remember Duncan Edwards. These considerations help to create a proper perspective of how remarkable it was that by the time George Best finally arrived in Manchester to give it a proper go at Old Trafford, the staff had created an environment where the weight of expectation carried by those young boys did not include the overwhelming load of the ghosts who invaded every sinew of the club – be it the pitch at Old Trafford, the changing rooms, the training ground or in the orchestra of the terrace. By 1961 – just three years after the ultimate of tragedies – the work done by Busby, Murphy, Aston, Armstrong et al had resulted in an education system for these boys that could have resembled any top-level football club. And, arguably, surpass it. If an individual had the propensity to dwell upon the players who had perished, that was not something encouraged by the staff, who concentrated instead on the relatively straightforward task of preparing for a career in the First Division.

"We never thought about Munich at all," remembers John Fitzpatrick, a full-back from Aberdeen who arrived at United the same summer as George. "It never entered our minds. We were picked because we were good enough to get into the team. There were plenty of guys waiting to get in there if you weren't up to it."

Willie Anderson – a Liverpudlian winger – concurs. "I didn't feel any pressure about Munich or the way the club dealt with it," he says. "It was the greatest dream I ever had. I was in awe of everything around me. I was always the best player around where I lived but I got to United and didn't think I was anywhere near good enough. The pressure was to be as good or better than the others. Twenty or 30 kids all there together, the club provided everything for us to do well. My dad was really strict and when I moved to Manchester there was a freedom, a liberation. It went from, 'Where are you going? Who are you going out with?' to, 'Here's your key, your supper will be on the table, try not to make a noise when you come in.'"

So George Best was far from the only player who had left home to try and make it in Manchester. His homesickness is remarkable in his own story, but it was merely a recurring feature in any out-of-towners. "I don't remember hearing about

George's story until much later after the event... I know that I suffered from homesickness too," recalls Stirling-born Jim Ryan. "I was in digs with Willie Anderson, and we often spoke about feeling homesick – and he was only from Liverpool! The club tried to help where they could, where it was practical, for example, getting the Christmas off."

It was natural that the boys from outside of Manchester gravitated towards each other socially because they were placed in digs with each other.

Ryan and Anderson were a stone's throw from Old Trafford, while George was housed at Mrs Fullaway's, first with one of the youth-team goalkeepers, and then when he was let go, a boy from Kent, Dave Sadler, arrived with one of the biggest reputations as a young player and became his room-mate.

"George was really quiet, but you could tell he carried an inner confidence after you got to know him," Anderson recalls. "Perhaps it was because you saw how good he was and how seriously he treated competing. It was quite hard to get to know him really, and perhaps especially so because Fitzy was fun, loud, boisterous and cocky. He'd drive you nuts. Dave Sadler, who shared digs with George, was so mature for his age. So you had these two personalties that were deeply contrasting with George's. I think it was a good thing that Dave was the one in digs with George, this really mature lad. I can't imagine the carnage if George had been living with Fitzy."

The social groups began to take shape and form their own dynamic. For those boys who were not from England, they were only permitted to sign as an amateur and not an apprentice – this meant having to take jobs as the usual apprentice stage. United, of course, were well-versed in working with suitable companies, and at first George tried his hand working at the

Manchester Ship Canal – he complained to Joe Armstrong about the laborious nature of the work, stressing that he just wanted to play football, and eventually an unofficial compromise was reached where George would effectively clock in for a local firm, and clock out at the end of the day, but generally spend most of his time training in the day and hanging out with his new friends in the evening, playing snooker, playing pitch and putt, going to the new bowling alley that had opened in Salford, and then going to clubs.

"George was an amateur when he first came and he lived in Chorlton whereas my social group was in Stretford," Anderson says. "If there was a group of you, he'd be the quiet one hanging at the back. We went to the Twisted Wheel. George didn't come out with our group that much, so I don't know why he was with us that night. We were there looking to meet nice girls. We hadn't been there long when George came over and told us he was leaving. We asked him why and just presumed he was bored. As he was walking out, the prettiest girl in the place left with him. He hadn't said two words to anybody. I don't even know if he'd even said two words to her."

There was an inner confidence about George which was developing from one of his very first practice matches in the summer of 1961. Harry Gregg described George's team as the "summer holiday lads", but had asked John Aston Jnr if he could take part in goal.

"We hadn't been training for very long when one of these young lads came through on a one-on-one," Gregg said in an interview with the author before he passed. "I used to throw a dummy before the player had a chance to do it to me. I would make it look like I was going to dive one way and then dive the other. This boy called my bluff, got past me and scored. A few minutes later he came through again so I tried to call his bluff. Same result. He did it another time and that last time, as I got up, I told him I would break his neck if he tried it on one more time."

This story is the one retold through the ages, so often that it has taken on a life of its own – for example, by Pat Crerand, who could not have possibly been at that first session as it was to be another 18 months before he even signed for the club. However, one should not dispute Crerand's recollection – because this was no one-off occasion.

"They had a great relationship, but George just used to love winding Harry up," Jimmy Rimmer, goalkeeper in George's youth team, says. "On the shooting practice when they'd lay the ball off and a player would shoot first time, George wouldn't – he'd keep hold of the ball and try and entice Harry out. One of Harry's strengths was jumping out and grabbing the ball at the feet of a player, he was a brilliant goalkeeper, but George loved that challenge of waiting and knocking it past him. Harry would say, 'No chipping the goalkeeper today', and George saw that as a challenge because Harry had basically dared him to do it, he just had to try. It worked a few times and Harry eventually got fed up and ran after him – it was a sight."

Gregg wasn't the only goalkeeper to suffer the torment. "Oh yeah, it happened to me all the time," Rimmer says. "He would take the mickey out of you. You'd go for the ball and he'd pull it back. It was great fun."

There was, however, a limit to George's early cockiness. "I can say he never took the piss out of me, I know it happened with Harry and the others once or twice," insists Dave Gaskell. "But George used to sit two places next to me in the dressing room – I think he knew better than to try it with me."

If he was capable of teasing an international player like Harry Gregg, George knew he had the capability to inflict similar embarrassment on players of his own age, no matter their size. "That was happening on a daily basis," Ryan says. "Everyone was a victim. He must have put the ball through my legs at least a dozen times. The worst thing was, he'd chuckle as he went past you! The saving grace was that you knew you weren't the only one who got it."

It was a significant boost in Best's settlement at Old Trafford. Five months earlier he had felt a tremendous sense of insecurity at being overlooked for his country, and then feeling like every scout was saying no, and finally the embarrassment of his first trip to Manchester. He had believed that doubt within him. It was probably as true of George Best at any time in his football career as it was in the summer of 1961 that his potential seemed limitless and pinned to an upwards trajectory. As an amateur on the professional developmental fields of Britain's most famous football club, George had discovered that he had a gift worthy of inclusion.

Soon after the incident with Gregg, the experienced stopper was asked for his thoughts on the new young boys by Matt Busby. Gregg enthused about George, but Busby lamented: "Pity he's too small."

George had not yet heard of these doubts, and might well have suffered if he did, but he was growing in confidence and his competitive nature was already being felt amongst his young colleagues.

"I was a cross-country runner at school, a good athlete, strong in long distance," recalls Anderson. "I was really quick. I would even say I was quicker than George, but then came his competitive spirit, and he would always be there right beside me, never giving up. I was competitive, but nowhere near in the same way he was."

Fitzpatrick would often be with them. "We would always be trying to outdo one another," he says. "From the age of 15 to 17, especially at Manchester United, you need to be concentrated and at your best every single day, and George was certainly that. He was brilliant in training. He was a fantastic trainer. George was a very competitive boy. He took playing snooker as seriously as anything. You might as well have been playing at Wembley. That spirit was there from the start."

Jimmy Rimmer felt George was the leader in that trio of lads. "He was the fittest player at the club," he says. "He wanted to be number one and he was number one. He definitely had that drive to be the best player around."

That is an opinion seemingly shared by Ryan. "George, physically, was a very strong boy and hard trainer," he says. "We would do the horseshoe runs as they were known and he would be at the front all the time. We should shout to him to slow down because the rest of us were running out of energy."

* * *

Training at United in those days consisted of plenty of running and physical activity. It is compelling to note that even in these ostensibly rudimentary times, there was still a nuanced approach to individual development, and the boys were evaluated on an individual need. Take Jim Ryan. Physically, he was similar to George; diminutive and skeletal. Ryan was put through an intensive individually-tailored programme.

"Because I was a small lad, I was singled out for more physical training," he said. "It was probably right. I didn't have the lung capacity that was required to be a top-level footballer, so Jack Crompton took me out after morning training and he would try and make me stronger. Two hours in the afternoon doing physical work, and then Jack would lay on top of me so that my objective was to push him off and wriggle out."

The story is interesting not only for the quirk, but also for the acknowledgement that George never had to go through the same procedure, as he was deemed strong and resolute enough. It should also be noted that Crompton's primitive approach was part of a fast-track to prepare Ryan for a first-team opportunity in the summer of 1965 – almost two years after George had made his own debut.

Back in 1961, Best's early exploits earned him an opportunity in the A team at the start of the 1961/62 season. His position was seen as an inside-forward and it was in the number eight shirt that he lined up against Stockport County's A team. It seemed like a big step up for the 15-year-old, who was then moved to the B team instead, scoring in his second game at that level against Bury as he found his feet in the most competitive standard of football he had known.

In December 1961, Real Madrid came to Manchester to play in an exhibition match. The clubs had been linked by the romance of the European Cup in the time of the Busby Babes; and after Munich they were linked as brothers, with the Spanish club offering to play friendlies at a reduced fee to boost the Old Trafford coffers and help United rebuild. In these earlier encounters, Madrid had initially steamrollered United on the pitch. Now, the tables had not quite turned, but the gap had narrowed.

United's first team were still struggling to get back on their feet, but they were three years removed from the disaster and had Matt Busby in complete control once more. Jimmy Murphy was still the official custodian of the youth team for competition but was spending more and more time with the senior players. Real Madrid, meanwhile, had finally seen their run as perennial European champions end earlier that year when Benfica defeated Barcelona in Switzerland. Los Merengues would have an Indian summer, qualifying for the final in 1962, but Benfica retained their trophy.

United won the friendly by three goals to one. Among the 43,000 at Old Trafford was a dreaming amateur by the name of George Best, whose hero-worshipping had extended to Alex Dawson and Harry Gregg, two players whose boots George took great care in cleaning. But the Spaniards brought with them an exotic flavour, as well as two players he'd often dreamed about watching in the flesh.

Were Francisco 'Paco' Gento and Alfredo Di Stefano really as magical in the flesh? Well, even if they could not inspire their team to victory, they certainly enthralled young George, who was keen to imitate the skills of Gento the following morning in training. More straightforward but less proclaimed than many credit was the work-rate of Di Stefano. George observed this legendary figure, the central star of all five of Real's European Cup wins and winner of five league titles to boot, treating this match as if it was a final – covering every blade of grass from his nominal position as a forward, dropping deep enough to evade the attention of Bill Foulkes when he grabbed control of the ball and smashed in a consolation goal from all of 25 yards.

Like a wizard discovering he has the power of magic the first time, George was astonished to find he could do just the same things as he'd seen Gento do the previous evening. It almost served as a further liberation, as George's form for the B team began to improve considerably. And watching Di Stefano work so hard to receive the ball in deeper areas so he could influence the game at his will also left a lasting impression.

"It was always an experience playing with George," Fitzpatrick recalls of playing as full-back behind him. "He would always be willing to come and help you. I would just try and get the ball to him as often as I could. Week in, week out, he was man of the match. I remember in one game, the ball was out of play and he just turned to me and said, 'Fitzy – I'm going to beat everybody and smash it into the corner.' He gets the ball and goes past one, then two, three, four, five players. Puts it in the corner. Runs back to the halfway line and says, 'Told you, didn't I?!' That was my favourite moment playing alongside him."

It wouldn't be the last time he did something like that.

It could be frustrating for some of his team-mates. "At first he was a very greedy player," says Manchester-born defender Eddie Harrop. "He didn't want to pass to anyone. When you're a young player, they try and encourage you to pass. When he got older, we all began to realise that he didn't have to pass it to anyone. It was obvious George had more talent. He could play a one-two with the corner flag."

The north-west football scene quickly started to hear the name of George Best when he scored two and generally terrorised his marker in a game at Rochdale where United won 10-1. The same team were victims of another brace in a 5-1 defeat in March 1962. Word was getting around about the slight kid who was making mincemeat of teams and the response was heavy-handed. His card had been marked, his reputation preceded him, and the tackling became immediately more aggressive. Another player might have buckled, but in a year of rapid acceleration, this was another step towards recognition of George knowing teams were fearful of him. Already, he was carving out a reputation to live up to.

"He just had that star quality," Anderson says. "God, he was a terrier out there, especially for such a little guy. He would go mad. Because of his style, players would be going at him but he would never be afraid. Opponents would go at him. He was the fiercest tackler on the team. He would be everywhere on the pitch, going for the ball and standing up to players. He was 15 or 16, and I remember being wowed by this fierce kid with this tremendous attitude."

Anderson and Jimmy Ryan were wingers, occupying similar positions to George, but their job descriptions varied massively.

"The great thing about being at United was the trust that the coaches seemed to have in you," Anderson says. "Straight away they might tell you how to play your position but from then on the team talks would be a case of – for me, as an outside-right – 'Willie, if you hit the touchline four times in a game and drive the ball across the box, you're having a great time.'

"There was no instruction to get back in to fill space and make sure the full-back doesn't overlap and all of that. They wouldn't tell George how to take players on. He was a natural. They would talk to him about his use of the ball, and he was such a quiet kid that you could see he was taking it on board. But the thing about George was that he had such a gift for figuring that sort of thing out naturally. Like a puzzle. He would work out what worked best for him. When you're a wide player you learn how to use your acceleration from standing and moving positions. George was like a wide player all over the field.

"He had a knack of knowing when to pause, when to slow

down, how to trick the defenders into stopping or turning on to an unfamiliar side. He was so good over that first five yards. I'm sure Jimmy Murphy and the other coaches talked to him but the speed of George's rise to the first team, the way he stayed there and how prominent his position came, those things are a testament to his footballing intelligence."

Ryan says that even in a team blessed with talent in wide areas, George brought an extra dimension with his individual quality. "As footballers do, he was doing the things that he was capable of," he says. "I would never try to flick the ball over people's heads, that was far from my reality. It was fantastic to watch and fantastic to play with. But he was a willing learner. He was willing to listen to the coaches to improve."

Anderson recalls one such game: "We scored a bunch of goals. I scored four and he scored three or four. We got a roasting after the game because we wouldn't pass the ball! We were both playing down the middle and because we didn't play the ball out wide we got absolutely slaughtered by the coach."

Best's growth in confidence had been observed by all of the staff. The most important men in the club discussed what to do with him. Busby and Murphy watched another training session of the first-team players against the kids, to get a proper look at George. Again, Best fooled Gregg.

"He got the ball on the halfway line, took it up to a much bigger, more experienced opponent, drifted past him, beat another, then another, and another," Jimmy Murphy recalled. "Then he blasted the ball past Harry Gregg from around 20 yards. Harry dashed out of his goal and held the boy aloft."

He was unplayable. Busby's concern was that George had a "congenital dislike of allowing anyone else to have a kick". Murphy was as loyal an aide to Busby as could be. In fact, he worshipped his boss in the same way he expected of others. This was one of the rare occasions where the Welshman felt he ought to interject. "Don't try to change this boy's style," he said. "Let him develop naturally. The rest will come in time."

It would be ridiculous to suggest that Murphy and Busby had not kept track of what had been going on in Best's first year but the interest became much more significant afterwards. "George rekindled some of the twinkle in my dad's eye," Jimmy Murphy Jnr says. "He was a genius. My father said, 'In my career there are only two players I have never coached. Duncan Edwards because he could do it all, and George Best, because it would have taken away from his genius.' They were instructed to leave George alone.

"I have a long-standing running bet with my pals that they can never find anything negative said about my father and the closest they tend to get is a quote from George who said, 'I couldn't understand the fuss about how good Jimmy was as a coach, because he never seemed to coach me!' He would call players like George, or Denis Law, a deckchair player."

Murphy was invested. So too was Matt Busby, who made a point of setting time aside to talk to Malcolm Brodie, the sportswriter of the *Belfast Telegraph*, who was in Majorca at the same time as United were on a post-season tour. It was worth following United as they were trying to sign Denis Law from Torino. Brodie, however, was given a scoop of a different kind. "I've got a boy from Belfast who will be the greatest," Busby told Brodie; though he asked him to keep it quiet.

Brodie agreed, and was as good as his word, but it was only a matter of time before the force of nature that was George Best was announced to the world.

MOVEMENT

Returning to the theme about potential, environment and all the variable factors that come into play to influence a person's path in life, it would be negligent to ignore the political factors, particularly as they played a prominent if still understated role in the life of George Best.

The Troubles in Belfast and the associated discontent in Northern Ireland is an obvious factor – Dickie Best had considered football as one of the few realistic prospects for a local boy to escape – but the global picture also came into play. George was born, almost symbolically, nine months after the end of World War II. There was greater public freedom to around the world and a feeling of positive times ahead.

George did not grow up in definite prosperity but neither was it poverty; yes, his parents had not been able to afford a television, but he had been able to watch one at a neighbour's house, where pictures around the world were beamed into living rooms. News was broadcast, as was entertainment

– and entertainment, in its different forms, encouraged dreams. Travel was easier. Communications were improving. There were movements around the world such as the San Francisco Renaissance out of California that propelled the hippy generation into modern culture, with freedom of expression and individualism prominent features. Creativity was encouraged, even if at Manchester United, the traditional value of hard work remained a staple of any youngster who wanted to make the grade.

"There was nothing glamorous about training for Manchester United then," Jim Ryan says. "That might have been how it was perceived by supporters but I can remember that it was a real slog."

Best embraced the slog. Having done the physical work in the morning, he would remain at the training ground in the afternoon, working on various parts of his game – such as his left foot, or trying to perfect the art of hitting the crossbar with every shot or cross. His development in his second year at United gathered some quick momentum.

His first nine games for the B team brought seven goals, some resounding victories and a call up to the A team – which, in this United setup, was effectively the team that would play in the Youth Cup and was led by Jimmy Murphy. He made an impressive start, scoring twice in a 3-0 win over Preston A, but was ushered back into the B team after quieter games against Manchester City, Liverpool and Burnley.

In December 1962, United's first game in that season's FA Youth Cup came against Bradford City at Old Trafford. Willie Anderson and Eddie Harrop were the lucky lads called up to play down the right. "Every level was taken seriously, especially the youth team – it was just as important as the senior side,"

Anderson recalls. "It made you feel great. Before a Youth Cup game all the preparation would be the same as if you were in the first team – you'd go to the same golf course for the pre-match dinner, and so on. The Youth Cup games would feel like a mini first-team game, especially if you were at Old Trafford under floodlights. You felt like a star. So many people came out to see us."

Best agreed, saying it felt like a "big step up" from the B team and that you would be watched by some "pretty big crowds". Almost 8,000 people came to see this game against Bradford where United scored a staggering 15 times. The forward line helped themselves to goals – Anderson scored, Ken Morton in the number 11 shirt got a couple, Barry Fry in number 10 got five, and Barry Grayson, in the number eight shirt Best normally wore, helped himself to two.

Clearly, George had some work on to get into this team. He resolved to do just that – in a freezing Boxing Day game at the Cliff against Blackburn, Best told John Fitzpatrick after a goalless first half that they should just take it upon themselves to win the game. Fitzgerald was flattered by inclusion as it was a royal we; the defender passed Best the ball, and George did the rest, running past three to score the game's only goal.

It was in March 1963 that Best's star started to ascend at an unstoppable pace. Two goals and a magician's display in a game at Bury had everyone at the club talking, not least because United won the game 8-2. The following week the B team played against Manchester City. George's performance was even better.

"It felt like he was scoring four or five goals every week," Eddie Harrop recalls. "It would be the talk of Monday morning after the weekend's game. I can clearly remember Fitzy came in telling us all about how brilliant George had been for the B team against City. 'He scored four goals but wouldn't pass to anyone!' It wasn't surprising – that was George as we knew him in training. He'd go past everyone."

United won that derby game 7-0. Two more goals in a 3-0 win over Bolton B was enough to earn him a shot in the FA Youth Cup team. Over 12,000 were at Old Trafford to watch Best, in the number 11 shirt, put in a fine performance as his side won 3-0 against Newcastle. He and Albert Kinsey were described as "the pick of a lively attack" by *Manchester Evening Chronicle* reporter Peter Slingsby.

Celtic midfielder Pat Crerand had just signed for United and was taking the opportunity to get familiar with his new club. The buzz was that they had a youth team that might finally bring the cup back to its spiritual home. Full-back Bobby Noble, centre-forward David Sadler and wingmen Willie Anderson and George Best were tipped to be stars, but one of those names stood out for United's new playmaker, Crerand: "I was sitting near Jack Crompton and I saw this remarkable player. I never saw a young player as good as he was on that day. 'Who's this outside left in the number 11?' I asked Jack. 'He's unreal.' Jack just looked at me and said, 'We know all about him. But we're keeping it quiet.'"

George had a quieter time as United were eliminated by Sheffield Wednesday in the next round but had, by then, netted two in a win over Tranmere for the A team. He had shown himself to be comfortable at that level and only closed the season in the B team because they had some extra fixtures – that poor City B team were put to the sword again as George scored two of his team's four without reply at the Cliff.

There had clearly been marked improvement and progression

but it was still beyond almost all comprehension that George found himself in the first team picture, making his debut in mid-September 1963.

In some ways, he could thank David Sadler. Sadler was a tall boy of tremendous composure and the intelligence to play in both a central defensive and attacking position. The controversial sale of Johnny Giles and the absence David Herd had presented opportunities in the side and Sadler had thrived. In his third game he scored against champions Everton in a 5-1 win at Old Trafford and then he got the first of his team's seven goals at Ipswich. His acclimation to first-team football suggested that maybe, just maybe, the player from his youth team who had been earning even greater reviews for his performances might have the requisite temperament too.

There was no doubt in Jimmy Rimmer's mind that George Best was ready. "He was a hell of a player even at that age… magnificent," Rimmer says. "He was born a star. He was just much better than anyone else around at that level. He was a complete player and I don't say that lightly. There were lads who went on to become internationals in our team, lads who won European Cups and other medals, and George was still above and beyond anyone. People will say they spotted a genius – I think that's even the quote that was used to describe him coming to United. But genius doesn't even cover it. There was only one George Best. I considered myself lucky to have played alongside him and watch him every day in training."

It is apparent that we have jumped forward a little so let's retrace our steps to cover the events of the previous few months. And, in doing so, we can take a journey through these snapshots of time to look deeper than the anecdotes to discuss George Best the footballer. What kind of player was he?

It does, frankly, seem absurd that we could say this barely 17-year-old boy was complete by the standards of First Division football, but Rimmer's words ought to be contextualised. He had watched as his team-mate had grown into life in Manchester and developed the confidence to do unpredictable things on the training pitch. Games provided a different education because the tackles that came in on a Saturday did not have Manchester United's best interests at heart.

There had been revelatory moments for George which seemed to act as an accelerant; teasing Gregg gave him the confidence that he not only belonged but that he could do similar things against his own age group. Watching Gento gave him both the ambition to imitate and the confidence to create on his own accord. Watching Di Stefano on that same evening left an impression that to be considered truly great you have to be better than everyone on the field and the only way to do that is to be everywhere on the field. There is a quote which fits, often attributed to Thomas Edison but the derivation is actually unknown: "Opportunity is missed by most people because it is dressed in overalls and looks like work."

It wasn't missed by George, but then, the true beauty of it was that he didn't see it as work either. The complaints about him always having the ball subsided as others started to realise at least half of the reason for him having it was because he worked so hard to get it in the first place. And, invariably, once he had it, he could create or score. The maturity of his body, increase in weight and hard work in the gym gave George the physical resolution to withstand the heavy challenges, and he was able to ascend through the youth teams with comfort.

As Eric McMordie had observed back in Belfast, however, those challenges could still leave some pretty nasty bruises and so, the decision rested with Matt Busby and Jimmy Murphy who had to consider two things – when would it be sensible to put him in without fear of being broken in half, and had he done so much at these lower levels that he simply couldn't be held back? Perhaps only Sir Alex Ferguson in British football history had a nous for such judgement as wise as those two, but it could fairly be said that even with the risks Busby had taken with putting the Babes into the first team en masse, none had been quite so physically frail as George Best.

However, to return to Jimmy Rimmer's observation, it is necessary to trace the qualities George possessed which made the decision so hard. Talent was no longer in question. He had started in that inside-forward role, usually on the right, but that quickly became a figure of footballing speech, as George would float around. His earlier games saw him stick to instruction and position, doing as he was told and waiting for the ball to come to him.

His athleticism meant he had the legs of any defender and his trickery and balance would mean he had the better of them, but it was upon learning that he could take the responsibility to go and get the ball himself that he took a significant step forward. He became as big a dream for the defenders on his team as he was an occasional frustration for the attackers he played alongside; working overtime to either recover the ball, or be in a position where he could receive it straight from the relieved defender.

It wouldn't matter where he was on the pitch. George enjoyed the challenge of receiving the ball deep in his own half. The further from goal, the more men to beat. It was a challenge. He was completing such challenges, set by himself, with such frequency at his own age level that it eventually began to turn into a headache for the coaches. Would he have the footballing intelligence to know that senior players on both teams would quickly grow frustrated with a youngster who tried to do it all?

There was some hope that becoming a professional at the age of 17 would give George a sense of settlement and maturity to maybe even slow down a little and understand he didn't have to do it all. At that stage, it was a formality that he would be offered terms, but it bode well that he didn't take it for granted.

"So many players wanted to play in my position, inside-forward, because that was the glamour role," George recalled in his autobiography *Blessed*. "Between the A and B teams, the youth team and the reserves, the club must have had 30 inside-forwards. So no matter how good you were, you certainly couldn't take it for granted that you would get the call from the management on your 17th birthday and be offered that precious piece of paper – the professional contract."

The fun and games of the time spent as an apprentice or amateur seemed to end as the season came to its conclusion. "When you were waiting to see if you would become a professional it became a little bit stressful, because you suddenly had the idea that this soon could end," Willie Anderson says. "If you got to 17 and they said they were going to wait a year to offer you professional terms, as happened in many cases, you knew there was a concern about being let go. I was one of the lucky ones. There were 20 of us when I arrived at 15 and by the time I signed professional, the players left from our group were John Fitzpatrick, George, and me."

On his 17th birthday, George was indeed given a professional contract. Fitzpatrick and George, still close friends, were taken down to Wembley to see Manchester United play against Leicester City in the FA Cup final. Best, who had only seen the famous stadium on black and white television, confessed that seeing it in its full technicolour glory was "mind-blowing".

United won 3-1 – a significant moment, as it was their first trophy after the Munich Air Disaster, and also came after a season where the club were fortunate to not get relegated. They finished in the final safe position in the league but yet now felt as if, with Denis Law's goals and Pat Crerand's scheming in the middle, a rosy future awaited.

The young boys had been included as part of the travelling squad, but there was not room for them on the team bus back in Manchester for the parade; little John Fitzpatrick and George Best, unknown to the majority of the thousands of United fans celebrating in Albert Square, waved down to them from a terrace at the town hall as if they had scored the goals themselves.

George admitted it made him "feel like royalty" and that feeling stayed with him as he travelled back home to Belfast for the summer to meet his newly-born twin sisters. He had trouble passing his driving test in Manchester but retook it in Belfast and was sure that the instructor was influenced by the fact he had a Manchester United player in the driver's seat.

Dickie was immensely proud that George had turned professional. But he had been apprehensive – on his visits over to Manchester he had sidled up to Harry Gregg to ask him if he felt George might be offered professional terms. Gregg, ever the straight-talker, would remind Dickie that he was not privy to such conversations but said that he felt certain that would be the case. With no official word from the club, Dickie prepared for his son's return, and again ensured he had a printing job waiting for him when he came home – only to be informed by his son via telegram that he had become a pro. Though Dickie was perturbed by finding out this way, Busby placated him by inviting him to Wembley too, and sat beside him on the train to London telling him how high his expectations were.

The Manchester United first-team squad had travelled to Italy, where Busby repeated his proclamation about the young starlet on the books, telling press members: "Young Best has the potential to be one of soccer's all-time greats."

* * *

The next crucial step of his development came with his biggest promotion yet. When he arrived back in Manchester after the summer break, George was placed with the reserve squad. This was the logical move – his form towards the end of the prior season had been so exceptional that it had tempted Busby and Murphy into considering whether they should give the Belfast boy his chance in the first team. The Central League would be an environment where they could see whether Best could cope against professionals of all ages and sizes. And this could be a tremendously physical testing ground – it would not be uncommon to find embittered senior players at this level, frustrated that they were not seeing first-team action.

The turnaround of players also meant opportunities were opening up. Best, who usually wore that inside-right number eight, started as an outside-left in a 4-0 win over Sheffield Wednesday in late August. He stayed in that shirt in a 1-1 draw at Chesterfield, before he was switched to the right for the visit of West Bromwich Albion on September 7, 1963. The game ended 1-1, but George scored his team's goal – and, after a quiet couple of games, he was now settling in.

Willie Anderson was playing at number nine that day and pays tribute to how his team-mate adapted to these changes. "George always played as an inside-forward in the A and B teams, he wasn't a wide player," he says. "I think he was played on the outside because it was easier to get him in the team. Not so much because he didn't have the quality... George progressed from there really quickly. It seemed like it was a run of games to see how good he was in the B team and the Youth Cup, and then really it was only a few games in the A team and even fewer in the reserves. And then bingo, he was in the first team and that was it."

Two days later, Best was back in 11, and Anderson back in seven, for a win up at Blackpool. The following weekend's game was at Newcastle, but when George finished training on Friday he noticed he wasn't in the team. He looked at the A team sheet and wasn't in it, and momentarily felt anxious that he had been dropped to the B side. When he wasn't there, he felt he had misread the reserves team, but his eye was caught by the word "Reserves" on the first-team sheet, which had his surname on.

His initial reaction was mixed. The 12th man in 1963 was not a substitute to come on to the pitch, as these were the days before those were permitted. "I considered myself dropped from the third team where I had started to enjoy my football," Best said. "I knew there was no injury crop among the senior players and figured that they only wanted me around to help with the boots and other dressing-room chores... I would rather have been playing for the third team than odd-jobbing with the big boys any time. Besides, I was so scared of most of them that I used to keep out of their way during the week and the presence of manager Matt Busby terrified me."

The truth was, George had felt a certain fear about most of the men in important positions at United, going right back to those first few months where he was too shy to even tell Joe Armstrong he wanted to go home, too shy to tell him he'd already eaten a breakfast, and beset by anxiety when he had to tell 'Uncle Joe' (the nickname the players had for Armstrong) that he didn't like the apprenticeship he was on. George Best was a living, breathing example that United's chain of command still made prodigies obsequious.

One of the understated successes of United's rebuild post-Munich was how closely they were able to keep things to how they were before the disaster. Yes, the concentration on giving young players a chance, but also the defined feeling of hierarchy, which would have been much harder to manage in the absence of Bert Whalley, Tom Curry and Walter Crickmer, three huge presences from the coaching and administrative side who perished in Germany in February 1958.

Jimmy Murphy could be credited with organising that and was pulling double-duty; that is to say he had doubled his regular workload to commit not only 24 hours a day to Manchester United – he somehow found 48. Aided by Joe Armstrong, Jack Crompton and John Aston Snr – and then a little later Wilf McGuinness – there was a reorganisation of responsibility, but slight enough that it did not have a long-term impact on the way the players felt it.

Before February 6, 1958, Murphy's main responsibility was to have his fingerprints on everything below first-team level. He was an aide to the players but was seen as a real firecracker, a man so passionate about his beloved Manchester United that he would pin young players up to the dressing room wall if he felt they had performed out of turn. If he wanted more physicality on the training pitch, he would often run on to the field and take out a player to show them how it should be done. And, when it came to a player being ready for first team action, Murphy would treat the prospect of Matt Busby deeming a player good enough as being selected by the King himself. There was a special reverence given to the manager.

Busby had, of course, been in Munich, but survived – only after being read the last rites twice. Murphy had not been involved in the crash as he was in Cardiff for a World Cup qualifier as part of his role as Wales manager. Murphy took control of most affairs at the club while Busby convalesced.

When the boss returned to Manchester later that year, he appeared older. Haunted. It took some time for that aura to disappear – for some, it never did. There was an ethereal quality which existed around him after the disaster, and for those younger players at the club, that feeling made Busby more imposing than ever before. Wilf McGuinness shared that feeling and when he became reserve-team manager, also conveyed that message.

In those first years after Munich, Murphy had to alter his own personality. The firecracker approach had to be watered down. Clearly, the emotional toll for players such as Alex Dawson, Shay Brennan and Mark Pearson had to be handled with sensitivity, and Murphy too was carrying his own considerable grief at the same time as trying to serve as a motivator for these players in their quest to carry on. In 1963, the simple passing of time had permitted Murphy to return to his earlier ways, although his time was split between the groups of players.

"The first team trained at Old Trafford and we were at the Cliff with John Aston Snr," Eddie Harrop says. "We'd normally only see Jimmy when we had to go to the ground after training and clean all the first-team players' boots and the dressing room. Other than that, Jimmy would come in to see us before Youth Cup matches to give the team talk."

Murphy's presence, however, was still the real deal, and treated seriously. He would still attend training when he could and give the players an "occasional boost" and tactical walkthrough, according to Jim Ryan.

"John Aston was a big force for the youth team, and the A and B team, he was the one who dealt with us at the Cliff," Willie Anderson recalls. "Wilf would deal with us if we moved up to the reserves. Matt was this big god and Jimmy was in your face. He had a lot more to do with us than Matt…

"Jimmy still possessed that fire. I used to live at home on weekends and come in on Monday. One time I missed the train, so rushed to Old Trafford. As I was approaching the stadium Jimmy Murphy was there, angrily waiting for me. He physically got hold of me and screamed at me about missing practice. I was 16, 17. He frightened me to death."

Murphy was able to use the fear he knew he instilled into those kids to propel Busby into an even more intimidating position. It was simple, and yet unfailingly effective.

From the perspective of George Best, one could reasonably assume there was a certain trepidation about leaving his comfort zone. The evidence – and there is more of it to come – suggests that George had found his feet and was enjoying his football so much that at this moment in time he was still viewing Central League football as a challenge to overcome.

On the management side, the reserve team was little to do with talent and more to do with temperament. The youth teams were designed to see how players of similar ages competed against each other but the reserves could field a player aged

17 or 37. Murphy and Wilf McGuinness determined that George was ready to make the step up to first-team football, and it was clear that the boy himself did not share that feeling.

George travelled to Old Trafford on the morning of the first-team game against West Brom to join up with the squad before they would go to Davyhulme Golf Club. Groundsman Joe Royle wished George all the best for the afternoon, which he found peculiar. And then Joe Armstrong was the next to bump in to him, and the next to congratulate him and wish him the best of luck. On the coach to the golf club, Pat Crerand, who had taken it upon himself to sit alongside George, told him that he had better not hit his crosses too long. George asked what the Scot was talking about, to which Crerand replied: "Ian Moir is injured today. You're playing."

George learned – and appreciated – that the news had been kept from him to stop him worrying too much the night before. He said he did not feel nerves, but instead was caught in a daze, so much so that he could barely touch his pre-match meal, while on the ride back to the ground the senior players tried to wind him up by talking up the defender who would be marking him – Graham Williams, the seasoned pro with a hard-man reputation.

It was at Old Trafford when Matt Busby finally made it official and asked to see George. "He just told me in that quiet, persuasive way of his to go out and play the game that came naturally to me," Best recalled.

As he ran out on to the pitch in the number seven shirt, George looked for the imposing figure of Williams, who he had imagined would be seven feet tall and breathing fire. He was surprised to see a player of regular build and only an inch or two taller than him. He was human after all.

Crerand, a relative veteran who had seen much in his time with Celtic and Scotland as well as these few months at Manchester United, was shocked by Best's calm that afternoon. "I don't remember him ever showing any signs of being under pressure, it just wasn't in him," he says. "In the dressing room before his debut you could have sworn he was just a regular first-team player. He was not bothered one little bit. Graham Williams was a terrific full-back. But he could be a nasty fucker as well. There was nothing he could do about George, though, and to be fair to Graham, there weren't many who could deal with him. From that moment he was a star."

And from that moment, legend was born.

The story goes that Williams ran roughshod over the teenage debutant. Not quite, according to Williams. The West Brom man found out just that day who he would be playing against, although Best's reputation had preceded him kicking a senior ball. "My first impression of him was that he wasn't very good!" Williams says. "I had heard about him. Everyone was starting to hear about him. He came with a reputation, people had been saying he was going to be one of the greats.

"He started on the right wing and he wasn't getting the ball. Bobby Charlton was playing outside-left so they were playing through him mostly. Georgie was stood on the wing, and it was easy to tell he was getting frustrated at not being played into the game. At one moment he just said, 'Fuck it, I'm off!' and he wandered off into the middle of the pitch to look for the ball. And that was Georgie, pretty much for the rest of his life, wasn't it? He wore seven on the back of his shirt but he played wherever the ball was. He wanted to be with it."

George did attribute a heavy tackle that hurt his ankle to West Brom's number three after he had shown the audacity to nutmeg him and he later wrote a letter home to his parents where he described Williams as a "madman" and that he "nearly broke my flipping ankle". (He would however say in his 1968 book *Best of Both Worlds*: "Williams couldn't have been nicer. He was firm and hard, but treated me as fairly as any debutant could have wished.") At half-time, Busby decided to move Best so he could go head-to-head with the opposition's fellow debutant, left-back Campbell Crawford.

Crawford had played in the previous week's reserve game, but George had played from the opposite side in that match, so this was their first (and last) direct confrontation. There were moments of excitement from the home player, but the United team used him sparingly after the ankle knock. Bobby Charlton said his new team-mate's first impression did not 'linger in my mind'. "I'm sure he showed some nice touches, but the overall impact was not overwhelming," he said.

It was another youngster, Sadler, who got the game's only goal – but the hype around the club had been on Best for a few months, encouraged of course by Busby himself, so it was natural that he would be the subject of discussion post-match.

"It was unfortunate that George should take such a heavy knock on his ankle, but despite this I was very pleased indeed with his first game," the United boss said. "He certainly showed us what he could do. Believe me, this youngster is not going to be just a good player, but something out of the ordinary, possibly a very great one. We shall try to bring him along without rushing him, but there is no doubt he has a great deal of talent and is one of our most outstanding prospects."

It was reported by the *Coventry Evening Telegraph* that the "tackles became far too fierce on both sides" but this is again something disputed by Williams. "They reported that I kicked lumps out of him but that became a standing joke between George and me," he says. "His father once showed me the letter George had sent home after his debut. In it he said he'd played against me, the mad Welshman, and that he was meant to play in the midweek game but he had picked up an injury. That escalated into this story that I'd kicked him all over the pitch, but nothing could be further from the truth. I didn't have to kick him, they didn't give him the ball!"

Two things were certainly true – Best's injury would rule him out of the next game, and Busby's positive takeaway had more to do with the youngster's willingness to keep going and complete the game than his contribution. He might have questioned that mental resilience if he had known Best was concerned about the "treacherous slide" he felt he suffered over the following weeks.

In the reserves, George might have felt he was doing well enough – goals in consecutive draws against Manchester City and Blackburn showcased his ability. The game at Blackburn had been a different experience – George explained how the crowd had been comprised of patients from a nearby hospital that specialised in looking after those who suffered with epilepsy, which made him thankful for his own health. But he still confessed that he "always seemed to be leaving the pitch with the same flat feeling of dissatisfaction".

George saw it as a demotion when he went from the reserves to the A team but it seemed to be a tactic to help him enjoy his football a little more. "When George got into the first team he still wanted to train with his mates in the youth team," Eddie Harrop says. "He properly broke into the first team at the start of the season but stayed for as long as he could with us. You didn't see that much of the first team – I only got to know the first teamers after I had an injury and had to go to Old Trafford for treatment. George would have been the same as me until he started moving up on a regular basis."

Back in the A-team, it was evident that George was playing at a level he was much too good for. Burnley were put to the sword when he scored a hat-trick in a 6-2 win. Then there were two goals in a staggering 10-1 win over Tranmere. George was told he would be allowed home for Christmas – something he took as proof that he had really slipped down the pecking order. Before he went to Belfast, there was one more game to play; an FA Youth Cup game at Old Trafford against Barrow. The talent was on show again as he scored two goals before the half-hour mark, while he also netted in the second half, but the humiliation did not stop there for the visitors, who were on the end of a soul-destroying 14-1 loss.

"I can remember Emlyn Hughes coming up to me years later when I was at Swansea," Jimmy Rimmer, goalkeeper on the day, says. "He said, 'Jimmy, do you know, I played against you lads in the FA Youth Cup. I marked Bestie. We lost 14-1. I thought I had a good game against him!'"

The *Manchester Evening News* described the combination play of Best and fellow forward Albert Kinsey as "devastating". One month later, United would play their next game in the competition; by that time, the star of George Best was ascending once more.

THE SECOND
COMING

O n Boxing Day 1963, George Best felt embarrassed as he was encouraged to talk through his experience of playing with the likes of Bobby Charlton and Denis Law to excited neighbours and family members who had piled into his family home.

Well, there was certainly nothing great to discuss from recent events – United had lost their last game before Christmas by four goals against Everton, and as the festive celebrations took place the team were losing 6-1 at Burnley. Furthermore, despite those recent hat-tricks, it felt almost embarrassing to discuss them when he had felt every single one of the 103 days that had passed since that sole first-team appearance.

The following morning, United sent a telegram to the Best home instructing George to return immediately and to go to the airport. It would be his first time on an aeroplane. He didn't understand at first, and certainly didn't agree with his family's excitement that he would be playing in the next game. Again, that confirmation didn't arrive until the day of the game. But Matt Busby was planning something that would shock the First Division.

"After training on December 27, we did as we usually did and checked to see what team we were in," says Willie Anderson, who was 16 at the time. "I naturally looked in the reserve team for my name, and I felt deflated that I wasn't on the team sheet. I thought I'd been dropped to the A or B team but my name wasn't on those either, and I was still processing that when someone said, 'Hey, Willie, you and George are in the first team squad!' At 11am on the day of the game at the golf club, Busby pulled us aside and said we would both be playing. We didn't have long to freak out. I didn't even have time to tell my family, they heard it on the radio."

George said that all morning he "found people doubting Mr Busby's wisdom in including two comparative kids for such a stern match". His opponents this time (he and Anderson would have freedom to switch) would be fellow Northern Irishman Alex Elder, an international renowned for the fantastic timing of his tackles, and Englishman John Angus, who had played for his country in 1961, as just reward for his performances in Burnley's First Division Championship side of 1960. Angus, a right-back, was the player Best would start against.

Anderson and Best's cause was helped no end by the fact that their team-mates were in the mood for revenge. Not that this allowed any dereliction of duty.

"Before the game Bobby Charlton said to me, 'Don't worry about anything. Whenever you get the ball, I'll be ten yards from you. You can always give it me if you need help.' We were running on adrenalin," Anderson says. "Against Burnley I was on the right and George was on the left. Because he was right-footed, he tended to come inside a lot. He of course scored a great goal and then that was it – he was an ever-present in the first team of Manchester United."

Best recalled his goal – United's third in a 5-1 win – as a "right-footed shot from the edge of the penalty box which flew into the corner" although the *Football Post* recorded it as an "open goal from six yards out". It was 3-0 United at half-time.

George had embarrassed Angus; Busby advised the wingers it was now time to switch. He gave George a sage piece of advice, hoping it would give him greater composure, control, and better use of his natural gifts. He advised Best to go at Elder with a little more caution, lure him into a tackle and then use a burst of acceleration. George had excitedly been running at full pelt whenever he got the ball. But he listened to the advice, took it on board, and the result was an even more thrilling performance in the second half.

United won 5-1. It was revelatory for player and manager. Best discovered a new and devastating way to utilise his talent in just his second game. Busby, as well as realising he had a new star, was reassured that even if the boy had a talent that was beyond coaching, he was not above listening to good advice.

Following the game, George flew back home to spend the New Year with family. On January 1, the *Belfast Telegraph* carried a picture of the hometown hero on the top of their back page. "That newspaper must have passed through a hundred sets of hands and my goal was a big talking point on the estate," George recalled. "It was as if I'd scored for them, too, which made me a bit weepy."

Malcolm Brodie, reporter for the newspaper, wrote: "Best, who made a tremendous impact in his second senior game for

Manchester United last weekend, is almost certain to keep his place for the difficult game at Southampton... Busby was most impressed with Best's display against such a fine full-back as John Angus, Burnley's English international. Indeed, George's development is considered remarkable at Old Trafford."

He returned to Manchester as he had been informed he would be involved in the FA Cup trip to the Dell on January 4. As they travelled down south, Busby took special time to congratulate the 17-year-old on his performance. "I felt as if Jesus Christ had spoken to me," Best recalled.

He was about to become the exclusive property of the first team; he certainly didn't play for the reserves, A or B team again as a rookie on the way up. But there was the small matter of the FA Youth Cup; United had progressed with routine wins over Sheffield United and Wolves. Jimmy Murphy called upon Best to play in the semi-final against Manchester City. There were the predictable complaints about a player who could now be described as a bona fide first-team player (when he played against Aston Villa in the First Division two days before the first leg of the semi against City, it was his 23rd appearance for the senior side) but Murphy had heard it all before.

In the 1950s United had set a standard in the FA Youth Cup with their five consecutive wins. It felt, sometimes, as if the competition had been set up solely for Murphy to showcase his "golden apples", as he liked to call them. One was more ripe than the others; in fact, when Duncan Edwards made similar 'guest' appearances for the youth side after playing in the first team, opponents would complain as the Midlander inevitably dominated proceedings. Like Edwards, Best was the most highly-hyped name of his group, and so comparisons were inevitable, even if only really applicable when made in reference to their peers rather than each other, certainly when it came to assessing their individual qualities.

"Duncan and George were different animals," David Gaskell, a goalkeeper who played with them both, says. "Duncan was big and forceful. A huge man. George was like silk. Duncan would surge forward, George could beat you on a sixpence. He was just the same in training and on the pitch."

Graham Williams – the West Brom player who played his career close to Dudley, where Edwards grew up and was now canonised following his tragic passing in Munich – had a similar outlook. "You can't compare them," he says. "Duncan Edwards was a giant of a boy, a man at 18, a player who would play in any position and be the star of the team. George was like a ballerina."

One thing they had in common was the fear they would strike in the heart of an opponent when their name was seen on the team-sheet, certainly at youth-team level. But Manchester City had some talented players of their own, who wanted to make an example out of the player who had been the talk of the town in the second half of the campaign.

"City had a defender called Alf Wood," Willie Anderson recalls. "He would run through a brick wall, and if you were in the way, he would run through you too. Those games were physical battles." Anticipating a rough encounter, Murphy had sent his boys out to "batter these Blue bastards", and a tough contest ended with United winning 4-1 in front of almost 30,000 people at Old Trafford. The aggregate attendance was over 50,000 including those who were at Maine Road the following week to see United win 4-3 on the night. Best forced the first goal and then brought the crowd – home and away – to their feet for the third; weaving through a number of City players before firing the ball home. *Manchester Evening News* reporter Eric Thornton said he awarded Best "the top marks of the night for a personal display".

So there was some semi-final joy, which was more than could be said for the luck of the senior side, even if Best himself had been a shining light. He played well in the FA Cup at Southampton and then faced a rematch with Graham Williams at the Hawthorns; this time, there was no disputing the winner of the duel as Best scored in a 4-1 win. Another goal followed in the 4-0 win at Barnsley in the Cup, and in the next game, two goals against Bolton in a 5-0 win capped off a display described as "particularly impressive" by Frank McGhee of the *Mirror*.

The FA Cup run continued with a thrilling triple-header against Sunderland with United eventually coming out on top after a second replay. That set up an FA Cup semi-final with West Ham at Hillsborough – the talk of the weekend was the prospect of Best and Howard Kendall, the Preston North End player born on exactly the same day as George, potentially becoming the youngest ever players to compete in the FA Cup final. In the end, Kendall earned that distinction alone, as Best's United were comprehensively beaten by the Hammers.

George was hoping for better in Europe. He had made his European debut at Old Trafford against Sporting Lisbon. They won that third round, first leg tie 4-1; a handsome victory under the floodlights where Best, still three months shy of turning 18, fulfilled another dream, with memories of those Wolves games against Honved still fresh in his mind.

A crushing disappointment followed, though, as Lisbon dominated the second leg from the first minute, scoring five without reply. It was one of the most calamitous results in the entire Busby reign. "Our performance was disgraceful," Best recalled of an evening where he first heard the manager raise his voice. The team went back to their hotel; half of the squad went out to drown their sorrows. George retreated to his room, where he dwelled upon the defeat. He took solace in the hope that he was still young and further opportunities would follow.

Busby, as big an advocate as there had ever been for the adage 'if they're good enough, they're old enough', had tried where possible to exercise some of his own caution, as he didn't want to rely too heavily on the new kid on the block. He made a point of telling reporters he was going to rest George for a league game at Upton Park, saying: "He is only 17 and it is asking too much of him to play at West Ham after the heavy pressure of European Cup Winners' Cup and FA Cup ties."

Still, Best had been present for each of the team's major disappointments towards the end of the season, and that included a chastening 3-0 defeat at champions-elect Liverpool. United would eventually finish second – ambitions were for greater things, but this was still the most promising season by far since the disaster, and certainly a complete transformation from the previous season's league campaign.

And a complete personal transformation for George, who had been so downbeat about his future at Christmas that a spot in the first team seemed a million miles away. He could never have imagined by the end of the season he would be not only a fixture in the United side, but also for his country, too.

He was selected for the first time to play in a game against Wales in mid-April 1964. There was some irony here, considering Jimmy Murphy still coached the Welsh national team, and it was Murphy who had played a big hand in Best's inclusion, when he had disbelievingly laughed at the doubt expressed by one of the selectors on the Northern Irish committee. Murphy's eye for talent was legendary; George was called up to the next squad.

His opponent in the Welsh team? Graham Williams. "Jim Murphy was going around the team giving us an individual chat," remembers Williams. "He'd come around giving us instructions about the player we were playing against and then offer us a sip of whisky from his flask. He came to me and said, 'Oh Graham, you've already played against George, haven't you?' I said yes Jim, I have. 'Good luck!' he laughs… He never told me how to play against him! It was like I was being sentenced to the death chamber!"

Williams had been close to Best twice already this season. But the ascent of the young forward had seen him grow in confidence every week. Experience only came with exposure and so George was apparently learning how good he was at the same time as everybody else. Now, with a couple of dozen first team games under his belt, Best was keen to go one-on-one again. "He wound me up, and he knew it," Williams recalls. "He would go past me and the next time he was walking by me he'd just smile at me. It was a wind-up. 'You didn't catch me then!' If I could be crude, I would say he was like dog shit, he was everywhere."

Northern Ireland won 3-2; Best was included in the squad for the next game, against Uruguay at Windsor Park two weeks later, on Wednesday April 29. One problem – the second leg of the FA Youth Cup final would be played the day after that match. United drew the first leg at Swindon on Monday April 27 with George getting their goal. Busby had put a temporary block on United fielding Best for that second leg (he had also played in the senior side's last league game of the season the previous Saturday); the player responded by joking he would put in a transfer request, so the manager relented and said he would wait and see how fit he was following international duty. Best was electric in front of his native crowd, thrilling the fans and tormenting his opponent in a 3-0 win.

He did indeed play against Swindon, and was a constant menace; Sadler scored a hat-trick, and had George's genius to thank for all of them, with two goals coming after Best had dribbled past a number of players and seen a shot parried.

"As early as winning the FA Youth Cup, from that point on it was obvious that he was going straight to the top. The very top," Jimmy Rimmer says. "He had a wonderful relationship with Jimmy Murphy. Jimmy would say to him before the ties, 'Just go out and do the usual, George.' When you have a player of the natural ability George had, you don't really have to tell him anything. He's the one who wins the game for you."

On the night, United won 4-1 to claim their first FA Youth Cup since 1957. Best had completed four full games of football at three different levels in six days but later confessed: "I would have played seven days a week if they had let me."

Not that he needed any exposure for recognition. There were already rumblings of comparisons to great footballers of the past such as Tom Finney or Sir Stanley Matthews. Best confessed to being embarrassed and felt he was "just a nine-stone novice having more than his fair share of beginner's luck".

Noel Cantwell, United's club captain, warned Best at the end of the campaign that he was no longer an unknown quantity. He had played half a season, and that was long enough to put defences across the country on alert. George Best was a marked man – or should that be, a marked boy.

TEEN SENSATION

The world saw plenty of seismic change during the football season that George Best made his Manchester United and Northern Ireland debuts.

The assassination of US president John F Kennedy on November 22, 1963, the increase of the US's involvement in the Vietnam War, as well as escalating racial tensions, all contributed to political unrest in America which reverberated around the globe. A significant element of that unrest was the voice of the post-war youth who were now emboldened to speak for themselves. This had been carried on a tidal wave caused by Beatlemania, and the rise was intrinsically tied to George Best's own.

In early 1963, the Beatles had embarked upon three nationwide tours. Their popularity skyrocketed. On the day George Best made his senior debut, *She Loves You* was at number one in the charts. Fans had been ordering the single for months, before the title of the song was even known. The term 'Beatlemania' was first used in a headline by the *Mirror* on November 2, 1963 when the band returned from a tour of Sweden and a thousand or so fans were waiting to greet them at Heathrow Airport.

That was nothing compared to the 4,000 waiting for them in New York in February 1964 ahead of an appearance on *The Ed Sullivan Show*. Some 73 million viewers tuned in; when the band returned home that month, 10,000 screaming fans were at Heathrow. *The New York Times Magazine* suggested this was a "religion of teenage culture", a "self-identifying culture when they need not transcend in order to find the values that reflect their own aspirations". The conformity and uniformity of what had gone before was no more.

The lifestyle of a music star meant late nights, with drinking and drug-taking often prevalent, most certainly in the audience. Loosened inhibitions and greater freedom of expression led to a more promiscuous way of life for many, and the increased ability to travel all over the world created a universal sense of liberation. Because they wrote music that people could relate to, and because they were on a stage right in front of people's very eyes, these music makers were seen as infinitely more accessible than the movie stars of the day.

It was this landscape into which George Best the footballer was introduced. The world of a sportsman was markedly different to that of a pop star, even if the link between being a professional athlete and having a healthy lifestyle wasn't as clear as it is today. For example, steak and chips would be on the menu three hours before a game, while George was surprised by the frequency with which some of his team-mates in the senior United side would take a sip from Jimmy Murphy's hip flask before a match to calm their nerves.

Drinking was very much a part of British football culture. It was much more complex than the following description will reduce it to, but footballers were not set for life by their wage as a player and after retiring many became publicans, embracing the terrace culture that was such a part of football. Drinking was a part of the game, part of the way of life in Britain; from the Sunday leagues that featured more time in a bar lounge than on a football pitch, to the fans drinking before, during and after a game, right down to the players going to pubs after a match because there was not the distance between a footballer and a supporter that you would expect today.

George Best went on his first 'tour' in the spring of 1964. It was his last official duty as a Manchester United youngster; a trip to Zurich for the Blue Star tournament. United had been taking trips there for years; it was a way to test their own kids against the potential stars of tomorrow, and also a chance to scout players for the future.

The major takeaway from this trip wasn't anything that happened on the pitch. It was George's first experience with alcohol. "Willie Anderson and Fitzy said they were going to the pictures, so George went with them, but the rest of us all went out," Eddie Harrop remembers. "We were in a bar, we all put a pound in the kitty and got two or three drinks. George and the lads came back early because they didn't realise the movie was in Swiss! We said if they wanted to join us they had to put a pound in the kitty. George said he would, but only if he had as many drinks as we'd had already. So he downed a few to catch up. He was absolutely bladdered. It was a job getting him back to the hotel past Jimmy Murphy, John Aston and Joe Armstrong, I can tell you."

George was now 18; as all 18-year-olds do, he swore off

drinking pints after that experience. He went back to Belfast over the summer and was pictured in the local newspaper presenting trophies at the same Cregagh Youth Club he had cut his own teeth. When he was back at Old Trafford for the new season, he was like a different animal.

"I think the first time he really stood out to me was when he started to look as if he was taking himself more seriously. It was that summer," Willie Anderson says. "We all met up at Old Trafford to find out what groups we'd be starting in. I'll never forget seeing George at the end of the corridor with a red turtleneck shirt and long hair. He looked like a rock star. He was always a good-looking kid but with his short hair he presented himself as prim and proper. And he went from that to me having to take a second glance. He really did look like a rock star and it seemed like he started to live up to that."

George's supporting act was not going to be Willie Anderson and the A team this time. There was Dave Gaskell, the capable goalkeeper who had been the youngest of all the Busby Babes when he made his debut in 1956. Harry Gregg, the first choice, was suffering from recurring shoulder issues. Pat Dunne, the goalkeeper from Shamrock Rovers, had been the only transfer in. The experienced defenders Shay Brennan, Tony Dunne and club captain Noel Cantwell were quick and uncompromising, whilst centre-half Bill Foulkes had an unassuming and unflustered demeanour to project assurance in the back-line.

In midfield, the team could boast the tigerish quality of Nobby Stiles, and the class and guile of Pat Crerand and Maurice Setters. There was considerable goal threat in the forward line of David Herd and Denis Law, ably assisted by the creative talents of Bobby Charlton, new signing John Connelly and, of course, George Best on the wings and at inside-forward.

Gregg, Crerand, Law and Charlton could easily be categorised as four of the best in the world. Dunne and Herd were certainly two of the best in the First Division. How good was George Best? Well, that was still a matter to be discovered.

Matt Busby's ambition after coming in at number two was to get his own act back to the top of the charts, but the start to the season was sub-par to say the least. Two defeats and three draws from the first six games left United in 16th. The bright spot had come at home to West Ham on September 2 where Best thrilled and was man-of-the-match; dancing past defender John Bond in the first minute to create a goal for Connelly, and then later scoring himself in a 3-1 victory.

Confidence was gained when Nottingham Forest came to Old Trafford and were beaten by three goals in the first 30 minutes. Victories over Everton, Stoke and Spurs had United in positive spirits as they prepared for a visit to undefeated table-topping Chelsea at the end of September.

With the stakes high, and the intensity to match, Busby and Murphy gave their customary team-talks; enjoy yourself, but make sure you are not outworked. There was no danger of that with the insatiable Best, who viewed this as the biggest game of his young career. Attacking from the front, and roaming out of position, he was a nightmare for the Chelsea defence – particularly as he was in their faces, pressing them, trying to win the ball as soon as they had it. The home team couldn't settle, and just after the half-hour mark, they were pushed into making mistakes in possession; Best seized advantage and powered the ball in to the net.

A victory for persistence. And an epiphany.

Chelsea were the leaders of the First Division. This was not a matter of playing boys of the same age, or even slightly older boys. These were the best players in the country, and they were terrified of him. The confidence surged. Out came the tricks. Eddie McCreadie and Ken Shellito, the home full-backs, only found relief when Best decided to inflict torment on the other. McCreadie was the unfortunate victim of more harassment in the second half, as Best stole the ball from him, invited the defender back just to go past him again, and then clipped the ball into the box. It was a cross-shot; it bounced off the crossbar and back to Denis Law, who headed in. United's result was secure, but Best continued to run riot until the final whistle.

It is rare for a footballer to receive applause from opposing supporters; rarer still when it comes after a game of such importance. So it is a testament to both the magnitude of the performance of George Best, and the grace of the Stamford Bridge crowd, that the entire stadium rose to pay tribute to the miraculous display they had just seen from the teenager.

"At the end they stood and acclaimed him," Ken Jones wrote in the *Mirror* – before comparing Best to Brazilian legend Garrincha. "They gave him their hearts because he had won them with every bewitching swerve, every flick of his magic feet. It was that way at Stamford Bridge last night. A night that belonged to a bundle of brilliance called George Best."

Blues manager Tommy Docherty could do nothing but confess Best had been "fantastic"; that was nothing compared to Shellito, who made it a personal objective, as the teams walked off the field, to get closer to George than he'd managed to during the game and congratulate him. "He'll be better than Bobby Charlton and the other top wingers of today," he told reporters afterwards. "He's the fastest player I've ever seen over the first five to 10 yards. He takes the ball right up to you and stops. His eyes are glued to your feet. You think you've got him and adjust your position, but the second your heels touch the turf he's gone."

Speaking four years later, George said he still felt the Chelsea game was the best he'd ever played; others would say different – he was to become a player of such significance that, like a pop band, everyone had their favourite hit. Still, it felt important – that Chelsea away in September 1964 was as much a statement of arrival of George Best in the First Division as the training ground introduction to Harry Gregg had been a statement of arrival at Old Trafford.

"That was when he came on to the national scene," remembers friend and one-time team-mate Rodney Marsh. "I remember picking up the newspapers the morning after and seeing all the headlines about him. There were many great players around at the time. George arrived with a flash, I remember it vividly. But there were plenty of players who might make an impact on their debut and disappear. After five or six games everybody realised George Best was the real deal. It was as soon as that. He was unplayable. He was un-markable."

In January 1965, Denis Law, in his column syndicated in the *Coventry Evening Telegraph*, reflected on the display as the "best I've seen this season".

"If I had any doubts about the future of this 18-year-old Irish-born winger, they were swept away that night," Law wrote. "If he had been beating them with one single move, they would have checked the danger. But he seemed to beat them with every single move in the book and a few of his own. He has the speed, the control, the flair, the inspiration that is given only to a few. I would have found the experience exciting if he had been in a rival team. But when a fellow on your own line-up hits this kind of mood, you have a right to remember."

A few days later, Best played for his country in Belfast against England; the Three Lions stormed into a 4-0 lead at half-time, but the hosts restored some pride with a thrilling second-half performance led by Best; a 4-3 final score meant that both sets of fans would have some fond memories of an eventful game. Before the game, Wolves defender Bobby Thomson – due to mark Best – was tipped by the *Mirror* to have "the toughest task in soccer". "I played against Best once last season and thought he was a good player," Thomson had said. "I think he'll go right to the top… I'm looking forward to our tussle."

Having made an enduring impression on the domestic game, Best was keen to test himself on the continent. The first examination had been passed well, with a goal and a fine performance against Djurgardens IF of Sweden in the Inter-Cities Fairs Cup; George's goal was the last of six, five of which had come in a stunning 23-minute spell in the second leg at Old Trafford. The performance confirmed the fears of Djurgardens chairman Sigvard Bergh, who had marvelled at Best's display as a guest of United at the game against Everton, saying: "It was amazing to see such confidence and ability in so young a player. Best could give us a lot of trouble."

In the league, United had been in scintillating form since Chelsea – they drew their next game at Burnley, and then went on to win six in a row, including one at champions Liverpool which put Busby's men on top of the league. Before that game, Leslie Edwards of the *Liverpool Echo* had described Best's ascent as being "like a meteor" and tipped him to become the most successful player to ever come from his country.

United then travelled to Germany to face Borussia Dortmund. The teams had faced each other in European competition only once before, in the 1956/57 season. On that occasion,

United had emerged victorious, and the Busby Babes had been declared as the best team in the world. George set about receiving similar individual acclaim and if the competition the teams had been playing in had been the European Cup, he may well have done. Once more Best was unplayable. He came up against the experienced German defender Gerhard Cyliax and gave him, according to the *Belfast Telegraph*, "the father and mother of a roasting". United won 6-1 at the Stadion Rote Erde, with Best getting the third goal.

Perhaps setting the pattern for a career to follow, George was as inspirational in defeat for his country as he was in victory for his club; the same month, he scored a wonderful individual goal against Switzerland in a 2-1 loss. He was not done with Cyliax either; one minute into the return against Dortmund, George stole the ball from him and created a goal for Charlton – United went on to win the second leg 4-0.

* * *

Sooner or later, Noel Cantwell's warnings at the end of the prior season – that opponents would seek Best out to hurt him – were bound to have some substance. Leeds came to Old Trafford in the first week of December in good form. They also arrived with a contrasting reputation to their hosts. Commentators had been thrilled by Busby's side, loving the invention added by Best; there was an admiration for the workmanlike quality of the Leeds side, but some dissatisfaction at their aggressive approach.

This was an introduction into life playing against Paul Reaney; and, for the first time, some genuine foundation for the concern over George's slight build. It had seemed impossible that this tiny magician could dance his way through games in the First Division and come to no harm – and Reaney, seven months older than Best, was in no mood to marvel.

"You wouldn't have thought George was physically cut out for league football just to look at him," Willie Anderson remembered. "But he had this strength about him. I remember watching the game against Leeds from the bench. Paul Reaney kicked him to death. George came to the bench after 40 minutes with tears in his eyes, he had been given such rough treatment. I can remember that vividly. And the kid still went out for the second half.

"Reaney was an animal. Leeds were a much too aggressive team. The only way to stop George was by kicking lumps out of him. But there was still that fierceness, that fearlessness, that I recognised in him from the lad who had been in the B team, that inner strength that said, 'I'm still going to come at you. You're just going to have to kick me again'. I lost count of the number of times he would be fouled for a free-kick, and then he'd demand the ball straight from the kick and go right back at the guy who had just kicked him. For me that was his biggest strength. You could not frighten him out of a game."

The brutal approach worked for Leeds on the day. They scored early in the second half and Busby's side couldn't get into it; the visitors weren't even distracted by the temporary suspension of the game for fog. There was an urban legend that whenever United were losing at home, steam and fumes would mysteriously pour into the ground from the local factories and warehouses. Even if there was any basis to this mischievous rumour, it did not have any benefit on this day, save for temporary respite for Best's bruised limbs.

Those who played with him every day were not concerned.

"I never worried about him being too slight," insisted John Fitzpatrick. "He was brave as a lion. He would tackle just as hard as the opposition used to tackle him. You were allowed to tackle in those days – and he was often targeted by the opponents. He took a lot of abuse."

A lot of abuse in the context of the 1960s was significantly different to how that would translate into today's sport. David Gaskell's experience reads like the medical history of a doomed stuntman. "I'm sure that some of the injuries we picked up were made worse because we all came in to the side so early," Gaskell says. "My body is full of metal. I'm sure that's because of being put into the team at such an early stage and I have no doubt that others have experienced the same sort of thing.

"Six Achilles tendons, two replaced knees. A plate in my wrist after I broke it in the Charity Shield. That was in the warm-up! David Herd had one of the hardest shots in the league, he was hitting shots at me. I saved one and broke my wrist. I strapped it up and played with it all season. I've lost all feeling in it now. I was kicked in the head in Helsinki. George would get similarly rough treatment. But he could look after himself. He was so agile and quick, he would rarely get hurt."

Paddy Crerand – a midfielder certainly able to look after himself – felt no concern about George's capability to deal with it. "I never worried about his slight frame," he says. "Playing out on the wing it didn't matter so much. If he was in the middle of the park it might have been a different matter. Despite his build though, George was as tough as nails and he was as game as anything. Even at that time, when there was nothing of him, he would never pull out of a tackle."

The Leeds defeat temporarily derailed United's runaway form in the league; they won just once in two months, at

Bramall Lane on Boxing Day where Best scored the only goal. George – the dreamer that he was – had cast himself as the protagonist in his own play. He had a fearlessness thanks to his youth and a confidence thanks to his meteoric rise; it was also to his, and the game's, benefit that he hadn't yet properly matured emotionally.

If he had, then he might have looked to the respectful professionalism of a Bobby Charlton and decided that a more sportsmanlike approach might cut him some slack against some of the more intimidating opponents. But no, the stubborn side of him – the side that said those rough tackles were merely evidence that opponents were not good enough to shackle him within the rules of the game – won out, and there developed an extra resolve to exhibit the sort of skill and imagination that nobody else appeared to have.

In the winter and spring weeks of early 1965 there were three extraordinary events which underlined Best's amazing skill and eye for footballing trickery. The first came against Burnley in the FA Cup. The previous week, the two teams had competed in a tight game that had been won by United – Best scoring in a 3-2 win. He would not score in this second encounter, but his contribution would live longer in the memory.

Burnley took an early lead through Andy Lochhead and seemed set to earn an upset. With time running out and United desperate for a way back into the game, Best moved down the left; he was challenged heavily and his left boot came off. As he tried to put it back on, the ball came back towards him. There was no time to do anything but play on, and George kept his balance and hit a cross with his stockinged foot. His previous crosses had been overhit, but because he wasn't able to generate the same power, the ball went into the box, and hit a defender before looping up. Denis Law had a trademark trick of his own – the bicycle kick. He performed it with class and accuracy, snatching an equaliser.

Burnley were not done. Sensing an opportunity with Best bootless, they raced to take the kick-off again. George threw his boot into the crowd but well-meaning United fans threw it back. In his own half, he scrambled unsuccessfully to put it on before Burnley kicked off. But the Clarets' plan backfired within a minute – and the ball once more found Best on the left. Encouraged by the crowd, the forward raced towards the box, crossed the ball again with his left, and there was Crerand in the middle. The Scot fired the ball into the net, sending Old Trafford into a greater state of frenzy and disbelief.

Best responded; playing out the rest of the game with one boot on and the other in his hand, much to the delight of the supporters. Clearly, all that practice to improve his left foot – going right back to his days on the local playing field – had paid off.

"Yes, that was George Best, every bit of him," Jimmy Rimmer says. "You could say it was George Best the showman but what it really was, was George Best the winner, so preoccupied with trying to win the game that he didn't even have time to put his boot back on."

After the game, Best was keen to praise Law for his theatrical effort. "I lost my boot in a tackle and I dropped it over the touchline," he explained. "But people kept giving it back – I just couldn't get rid of it. I didn't put it back on as there was so little time left. Perhaps it was just as well that my boot came off, for I had been hitting my centres too far. Still there seemed no chance Denis could score with his back to goal. How he managed that wonderful overhead kick I'll never know."

There was, however, some controversy. It was stated in the referees' chart that a player should not be permitted to "appear without boots when others are wearing them". The referee on this occasion was George McCabe, one of the league's most distinguished officials. "The first thing I noticed was Best bending down on one knee as if to replace the boot," he said in defence. "My attention went back to the game, which was in a tense state. Near full-time I noticed Best was carrying the boot. Looking back, I suppose I should have ordered him to put it back on, but I could not relax for a second."

United were through to the quarter-final where they would play against Wolves. In these days where football on television was still in its relative infancy, this was a game the cameras were sure to be at. Best was desperate to do something that would leave viewers gasping.

Jim Ryan recalled the events of the day. "I wasn't in the squad but George was. They were going down to Wolves in the Cup, and I told George I was going to go down in the car. He said he'd get me a ticket, but before he did, I had to wait on him as he was practising these bloody corner kicks. He's got half a dozen balls and he's taking kicks from the left wing. There's no goalkeeper. He's taking them over and over again. Curling them into the net from the corner. 'George,' I said, 'come on, hurry up.' I didn't know what he was doing it for.

"Eventually he finishes, gets me the ticket. I went down to Molineux and the atmosphere was great – this was a time when Wolves were a really top team. After about an hour of a great contest, United get a corner out on the left. George goes out to take it. It instantly came to my mind what he was going to do, but I could barely believe it. 'Don't tell me he's going to shoot from here,' I thought. He surely couldn't. He did. He curled it directly into the goal – it was like a self-fulfilling prophecy. It almost felt like he had been practising it to show me what he was going to do later that day. It was unbelievable."

United won 5-3 in a tie for the ages, but George's remarkable moment of invention was so ingenious that it even caught out the cameramen; so, in the footage of the game which aired on television thereafter, a crudely edited clip shows Best arriving in the box in an open play scenario, and then the frame cuts to the ball arriving in the middle of the goal from the corner.

If Best had scored the goal that was suggested from the television replay, it would have defied Newton's law of universal gravitation considering it started out as a low drive into the corner and then the ball suddenly jumped three feet into the air and at least three yards over to the right! Then again, if any player was capable of such a feat…

Still, for posterity and accuracy, we can take Ryan's testimony and also the somewhat dour report from Derek Wallis of the *Mirror* – "George Best curled a corner into the net" was an accurate description of a moment that deserved an explanation much more spectacular. Surely the football world hadn't become so accustomed to his brilliance already that it was reduced to such a monotonous account – the writers would just have to find new ways of describing Best's feats, although perhaps the prevailing point is that his superlatives were becoming so frequent and breathtaking that no dictionary could keep up.

* * *

Three days later United welcomed Chelsea to Old Trafford. George, already on a high, was more keen than Eddie McCreadie to resume acquaintances, and re-introduced himself almost straight from the kick-off. McCreadie was given the ball by Peter Bonetti and his clearance was immediately charged down by Best. George got to the bouncing ball first, nudging it high and away from his opponent's control. The Chelsea man was still goal – and ball-side, but anxiously slipped, unable to tell which way the forward was coming from.

Now with complete control and just inside the box, Best impulsively took another action. The Stretford End was going bananas; they could almost reach out and touch the number 11 as he neared the byline. Impossibly, Best lofted the ball above Bonetti and it floated into the far corner. From that moment it was exhibition stuff from the Northern Irishman, with the United faithful treated to a repertoire of tricks; killing a long ball with one touch, spreading the play wide from the middle of the park, teasing opponents before jetting past them.

At half-time, visiting boss Tommy Docherty was fuming. "Doc told me to mark him," Ron Harris, the legendary Chelsea defender known as 'Chopper', recalls. "He said, 'If he goes to the toilet, hold his hand.' I tried, but couldn't get near him. At half-time Tommy said, 'I thought I said to get close to him?' So I asked what I was supposed to do – break his leg? What if I got sent off? He said, 'Well don't worry about that, they'll miss him a lot more than we'll miss you!'"

United won 4-0; Chelsea were so wound up that Harris decided to exact some retribution on behalf of his tormented colleagues by racing out of position and giving George a knee in the back – earning a booking for his trouble. If Harris was to describe it as a challenge he might face action under the Trade Descriptions Act – he was fortunate, then, that the Act would not come into formation until 1968, and also that referees took a far more lenient view of such incidents at the time. Indeed, it was altercations such as this which led to a revision of the rules on tackles. It's worth pointing out that Harris was aggressive, but not out of place for his time.

"My job was to man-mark players, centre-forwards like Denis Law and Jimmy Greaves," he explains. "I was given the job of trying to follow George around the pitch. How the game was back then, you would always try and get in nice and early with a couple of late tackles. He was a frail fella who didn't weigh ten stone so I would say he was a very brave man. He had a terrific knack of riding tackles… you would know with certain players that if you made that early impression you'd be in for an easy ride, but George would always come back for more."

Despite Best's emergence as a modern problem in terms of the type of opponent he was, it is indicative of his exceptional difference rather than the start of a new trend that Harris – only young himself, at the time – did not feel the need to change his own approach altogether. "I didn't really," he says. "I mean, you would generally slide in, and he was such a tricky lad that you had to stay on your feet. If you slid in he had this balance, the body swerve and those two good feet that would leave you in the mud. He was in an exceptional front line. But he was a magnificent dribbler. I'm not saying that Denis and Bobby weren't brilliant in their own right, but it was George's special talent that he could turn on a sixpence. Until you marked him you didn't know how good he was."

But word was getting round. It seemed as if George's cup heroics from the earlier rounds against Burnley and Wolves had United's name on the cup, but the menacing sight of Leeds United was laying in wait for them in the semi-final. "The man was played as often as the ball and the fouls tally mounted up to awful proportions in a game that was an absolute disgrace,"

Best recalled of that match; and, though the tie went a replay, Billy Bremner's last-minute winner for the Yorkshire side meant there were no fond memories to be found there, either.

It had become a bitter rivalry, and Leeds had emerged as the primary rivals to United for the First Division title too. But Busby's side responded well to FA Cup disappointment, winning 5-0 at Blackburn and then 1-0 against Leicester to set up a titanic struggle with Leeds at Elland Road on Easter Saturday. John Connelly scored early on another physical afternoon – it was the only goal of the game, and with three games left, United now had a point advantage at the top.

Two days later, United played Birmingham at St Andrews. It may have been Easter Monday, but snow was falling in the Midlands, and it was against this backdrop that George scored an early goal. The hosts were bottom of the table, doomed to relegation, but fought back to be level at the break and then scored in the 62nd minute. Soon, the snowstorm wasn't the only flurry the home team had to cope with, as that goal provoked United into an angry bombardment – Best equalised within 60 seconds, two minutes later Charlton gave his side the lead, and ten minutes after that skipper Noel Cantwell capped off the comeback with the security goal.

Next up was Liverpool. Leeds had returned to the top of the table so United needed a win. The result was more convincing than the aggressive approach of the soon-to-be-dethroned champions would have suggested. Sam Leitch of the *Sunday Mirror* praised a "brave and skilled 90 minutes from left winger George Best – what a black-and-blue time he had with thumps galore in a no-nonsense match"; United won 3-0 with a brace from Law and a third from Connelly towards the end.

The penultimate game was at home to Arsenal; this would

have been the last match of the season, but United had a rescheduled game against Aston Villa still to play, and so they could effectively be playing a cup final in that match in the knowledge that Leeds would have concluded their own season.

The other challengers had been Chelsea, but they had undermined their own position. Their last three games were all away, against Liverpool, Burnley and Blackpool, with the Blues needing to win at least two of the three to stand a chance. But after losing at Anfield, several young players broke a curfew by going out in Blackpool, and manager Tommy Docherty dropped eight of his team as punishment. It hit their chances – the mostly reserve side shipped six at mid-table Burnley and Docherty was cast as the man who had cost his team the league on a matter of principle.

In truth, Chelsea could have won both of their final league games and it wouldn't have mattered. This is because United were business-like in their execution of Arsenal. Best was the man who got the ball rolling with the opener. Denis Law played the ball to him in the box – George took control of it and, in the hustle of the penalty area, paused.

The ensemble of the visiting defence moved to the beat of the song they thought they were listening to. Best, as he was wont to do, changed track without them even realising. This was not a matter of audacious skill; but it was an audacious manipulation of timing, catching the entire opponent – to a man – off-guard, and consequently catching goalkeeper Jim Furnell off-balance.

He wasn't finished there. He shot towards goal with an effort that was weak enough to tease Furnell that he could get there if he readjusted his body quickly enough. The Arsenal stopper almost got to it too. But almost wasn't enough. George – the irrepressible showman – had provided a moment worthy of the occasion. To do so on such a day was one thing. This was just seven minutes into the biggest game of his career.

Law added another two in the second half. United won 3-1 and were delighted to hear that Birmingham had managed to hold Leeds to a 3-3 draw. The Yorkshire club were level on points with the Lancashire side, but Manchester still had one game left to play. Busby's side had a superior goal difference but in 1965, teams finishing level were actually separated by goal average – goals scored divided by goals conceded. So long as United avoided defeat by 19 goals at Villa Park, they would be champions, and George Best – celebrating with a lemonade – told *Belfast Telegraph* reporter Dennis Edwards "I think we can safely forecast that will not happen" and United's celebrations began with that win over Arsenal.

"I felt it was going to be our night once Denis Law gave me that great pass for the first goal, but it was difficult to concentrate on the game in that tense atmosphere, particularly with the news coming from the Birmingham game," Best said. "What a night, and what a way to round off a great season. It's a pity my father could not be here for the game. He came over from Belfast for the Liverpool match on Saturday but had to go back to work. Still, I'll have a story to tell them all at home."

Indeed he would – as would Alfredo Di Stefano and Ferenc Puskas, the Real Madrid legends who were guests of honour at Old Trafford for the Arsenal game. They may not quite have seen the official coronation of the new champions, but had most certainly witnessed the actualisation of Best's potential into the tangible influence in his team's success.

George was a few weeks shy of his 19th birthday and had seemed like the most composed player on the pitch. Frank

McGhee of the *Mirror* admired how he had maintained "an incredible icy calm when more experienced men showed how the tension could cause talent to wither and wilt".

There was no intensity at Villa Park, however. The hosts won 2-1, but United were clearly caught between the celebratory hangovers and looking ahead to the Fairs Cup games against Strasbourg which were shortly approaching.

Meanwhile, between the end of the domestic and conclusion of the European season, Northern Ireland had a World Cup qualifier against Albania. At the start of the campaign, club-mate Willie Anderson had expressed amazement at the seriously stylish way George was now presenting himself. And now, at the end of it, some of his international team-mates were in similar awe. One was caught within earshot of a reporter saying, "Let's see what the best dressed teenager of today is wearing" in anticipation of George's arrival at the team hotel.

Johnny Crossan scored a hat-trick in a 4-1 win, but George, who scored the other in the 85th minute, was once more the player who elevated his side to another level.

Northern Ireland "owed much to the sheer genius of George Best", according to sportswriter Bill Ireland of the *Belfast Telegraph*: "Best persistently baffled the Albanians with his swerving runs and used the ball with the utmost intelligence – his cross-field passes and accurate lobs often causing consternation. He is every inch the natural footballer, but the response from some of those around him left a lot to be desired."

The European defenders George facing in a United shirt took the rudimentary approach as guided by Paul Reaney; United faced Strasbourg and paraded the First Division trophy to the Old Trafford crowd before kick-off, but the visitors were not going to stand on ceremony after being humiliated in the first leg by a five-goal defeat in front of their own fans. One report described Best as being floored by heavy tackles "time and time again". The 0-0 draw was a battle of endurance in more ways than one.

This was nothing compared to the tempestuous affair with Ferencvaros in the semi-final. United won the first leg 3-2 and should have had the chance to make it four when Best was brought down in the box; the referee, who had already given Busby's side a penalty earlier in the game, did not award a second. This turned out to be crucial. The Hungarian side won the second leg 1-0, with George coming closest for his team with a header that was cleared off the line.

Midfielder Pal Orosz decided that he had a more straight-forward method of stopping George Best; a fist to the face startled the United kid, and within seconds Pat Crerand had arrived on the scene to throw punches of his own. Orosz and Crerand were sent off – but both were back for the play-off (before ties were decided by away goals). Ferencvaros won 2-1 to finally conclude United's season on June 16.

"We may have gone down, but we have plenty to cheer about after United's best season for years," said Best, with some dis-appointment but no little perspective.

It was an undeniable truth. United had won their first league title for eight years, which was remarkable in its own right. George Best's importance to that success was indisputable. Life had changed so much for him in the previous 12 months – and in the 12 months before that, too. So perhaps he could have expected a repeat – but, as was par for the course with George Best, nobody was predicting what was about to happen in the 1965/66 season.

KINGMAKER

Winning the First Division championship in 1965 was the fulfilment of one of Matt Busby's ambitions after the Munich Air Disaster. The man who had created the dynasty of dynasties – who had worked fastidiously to plan – had more vague aspirations the second time around.

"I don't think there was a specific goal, but he wanted to build something comparable with the Busby Babes," journalist Paddy Barclay explains. "Something that was expected to win titles at home and abroad. Bear in mind the standard that was set – European semi-finals were beginning to be taken for granted. It was also the era where the FA Cup really mattered, so the victory of 1963 was a big prize and a big step on that road. The big two for Matt were the league title and the European Cup because they implied undoubted supremacy. He wanted United back there."

By whatever measure you use to determine such matters,

Busby had succeeded in his quest to create another great Manchester United team. That it followed Jimmy Murphy's deliverance of a youth team worthy of the club's grand history was no coincidence. The achievement was as unsurprising as it was remarkable. That is to say, the pair knew no other way than to construct a football team with these qualities.

"The most amazing of them all," was how Bill Foulkes described the 1965 championship side. "We felt we had the makings of a top team already, but then George appeared and kicked us into a new dimension. His footballing make-up was practically flawless and he could have excelled in any position."

United won the FA Cup in 1963 with the essential structure of a great team in place. A team with the potential for greatness but yet with a sadness attached to it. There were one or two players missing, but most of all, it was the intangible something, that certain sense of personality which had been sucked out of the club after Munich. There was a tremendous dignity with which the club carried itself, and of course that in its own right was a commendable trait, but the braggadocious extroversion which seemed to personify the Babes appeared to have been sacrificed for it.

Busby and Murphy could create a team which possessed many similar qualities, but even men capable of moulding extraordinary things as these two were, they could not manifest the sort of stardust that comes from the personality of a player like, for instance, Duncan Edwards.

A good player, a great player, added to the 1963 FA Cup final team could have made United great. He might have taken them to another league title. He might even have taken them to the Holy Grail of the European Cup. But it was the extraordinary personality of George Best that elevated Busby's last wonderful team into the pantheon of the true greats. We know that it is so because the returns down memory lane have often skewered the conversation so far the other way as to suggest it was only George Best who was responsible for the positive fortunes of Manchester United in their last glory years under Busby. It is a revision that tells us simultaneously just how underrated that United team was and how big the final explosion of George's United career was.

All of what was to come may never have happened if not for some timely intervention from Matt Busby at the start of the 1965/66 season. There could be no doubt George was living up to his personality. To this point in his career he had always been encouraged to do so. In the star-studded attack of Old Trafford, he was the wildcard while others, such as Denis Law and Bobby Charlton, were the established stars.

Law was a goalscorer supreme. In 1963/64 he set a post-war record of 46 goals in 42 games and followed that with 39 (28 in the league) in United's title-winning year. It was an accomplishment that earned him the Ballon d'Or – also known as the European Footballer of the Year Award – for 1964.

Bobby Charlton did not score as many goals, but was just as reliable when his team needed him – and, as the heartbeat for his club and country, this was going to be a big year indeed for the man synonymous with the number nine shirt. The 1966 World Cup was to be held in England, and much was expected. If Charlton could keep up those contributions in a successful side (spoiler alert: he could, and did) then the Ballon d'Or could be his in 1966.

These were the ceremonial and official titles bestowed upon individuals for achievements in a sport that still prided itself on class, prestige and rite of passage; the old boy's hierarchy of the way things were done. But Best was no respecter of rule or reputation; although he quite clearly possessed some awe for celebrated figures, at the same time he was not afraid to challenge the orderly way in his own manner. In the early weeks of the new season, it is fair to say that George was not conducting himself with the professional dignity of a champion in the same way that Bobby Charlton had done when he himself was a prodigious youngster.

Excess is a topic deeply connected with the story of George Best. To steer away from the subject as much as possible is a deliberate path taken in this book; however, to completely dismiss it would be ignorant to its importance, and therefore doing a blind disservice to the subject. And, upon the first real encounter with the subject in George's life, it ought to be confronted and addressed for what it was.

Let us not confuse this with a tale of origins. It has been covered in this book and elsewhere that George's first real taste of alcohol in the football fraternity was on the trip to Switzerland with Eddie Harrop and David Farrar. In his book *A Strange Kind Of Glory*, Eamon Dunphy tells a story of how, as a youth team player, George 'stole' Jim Ryan's girlfriend and joked about it in a cruel manner in front of the other lads.

These tales only have true relevance when put into the context of George's perceived vices in later life. Taken for what they were at the time, they are not particularly extraordinary. For example, speaking in an interview for this book, Ryan was quick to downplay the significance of his fallout, insisting it blew over in a week or two and that he and George were best of pals again afterwards. Of course, the stories have some connection greater than merely tenuous to George's life story. They do form part of the origin for issues in later life.

In the mid-1960s, these were normal issues in a life that was becoming less than normal which each passing week.

Take, for example, George's supposed womanising. "We would often go to a park, and then maybe a bar or a pub but we never had a drink, and George certainly didn't," Ryan says. "We would go to look at girls, that's the only way I can put it." So, when does normal behaviour cross over into being a notorious personality trait? On one hand you could safely assume most people in George's position would have taken advantage of the attention. On the other, it was also reasonable to deduce that the boy who had only turned 19 in the early summer of 1965 was still maturing in an ever-changing world; he was lauded and loved for his risk-taking on the pitch and it is natural it followed that he would feel suitably emboldened off it.

Take the story Harry Gregg told about the teenage 'little fella' having an affair with a married woman and losing lots of money gambling at the Cromford Club. George had tried to bluster his way out of it but, as the club was owned by Matt Busby's close friend Paddy McGrath, was unable to. He promised to change his ways, but as was the case with any teenager, changing his ways only meant committing the crimes in a way that he wouldn't be found out.

And so he continued to burn the candle at both ends; a process that only ever truly results in diminishing returns, a result that is only appreciated when the candle is gone and all there is left is a burnt wick. When you are young, you think it will burn forever, and while you still have your faculties, there is never a reason to believe it won't.

Despite being a firmly established member of the first team, George remained close to the players he had come up through the youth team with and socialised with them.

"One night George and I had been out and we were called into the manager's office the next morning," Jimmy Rimmer recalls. "Matt Busby would turn out the lights in the corridor so that only the light on the door that had 'MANAGER' was glowing, just to add to the atmosphere and make you feel intimidated. We got in there and he said, 'I know what you lads are doing. You've got to control yourself a little bit.'"

The plea fell on deaf ears. It was a true summer of indulgence for George. "Like a fool, I let the glory get a grip on me," he said. "All the proud plans for a stirring, successful entry into Europe spluttered to a sickening halt after just a month of the 1965/66 season. The crash came after a string of late nights that could have ruined my career. Suddenly the life of fame, photographs and big money had made me the prize to have at any party. And I loved it. Dances that finished before midnight usually developed into parties that went on into the next day. I was living 24 hours a day and letting myself get really run down. My play was suffering yet I didn't seem able to do anything about it... I was going on to the field tired; coming off shattered."

At first it seemed as if it could be sustainable. Best had opened United's season with a goal in the drawn Charity Shield encounter against Liverpool, his strike described by Sam Leitch of the *Sunday Mirror* as "a masterpiece of gentle timing". But a string of indifferent performances followed in the league, with one particularly miserable afternoon against Newcastle in mid-September where United were lucky to get a point, thanks to a late equaliser from Nobby Stiles.

In training the following Friday, George admitted he was not surprised to see he had been dropped from the team to face Chelsea at home. He was however surprised to be told Busby wanted to see him again. "It was not a snarling chastisement," Best recalled. "Mr Busby is not like that. He spoke quietly and effectively... he told me why he was leaving me out. He said he didn't think my mind was on my football. He said I had a great future if I looked after myself. He wanted me to take life easy for a week or two... I left that office an older and wiser man. I must admit that I had been a fool. I was only annoyed because I had been found out. I reckoned that nobody at the club knew what I was up to and the fact was that everybody did."

Best admitted that Noel Cantwell and Pat Crerand both tried to talk to him about taking early nights – that, according to George, "only made me feel ratty about their interference into something that was strictly between me and my shadow". But when United took Chelsea apart 4-1, with Charlton getting the first and Law scoring a hat-trick, a different mood struck the youngster. "I realised I was extremely dispensable," he admitted. "The thought terrified me and I vowed I would never again put pleasure before playing."

George had been a student attending the lesson, and even if the lesson had not really been learned, there is no doubting that for a while his dedication to making sure he did was sincere.

He was dropped for the next two games – left out of the team for the trip to Helsinki as United began their European Cup campaign, where his absence was not felt in a 3-2 win – and then, at Arsenal, where it perhaps was, in a 4-2 defeat. His recall had an immediate boost. First of all, he scored the second of his team's six against Helsinki in the return game, and then, he scored the opening goal against Liverpool in a crucial 2-0 win at Old Trafford.

United's mixed start to the campaign took another turn for the worse one week later, although Best could be absolved of the blame at White Hart Lane when his team lost 5-1. The game has gone down in club history as John Fitzpatrick became the first ever substitute in United colours when he came on for Denis Law – though the result is conveniently forgotten in modern recollections when retold through someone of an Old Trafford persuasion! The match has been immortalised in the memories of all associated with Tottenham because of the way Jimmy Greaves dribbled through the United defence to score one of the truly great goals of the era.

The champions' response to this humiliation was strong. A run of six wins should have been seven and only wasn't because of a very eventful game at Old Trafford against Blackburn. United had a first-half lead through Charlton, but late on, Harry Gregg kicked out at Rovers defender Mike England and was sent off. David Herd went from goalscorer to goalkeeper and the visitors took advantage, scoring twice in the last seven minutes. Fortunately Denis Law also netted to salvage a 2-2 draw. Progress up the table was coupled with progress in Europe with Herd contributing in more conventional form, scoring a hat-trick against ASK Vorwarts of Germany (now FC Frankfurt) to secure qualification to the next round. The opponents there would be the formidable Benfica of Portugal; led by the great Eusebio.

In order to prepare, Matt Busby flew out to Portugal to watch them play, causing him to miss his own team's match with Tottenham one week before Christmas. Jimmy Murphy took charge and ordered the players to exact revenge. They did it to a tee – winning 5-1.

Having got back into contention at the top of the table, United ended the calendar year in third place, five points behind leaders Liverpool, ahead of the New Year's Day trip to Anfield. Around 10,000 supporters were locked out and missed the drama as United scored after 90 seconds through Law, but conceded a goal similarly close to the end to lose the game. With the chances of retaining the title receding, league form became more patchy, with a run of just three wins from nine games taking them out of contention.

* * *

The temporary dip in fortune for United did nothing to disturb the skyrocketing trajectory of George's profile. "When you live around it he was just one of the guys," says Willie Anderson. "But the thing which really opened my eyes to his level of celebrity was when Matt Busby asked George and I to play in a benefit game over the Pennines for the widow of a player who had died. We were in a select XI against Liverpool.

"George said he would drive, so we went together in his big white Jaguar. We play our game and at the end the police came up to us and said 'Hey, George, you can't go out that main entrance.' There were 3,000 girls waiting! I was taken aback. This was my mate, just George Best. We were pushed through a turnstile into the parking lot – it was a rush to try and get to the car before the girls saw us. George made it, I didn't. They were dragging me all over the place to try and get to him. I finally got into the car and we made our getaway."

George's form had recovered from that early dip, but this added rise in popularity coincided with a period where he was being scrutinised for the first time. He was the subject of hyperbolic criticism for a performance for Northern Ireland, with one critic describing his display against Albania as his "worst ever international". It was his 12th cap.

Better fortune seemed to wait for Best and his club in the cup competitions. He scored twice in a 5-2 rout of Derby County in the FA Cup – to make it 13 in all competitions by mid-January – and then Benfica came to Manchester in early February for the first leg of their European Cup tie. They arrived not only with Eusebio but with arguably the strongest recent record of any team on the continent, with their two wins and two defeats from the last five finals.

If you are even at least remotely familiar with the story of George Best then it is no spoiler to discuss the significance of this tie in his career and indeed in his life. It became one of those 'explosions' he spoke about. However, it does not therefore follow that it was so unexpected. Take the words of António Simões, the then-Benfica left-winger, who insists that Best was one of the danger men they were preparing for.

"Of course we knew about George before the tie," says Simões. "He was already a great player. It was only the beginning of his career but the talent was there. Nobody had doubts about that. He was destined to be better than just great."

But the word 'destined' suggested the moment of realisation was still to come. And at times in the first leg it seemed as if it would be a way off. Best confessed to being struck by the "bewildering pace" of the game and it was the maturity of Charlton, Herd and Law which helped United overturn an early goal to lead 3-1.

The major talking point had been the clash of Eusebio and Nobby Stiles. Stiles did a competent job until the 70th minute, when the legendary forward demonstrated the sort of instantaneous class that sets true stars apart from the ordinary. The sort of class which had seen him succeed Law as the European Footballer of the Year. His quick change of feet finally earned him some space and everyone including goalkeeper Harry Gregg was wrong-footed. The cross was converted by Jose Torres; the goal was seen as one of the most significant reasons United needed to sign a goalkeeper, as the imposing Gregg of years gone by would have surely commandeered his box to seize control. Sadly, a succession of shoulder injuries had impacted his ability to do so.

United won 3-2 but that late Benfica goal felt like an equaliser. They had never suffered defeat at their home ground, the Stadium of Light, in European competition. "When we lost 3-2 we felt we had created a good hope for our chances of progressing," Simões confesses. "We thought we could probably go through."

For their part, United knew it was crucial to go into the second leg in confident mood. They also needed to be sure they had their shooting boots on, because it was almost certain they would need to score in Lisbon. In the six games before the return, United did exactly that, winning four and drawing two, and scoring six, four and four in different games. Charlton and Herd grabbed hat-tricks. Law twice scored two. John Connelly helped himself to three. And, in an eventful FA Cup clash at Molineux which served as the warm-up to United's trip abroad, George found his own scoring boots for the first time in two months, netting the decisive goal in a turnaround 4-2 win from two goals down.

In the pursuit of complete preparation, Busby took his side out to Portugal on Monday instead of Tuesday. It had a positive and relaxing impact on the squad, although the late kick-off time of 9:45pm induced some nerves. A strange feeling encompassed the dressing room. This was, undoubtedly, the biggest occasion the club had faced since Munich. Since they had faced Real Madrid in the 1957 semi-final. This was what Busby had strived for. He had his Holy Grail and still dreamed of success as a winner, but he had already succeeded in the challenge to make Manchester United competitive at this level again. The first leg win had proven that. Whatever happened in the 90 minutes of football was not going to detract from this accomplishment. Harry Gregg, Bill Foulkes and Bobby Charlton could sit in the dressing room and appreciate that it was enough to be competitive. They had ambition, of course. But they had already accomplished and overcome so much.

On the other end of the spectrum was George Best. The 19-year-old did have something to prove. He was still writing his story. He had the same blank canvas that the Babes who perished had; only George was able to paint upon it. Just as those young men in 1956, who had taken domestic football by storm, had been declared the best team in the world, George was in a position for the first time where he could stand among the greats and make an impression of his own.

He had been through the same system as everyone else. The youth team, the reserve team, the first team. On each occasion he had almost appeared to be as bewildered by his own brilliance as the company he was now keeping were. Lightning just kept striking where George Best was concerned. Now, in Portugal, he had an opportunity to illustrate that his potential was so great that even his ability at such a precocious age, with so much left to learn, meant his name was worthy of discussion amongst the greats he had been compared to.

In the half-hour before kick-off, all thoughts were on the game. The team were ready to play by 9:15pm. George himself was developing a reputation for coming in shortly before kick-off. "He became so laid-back that Matt Busby would often be asking everyone where he was 15 minutes before the game," Jimmy Rimmer says. "He'd be in the lounge talking to anyone, he was that relaxed and confident in his ability to just get his kit and boots on and go out. He was never flustered."

Tonight, though, he was ready much earlier. Pat Crerand would wait until the last seconds before leaving the dressing room to tie up his bootlaces but even he was ready.

The dressing room of a football team is a cauldron of superstition at the best of times. "Some of the lads were kicking a ball about, whiling away the time in the dressing room," George remembered. "I saw it bounce across to Crerand and, like a man who could restrain his pent-up emotions no longer, he rapped it erringly into a full-length wall mirror that exploded into a thousand pieces. As soon as the slivers of glass stopped tinkling to the concrete… silence. Until Bobby Charlton said quietly, 'Now everyone just forget that ever happened.'"

The moment interrupted the tension. The identity of the person lightening the mood was poignant; Charlton was a man who could appreciate true misfortune. He had played 398 games for Manchester United before this. Many had been lost. Losing a game of football was not a disaster, even for Manchester United. Having the opportunity to play a game for the club was a blessing.

The team-talk given by Matt Busby has taken on a legend of its own. Almost all recollections include a variation of the following: that he instructed his players to be safe and keep everything tight for the first 20 minutes. Harry Gregg disregarded this as "nonsense – absolute, complete rubbish" and insisted "no Manchester United team I ever played in was told to defend". Maybe it was a matter of interpretation; the nuanced difference between discipline and being defensive as an attitude. Either way, Busby could be grateful that everyone was singing harmoniously from the same hymn sheet; for, though the night would belong to one man, it is undeniable that he required stellar performances from a high-class supporting cast. Before the game, Eusebio was presented with the trophy for his recent European Footballer of the Year award, setting the scene for a performance worthy of it.

"A tremendous roar greeted the first whistle," remembered Bobby Charlton. "From that moment it was George Best's game, football history will always be sure about that, but in fact the whole team functioned beautifully."

* * *

It seemed as if both teams were wary of the other. Benfica had seemingly decided to sit back and wear United out. It was a gamble doomed to fail. You can call it a team unity, you can call it fate, you could even call it a capitulation. You could call it the greatest 90 minutes from any British footballer. But more true than any of those statements was the shell-shocking devastation George Best inflicted on the home defence for the first 15 minutes. He was a man on a single-minded mission.

In the first moments of the contest he latched upon a defensive header that went awry, and he would undoubtedly have stormed through on goal had he not paused to defer to Herd's seniority. Herd, to his credit, tried to play a through ball but the momentum had gone. Then, as United poured forward again, Best again anticipated the bounce of a home header. This time he observed as a defender came towards him, and he poked the ball around him as if he was a player from the Fourth Division and not one of the strongest teams in Europe.

As Benfica tried to attack, there was Best again, on the edge of his own box, intercepting a pass with his head and accelerating past one man, only over-running the ball 40 yards up the field. There were not even five minutes on the clock, and already there was a deep panic within the home defence.

"With Benfica clearly convinced that we would go for their throats as usual, the strategy worked a treat," Bill Foulkes said. "Playing so deep, George had never been given as much space in his life and he was rampant."

Happening at the Stadium of Light, in real time, was another awakening of George Best. There had been such proclamation of the level people felt George would one day ascend to but that was one day. And one day was supposed to be in four or five years. Not now. Not tonight. But here it was, sure enough.

And when we say here, there is no greater declaration than that of Paddy Crerand. "Already by then, I felt he was the best in the world. I honestly did," says Crerand. "He won the European Footballer of the Year award in 1968 but in 1965, 1966 and 1967, as young as he may have been, he was the best.

"Matt and Jimmy were telling us to keep it tight for the first 15 minutes. Keep it tight, keep it level and we'll go on from there. Quieten the crowd. Sensible stuff. We were three-nil up in 15 minutes. That was the night George became known to the world, even though what he did was of no surprise to any of us. The goal he scored with a header – Tony Dunne took the free-kick. Tony wasn't the longest kicker of a ball you could wish to meet. I said to George, 'Don't stand out there on the wing – Tony'll never reach you. He can't kick it that far.' I didn't know I was a genius! George goes in-field and only goes and heads the ball straight into the back of the net."

Six minutes gone.

Three minutes later he had the ball in the net again. Charlton fed through a fantastic pass, and George was much quicker to anticipate it than the two defenders either side of him. He received the ball and controlled it on his left. It seemed a heavy touch, but he was able to turn, get there ahead of the defender, and slide it into the net. The linesman, however, had his flag up for offside – despite Best clearly being on. His speed had been too much for even the officials.

In the 13th minute, another long ball is headed down by Herd for Best to run on to. The winger's first touch is again heavy but perfect. There are three defenders between him and the goal as the ball bounces. He is able to accelerate away from the first. There's no point him even trying to catch Best.

What follows is a majestic, physics-defying example of gravity and movement. Cruz and Germano think they have the space covered. Cruz, the left-back, stands his ground. Germano, the centre-half, decides to commit to a sliding tackle.

It is the improbable speed with which the following movement is executed that still causes the jaw to drop. Best, anticipating the heavy tackle, touches the ball past the defender, the same way he had already done plenty of times in his fledgling career. But it is his balance which truly enthralls, surely only made possible by his speed of thought and his small frame, enabling him to arc his body in one movement – first left, away from Cruz, and then right, away from Germano, and then straight on again to regain control of the ball to take him towards goal. It doesn't seem possible. Performed with the agility and grace of a world-class ballet dancer or figure skater; with the sleight of hand of the world's greatest magician; with the flight and navigation skills of a bird dodging an unavoidable obstacle at top speed. It's breathtaking. It's marvellous. It's magnificent.

But this move alone is not affirmation of Crerand's premature coronation. It would be a trick of the light, perhaps consigned to word of mouth and the protestation of a spectator insisting one night they saw this occurrence, if there was not a reason for it to be captured.

And that reason was the goal which rounded it off. In less than three seconds, George had stolen control of the ball and performed this routine on instinct yet with the cold and calculated precision of someone who had planned every moment, every bounce, every change of direction. As if he was the one controlling everyone else. It seemed to be the only explanation for how perfectly time and space was manipulated to bend at his will. And then, suddenly, he was through on goal, and with so much time it would have taken much longer than three seconds for anyone to even get close to him.

The goalkeeper tried. But what could he do? He was caught under the same spell as the 75,000 in the stands and his ten team-mates. Pereira tried to narrow the angle. George shot low, straight across him, and for added visual quality the ball struck the tight netting just inside the corner and bounced back out with so much force that the right-back, Dominicano Cavém, could only kick it back into the net.

"The Boss had told us to take it steady for 20 minutes," Nobby Stiles recalled in his book *After The Ball*. "When Benfica were a heap of smouldering ruins, Bill Foulkes said to me, 'Didn't anyone mention the plan to George?'"

United were two goals up on the night, one up on aggregate, but if this were a boxing contest the referee might well have intervened in mercy. Punch-drunk and bamboozled, the Benfica defence were almost like statues as Herd and Law created an opening for Connelly to make it three in the 16th minute. Only then did Busby's side take heed of his advice and slow the game down. At half-time, Law remembered Crerand quipping, "Anyone got another mirror?"

With a 6-2 aggregate lead they could even afford the mishap of an own goal when Shay Brennan miscalculated a lob back to Gregg. Suspect goalkeeping was at play when Crerand scored the fourth United goal in the 80th minute, but Pereira was not at fault when he fell for Charlton's clever shimmy to make it five in the last seconds.

Thus concluded the evening's proceedings. George did not play a part in his team's final three goals but all anyone could talk about was the seminal mark he had made on the game. Busby, Murphy, Manchester, England, the world. All had been robbed of a similarly defining performance from a Babe. George was not only fulfilling his own potential, he was justifying that of those who had gone before him. He was Duncan Edwards rampaging unstoppably through the Madrid midfield. He was Tommy Taylor plundering goals against Inter Milan.

* * *

United had scored goals at such a frenetic pace that night in Lisbon that for years afterwards Jimmy Murphy had been convinced that George's disallowed goal actually stood. When writing his book *Matt... United... and Me*, the Welshman wrote of the Benfica match as "the greatest I ever saw Best play. He scored three goals, taking the ball from the halfway line for one of them, and beating several opponents before hammering it in from 20 yards. The touch of a master.

"Yet on that night of triumph, I don't think George Best was even aware there was a fellow named Eusebio playing for the other team. This is his secret. I am sure if it was possible for him to play in a forward line of Puskas, Di Stefano, Pele and Eusebio, George Best's attitude would be: And now watch George Best of Northern Ireland play!"

George would plan for things he wanted to do on a matchday. He would try new tricks all the time. This quality made him stand out against the ordinary. But it was the instinctive skill observed in the second goal – the ability to do something so extraordinary, so outrageous in the heat of the battle, with no time to think, against the very best of opponents – which set him apart as one of the truly great players.

And so, even at the age of 19, those heady tributes about George being the best player in the world did not feel unreasonable. In fact, one might even consider the moment where he swerved impossibly between two defenders, only to retain full composure, as the very second where he could lay claim to that title.

"George was so different," Willie Anderson says. "If the team wasn't successful then you would say George was just another great player. But it was a great team, and there was even an argument to say that George carried them at times, which tells you just how good he was. Denis and Bobby were fantastic players in their own right, straight guys, and here was George with long hair, dating television stars and models.

"Bobby could glide, or surge, past a player, and Denis was as quick in the box as anything. But I think you could say George could do that and had strings to his bow that even those two didn't have. George had this tremendous sense of creativity that nobody else had. There was nobody in the world like him. We realised he was different the more time we spent with him as a kid. He got better really quickly, but you could also say that it was just a case of that opportunity presenting itself, and it was a case of proving himself – so he had always been that good, it was just that in 1963 Stretford knew him, by 1964 the entire country did, and in 1966 the world did.

"He grew in confidence, he developed in maturity, he worked to improve, he was playing at a higher level and knowing he could star, playing with better players like Crerand, Charlton and Law, these players who could create different openings and different space. This was a kid who came into a team like that and made them even better."

It is perhaps most pertinent of all to consider the passionate recollection of Simões. "Everything was perfect for them and we had a nightmare. When they started to score goals and play in the way they did, it was very difficult for us," he said.

"When the game is over you have to just offer congratulations because they were better on the night. It was that simple. Sometimes you can play better than another team but you don't score, and the opponent has a chance to survive. Manchester United gave us no chance to survive. They were ruthless. We tried to do our best but it was not our moment. It was their night. I would always think, 'I just hope George doesn't get mad'. You don't want to give a great player extra motivation.

"But he was mad that night and it was a big problem for us. He was so mad there were two George Bests. It's hard enough to play against one – how are you going to play against two? It is very hard to stop a guy like that when he is having this kind of experience. Nobody from Benfica will ever forget that game. In the end they gave him applause. I think about the great privilege that I had to be a part of this occasion.

"What means more to me was that I had the experience to share the field with one of the best players ever, having one of his most special nights, doing all the special things, all the magic things, and I enjoy remembering a player doing this. It didn't matter if we played with 11 or 22 players, we could not have beaten him. He was a tornado in that game."

Harry Gregg agreed: "George played many great games, but the evening he transformed from potential into a genuine superstar was when he destroyed Benfica."

The grace displayed by the Benfica team was on show that night. They were yet to even endure their first sleepless evening and they invited the United contingent out for a meal and a drink. "The Benfica players took us out for dinner after the game, if you can believe it," Paddy Crerand recalls. "If we'd just been beaten 5-1 by them, we wouldn't have fucking gone out anywhere. We would have gone home and cried! They were fantastic. Different class."

Leaving the Casino Estoril restaurant, George walked past a market stall and bought a sombrero. On the plane, he talked about his intention to wear it so that he would be photographed by the press when they arrived back in Manchester. He put it on in preparation; Gregg told him to stop being so foolish and to take it off, but the other players, triumphantly celebrating in the same way George was, told the goalkeeper to keep quiet.

Sure enough, George walked off the plane donning the sombrero as though it was a scalp. Some in the press had described him as 'El Beatle' due to his likeness to the pop group taking the world by storm. There could be no doubting that the minute the plane touched down in England was the moment George's life changed forever more.

"I started believing what they were writing about me," George later said. "So I actually did it on purpose. I knew they were going to take my photographs. I wish I hadn't have done, but I did. I thought I was taking advantage of something but it backfired. You end up living like you're in a goldfish bowl."

So, to that press reaction. Portuguese newspaper *A Bola* – who had published that Beatle reference – were seemingly as gracious as the Benfica team, describing United as "the greatest club team that European football ever produced, after the fabulous Real Madrid". The *Belfast Telegraph* could scarcely contain themselves with the excitement of their favourite son's display: "It was fantastic, hardly credible. Best got two of them with typical pieces of audacious brilliance."

And Frank McGhee of the *Mirror* showed that even with the considered judgement of an experienced sportswriter, he could not deny the frankly unbelievable sight he had witnessed: "The player at the sensational centre of it all was that wilful, skilful waif George Best. Now surely he is the young pretender to the 'King of European Football' title awarded to Benfica's Eusebio before the match."

Perhaps the most understated comment of the coverage came from Best himself, who was more sheepish in his conversation than his presentation: "We were lucky at the beginning and they could not stop us from then on."

"The scribes dubbed him 'El Beatle' and from that day on his life became a goldfish bowl," Gregg said. "There were many occasions when I felt George's team-mates were often his worst enemy. There was nothing deliberate, or malicious, but they seemed incapable of realising the need to protect George from the fame that was engulfing him."

There was nothing in the short term which suggested George was affected by the new adulation. To get the real feeling on that score it's best to consider the opinions of those who had been with him in those first couple of years at Old Trafford.

"I couldn't say that he changed," says Jim Ryan. "By that time he had moved into a different group and had a different circle of friends. When I played in the European Cup with him I couldn't say he had changed very much as a person to the lad I was with in the youth team with."

An episode recalled by Eddie Harrop – the young full-back who never made it into the United first team – reveals much, both about the way George was and the things he was going through. "A couple of years after I was out of the game, I was walking with my girlfriend, now wife, down Market Street in Manchester," Harrop says. "On the other side of the street, George was walking – he was being trailed by at least ten people. Girls, hangers on, that sort of thing. He spotted me, and didn't just wave. He came across the road – in those days, Market Street was a two-way street. He dodged all the cars and buses and nipped across, found me and gave me a big hug. He hadn't seen me for two years. He was a big star then. That was the type of person he was, that was the George I knew."

John Fitzpatrick concurs. "He certainly was the best player in the world after Benfica. He went from being a name that a lot of people knew to suddenly being the star player of Manchester United. As a person, he didn't change, and as a player, he was just the same, it was just the target on his back grew as big as that star… I say this not only because he was my friend but George Best was the best player in the world at the time. Whenever he went out on a Saturday afternoon, nobody knew what to expect. He was such a great player. I used to feel a wee bit sorry for the full-back he'd be playing against. You'll never see another player like George again. The best player I ever saw. By a considerable distance."

The pride of the players he had graduated with is obvious

and palpable. The thoughts of Jimmy Rimmer are no different. "It was marvellous," he says. "We all knew that he was going to be a star, we all knew he was going to be the best in the world. It was one thing for us lads to be talking about him but it was another for someone like Eusebio to start acknowledging how good he was."

For that to be proven, United would need to achieve. But the evening in Benfica would remain the highlight of the season. The league form continued to be poor and although there was progression in the FA Cup, it came at a considerable cost. In the sixth-round tie at Preston North End, Best was given some rough treatment, and hurt his knee in one particularly rough challenge. He felt it had eased but as he went to take a late corner he remembered his knee "collapsing".

That game was drawn – Alex Dawson, the former United striker, scoring for the hosts, and Herd levelling for the visitors. But Best missed the replay as an x-ray on his knee had revealed cartilage damage. Physio Ted Dalton told Busby that an operation was probably necessary; George thought they were joking at first and insisted to Jimmy Murphy that he would see out the season. Dalton acquiesced that they would see how it went with treatment three times a day and plenty of rest, with the European Cup semi-final against Partizan Belgrade in mind.

And so George was 'rested' for a couple of league games but played against Leicester City in the game before the team flew out to Belgrade. He was uninspiring in a 2-1 defeat but made it through the 90 minutes, so also made the trip.

In the evening training session before the game George was put through his paces. One exercise included carrying Denis Law on his back, which only exacerbated the pain; George privately knew this, and was gingerly striking the ball with minimal power, so desperate he was to avoid further pain. In the European Cup, the substitute rule applied only for goalkeepers, and so George knew it was start or nothing.

Early in the game a cross flew across to Best. His swing was sincere but he failed to connect. Immediately he winced. Trainer Jack Crompton rushed on to the pitch to massage and adjust the bandage on the knee. Momentarily, George felt better, and in a sole moment of freedom was able to dribble and create a chance for Law to strike the crossbar. It was as close as United came. Having withstood the early approach, and realising this was not the fit George Best that had terrorised Benfica, it was a confident Partizan who came out for the second half and they scored twice within 15 minutes to secure a 2-0 win. Late on, Crompton again had to see to the knee, and it was all George could do to see the game out.

"Best's inclusion was a gamble that didn't pay off," Frank McGhee wrote in the *Mirror*. "In the 75th minute he had to have treatment and limped along for the rest of the match.. and so did United."

On the way home, there was a 10-hour stopover in Vienna, and so the United players wandered around the local area. Best, of course, was hobbling, and hoping against hope that he would be fit to play in two semi-finals – the return leg against Partizan, and then in the FA Cup against Everton.

Busby gave it a couple of days back in Manchester until making a final decision. On the Monday before United played Partizan, George went to see a specialist, who advised that he must have an operation and that he could not play again until that time. The date for surgery was set for FA Cup final day.

United's attempt at breaking down a resolute Partizan was

admirable, but all they had to show for it was a late Nobby Stiles goal and a 1-0 win. The destiny which seemed at hand a few weeks later would have to wait. There was no consolation in the FA Cup – it was bad enough that United were beginning to feel the physical strain of the season, but Everton rested their entire team in the preceding league fixture. They were fined heavily by the FA but those fresh legs made the difference when the Toffees scored late on.

In the league, United finished fourth. And so a repeat sojourn to face the elite of European competition would also have to wait for another year at least. A silver lining for George was that he was named third in the Football Writers' Footballer of the Year award – Bobby Charlton won, but he would get his hands on a more special trophy that summer.

The World Cup was played in England, and George was at Wembley with David Sadler and Mike Summerbee to watch Charlton lift the Jules Rimet trophy. Although happy for his friend, George felt Alf Ramsey played "without flair and imagination"; he also felt Northern Ireland ought to have been there. He was angry at the referee in the qualifier against Albania in which his own performance had been criticised. "We played badly and allowed them to draw," George observed, before saying, "Correction: We played badly and the referee allowed them to draw." He was also critical of Arsenal for not releasing Terry Neill and Billy McCullough, two of Northern Ireland's most important players, for a game in Switzerland. Best had scored a fine opener but his team lost 2-1.

And so, with the number of competitions limited for the 1966/67 campaign, George's objective was simple – to win the First Division again.

CHAMPIONS AGAIN

George Best was not superhuman, though it may have seemed so on that March night in Portugal. No – he was torso, limb and pulse, just the same as any mortal walking the planet. That realisation had been all too painful when one of those unceremoniously brutal tackles he was growing accustomed to finally caused the damage they'd threatened to, and buckled the back of his knee, ending his 1965/66 season prematurely.

It is one of sport's most unfair rites of passage; a competitor discovering that an injury picked up in any given moment can have far-reaching consequences. And whatever punishment is doled out to the culprit, it rarely compares to the indeterminable length of time the victim could be out for, nor does it account for the indiscriminate time when the incident could occur. In that respect, Manchester United were hurt just as much as George Best was; as the forward recuperated from his surgery, watching Real Madrid overcome Partizan Belgrade by a single goal in the European Cup final, it was natural that everyone at Old Trafford felt that it could, and even should, have been their time.

George was comforted by his youthfulness. It would have done his confidence no harm at all to see journalists suggesting United's relative failure was because he had been injured.

If he had felt emboldened to ask for an improved salary following such praise, then the travails of Denis Law over the summer would probably have caused him to reconsider. In June, Law had demanded a new contract with an ultimatum. Matt Busby called his bluff and put his star striker on the transfer list. The matter would eventually be resolved – Law would get improved terms, though not quite so high as he had hoped, and only once the matter had escaped the attention of the newspapers.

The case of John Connelly, however, proved to George that the manager could still be ruthless. In September 1966, Connelly was told he was being dropped and in front of others, Connelly told Busby he must be joking. When the boss confirmed the news, Connelly told him to "stick your club up your arse" and before the month was out, a hastily arranged transfer to Blackburn Rovers of the Second Division signalled the premature end of the winger's brief career at Old Trafford.

The start to the new season had certainly been less than harmonious. The results in the pre-season were insipid; a 4-1 loss to a Celtic side emerging as the best in Europe was followed by another defeat by the same score to Bayern Munich four days later. It was a humbling reminder that Benfica was already old news. A 5-2 defeat to FK Austria followed that, though at least George saved some blushes on the continent with the winner in the final warm up game against Florence.

United's first league game of the season came against West Bromwich Albion at Old Trafford. In the number seven shirt, he would once more line up against his old foe, Graham Williams. As it turned out, this was not the first occasion the pair were close that summer. George had spent a couple of weeks in Majorca. Pat Crerand went along. It was clearly a footballer's retreat, as the United players bumped into some West Brom players on the beach.

"I was away with John Kay and John Talbot and I know for sure Pat Crerand was with George too," Williams recalls. "I asked to be introduced to George and then he said, 'Oh yes, we've already met, I've got your autograph on the back of my leg!' There were boats coming into the island and people would jump off just to take a picture of George and then get back on the boat. I never saw him refuse an autograph, or a photograph, but I do remember that he spent a lot of time sitting and talking to my mother-in-law, and playing with my son, hoping he wouldn't be disturbed."

George's recovery had apparently worked a treat. The ball was played to him as soon as the United players could get it there. Within 45 seconds of the new season, Best had given his team the lead.

"I enjoyed playing against him, I looked forward to playing in those games," Williams says. "It's a little bit strong to say that he was the best outright, because you had players like Pele and Eusebio, but he was definitely one of the best, right from those early months. And I mean one of the best in the world - you would pay money to watch him. You never saw him on his arse. His balance was unbelievable. Yes, the standard practice for a full-back in those days when you came up against a player of George's calibre was to hurt him. Or try to. In most of the footage you see of him you see players swinging at him with wild tackles. That was what he got every week. And you never saw him on his backside. He could play any position on the pitch and play it well."

United started their season with a flurry which would become a trademark of this team when they were at their best. They were irresistible in the first quarter of the game – scoring through Stiles in the eighth minute, Law in the 16th, Herd in the 17th, and Law again in the 22nd. Amidst all that, West Brom even managed to get a goal in the 10th minute, and scored two second-half consolations to earn a 5-3 scoreline that was rather flattering to them. And this was the tone for United's start to the season. Busby had dropped Gregg, who had featured in the friendlies and faced much of the blame for the most of the goals, and David Gaskell started the league campaign in goal.

Gaskell was now 26 – to many, he would be approaching prime, but he had been in and out of the team for 10 years already and it seemed obvious that those physical injuries sustained earlier in his career would prohibit him from having the physical prowess that Gregg had exuded in goal prior to his own injuries. Gaskell conceded seven goals in the first four games and was replaced by Gregg. But Gregg lasted just two more games for United – letting in two against Newcastle and then three at Stoke in his last-ever outing for the club.

Gaskell was recalled but conceded two at Spurs as United lost their third league game of the season already in September. At White Hart Lane, even George's miraculous intervention for an assist couldn't earn his team a victory. "Just before the break, George Best chased a loose ball towards the corner flag, controlled it superbly and flicked a glorious overhead kick into a crowded penalty area," wrote Ken Montgomery of the *Mirror*. "Denis Law rose above the lot to crash his header past Pat Jennings with the ferocity of a full-blooded drive."

But in the last five minutes, Alan Gilzean and Jimmy Greaves gave Spurs a dramatic victory. Pat Dunne was brought into the side and then let five Blackpool shots go past him in the League Cup. Eight games of the season gone, one clean sheet, and 17 goals conceded. There was no escaping the fact that the goalkeeping situation had reached a state of emergency.

The goalscorers in the team were having to truly throw out those quick combinations to stand any hope of getting results; three goals were scored in each of the home games against Everton and Newcastle, within 16 minutes in the former (either side of half-time) and 19 minutes in the latter.

Even Matt Busby, with his enjoyment of attacking football, realised that there was a difference between carefree and suicidal. But he was initially caught between a rock, a hard place and tradition. Tradition dictated he should give another player a chance but all three senior goalkeepers had been given a run already, and it was much too unfair to put that weight of expectation on 18-year-old Jimmy Rimmer. The hard place was the rotational aspect of the goalkeeper selection and the rock was United's financial situation, which did not allow for recruitment. However, the unexpected contretemps with Connelly had provided a £40,000 boon in the accounts and Busby immediately sought to use it.

There was a logical solution due to a series of events at Chelsea which had left them with two world-class English goalkeepers on their roster. Peter Bonetti had requested a transfer and so manager Tommy Docherty had pre-empted the disappointment by signing Millwall's Alex Stepney for

£55,000. But then Chelsea chairman Joe Mears suddenly died, and his replacement Charles Pratt refused to sanction the sale of Bonetti as he was such a popular figure at Stamford Bridge. When United enquired, they were informed they could have Stepney, and the deal was swiftly concluded, although it did cost the club a world-record fee for a goalkeeper – £55,000. Stepney was in the stands for the Blackpool capitulation, which confirmed just how urgently he was needed.

George approved of the signing, later explaining that he felt United had "improved out of all recognition in defence. Perhaps this can be traced to the signing of Alex Stepney... he is probably the biggest single reason for the improvement. He has given the rest of the defence complete confidence where nerves used to rule."

For those requiring a modern comparison Stepney was to Busby very much like Edwin van der Sar was to Sir Alex Ferguson in 2005; he was calm after the chaos, an unfussy and uncomplicated goalkeeper with fine agility, unflustered composure and a keen eye to start play moving again. He might have seemed timid in comparison to the fiery Gregg but that belied a steely inner-confidence that quickly exuded through the new-look defence, which included the repositioning of Tony Dunne to right-back and the young and supremely talented Bobby Noble at left-back.

Brennan's days as a mainstay in that right full-back position seemed numbered when United went down 4-1 at Johnny Carey's exciting Nottingham Forest in just Stepney's second game. Busby, a loyalist to the point of being extreme, reluctantly dropped the veteran Brennan for Noble, and United's improvement occurred almost overnight.

There were six wins on the bounce in October and November

1966; the second of which came at Stamford Bridge against league leaders Chelsea – already something of a happy hunting ground for George Best. United had a half-time lead given to them through John Aston Jnr, the winger who had seized a chance in the team following Connelly's departure, and 18 minutes into the second period Best once more left a lasting mark on this piece of West London turf.

In the home defence was Eddie McCreadie, who by now must have felt George held some personal grudge against him. That feeling would have been strengthened here. George went at McCreadie, and caused audible gasps in the home crowd by leaning over but actually feinting to move to the other side with the ball. By making himself seem off-balance, McCreadie had been utterly confused, and Best played a one-two with David Sadler before powering home a left-foot drive past Bonetti. Describing the goal for the *Mirror*, Ken Jones said it had "seemed impossible". United won 3-1 to close the gap to two points.

Best netted the winner at Leicester and then was the man-of-the-match against champions Liverpool in a contest that could easily be billed as the game of the season. George scored both of United's goals in the 2-2 draw at Old Trafford and was also booked for retaliating against Ron Yeats. It was intense business. Liverpool's league victory the previous year meant they were now tied with Arsenal as the most successful league team in English history, with seven titles apiece. United were on six, level with Sunderland and one ahead of Everton. Winning was everything; it was the only way to guarantee entry to the European Cup, other than winning that competition and qualifying as holders, of course.

The tighter defence had enabled United's goal power to

catapult them back into contention at the top of a competitive league. David Herd scored four goals against Sunderland and then another three at West Brom either side of the Liverpool draw to put United at the top of the table at Christmas. A 2-1 defeat at Sheffield United on Boxing Day caused a moment of introspection from Busby. His team were too open on the road – they had won six and lost six.

Players and coaches from this era would often discuss their philosophy of collecting points. Two were awarded for a win and one for a draw. With narrower margins, it meant away draws were usually seen as good results, and playing for one would be seen as a positive approach. Busby advised his players to begin away games cautiously, so that they could both read the tempo and then dictate it. "The defence became mature, sophisticated, so that in the run-in we drew eight away games," recalled Best. "John Aston and myself would drop back for the first 15 minutes in order to keep it tight and then start to attack out of a settled rearguard. In those early minutes the opposition gets plenty of the ball and you can see what they have to offer. For the first time that I can remember there were vital matches in the championship season in which we decided to play it tight all the time."

It was, perhaps, the first time Busby had studied his team, considered the limitations within, and sought to compensate rather than strengthen. One might even say that the trust he had with the squad was so strong that it played a part in how he built his side. The plan to stifle them away and go for the kill at home was working a treat and paid dividends again when David Herd scored two minutes into the home game with Leicester on March 18.

However, in the act of scoring, Herd broke his leg when Foxes defender Graham Cross tried in vain to tackle; an injury that would prove catastrophic for his career. By now a veteran at 33, Herd sometimes divided opinion among fans as he wasn't as prolific at his peak as a Law, nor as versatile as a Charlton, or for that matter as ingenious as a Best.

But he was a reliable scorer to complement the trio and his contribution would be sorely missed. Not least because Best himself had been off the boil, by his own admission, since that game against Liverpool. He hadn't scored a single goal in the three months since and even received mail blaming him for United's FA Cup defeat to Norwich City in February.

"I've had these anonymous letters telling me in no small way that I'm to blame for United going out of the cup, but they went straight into the fire," he said, before admitting, "I'm not pretending I didn't have a terrible game against Norwich and I haven't really hit form for a while."

Busby's latest reshuffle meant calling David Sadler into the team, but playing him alongside Foulkes in defence, and pushing Nobby Stiles into midfield. It did the job at Anfield as United played the game and not the occasion to get a 0-0 draw and stop the momentum of their opponent.

* * *

Best needed to recoup some momentum of his own. Those moments against Chelsea and Liverpool hadn't been enough to justify the hype that had come with his performance against Benfica, but that had owed much to a learning curve he was still on. It wasn't Herd's injury that prompted George's acknowledgement that he needed to step up; it was a team meeting Busby called after training the day before the Leicester game.

"That was a warning in itself," Best recalled. "For Mr Busby to keep us back to talk to us himself mean that something important was to be said. Something strong, perhaps, since the meetings are always deadly serious affairs... He went through the team and then came to me. He tore into me more hurtfully than any full-back had ever done. Oh yes, he had heard all about my late nights and free-for-all philandering. Everyone was telling him that it was all affecting my play.

"Then he dropped the bombshell. Without blackening my character completely, he seemed to side with the gossips for the first time when he added that, so far as he was concerned, there was no smoke without fire... I didn't answer back. I just felt sick at heart. As I sat there blushing to the roots of my long hair, he quickly changed the subject and rattled on to attack the next United problem. But he had wounded and shaken me to the very core."

George confessed that the following day's incident with Herd reminded him that "all the gold and glory is never very far removed from a hospital bed". He had been especially upset with Busby's remarks because he had been with a girlfriend for a couple of months, practically a long-term relationship for him at this point. It was nonetheless true that there had been a migration of sorts in the latter months of 1966.

George would never not be friendly and warm with the boys he grew up with at United; he simply moved in different circles now. Life now involved discussing business opportunities with Mike Summerbee and not hanging around the bowling alley with the youth team lads. Summerbee became one of George's closest friends but the other people involved in the business world did not always have the Northern Irishman's football career at heart. That's not to say they necessarily had negative intentions, certainly in the beginning, but it's almost certainly the case that their thoughts were self-serving rather than in George's best interest.

"While he was still one of us we'd treat him exactly the same, so if he was acting out or anything like that we'd just tell him to stop being an arsehole," says Willie Anderson, who moved to Aston Villa in January 1967. "But then the in-crowd in Manchester became his friends, guys who would tell him he was incredible and he was always right, just so they could go into work the next day and tell them who their new pal was. There was nobody to talk any sense in to him."

Nobody except for Busby, it seemed. And, just as had been the case in the early autumn of 1965, a short sharp shock from the boss was all that was needed to inspire. The George Best of the final five weeks of the season was most definitely influential in a positive way. His first goal of 1967 came two days after the Liverpool game, down at Craven Cottage, as United got another away draw. Back at Old Trafford, when United welcomed West Ham, Best put in arguably his best display of the season. In the second minute he was hauled down in the box by full-back John Charles and Charlton – newly crowned European Footballer of the Year for 1966 – put the penalty away. With tension high late on, George scored the vital second goal in the 86th minute, and then created a goal for Law two minutes later.

Charlton then scored two in another away draw, this time at Hillsborough, and George would have had some serious concern that the fickle finger of fate was pointing menacingly in his direction once more when he was carried off in the last minute with an ankle injury. His injury only kept him out of Northern Ireland's game with Wales in the following midweek.

A win over Southampton and a draw at Sunderland's Roker Park (following which Bobby Noble was involved in a car crash that ended his season and ultimately his career) gave United a powerful advantage at the top of the table as they prepared to welcome Aston Villa. Villa took a first-half lead – ironically through the returning Willie Anderson – before George put on a second-half performance to behold. According to the *Birmingham Post*, Villa defender Charlie Aitken suffered a "bewildering afternoon" at the hands of United's number seven. Aston and Law scored to turn the result around and Best made the result secure ten minutes from time.

Busby's side now needed one win from their last two games to secure their second title in three years. Nottingham Forest had emerged as the sole contenders but they had trips to Southampton and Fulham as their final two games. Leeds had games in hand but they were at Manchester City and Sunderland. United could probably even afford to draw at Upton Park, but for once on the road – and when it really mattered – they were in clinical and not conservative mood.

This was the breathless United of Benfica and of the opening day; tearing into opponents with such a relentless ferocity they didn't know which way to turn. John Charles again tried to leave a physical mark on George early on but it was no use. Bobby Charlton scored after two minutes. Pat Crerand after seven. Bill Foulkes after 10. And in the 25th minute, Stiles led a forward surge and played the ball to Best, who moved past Charles with ease – teasing him by shifting the ball from one foot to the other – and fired in the fourth.

United had been wearing a new white kit with a red V-neck. "I couldn't help wondering if the V stood for victory," recalled Best. "Actually Denis Law and Pat Crerand upset the pattern at half-time by changing into crew-neck shirts, but by that time we were in an impregnable position." The change certainly helped Law feel more comfortable, with the Scot scoring two in the second half to crown United as champions with a resounding and historic 6-1 win.

The occasion was marred by crowd trouble ("Every time I looked towards the crowd I seemed to see fans being led away with their faces bleeding," remembered Best) and hasty celebrations. Busby brought champagne into the dressing room but the team had to shower, change, toast with a celebratory drink, pose for photographs and also give comments to reporters all in the space of 15 minutes so that the team could get the six o'clock train back to Manchester. They made it in time; and the Stoke City team, down in the capital after facing Arsenal, and also due to face United in their last league game at Old Trafford, sent complimentary drinks to the new champions from their carriage further down the train.

George had noticed a "sun-tanned beauty" board the train in London and invited her to join them on a night out in Manchester. The invitation extended to joining the squad on the team coach from the train station to the stadium, at which point the girl was spotted by Matt Busby. "I might have known," Busby smiled. "It's a good job we won the league."

So much for the steady girlfriend!

The prevailing matter of importance was that Manchester United had qualified for the European Cup again. Best recalled how "for year upon year one goal has driven Manchester United on more than any other... to win the European Cup. That competition has stood supreme among all others". "Where, in Europe, is there a side to match our skill?" he asked. "We have the beating of any club side on ability and now that we

The Belfast boy: From the very beginning of his life, George Best and a football were the closest of friends. This image of Best, from 1948, shows his preternatural footballing instincts

Fresh faced, but brave: As these photos from 1964 attest, it is easy to forget how young, and slight, Best was when he made his entrance into a brutal footballing era. From the very start, Best was a marked man on a football pitch but his youthful looks betrayed a tough young character eager to make an impact

Gunning for it: Best warms up at
Highbury for United's match away
at Arsenal in November 1964

Taking a dip: Best in the communal bath at Old Trafford after a home victory in April 1964

Leaving them to it: Best, left, wisely decides to opt out of a clash between his United teammates and Leeds United during their FA Cup semi-final at Hillsborough in March 1965. Denis Law had his shirt ripped during a fracas with Jack Charlton and Bobby Collins. The horrendous condition of the pitch was the norm for the 1960s

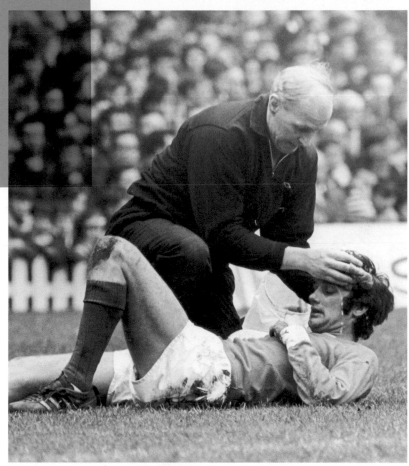

Magic sponge: United trainer Jack Crompton attends to Best during a match in 1966. No matter how many times Best got clattered, more often than not he climbed back off the floor and re-entered the fray

From the spot: Best scores a penalty against Liverpool at Old Trafford in December 1966

A coming of age: Best slots home his second of the game, after just 13 minutes, as he singlehandedly dismantles Benfica in the second leg of their 1966 European Cup quarter-final. Best was simply unplayable on a night where United won 5-1 and where Best truly announced himself as a great of the game

Two legends: Best greets Eusebio before the Benfica game. Eusebio was awarded his European Footballer of the Year trophy ahead of the match - Best made sure that was the highlight of his evening

Media darling: With his photogenic looks, Best soon became a dream for Fleet Street. After the Benfica win, he dons a sombrero on the way home. The nickname 'El Beatle' is born...

Busby, the genius: Manchester United manager Matt Busby (fourth from right) holds the 1966/67 League Championship trophy aloft as he and his players parade it around Old Trafford in May 1967: (l-r) Denis Law, Bill Foulkes, Shay Brennan, David Sadler, Bobby Charlton, Jimmy Ryan, Busby, Alex Stepney, Tony Dunne, Pat Crerand, George Best

A national icon: Although glory with the Northern Ireland team was always going to be unlikely, that never stopped Best from giving his all when wearing the green of his country. Here he is in action against Scotland at a crammed Windsor Park in October 1967

Aerial prowess: Best might be remembered as a genius on the floor but he was such a fantastic athlete that he also represented a real goal threat in the air as well

had found those lost chords in defence I knew that you could back us to go winging our way successfully over the Continent next season."

And if the summary of the West Ham destruction by *The People*'s Joe Hulme was anything to by, George's optimism was shared by many. "Matt Busby and his magnificent XI swept back into Europe on a wave of emotion and the most devastating spells of soccer magic I have seen in 44 years in the game," Hulme wrote. "If I carry on for another 44 years, I can't hope to see anything better than the first 25 minutes which produced four United goals. George Best was a genius. His goal, United's fourth after 25 minutes, was a piece of soccer joy. He picked up a through pass from Stiles and juggled the ball on both feet before shooting."

Ambitions were high – but this time around, George Best was well aware of the standard he would need to reach on a consistent basis if he was to achieve his dreams.

THE IMPOSSIBLE DREAM

Nothing lasts forever. In sport there are purple patches where everything comes together perfectly at the right moment; a combination of factors that align for a period of time, however long or however short, which can thrill in the moment and only truly be appreciated with the benefit of hindsight once it is over, forevermore the subject of conversation, comparison and procrastination.

For George Best, the 1967/68 football season was the true beginning of this period, because this was the campaign which finally earned him the accolade which had unofficially been awarded to him by many of his peers some years prior. But more importantly, it was a period of George's life where he maintained a healthy enough balance between all of his interests so that he could thrive. There remained plenty of the naivety and exuberance of youth so that the freshness of his brilliance could astound, yet there was now enough experience for a still-young dog to learn new tricks. There was enough time served for him to understand what he could do.

One strong thread that bound this season together was George Best's confidence that he could imagine and he could do things that no other player was capable of. It was an internal revelation; a discovery of power. You will recall the story told by John Fitzpatrick – when George told him he was going to beat everyone and score a goal, so he did. Or that of Jim Ryan, who spent time watching George practise scoring from a corner a matter of hours before doing it for real in a match.

George was now 21, and confident enough to regale his team-mates with his dreams and ambitions of what he would one day do on a football pitch. They were almost predictions, or spoilers. Many of the older men would laugh dismissively at the cocksure way in which George would express what he wanted to do. It could be finding a new way to go past a player. It could be the way he wanted to score a goal. But these were not flippant daydreams. Those senior professionals in the Manchester United dressing room were quick to understand and appreciate the intelligence and intent – even if sometimes they were left as confused on the pitch as George's opponents.

"He was a very intelligent player – and as a person off the pitch, never mind on it," Paddy Crerand says. Jimmy Rimmer recalls: "He would tease us before a game, 'I'm going to do something new today, something different.' And the first time we found out about it was when he did it. Sometimes it would be more elaborate. 'I'm going to try and take on every single player today.' He would want to do something different, something that would entertain people and give them something to talk about.

"After one game Denis was complaining that he did more short burst runs into the box waiting for George to give him the ball than he would do on the training pitch. But George would just hold on to the ball and go back at his player. George was George, though. He did things people didn't even know was possible... but, to balance that, Shay Brennan would say his job had been made 50 per cent easier whenever he played behind George because he'd be back tackling the winger Shay was meant to be marking! Shay was a very good player but he described playing with George as a pure luxury."

United's latest defence of their league title began with a mixed bag of results. With Bobby Noble out, Tony Dunne moved back to the left and the veteran Brennan was back in his normal position. Nobby Stiles sat alongside Bill Foulkes to complete an experienced backline. Pat Crerand and Bobby Charlton patrolled the middle of the park with George from the right, John Aston on the left and Denis Law accompanied by Brian Kidd, the 18-year old homegrown striker promoted to fill the boots of David Herd. Busby tried a 4-2-4 formation. When results were not going United's way, youngsters Francis Burns and Jimmy Ryan were given chances for Brennan and Aston respectively; Ryan, a predominantly right-sided player, wore seven and George moved to the left to wear 11.

Two draws and one defeat from the first five games was hardly convincing and United were staring down the barrel of a home defeat to Burnley on the September 9, trailing 2-0 with five minutes to go, until Burns and Crerand scored to salvage a dramatic draw. This was a confidence boost and in the following game, George registered his first goal of the campaign to earn a 1-1 draw at Hillsborough.

In a game of such fine margins, a positive result or performance can go a long way to influencing the momentum of a team. The next opponents for United were Hibernians of Malta; the first game of that season's European Cup, and a convenient visitor to Old Trafford to build some of that confidence. Busby's side won comfortably with two goals apiece from Sadler and Law. Sadler's second was the highlight of the evening, with Frank McGhee of the *Mirror* explaining: "George Best laid on the goal of the game in the 58th minute, wriggling past three defenders before Sadler finished the move."

George was becoming notorious for his love of sleep and his late-to-rise attitude, while it seemed he had taken a while to stir in the campaign. But once he had roused himself, he was in fine fettle. There was some fun to be had in training that week. Nick Murphy, son of Jimmy, was a forward for the reserve and A team. "We went through a drill where we were only allowed two touches of the ball," Nick recalls. "And yet George still never lost the ball. Because he had mastered the art of knocking the ball against you with his second touch and reclaiming it. You couldn't get it off him."

Spurs came to Old Trafford the following weekend and took an early lead through Alan Gilzean. That simply provoked Best into action. Within five minutes he raced past Cyril Knowles to equalise. Spurs held out until the last stages of the game. But with five minutes remaining, Best stole the headlines with a blistering spell, first creating a goal for Law then scoring another himself to make the result secure. His performance had been so extraordinary that even visiting defender Mike England could only admire what he was watching. Best was replicating what he had done in training that week.

"Every time we played against United, Bill Nicholson would bring up the names of the players we would be playing against," England says. "They'd get specific jobs to do. We would sacrifice a player to mark George Best. That's how good he was. Bill would normally pick a midfield player and ask him to stay with George and annoy him as much as he could. 'If he goes to the toilet, you go with him,' Bill would say. He was so outstanding that he learned how to lose the extra markers.

"I've never seen anything like it. He was playing one-twos off a defender. He was a tremendous athlete. He was quick and agile; a nightmare to play against. A lot of people admired his fantastic control but he had such wonderful balance. He would skip past players on pitches subjected to torrential rain... I would admire him moving. I could stand there as a defender and think, 'That is quite something'. Even as an opponent. If you had him coming at you with the ball, you knew he could go either way. So his feinting was unpredictable. He could make out like he was going left and he would get you off-balance and pirouette in the other direction. He would make it look easy and make good defenders look clumsy."

England recalls George was the talk of the nation: "He stood out from an early age. He was something different and people wanted to go and watch United just to see this new boy play. It was clear from the start he was very special. Players like him don't come along very often. He had his own personality, his own unique style, and his genius made defenders look silly. He did things you didn't think could happen on a football pitch."

United's absence from European competition meant that it was only on the return to the stage when George's separative level of stardom, compared to even his most illustrious Old Trafford team-mates, became truly apparent. Busby's travelling party to Malta for the return leg included the world's most expensive goalkeeper and two European Footballers of the

Year but they could not compete with the attention reserved for George Best. Stewardesses at the airport could not maintain their professionalism and asked for his autograph. He recalled the warm welcome on the island as unlike "anything we ever received". It was inevitably Best who had the most significant involvement, striking the bar from distance in a 0-0 draw.

Back home, United recorded crucial league wins. First against a Manchester City team who were in the throes of developing one of their greatest ever sides, and then against Arsenal in a controversial encounter where Denis Law was sent off and suspended for six weeks. Law's absence placed extra responsibility on the shoulders of Best and he stood up to it, possibly emboldened by the events of the following fortnight.

A couple of weeks after the game against Arsenal, George was back in the Northern Ireland set-up for a game against Scotland at Windsor Park. This was his first involvement with the national side since that 'worst international ever' against Albania. Best, the boy with the penchant for the extreme, put in a performance that was so magnificent that the game was named after him. His direct opponent on the day was Tommy Gemmell, a 'Lisbon Lion' and bona fide Celtic legend.

Scotland started well. Gemmell had a shot from distance. But the hosts soon settled down. Windsor Park buzzed with anticipation whenever their team got the ball to their number 11. Three times he received it and turned away from markers to fire long shots which tested the goalkeeper Ronnie Simpson. Then he turned his attention to Gemmell, targeting him with mesmeric wing play, turning him time and again to supply crosses that were narrowly missed by team-mates.

Gemmell suffered a torrid first half. He asked his opposite number if he would mind switching positions. But that man was Chelsea's Eddie McCreadie, who had been there too often to fancy being tortured again, and he replied, "Not on your life!" Cue more misery for Gemmell as Best sensed his vulnerability. From one dribble that took out three players, George played in Derek Dougan who was unceremoniously taken out in the box, but no penalty was given.

Soon after, Best's brilliance engineered the breakthrough. He went over to McCreadie's side, but McCreadie left the job to Bobby Murdoch. Murdoch couldn't get close; Best's cross was converted by Dave Clements. As the game drifted towards the conclusion, Scotland's defence grew weary, frustrated by the endless tenacity of Best, who was tracking back and winning the ball before setting off on another dribble. Scotland were in theory searching for an equaliser. Gemmell couldn't wait for the final whistle. "It was 1-0 going on five," he said. "I couldn't get close to him. It was like trying to catch the wind. I tried to body check him, trip him, kick him... nothing worked."

In those latter exchanges, George's mood changed from the deliberate conservationist – waiting to draw the tackle – to elaborate runs, with one right at the end of the game very nearly concluding in a goal. When the referee finally called time, the scoreline read 1-0 Clements, but the game would forever be eponymously Best's.

Billy Bingham, only recently installed as manager, beamed about his star man's role. "Best was a master," he said. "The Scots tried everything to stop him but they failed miserably."

The acclaimed sportswriter John Roberts, who would later ghost a newspaper column for Best, knew it was one for the ages. "George played in every position that day," he says. "Billy Bingham told him to keep Gemmell busy. He destroyed his confidence within 15 minutes. I saw him knock the ball through his legs, get the ball, and go back and do it again. After that he didn't have to worry about Gemmell and he was all over the pitch. I remember saying at the time that when I was old I would bore the younger generation telling them all about the time George Best played like this at Windsor Park."

Sam Leitch of the *Mirror* described it as "one of the truly major individual playing performances of the decade." Malcolm Brodie of the *Belfast Telegraph*, a champion from the early days, found this outing barely credible. "The whole fascination of his performance was like a dream," Brodie wrote. "It was all so staggering. He entranced the crowd with those delicate touches as he dispossessed Scottish players to begin his build-ups, for he rarely got a service from his colleagues. He had to do it alone, do it his way."

Brodie's idolatry of George grew even further after the game. A young boy by the name of John Doherty wrote to Malcolm as he knew he would miss the game because he was ill in hospital. He asked if the journalist could get George's autograph for him. George insisted on going to the hospital, so the morning after the match the pair went to see John, where George presented him with his shirt from the game. (Years later, on a television show where George was a guest, Doherty was present in the audience and retold this tale; Best was evidently emotionally affected.)

* * *

Back in United colours, a buoyant Best put Coventry to the sword – his contribution in a 4-0 win was described by Frank McGhee of the *Mirror* as "magic"; his game was rounded off by a magnificent chip just under the crossbar. This magic was also in evidence when Best was required to fill in for Law at Anfield in mid-November. Busby fielded a 4-3-3 with Best given a free role, in Law's number 10 shirt, alongside Aston and Kidd. A tough ask was made even tougher by the absence of United's clinical goal getter (compounded of course by Herd's injury issue). George, however, was a man with a plan.

"We didn't do a lot on Fridays," Alex Stepney remembers. "You'd have a warm-up, a five-a-side. During the week George would be trying things out. The day before we played at Anfield we had finished our training and he came up to Paddy and I and asked if we would stay with him to go through a routine.

"Now, I just have to remind you that there were few games shown on television. *Match of the Day* was quite new. You got to know players by playing with and against them, not really by watching them. But what we would do is sometimes go to games locally. So I can only think George had come up with this by going to see Liverpool play. He started talking about Bill Shankly's back four and Tommy Lawrence in goal. The defence played high up the pitch and George said he felt that was the reason they didn't let in many goals at home. If the ball was close to the halfway line they'd grab you and foul you if they couldn't win it in a clean tackle.

"George gave the ball to Paddy and told him to drop deep into the old right-half position. He told me to go in the goal at the other end and stop him. 'Do what you'd do in a game, Al.' He told Paddy to hit a long pass that would come in around 20 yards from the left-wing position. He would start on the halfway line, close to the touchline, because he knew from such a position he couldn't be offside. Paddy hits this pass and George comes in from the angle. He kept coming straight at me. I was trying to push him out of the way with my position but the ball was never more than six inches from his toe. As a goalkeeper you are forced into making a decision. Mine was to dive at his feet. As I was about to do so, he played the ball against my shin, got on to the rebound, and tapped it into the empty net. He turned around and said to me casually, 'You didn't expect that Al, did you?' I said no. He said, 'That'll do.'"

At the time Stepney put it down to just another episode of training with George Best; a ritual anyone at the club could experience any morning. "I couldn't say I was especially embarrassed by him – but that's because everyone got it," Stepney says. "It wasn't something reserved for the goalkeepers. But being on a training pitch with him was an experience in itself. He would come up with ways to beat a player, something different from what had ever been seen before."

In the midst of the battle at Anfield, George had already made an impression by netting in the 18th minute. Liverpool were pushing for an equaliser before the break and won a corner in the 39th minute.

"I was a goalkeeper who would try and keep possession with my team," Stepney says. "Paddy wasn't the quickest player but he was always available and would always want the ball from me to open the game up. I claimed a corner at the Anfield Road end and threw it out to Paddy. I'd seen him receive the ball and turn a hundred times. We were playing this hugely competitive game and your concentration level has to be so high that of course you just simply forget about what you felt were minor incidents on the training pitch. Now, though, I saw him hit a pass almost identical to the one he had played the day before. The ball dropped behind Tommy Smith and Chris Lawler. George had anticipated it and got to the ball so quickly they were out of the game. Emlyn Hughes on the other side didn't have the pace to catch him. I saw Tommy Lawrence caught in the same dilemma I had been in; I watched as he fell for it the same way I did. Goes to dive. George pokes it against his shins, gets the rebound, and puts it in the Kop end goal. He stood there and laughed with his arms raised."

...to run where the brave dare not go...

The second goal was the security. United kept Liverpool at arm's length save for a late consolation – George's ingenuity had decided another big match for his team.

"He talked about scoring different types of goal," Jim Ryan says. "We all did, really. That you would take it around some players and then flick the ball in the net – I suppose you could say it was a way of insulting your opponent. But there was talking about it and then actually trying to do it, and I don't think anybody ever did, except for George."

It came with a price. Some were terrified of Best due to previously inflicted wounds to their ego. Others were so enthralled that in their reverence they stood on ceremony and in admiration. But there remained a significant number of defenders who were not so submissive. Best's reputation preceded him and the news of his exploits was circulated around the country and around the world. A few days after going to Liverpool, United faced a similarly hostile reception in Sarajevo in the European Cup. There, a 0-0 draw was seen as a lucky escape, with the usually reserved Busby blasting the "most disgraceful exhibition of tackling I have ever known".

"The Maltese weren't vicious, but the Sarajevo team were pretty brutal," Alex Stepney recalls. "But you would find that with teams where the quality gap was so big; they had to find a way of bridging that gap and it would often be with aggression. But then you would play against a Real Madrid or a Benfica, a team with great ambitions of their own, and the objective was more fair. They would put an extra player on George but it wouldn't be with the intention of hurting him."

Similar was waiting for him against Southampton, where he picked up knee and ankle injuries that were so severe that they would keep George out of "the one game I don't want to miss"- the Home International against England at Wembley. Jimmy Murphy told reporters he didn't even think Best would recover in time to face Chelsea for United the following week. He did, but this time – with an already bruised and battered body – Ron Harris had a rare 'victory' of sorts. United still drew at Stamford Bridge but Harris, criticised by the media for "kicking and battering" George, was booked. Best did have some positive involvement – his clever back-heel started the play for United's equaliser, scored by Kidd – but he was largely aggressively sidelined and was even booed by some sections of the home crowd because of the time Harris had previously been booked for those hard tackles at Old Trafford.

There was no rest for the wicked – next up was Sarajevo, who came to Old Trafford in even more vicious mood. George was targeted from minute one. In minute 16, Fahrudin Prijaca was dismissed for a kick that was described as "brutal" by some journalists. By then, United were 1-0 up through John Aston. Soon after half-time, it all kicked off again. "It was Best himself who sparked off the trouble in the 58th minute," read the *Mirror*'s report. "He was tackled as he had a header palmed from the line, collapsed with exaggerated drama and then, as 'keeper Muftic tried to hoist him to his feet, Best swung a punch. Muftic collapsed dramatically. Ref Roger Machin

(France) mildly cautioned Best… and from that moment the Sarajevo players were after the Irishman."

Five minutes later the visitors were incensed when Best himself scored the crucial goal – Aston had created a goal from a cross that was, by his own admission, at least two foot out of play; from then on, they had to concern themselves with sporting revenge but could not manage more than a late consolation. United were relieved to qualify and Best was relieved that his next opponent was only Graham Williams of West Brom, by now more of a pantomime villain in comparison to the assassins of recent weeks. Best netted twice in a 2-1 win.

* * *

George had clearly been the player of the season so far – and was named Ireland's Footballer of the Year – but it seemed the first part of 1967 had counted against him when it came to global recognition as he came only eighth in the European Footballer of the Year, with Florian Albert of Ferencvaros as the winner, even though it would be safe to say everybody on the continent paled in comparison to the Northern Irish forward at the time. There was no sulking; Best was in scintillating form over Christmas, scoring six goals in five games. The last of those was an FA Cup third-round tie with Spurs.

George was dreaming of Wembley that year. He had been particularly stung by the criticism after the Norwich exit and seemed to have a personal mission to get to the FA Cup final. In his book *Best of Both Worlds*, George opened a chapter describing his fantasy of a Wembley moment.

"I see us get a couple of goals up and then George Best will produce the greatest show of individual talent ever seen on a football field," he wrote. "Only the last 20 minutes remain and with United in such superb and invincible form it is time to show off." Best describes how the move will begin with a long kick down the field. George will then trap the ball against the turf – with his backside. "Imagine the roar… the cheek of it."

He jumps up, only to be scolded by Denis Law who is wagging his finger and telling him to stop taking the mickey.

"I step past the left flank of the defence bouncing the ball on my thighs and never letting it touch the ground." When United are awarded a penalty in the last minute, he tells the goalkeeper he is going to score in off the crossbar – and does.

"The crowd is in ecstasies. The magic has them almost delirious. It is preposterous that anyone should dare to attempt such outrageous tricks at Wembley. But the best is yet to come. The final rite is reserved for the closing minutes for a stunt that would be regarded as fantastic even in the circus ring."

George then explains how he will latch on to a cross into the box and perform a handstand and volley the ball in.

"That is how I see myself in the future. Such tricks with the ball are not impossible for I have done them all in training and have kept the ball off the ground in a lengthy dribble during a league match against West Ham. And that got me a wigging from Denis Law. But I was delighted with myself."

Nobody, then, was more determined to make Wembley a reality. George scored in the fourth minute – equalising a Martin Chivers goal in the second. And then Bobby Charlton scored in the 73rd minute, but Chivers equalised 60 seconds from time to take it to a replay. Best was the best player on the park at White Hart Lane. But Spurs held on for extra-time and won with a goal in the 104th minute. "Although George Best produced moments of sheer magic, they were not enough to drive a hole in Spurs' defence," wrote the *Mirror*'s Ken Jones. Best could not be blamed this time, but once more, the result was the same – no FA Cup final.

United were down at the same ground three days later for their return league game. Chivers scored in the second minute again – but Best was in the mood for some revenge and achieved it in memorable fashion. He was described as "untamable" by the report in the *Sunday Mirror*, which continued: "The Best equaliser in the 20th minute was one of those magical moments in football when even the players wonder how it was done. Four Tottenham defenders plunged on Best when he took a clever pass from David Herd. George's brilliance seemed faster than the human eye. I saw how he beat three men, the fourth Spur was lost in a blur of impish Ulster."

Again, he found only appreciation from the Spurs backline. "He just went past one player and then another, and another, and then he put it in the net – even as someone on the other team, you just had to marvel at how wonderful he was," says Mike England. United won 2-1 thanks to a late Charlton goal.

At the end of the month United were back in the capital to face Arsenal. Best was inspirational in a 2-0 win. "United won with a goal that was a gift and another that would rate as golden in any circumstances," wrote Harry Miller of the *Mirror*. "Inevitably, George Best was involved in both. After 23 minutes, he hurried Storey into a back pass that bounced over the goal-line. Then, after 55 minutes Best cracked in a tremendous left-footer."

In his *Sunday Mirror* report, Roy Peskett wrote of the performance that Best thoroughly "mesmerised the Arsenal defence, twice showing them the three-card trick, which was enough to produce two match-winning goals" and of the second goal, "in moved the Irishman to sell three different dummies to Neill and McNab before slashing the ball home".

George was relentless and unstoppable. Reports of his excellence put the fear of life into opponents who were not able to see highlights every single week; and, when highlights were shown, they merely confirmed every superlative.

"Because of his reputation that had been growing so much since that game against Benfica, managers started to put two players on him to stop him from playing. But they couldn't," Alex Stepney recalls. "It was being with George every day in training that mesmerised me more than seeing what he did on the pitch. Matt gave him a free role. I think he wanted everyone to show their talent. There was never an instruction of what to do. You could say George was the best in the world.

"Denis was the best around at scoring inside 12 yards. He was lethal with his feet, great in the air, fantastic acrobatic skills. Bobby scored his goals from 25 yards and never stopped running. But George could do everything, beat players, score goals, he was good in the air and he could use both feet. He could play anywhere. And because he had a free role he did what he had to do. It was a dream to play with him.

"He was the outright player who would beat players. It was an extraordinary talent. Other players would perhaps glide past or run past a player. George would stand up to them with the ball and beat them. So much of that was down to George himself but you also have to commend Matt for being brave enough to give a player such a free role and also the other players for going with it."

Best was actively present on the Manchester nightlife scene. He appeared in commercials for all sorts of products, including one infamous advert for Cookstown sausages filmed in the Best family home; he was by now earning more from these endorsements than he did from his United contract. Those earlier incidents where concern was expressed were no longer applicable because George's form was not, apparently, negatively impacted. George himself was keen to go on weekend talkshows because they increased his public profile.

"We were all married, and he wasn't," Stepney says. "The boutiques and agents, the television shows, certainly for a time, I wouldn't say distracted him. I thought for a while it almost motivated him. I didn't think it affected him when we played." It ought to be said, too, that whilst there was a working balance, George was undoubtedly conscious of ensuring he was grounded. In David Meek's *Manchester United Football Book No. 2* published in 1967, Best had told the author: "My manager, Mr Busby, is fully alive to the temptations that can befall a young lad like me and he is all in favour of my parents coming to live in Manchester from Belfast."

This was the first time George had publicly expressed such a wish, though it wouldn't be the last. The Best family, however, whilst obviously immensely proud of George, could not comprehend the level of attention he was receiving; especially the way it would exponentially escalate so following each 'explosion'. The sausage advert had been uncomfortable and that was small fry compared to the attention he was now getting. The prospect of moving to Manchester did not appeal.

A little later down the line, after a UEFA representative game in Cardiff in which George played with Bobby Charlton, the pair travelled back to Manchester together and Bobby asked his younger colleague if he would like to go to his house. There, Charlton recalled "a strange and poignant evening, adding: "I saw a different George, inquisitive, warm, and maybe a little insecure in himself. I didn't think his lifestyle was compatible with being a professional footballer."

George – who still had his bedroom at Mrs Fullaway's – asked him questions about being married, having a house, the domestic life. If he was seeking direct advice, he didn't get it; Charlton would lead by example and not instruction. But Charlton was nine years older anyway. Yes, they were involved in the same sport, for the same club, at the same level, but even Charlton could not truly comprehend the spotlight George was under now. To an extent, neither did George. Still, there are at least these two examples of him proactively reaching out. And writing this in hindsight is not to attribute blame. Nobody could have forecast the way things would turn out.

That is because there were still elements of George Best's life which seemed normal within the parameters of a football career. At any time, one player has to be the best around, and it just so happened that in the early months of 1968 many believed that the identity of that player was George.

Included in that number was Géza Kalocsay, the coach of Gornik Zabrze, United's next opponents in the European Cup. "Best could have played at any time in any of the world's great teams," Kalocsay told reporters. "He is the best winger in the world. He will be very difficult to contain. He does not need room to work. He is a good dribbler, and has a very sharp shot with either foot."

The greatest show of appreciation came for visiting goalkeeper Hubert Kostka; Old Trafford gave Kostka a standing ovation for an inspired performance. Unfortunately for him, his efforts did not result in a clean sheet. On the hour-mark, having been shadowed by Henryk Latocha for the entirety of the match, Best had one moment of inspiration. He finally wriggled free of Latocha's attention and turned smartly to beat two more opponents; with an opportunity to shoot, George took aim. His effort deflected in. Late on, Brian Kidd scored a second.

Sandwiched between the legs was a visit of Chelsea to Old Trafford. It was an eventful game, with Ron Harris once more as close to Best as the referee would allow. Closer, most of the time. The Blues had a new manager, Dave Sexton, who was already establishing a reputation as a tactical coach of the future. Harris insists he wasn't given any detailed breakdown by Sexton; instead he was asked to do what he did best, to Best. "Dave didn't give me any specific instructions," says the former Chelsea man. "I just remained as a man-marker to stop the opposition from playing, that was my job."

Bobby Tambling scored for the visitors in the first half. In the 52nd minute, Brian Kidd levelled, and then shortly afterwards, Tommy Baldwin put the Blues back in front. Three minutes later United were awarded a penalty. What followed was bizarre. Denis Law, the usual taker, decided he didn't want to take it because he didn't think he was playing well. Best stepped up – and missed. Chelsea scored a third late on to secure their win. It was a blow, although the champions still led the First Division.

Attentions turned to the second leg against Gornik. Busby was so unhappy with the pitch in Poland that he described it as "not fit for football" and wanted the game postponed. Best echoed those thoughts to Malcolm Brodie, telling him: "This pitch is almost as grim as the place itself." United lost 1-0 on the night, but scraped through on aggregate. The prize was significant. Real Madrid in the semi-final. Still, losing games was becoming a worrying trend, and worse was to follow. In three consecutive games George scored within the first two minutes – United's habit of making sure he got the ball straight from kick-off was working a treat – but in the first and third of those, at home to Manchester City and Liverpool respectively, the local rivals turned the game around to take all the points away from Old Trafford. That was now five defeats from eight league game and it was enough to make Leeds, Liverpool and Man City slight favourites to win the title.

Best's own form remained supreme. Those early goals were followed by two against Fulham at Craven Cottage, one at the Dell from an impossible angle to earn a 2-2 draw against Southampton, and another as Fulham came to Old Trafford. The flurry of seven goals from six games – and 26 in all competitions so far that season – invited yet more praise. Leeds United manager Don Revie managed to find a new frame in the decreasing number of superlatives left to offer Best in his *Football Post* column. No longer must he solely be compared to his contemporaries. According to Revie, George was "obviously even at the age of 21, one of the all-time greats".

...to fight the unbeatable foe...

Decades before Sir Alex Ferguson angrily declared he "wouldn't sell that mob a virus", Manchester United did of course have a very good relationship with Real Madrid. Santiago Bernabeu's act of brotherhood in United's greatest hour of need would never be forgotten by those of the time. But some things were just the same then as they are today. Real were seen as the glamour club and Manchester United versus Real Madrid in the European Cup was seen as the ultimate tie. Had Munich never happened, it seemed the two clubs would be fated to have an annual battle in the European

Cup. Real had eliminated United in 1957, and the disaster robbed those Old Trafford boys of an opportunity to show the benefit of a year's education in a repeat match.

When the clubs were drawn together in the 1968 semi-final, the only sadness was that it wasn't the final, although it was fitting that there was at least this one more opportunity for them to compete against each other in this era. Two years earlier, Real had won their sixth European Cup (defeating United's conquerors Partizan in the final), so while their own peak might have been and gone, they were still of the requisite quality one would expect at this stage of such a competition.

Even at their strongest United would be facing a difficult proposition. But Busby had headaches when it came to the players who would scare Madrid. David Herd had returned from his leg injury but wasn't the same. He played eight games and scored just one goal. His appearance in the recent home defeat to Liverpool would be his final game for the club.

Another pressing concern was that of Denis Law. The striker had long-standing knee problems which now required regular cortisone injections just to get him through games. Law visited a specialist in January who found that a previous operation the player underwent, to remove cartilage from his knee, had failed. The specialist recommended another operation but United chose to delay it. Law was able to take to the field for the first leg against Madrid at Old Trafford.

United's players were at once surprised to see Madrid retreating from kick-off completely of their own accord. They were encouraged to take the impetus in the game and did so, smothering the visitors and penning them back. Their only reward for such ambition was inevitably started and finished by George. His wonderful 'around the corner' flick created space for Kidd to turn with the ball in front of him. He played the ball to Aston, who got to the byline and pulled it back.

Best was there, 12 yards out, showing composure that defied the occasion and the bobble of the ball with a thunderous left-foot shot. The ball flew into the top corner. In initial reaction, George's celebration was almost arrogant, with a nod of the head and a raise of the right arm; but the emotion of the players around him, not to mention the incredible roar of Old Trafford, made him a little more animated.

It seemed then that there would be a rout. It was not forthcoming. Madrid withstood the waves of attacks and got away with just a 1-0 deficit. "We were all over them at Old Trafford," Stepney says. "We should have scored three or four. The one we did get was a fabulous goal through George. Boom. It was in the net before the goalkeeper even realised he'd shot."

The following weekend United went to the Hawthorns to play West Brom. "We won 6-3, it was the best game I've ever played in, and one of those games where everyone on both sides played very well," Graham Williams recalls. "It was our FA Cup winning team and of course their best ever too."

The entertaining game came at a cost – firstly, the result, which now gave Manchester City a firm advantage in the title race. Secondly, a recurrence of the knee trouble for Law. Although he scored, he was no longer able to continue playing under the pain and was told he must have the operation he had delayed. He would be ruled out of United's crucial run-in.

Where would the goals come from? George Best, of course. United responded to conceding six by scoring six in their next game. Newcastle were the unlucky recipients not only of that barrage but also of George's first senior hat-trick, which included two penalties and a tremendous 25-yard drive.

Brian Kidd scored two, and David Sadler the last, to reassure Busby that his team still had firepower. Still, Newcastle's soft resistance did not inspire confidence that the Magpies would be able to get a result against Manchester City on the final day. And so it proved, with City winning and therefore winning the title; United lost 2-1 to Sunderland at Old Trafford, with Best getting their goal, but even a victory would not have stopped their neighbours from getting the trophy on goal average.

There was considerable compensation laying in wait, so long as United's confidence wasn't too badly hurt. They could ill afford to give Real Madrid any further incentive. This time Busby was going to be cautious. He started with three men in defence in Spain – Foulkes, Stiles and Sadler. Kidd would be the lone front man. There was a lot of pressure on Best and Aston to make the most of their speed and any counter-attack. Suddenly, on such an occasion, the importance of age and experience seemed to show itself.

Shay Brennan and Tony Dunne – who might both have felt their days were numbered 12 to 18 months ago – were now going to play the biggest game of their careers. Jimmy Murphy had been giving them advice on the bigger occasions to better preserve their energy. He would be telling Brennan in particular to blast the ball out of play if he was being attacked so that he could retreat and not be beaten for pace down the line. Brennan was particularly nervous ahead of the second leg; Murphy told him not to worry as he'd seen a "lovely little bar" for after the game. Brennan was 31. Bill Foulkes was 36. Bobby Charlton was 30. Pat Crerand was 29. These were players at or past the prime of their career. The rarity of such an opportunity was not lost on them. In an attempt to centre their concentration Charlton had told his team-mates not to worry about losing the league title. "It's the best thing that could have happened," he said. "Now we have got to beat Real to get into Europe next season."

Playing in a conservative manner did not suit United. There was a mirror of the first leg, with Real feeling more and more ambitious; their reward was two goals, through Pirri and Best's erstwhile hero Gento, by the 41st minute. Busby's men were stung and sought to make instant amends - they did, but were helped by Ignacio Zoco who put the ball in his own net. Even that positive moment was soon forgotten when Amancio made it 3-1 on the stroke of half-time.

The break could not have come at a better time for the anxious United players; nor could one of Matt Busby's greatest team-talks. The man whose soothing words could extinguish a raging fire reminded his players of the straightforward reality of the scenario. They were only one goal down on aggregate. But Busby also had another ace up his sleeve. He decided to move Sadler up front, and said: "You've attacked teams all season. Why aren't you doing it tonight?"

On the pitch, the players conducted themselves with the professionalism Busby had hoped. The hosts were a little disturbed as United seemed content with the scoreline. Real Madrid had expected a similar urgency to that displayed in the first leg, with time at a premium. Fifteen minutes passed with this cat-and-mouse scenario. Then another. In the 75th minute, United were awarded a free-kick. Crerand took it and looped the ball into the box. Fifteen yards out, Best met it with his head, but due to the close attention of his marker, did well to flick it towards goal. There at the far post was Sadler, to force the ball over the line and stun the home crowd in the same way as he did the defence.

The purpose of United's game-plan now clear, Madrid were forced into an uncomfortable position of their own. But while they were still waiting for instruction, United struck again. Crerand threw the ball to Best on the right; the winger danced past the numerous Real Madrid challengers throwing themselves at him. On another time or on another day, George might have taken another touch, considered his proximity to goal and shot. He might have feinted again, causing the sort of frustration Denis Law had confessed to in the past. "He wasn't just a great scorer," Stepney says. "He made goals and knew when to pass. He went past a couple against Madrid players and still had the presence of mind to play the ball."

This time he took the mature route; with his head down, he did well to spot the blur of a red shirt arriving just in the periphery of his eye-line. He played the ball and looked up. It was centre-half Bill Foulkes. In 663 games Foulkes had scored just eight goals for the club. "I expected to see him blasting it wide or over the bar as he usually did," George remembered.

Not this time. To see Foulkes bounding forward unstoppably into the box with his considerable frame is reminiscent of the scene from the movie *One Flew Over The Cuckoo's Nest*, where Chief Bromden is playing basketball and does not possess the mobility to alter his momentum, thus can only run like a lumbering wardrobe until nature has taken its course. In the Bernabeu, nature was, in the context of all considered matters, a simple side-footed finish into the corner of the net. In the context of what it meant to Manchester United, it could well have been the most spectacular strike that there had ever been.

There was no answer from the Spaniards. United held on for a 3-3 draw on the night and a 4-3 aggregate victory. It would be regarded as one of the finest nights in their history and listed within the many great comebacks associated with the club but the contemporary report from Malcolm Brodie of the *Belfast Telegraph* was not quite so appreciative of the manner of the victory. "This was a wonderful result for Britain, an uplift in soccer prestige, but there was a hollow ring about it all. There was nothing decisive, no great fightback, no sheer display of skill or courage. It just seemed to happen because Madrid mysteriously crumbled," Brodie wrote, although he could not hold back from praising his favourite player: "It was Best's piece of genius, however, which earned that equalising goal… this was the only occasion Best had revealed that magic touch, that supreme class of a world player."

Such proclamations were nothing new to George; but, at the age of 21, he finally did receive some official personal recognition in England, when he became the youngest ever player to receive the Football Writers' Association Footballer of the Year award with 60 per cent of the vote. Nobody could argue that it was not well deserved.

* * *

Manchester United had set their hearts on winning the European Cup that season, particularly because the 1968 final was to be played at Wembley. "It really did seem to be our destiny," George said. He finally had the Wembley cup final that had dominated his daydreams for years.

It was understandable, then, that he became almost irritating to his team-mates with talk of his grand plans. "The daft things people have in their mind," Paddy Crerand laughs. "Before the game George was talking about what he was going to do. 'If I can get the ball and beat everybody, I'm going to go through, put the ball on the goal-line and then bend down and head it in the net,' he said. I said, 'Are you flipping mad? You'll get your head kicked in!' But I put it down to him just being a kid."

United's opponent in the final was Benfica, the team George Best had vanquished almost on his own two years earlier. Eusebio and company defeated Juventus in their own semi-final; and so, with history to guide, Matt Busby's team were installed as favourites. Not only because of that prior result, but now the ageing Portuguese side were perceived as well past their optimum ability. "It's barmy to say they are past their best," George insisted to reporters in the build-up to the game. "I think we will win, but it will be a hard, close game."

Nothing was going to be left to chance as far as Benfica manager Otto Gloria was concerned. Gloria was sure there were no lingering mental scars from the previous meeting: "We have put that memory behind us. But we do not forget that Best is a good player. But like Nobby Stiles will mark Eusebio, so Cruz will do the same with Best. He is very experienced."

António Simões recalls that the subject of George Best dominated his team's plans. "Our defenders spent much time preparing for George. It was straightforward. Stay close. Don't let him get the ball. Our defenders were trying to anticipate the moves that were going to him. We knew if he caught the ball, especially with momentum, there would be a problem."

Stiles, who would indeed be given to the task of Eusebio, told sportswriter Hugh McIlvanney: "There is one consolation. I'd rather play against Eusebio or Amancio or any of them than have to face Georgie Best. You should see what Georgie does to me in training. Splits me in two. It gives you heart to know that some poor character has to try to cope with him." McIlvanney described United as having a team with "undeniably ordinary players" with "an alarming vulnerability in defence" and "an excessive dependence on one or two men in attack".

But, as with all cup finals, particularly when the weather is warm and the evening is light, all pre-match expectations go out of the window and the sense of occasion just grabs you in a stranglehold. Manchester United had prided themselves on liberating their players of the weight of following Munich but there could be no avoiding it now. Everything tied together. A decade on. Wembley Stadium. The first English team to reach a European Cup final. And yet the conversation was never held between players and the management, it merely lingered in the air, filtering through to the conscious mind of all 92,225 spectators and the players, club representatives, officials and otherwise.

Busby lined up his team with a 4-3-3. Denis Law would be watching from his hospital bed as he underwent surgery, so Brian Kidd, on his 19th birthday, was given the start up front. John Aston was told to stick to the left side and pin down the right-back Adolfo. George was given a nominal inside-forward role on the right but, as ever, would be given freedom to roam by Busby. Of course that freedom was not afforded to him by the Benfica defence. They had players in a permanent state of awareness; defenders close to him, defenders standing off him to protect against that surge of pace, and more close by just in case the other two plans didn't work.

This approach resulted in numerous things. The first was, obviously, a frustrating evening for Best. The second was a lack of protection for Adolfo on the other side of the pitch. Aston enjoyed the freedom to attack the defender time and again, providing service from the left hand side. The third was a consequential freedom for other players, like Aston, to influence the game in Best's stead. Early in the second half, one passage of play summed up George's evening. He received a bouncing ball and turned to attack the defence – he flicked the ball over Jacinto Santos' head, but, as he did so, two more players came in from the right to close down the space. The goalkeeper, José Henrique, rushed out of his goal. It was enough pressure to allow Jacinto to fire the ball away and out for a throw-in. As the defenders regrouped, Sadler moved into space on the left to collect the throw. He cut inside and crossed for Charlton to head across the goal and into the net. It was a stunning goal.

Wembley was in a state of frenzy. Moments later, United broke through again. Crerand clipped the ball over the top to Best, in a rare pocket of space behind the left full-back, Cruz. He was offside, but didn't realise it; nor did Henrique or Jacinto Santos. George clipped the ball over the goalkeeper, who collided with his defender. As the ball bounced towards goal, George theatrically star-jumped, celebrating before it even touched the net; every bit the showman. On the goal-line, he could not resist thrashing it against the net, but mid-motion he had realised that the flag had gone up.

Benfica now had to attack and this meant being a little looser with their military-style defensive approach; Best sensed this and roamed left, causing havoc with their marking system. In one move he bewilderingly weaved through three players on the left-hand side and fired a shot at goal that Henrique saved. Benfica rode that particular storm and Best eventually returned to his starting position as United aimed to conclude the game with their lead intact. Benfica proved they were not there to make up the numbers when Jaime Graça arrived at the far post to convert a cross with 11 minutes to go.

The scene was set for a thrilling finale. It was clear that the trophy would be decided in dramatic circumstances; what could not be predicted by anyone packed into Wembley Stadium was that within 15 minutes they would not only bear witness to two of Manchester United's most defining on-pitch moments of all time, but quite possibly – and this is stated with no fear of hyperbole – the top two.

The first occurred in the dying moments of the 90-minute match. "Two minutes before the full-time whistle I hit an incredible pass to Eusebio," Simões recounts. "I think he will surely finish the game. But he doesn't. He shoots straight to Stepney. I have relived that moment many times and each time I expect Eusebio to score."

The ball bounced invitingly for the legendary forward to strike – and he did so, with no little power. Fatigue appeared to be a factor; for once the player who had scored more goals for his club than he had played games did not strike with his usual accuracy. It did not require cat-like reflexes or the dramatic extending of an arm, but it did ask two things of the goalkeeper – the first, that he be brave enough to stand up to the power, and the second that he was of strong enough assurance to hold on to the ball. Alex Stepney answered yes on both counts. In doing so he performed – by a considerable distance – the most important save in the club's history. There was precious little time for United to have recovered from such a blow.

Eusebio attempted to congratulate Stepney but the goalkeeper appeared to shrug him off. "I was thinking more of the friendly we'd played in Los Angeles," Stepney told Paddy Barclay in the latter's biography of Matt Busby, referring to an exhibition match in May 1967. "There had been a bit of trouble because they were still angry about the 5-1 in Lisbon. Eusebio scored twice. Put two penalties past me. And he had this habit of smashing them, then running into the net to get the ball. And as he ran past you he'd ruffle your hair."

United had one more attack in them. What happened goes a long way to explaining the mental and physical fatigue both teams were feeling. Cruz – the man meant to be marking Best – took possession of the ball, but was pressed by the man he was supposed to be marking. George cut in from the right and took aim. The ball hit the side netting. A tired effort, with John Aston and Dave Sadler expressing their frustration in the middle. Soon after, the whistle blew. Extra-time.

...to try when your arms are too weary...

As Manchester United's players sat on the Wembley turf, with trainer Jack Crompton and physio Ted Dalton tending to them as though they were victims of a literal physical battle, Matt Busby and Jimmy Murphy tried to inspire some new energy. "We thought we were all tired," Stepney recalls. "This was the old Wembley pitch that really took it out of you, especially in games in May, and it was about 98 degrees inside the stadium. The physio Ted Dalton was rubbing the legs of the players. One of the players remarked how they were shattered. Paddy and Jimmy Murphy quickly responded along the lines of, 'You are? Well have a look at them!' There was one player who didn't seem tired at all. George had a quiet game in normal time because of how worried Benfica were. But he was the player who..." Ah, wait.

It had come to this.

Ninety minutes, yes. An entire campaign, too. United did not win the league, so unless they were able to win now, they would not be competing in the European Cup again for some time. Of course, though, this went back much further than that. It went all the way back to Matt Busby's dream of pitting his team against the best players on the continent.

All the way back to Munich and the forever lost potential of Duncan Edwards and company. All the way back to the burden felt by players like Alex Dawson and Mark Pearson and many more. The pressures that were not placed upon the shoulders of those who followed, but nonetheless were felt and carried. Alex Stepney's composure had preserved the dream of winning the European Cup ten years after the disaster. His save had pulled the momentum back into United's favour. Now they needed to seize it.

Soon after the game restarted, United went through their most profitable avenue of John Aston – by some distance, the man of the match – and won a corner. Benfica cleared and knocked it out for a throw. Dunne played it to Stepney, who picked it up and played it to Brennan. Brennan, under pressure, knocked the ball back to his goalkeeper. This time Stepney decided he would go long with the kick. The ball boomed down field into the Benfica half. Brian Kidd leapt and flicked it on.

Suddenly, Jacinto was living his worst nightmare. George Best had drifted out of position and it was he cutting in from the left to attack him, and not John Aston. Nobody was close. Jacinto had no option but to commit. His decision was not to tackle, but to swipe at the ball as powerfully as possible. But Best got there first, nipping the ball between the legs of the defender, leaving his opponent swinging a right leg at thin air. By the time he turned around, he knew the cause was lost.

George's balance at the crucial moment was remarkable. His momentum should have carried him in a straight diagonal line across goal. If it had, Henrique might well have smothered it. At the split second before the seemingly inevitable collision, Best dropped his shoulder. Wembley had already erupted with the sense of anticipation when Jacinto had been beaten. Now, as George's body dropped to the left, and with the goalkeeper having left his goal, the roar was so deafening it was almost an indistinct white noise.

In a moment of instinct, George had created the moment he had been dreaming of. It was an actual living reality. He had made it happen. "I still have dreams about that split second where everything almost stood still," George recalled in 1985. "Those hundred thousand people knew I was going to score. But in that split second before going past him and it going in the net, something might go wrong."

That was one part of the plan. The next – according to the script he had prepared – was to get to the line and head the ball in. On instinct, though, he was going to do something different. He had decided he was going to stop on the line and back-heel it in. But Jacinto was now in pursuit, so it could not happen that way. With glory at his feet, George struck the ball with his left foot, strong enough so that it would bounce in and weak enough that Henrique would be tempted to perform a vain, heroic Superman-style stretch to pull the ball back. He couldn't get there. George had put United ahead again.

Just as he had done in the Stadium of Light in March 1966, George Best had left a permanent impression, in his own personal way, on a moment in time.

"I could only hold the ball for four seconds in those days," Stepney says, recalling the action. "The referee, Concetto Lo Bello, was in charge of the game in Gornik. He'd pulled me up on the snowy pitch because my momentum had carried me forward, only just outside the area, when I caught the ball. He gave a free-kick and they scored from it. I knew he'd be watching me closely this time so I had to get rid of the ball. I hit it long and Brian got a flick on. George was still running, still full of life. Their defence was flat-footed. They didn't want to deal with him. He nutmegged Jacinto Santos, one of the best defenders in Europe, and then went around the goalkeeper…

"I know he joked with Paddy that he nearly went to head the ball over the line… to reach the level where he could play in a European Cup final, with the intensity so high, and still hit the shot with just enough power that it would go in but fool the goalkeeper into thinking he had enough time to save it… that was George. I had the perfect view of it, watching it from the other end. I was thinking, 'For God sake, put it in!'"

Denis Law might not have been on the pitch to give George a scuff to the head, but Crerand was, and almost felt like it. "You could feel like killing him at times because he would take an age to put the ball into the net," he says. "I knew he would score when he went through but it was also typical George that he waited to tease them to make them think they could also get it. He was probably half-thinking about going down to head it. Maybe he would have been able to, but even if he did, he would have had a going over not only from the Benfica players, but from Matt and Jimmy Murphy as well."

Benfica were shattered. Within a minute, Brian Kidd scored to make it three. In the 99th minute, Charlton grabbed his second with a memorable angled drive. United were jubilant, but the realisation of victory after so many had been through so much began to take an emotional toll for those on the bench. Busby now had a full half of extra-time for it to sink in that his life's work was about to be crowned in the way he had always dreamed. "It was a very strong team," Simões admits. "They had four or five extremely good players and then the others were good players willing to work extremely hard. It's tried and tested over time. That combination and balance in a team, even today, is the best you can get. In the game, in the 90 minutes, it was very close between the teams. No big difference between us until George Best decides he's going to decide the game. Then he seizes the ball, dribbles past two guys, dribbles the goalkeeper and scores a goal. It happens as quickly as that. It's a moment and we're gone. It's the key of the game and George Best had the key all along."

And so if Stepney's save could rank as number two in the all-time list of important Manchester United moments, it stands to reason that George's goal is the event that beats it. Certainly, there is a long list of individuals prepared to argue that it remains the most important goal, at least, in the club's history. Jimmy Rimmer – substitute on the day – offers this thought: "You could say that the most important save and most important goal in Manchester United history were only about ten minutes apart."

"You would have to say it is," Crerand says after some thought. "Matt's dream in life was to win the European Cup. Then it became about Manchester United wanting to win it, and the fans were desperate to as well. So when you take that all into account, you have to say it's the most important."

For Stepney, there is no doubt, no reason to pause. And that owes much to the way the goal was scored. "It's definitely the most important goal in United history," he says. "Whatever a club achieves someone has to go first. There were three men in Munich who were still there – Bobby as captain, Bill Foulkes, and obviously Matt. As a group of players we never said anything, we never spoke of the emotional significance. But I knew, and I know for sure the others did, that we were playing for those three men, all of those who passed away, all of the people who suffered as a result of the disaster.

"This was the journey the club started under Matt, to be the first to win the European Cup. So to score the goal which brought the club to that achievement couldn't ever be anything other than the most important in United's history. And what made it better was that it was scored in a way that was so unique to George, it was a product of his imagination, and that was a benefit of the freedom given to him by Matt."

That is a feeling shared by many and articulated perfectly by Paddy Barclay. "The fact that he was the shining light after Munich elevates his importance to United," he says. "Definitely. Without question. Even more so because he was fundamental to the greatness of that great side. Even within that team he was the standout."

At the final whistle, the cameras focused on Busby and Charlton, as well they should have. Jimmy Murphy, never one for the spotlight, approached the crestfallen Benfica players to offer his congratulations for a good game and commiseration for their bad luck. One man made a beeline for George Best. António Simões. The Benfica winger asked for his shirt. "I was looking forward to exchanging jerseys with him because of the admiration I had for the man and the personality," Simões says. "He was probably the first football player who became a star. We were already idols of our time but he was a star. Why? Because he was very extravagant. He was like a challenge to society. I had incredible admiration for him."

Best, consequently, was the one player pictured in a white Benfica shirt in all of the celebrations, having received Simões' in return. For years, people wondered what had happened to Best's blue number seven jersey. Simões confirms it is still not only in his possession, but it is now a family heirloom. "I will never sell it and it will never leave my family," he says, his voice almost breaking. "There are few possessions I have. The money or the value of it, I don't care, because I have the most rich memory I could ever have when I look at the shirt.

"When someone is so special they become special out of the game as well. And that for me was where the problems began for George… for me, I remember the guy who played the game. I loved the game and so did he, and I appreciated the talent of the man who played it as well as he did. I loved a player who could surprise me… you don't have players like that anymore. There are no George Bests today."

To reach the unreachable star…

The praise was universal. People could barely be more effusive or as forthcoming in their platitudes for what George had done. And yet, as United's celebrations at the Russell Hotel in London went well into the night, with families of the Munich deceased invited to dinner with the new European champions and Matt Busby sang *What A Wonderful World*, George felt a certain pulling feeling of anti-climax.

His girlfriend of the time, Jackie Glass, who lived in Chelsea, said George made his excuses midway through the night to go to her apartment. She remembered that he seemed "drained of emotion"; in his autobiography *Blessed*, George simply says that he remembers nothing of the night after arriving back at the hotel because he got drunk celebrating, but did describe it as the "greatest day of my footballing life".

THE FINAL DAYS OF PARADISE

I t was just as well that the European Cup final was followed by the summer break because it took some time for George Best to unravel the events of May 29, 1968 so that he might begin to comprehend them.

His feeling of anti-climax had come from two key points.

The first was that he had been unable to play in his normal fashion because of the attention given to him by Benfica at Wembley. "I was looking forward to the match," he said to Eamon Dunphy for *A Strange Kind of Glory*. "I'd imagined 90 minutes of pure magic, I thought we'd hammer them. But I only played in snatches."

Even the Portuguese domestic press were critical of Benfica's spoiling approach. *A Bola*'s Murelio Marcio wrote "the battle of England ended in a massacre", continuing: "Benfica found so many difficulties trying to stop Best that they began to dislike him personally."

Ken Jones of the *Mirror*, meanwhile, felt George should shoulder some responsibility. "Best had a mixed-up match, displaying great skill but robbing others of opportunities because of his greed on the ball," Jones wrote, although he did add the caveat: "Benfica's treatment of Best bordered on disgraceful and full-back Cruz might have gone from the match long before the first half was finished."

George found it difficult to come to terms with the idea that Aston had enjoyed the sort of game he would have loved, without ever truly appreciating that it would likely not have happened that way if Benfica weren't so preoccupied with Best. He was a perfectionist, and that wasn't an excuse as far as he was concerned. This is not to say that George begrudged the fortune of his fellow winger. There ought to have been considerable solace to take from the fact that even with all of that, he still had the moment which would be replayed forever – the winning goal, scored in true George Best fashion.

Every single year one team would win the European Cup and one player would score the decisive goal. The chances of everything aligning so perfectly that the goal would be scored by the best player of the time in a manner that was a true reflection of their ability is so rare that only a few come to mind. Zinedine Zidane for Real Madrid against Bayer Leverkusen is one. I will leave you to think of others. The narrative for Wembley in 1968 had so many threads that George's goal might have quite understandably been somewhere down the pecking order when it came to how it was reported.

Instead, however, this was the other thing that ate away at George. In the days and weeks following Wembley, his frustration was that it didn't go exactly as he had planned. This was easily remedied. George may not have smashed it in off the crossbar or back-heeled it or stooped to head it in on the line, but the instinctive switch-up was so wonderful, so George, that he was able to appreciate the adulation for what it was. He understood that the praise for a goal only he could have scored was not gratuitous or facetious. It says so much about George the player, and George the man, that he had to be convinced that possibly the greatest individual moment seen in a European Cup final to date was a worthy addition to his catalogue. So, over time, he was able to accept the compliments with some contentment.

In Dunphy's book, he told the author "it was like something from *Roy of the Rovers*" with a smile on his face. Indeed, he would later complain that some broadcasters would only show the goal from the moment he moved past the goalkeeper Henrique, making it look like it was a mere tap-in.

George would have two opportunities to follow Wembley in the coming season. United were in the European Cup again as holders. The final would be at the Santiago Bernabeu stadium; a fitting venue to follow Wembley. And, by winning against Benfica, United would also face Argentinian side Estudiantes in the 'World Club Championship' which was officially known as the Intercontinental Cup. There was plenty of controversy surrounding that competition because of what had happened the previous year. Racing of Argentina took on Celtic in a series of games that were particularly violent.

Racing eventually won in a play-off after Celtic had four men sent off (the winners had two men dismissed themselves!). The disorder had been blamed on the competition not being under FIFA's jurisdiction, so just before the European Cup final, the governing body announced they were taking control of the event. European Union secretary Hans Bangerter said: "The proposals were drawn up after discussions with the South American Confederation and their main purpose is to tighten discipline and streamline the competition."

Before travelling the world, George went back home for the summer and was given the hero's welcome one would expect, which included a reception in the parlour of the Lord Mayor of Belfast. The Mayor, Alderman William Geddis, presented George with a tie and said: "We are all proud of the Belfast boy who has gone to the top. I am delighted to be here to welcome him on behalf of the citizens."

There was no place like home for George, who said: "I have been all over the world since I have been lucky enough to play football for the greatest soccer club. But no matter where you go, there are no people like Belfast people. It is always a great pleasure to return home. I will try and get home more often."

The honours were handed out liberally to those associated with Manchester United following their triumph. Matt Busby became Sir Matt Busby. Bobby Charlton was awarded the OBE in 1969. The emotionally overpowering night at Wembley was already feeling like Busby's crowning glory, the culmination of a life's work, and though that was undoubtedly true, George Best's life in football terms had really only just begun. He turned 22 a few days before the final and had a lifetime of ambition in front of him.

There was most definitely a shifting feeling of uncertainty in the first few weeks of the following season. Sir Matt Busby could be ruthless – John Connelly found that out – but he was also loyal to a fault. Loyal even if it came at his own cost.

Over the years, observers would identify this as a key difference between Busby and Sir Alex Ferguson, but that is not necessarily true. In 1990 Ferguson dropped Jim Leighton for the replay of the FA Cup final. In the 1994 final there was no space on the bench for outgoing legend Bryan Robson. In 2009, though, the manager had mellowed, and had to include Ji-sung Park in his Champions League final squad after omitting him the previous year.

By this time Ferguson – closer to the end than the beginning – had developed a more sentimental side to his approach. Busby was only 59, a relative spring chicken compared to the relentless man from Govan who took over in 1986. But Munich had aged him considerably, both physically and mentally. In any case, the landscape of football was different, and the perception of what qualified as achievement was much less aggressive – that is to say, legacies were not evaluated by a particular period where one club monopolised trophies.

When Ferguson took over at Old Trafford and made it is his aim to "knock Liverpool off their perch", the silverware-consuming aspect of the monolith had more in common with United's greatest rivals. When the number of overall trophy wins was relatively low and attainable there were three key factors; to become the best, to be the first and to do it with your own style. Busby's five league titles at United had tied them at the top of English football's historical pyramid next to Arsenal and Liverpool. After Munich his ambition to win the league was less about winning the championship and more about getting another shot at the European Cup.

Victory was fulfilment as much as it was vindication.

"Matt believed in the World Club Cup and wanted to compete in it, so it was clear he didn't have any plans to retire immediately after Wembley," Paddy Barclay says. "Jock Stein had told Matt not to trust the competition with a barge pole. Matt believed – maybe rather naively – that the power of

Manchester United extending their hand of friendship could end the warfare of previous years. It was well-intentioned, but as soon as they arrived in Argentina there was hostility. It wasn't one of Matt's better campaigns."

It would therefore be wrong to suggest that Busby was neglectful of his duty as United manager; that he had lost his desire to win or improve. But one thing he would not compromise on moving forward was the loyalty he showed to his players, particularly those who had provided him with his greatest moment. It was not necessarily myopic; Busby had a sound retort. These players won the European Cup. If you're the best, it is on other teams to improve to beat you.

And yet there is a compelling argument to suggest United had been in decline for a couple of years already. Bobby Noble's form had appeared to signal the end of Shay Brennan's career before one man's pain was another's pleasure. And so it was for David Herd and Brian Kidd. There were high hopes for Kidd but he was perhaps less of a cert than Noble and certainly less of a goal-threat than Herd, respectable though his goal return was. John Connelly's hasty exit had presented an opening in the team for John Aston. Aston was the subject of divided opinion on the Old Trafford terrace but his performance at Wembley won many over. Now he needed to increase his goal contribution to match Connelly's prior efforts.

So those were just three areas of the team in 1968 that could be said to be weaker than in 1966. Alex Stepney's arrival had papered over the cracks of an ageing defence. Faced with the two realities – one being to see his side as European champions, the other to note the decline for what it was – Busby chose the one which favoured a faithful approach with his players. Some would be critical of that approach. But even if it is true it is worth considering the following. Let us theorise a scenario where the goalkeeper wasn't the only member of the defence Busby was ruthless with in 1966. Let's suppose he looked at Bill Foulkes at the age of 34 and signed Mike England from Blackburn Rovers, before he went to Spurs, as some in the many years that have passed have suggested he ought to have done. There would be no Foulkes in Madrid, galloping to score a dramatic goal. No Foulkes at Wembley. It would have been as big a loss for Manchester United folklore as it would have been for Foulkes. Sometimes it pays to favour sentiment and romance. Other times, however...

United's first game as European champions came on the opening day of the Division One season against Everton at Old Trafford. George opened the scoring in the 21st minute. Alan Ball, another player linked with United who could well have improved them (and would have loved to have been given the chance, considering his father was a season ticket holder at Old Trafford) levelled four minutes later. And, four minutes after that, Charlton – promoted to club captain over the summer – grabbed the goal that earned the win.

The United train was up and running again but the wheels came off immediately. At West Brom, the hosts stormed into three-goal lead by the 18th minute and won comfortably. A trip was then made across town to Maine Road. Law had complained of soreness in his knee so he was out. Foulkes, Crerand, and Brennan were all missing too. So Frank Kopel, John Fitzpatrick, Alan Gowling and Kidd all deputised. A 0-0 draw at the champions was decent in the circumstances, but there was a further price to pay when Aston suffered a terribly cruel twist of fate, breaking his leg badly.

In the following game, United played Coventry at home.

George moved over to the outside-left position in the number 11 shirt. Jim Ryan wore seven, and scored the game's only goal. It kept him in the side for the next game against Chelsea where he lined up against the man the press were predicting would replace him – Bobby Tambling was a rumoured target for United as a senior name to replace the injured Aston.

Chelsea said no dice – and Tambling was among the scorers as the Blues inflicted a sobering 4-0 drubbing on the European champions. With no Law to worry about, Harris once more played as a personal minder for United's star man. Dave Sexton used the Benfica tactic – three men watching the danger man at all times. "Chelsea's pre-match analysis of United was searching, exhaustive and accurate," wrote Derek Wallis of the *Mirror*. "It would not surprise me to learn there was even a note on the way George Best ties his bootlaces."

Joe Harvey, Newcastle manager, was not quite as fastidious as the Chelsea coach. To his cost – Best was influential in a 3-1 win for his team in late September. His two goals included an effort which would go down in the top five of any other player's portfolio. He wriggled free of a tackle just inside the left-hand side of the penalty area. There were two more defenders between him and the goal. They were well-positioned. George was just a yard from the byline. Instead of going around them, George went for something so outrageous it would not enter the mind of a regular player. He scooped the ball over both of the players in front of him, and the goalkeeper – it should have been impossible. The ball went into the top corner.

By then, United had reinforced. They did not sign Tambling – but they did sign Willie Morgan, the Burnley winger who could have passed for George Best, for just over £100,000. Morgan was pacy and liked to take his man on but would most often do what normal wingers did – he would get to the byline and hit a cross in. Morgan wasn't normal – he was very very good. And he had the confidence that said he would not shrink on the stage.

"George and I were the two biggest names in the game," Morgan says. "It was unusual for players of our age to get to the first team as early as we did. I was going to go to Leeds but United came in with a late bid. I met with Matt Busby and he asked if there was anything I wanted. I said I wanted the number seven shirt, and he said that would be no problem. I arrived at training on Monday morning and met all the players.

"Bestie approached me and asked me if I wouldn't mind going to lunch with him. So we went to this place on Bridge Street in Manchester. 'Let's be friends,' he said, and when I asked why we wouldn't be, he said he felt the press would try and make us rivals. There was no preciousness, no complaint about me taking the number seven shirt. We got on, we'd often play snooker together, we just had an easy friendship."

George Best's 'shirt number' is something that has gone down in United folklore. At Wembley he wore seven and it is true to say that up until this period that had been the number he wore most often. In the earlier days, when he had not earned his freedom, George wore the number according to the position he played. Now there was an understanding he could play anywhere. That suited Charlton, who was a player who enjoyed space. It suited Law, too, who amusingly considered himself a box-to-box player rather than the instinctive striker everyone else saw him as, so liked to drift into whatever area Best wasn't occupying.

George would wear seven because Aston would wear 11 as a definite left-sided player. But, whenever that changed

– when Ryan, an out-and-out right-sider, for example, came in – George would wear whatever shirt was free. Sometimes eight, sometimes ten. Consequently, although he serves as the origin for United's marketing of the famous number seven, he became so associated with the number 11 shirt that others felt they were following him in that, too.

When Gordon Hill arrived at United in 1975 he was excited to wear "George's number". When Ryan Giggs broke into the side he was labeled as the "next George" and a large reason for that was the number 11 on his back. George made such an impact that he was seen as the man to follow in two different shirt numbers for the same club.

Not just any club. Manchester United. European champions. And, if all went to plan, world champions too. United travelled to Argentina to play the first leg. The Argentinian newspapers clearly did not get the memo about the hope for friendlier relations. Nobby Stiles was described as "El Bandido" (the bandit) following negative remarks made about Stiles by Benfica manager Otto Gloria which were reprinted in the match programme, and references were made to Denis Law's controversial disciplinary record. That was an equaliser, then – Carlos Bilardo, the home team midfielder not only had a reputation for being violent, he was said to carry pins on the pitch which he would stab opponents with.

"It may not be easy, but I know I have to accept it," George (who had been sporting a moustache at this time, something he later regretted, yet a facial feature that made him look more like the bandit than the labelled Stiles!) told reporters about his anticipation of some rough treatment. "The boss has constantly hammered the message into us that we must keep our heads. I will be reminding myself of that all the time."

"We have come to play a football match, not take part in a war," Busby told the press. Osvaldo Zubeldía, the Estudiantes manager, matched the conciliatory tone. "Like Sir Matt Busby, I have told my players to be calm and to avoid incidents," he said. "But, like Sir Matt I have also told them to win this championship. These are two instructions that do not always fit together very well."

They didn't. And it is all the more compelling when considering how the Estudiantes players saw themselves. Rubén Pagnanini was a young right back – spared from being fed to George because the experienced Oscar Malbernat, team captain, was in front of him. In an interview with the esteemed Marcela Mora y Araujo for Dutch publication *Hard Gras*, Pagnanini not only refutes the allegation about his side's philosophy, he tries to paint a different picture: "That stuff about Bilardo and the pins is a lie. Estudiantes were tough on the pitch. We were a hard team to face. But we walked onto the pitch with the rule book under our arm. Albeit with a little picardía criolla – creole cheekiness. People want satisfaction and one big way of achieving that is by winning. Our fans loved our style of play; agile. They understood the team and followed our style. We were tough, sure, but within the rules."

Bilardo, naturally, agrees. "Osvaldo changed football, in the world," he said. "Moves we now know as pelota parada (play based around stopping the ball) which everyone uses he used to implement in '65. Pushing all the players back so as to leave your opponent offside – he used that in '65. Kicking the corners with the opposite leg to the corner you're on, he did that back in '65."

Juan Ramon Verón, father of Juan Sebastian, the future United player, claimed Zubeldía was at least 20 years ahead of his time: "The way of marking, the notion that you should not allow your opponent to play, totally lacking in lyricism... in Argentina we had some great players but we hadn't won anything. Zubeldía was a visionary."

That seems to be backed up again by Bilardo's memory of the preparation. "They started to call us the laboratory; because of the corners, the free kicks... the critics and the press used to say 'it doesn't matter who you're playing against', and we would say yes, it does matter and a lot. We filmed matches on Super 8, we got hold of Super 8 film of Manchester United. And the press needed to knock us down at all costs because they were doing badly from us. Boca and River sold papers, sold advertising – say you paid 3,000 pesos for an advert with Boca, with us it would be 1,000. We'd win the Libertadores and it would be quite small on the cover."

Eduardo Flores, the imposing forward, said that he felt the negative reaction was borne out of resentment which began locally. "We started in '65 when we were 20, 21, 22 years old," he said. "Verón, Pachame, me, [we] came up from the youth divisions... Bilardo and Madero were older. The first three seasons were team building, evolving. Afterwards we had four years during which we won everything. When Estudiantes won the Metropolitan Championship in 1967 we became the first small club to win the championship in Argentine history. We defeated the big clubs. That's when the started to call us anti-football, to say we pricked our opposition with pins..."

Beauty is in the eye of the beholder, it would seem. There was no accusation of pins and stabbing but the tie was not lacking in violent altercations and this much is not disputed on either side. If it were a comedy sketch then the sight of the Argentine team targeting the diminutive Stiles in such aggressive fashion might have been amusing, but it was no laughing matter for the United players. Stiles was kicked, punched, even head-butted, and tried to maintain his calm, even after he suffered a blow to the head and needed stitches.

Bobby Charlton was the epitome of a sportsman but even he received a wound on the shin that broke his shin-pad. Bilardo seemed to be orchestrating the mayhem in the manner of the world's great conductors. But like all good leaders, he would not instruct his colleagues to do what he would not do himself. Best collected the ball deep in his own half and surged forward. Bilardo came at him. George was able to avoid him with some comfort, dancing past him with the ball as if he wasn't there. And, as if to prove he was there, Bilardo swung a leg with some significant force towards Best's crotch. The ball was on the floor. The referee blew for the free-kick but that was the extent of the punishment. George bent down, picked the ball up and offered it to Bilardo. "If you want it so badly, there you go," he seemed to be saying.

The hosts took a first-half lead. Stiles was sent off when he finally retaliated. The red card was for a push on Bilardo erroneously remembered by the home player. "In one incident, I turned my back and he kicked me up the arse," Bilardo remembered. "One of many kicks. But my philosophy was always that sometimes you give and sometimes you receive. If it was tough, you put up with it."

Still, United looked to have secured a draw when Dave Sadler scored. But he was ruled offside – despite there being two defenders on the goal-line. Sadler and Best faced the press afterwards and as the Londoner stated his case, George interrupted: "He disallowed it because it went into the net."

FIFA President Sir Stanley Rous was in attendance and

remarked that "the outstanding feature of the match was the quite remarkable tolerance of the United team".

If United hoped that on home soil things would be calmer, they hadn't accounted for the particularly boisterous personality of their opponents. They were bound to be aggravating guests. "We looked forward to a better game at Old Trafford, thinking they wouldn't dare play with such violence at our place," George recalled.

They did.

Law was forced off the pitch with an injury to his shin before half-time. With Stiles suspended, George became the primary target. Oscar Malbernat spat at him. In the last minute, José Medina punched him right in front of the official. Best waited for the referee, Konstantin Zeevi, to send him off. But he took an age, and, thinking that it wouldn't happen, Best threw a punch back at Medina. Both were sent from the field. "It was the most satisfying red card I've ever had," Best wrote in his book *Blessed*. "It was also a relief that we only drew 1-1 to lose on aggregate because Sir Matt would have had a problem getting 11 players willing to turn out for a play-off."

Oh yes – there was a football match that occurred. Verón – whose son would later score a fair few more on this ground – netted early on to give his side a 2-0 aggregate lead. United actually staged an incredible response after Best's dismissal. Morgan equalised, and then Brian Kidd thought he had forced the ball over the line to win it, but the referee thought otherwise.

When the dust settled, as George said, the players would not be so bothered that they would not be playing again, but in the heat of the battle such controversy to end the game only served as further fuel for the fire. The unflappable Alex Stepney had seen enough, and as the teams left the field and went up the tunnel to the changing room, the goalkeeper threw a fist at the head of ringleader Bilardo, who had earned the nickname 'Bastardo' among the United players.

"It was frightening," Stepney recalls. "We anticipated it would be an aggressive encounter but they were a much better team than we'd realised. In the second game it was different, there was an angrier atmosphere, and there was all that aggression that we'd thought was coming first time around. I wasn't happy with the way they were literally kicking lumps out of George and Denis so at the end I confronted Carlos Bilardo, their captain, in the tunnel to let him know what I thought."

Busby was furious with Stepney and did not see it as acceptable retaliation. The goalkeeper was called into the manager's office where he was told he'd let the manager, Jimmy Murphy, his team-mates, the supporters and the club down, and was left in no uncertainty that a repeat offence would end his career at the club. The manager clearly still had an iron fist. It made the headlines which shocked the nation in January 1969 – "I'VE LOST MY GRIP" – all the more dramatic and stunning.

* * *

George's form in the early months of the season had generally held up. Eight goals before Christmas was a solid return and there were some strong performances, as always – most notably against QPR where he was credited with two of United's goals in a 3-2 win.

Here he had felt in particularly tortuous mood, according to the *Sunday Mirror:* "Twice Best bamboozled everyone to pave the way for a goal from either wing. He could be credited with both, but Ron Hunt helped in the first in trying to clear and Tony Hazell finished off the second when attempting to head for a corner."

Despite the difficult team form, George was not foreseeing the turbulence to follow. Who could? His contentment was reflected in his forecast for the future in his book *Best of Both Worlds* which was published that year. He spoke about maximising his earning potential outside of football for two more years, and from the age of 24, he said, "I will then be able to concentrate solely on becoming the world's best footballer." He thought that by that time, he would be able to afford to "have a man to clean my shoes, another to drive me about and other people to look after my personal and financial affairs". He spoke of becoming a millionaire and then flying off to Bermuda where he would settle down.

Still, it's hard not to think that as far as Best's personal ambition for the year was concerned, it was job done the second he scored at Wembley. He had watched for years as the European Footballer of the Year award was given to the man who had starred for the team who won the European Cup.

It wasn't a hard and fast rule – there were occasions where you could upset the apple cart, particularly in a World Cup year, and George had two team-mates he could use as evidence – but generally speaking, your chances would most certainly improve. On Christmas Eve, what had unofficially been the case in many eyes for two and a half years was made official – George Best was named the European Footballer of the Year. Once again, he became the youngest ever player to do so.

He had reached a peak, but had not stopped learning. Soon after the Estudiantes game United came up against Leeds. Sometimes it didn't matter how good George was; if a player had the single-mindedness to stop him from playing, it could be difficult. Paul Reaney was that man. George had missed both games with Leeds the prior season and observed how Aston seemed to have more joy. Before the game he approached Willie Morgan. "We very rarely switched," Morgan says. "Only when we played against Leeds and Paul Reaney because he hated playing against him, and I had a guy at Newcastle who was useless most of the time, but could I beat him? Whatever dummy I threw him he'd go the same way as me. It was like he was that bad he was world class. So I asked George to give him a hard time, which he inevitably did. And I would sort out Reaney for him."

The switch didn't have the effect either would have truly hoped – the result was 0-0, and, for the first time, it suggested that George was fallible. Willie Anderson rejects the idea that the move was in any way evidence of self-doubt, and reiterates that it was in fact against his spirit. "As he matured in the game he would switch but it certainly wouldn't have been through fear of the opponent – it would have been a case of knowing he would have more joy if he moved around, and therefore be better for his team," Anderson says.

"That was a sign of intelligence because it would mean his marker would either have to follow him and leave a space, or, pick another player. Look, he could ride tackles better than anybody I ever knew. People would try and tackle him and they couldn't get near him. So they'd try and kick him, but he'd be gone. He just had this wonderful sense of space and timing, the ability to not only time his own movements but anticipate the lunge of an opponent to make them look like a fool. It came so totally naturally to him. Anything you played him at, he wanted to beat you, and he'd get pissed off if he didn't. Clearly, that competitiveness stayed with him as part of his personality and not just on the pitch. He was good at every sport. I'm sure whatever he put his mind to he would have excelled at."

* * *

Let us return to the theme from the start of this book about the combination of factors that often have to align in order for things to turn out a certain way. From May 22, 1946 to January 14, 1969 these events had all seemed to be beneficial for George Best's career. Even the trials and tribulations, like Paul Reaney, were merely challenges where the public would wait to see how and when – not if – Best would overcome them in his own irrepressible manner.

On that day in mid-January everything changed when Sir Matt Busby informed assembled press that he would be retiring at the end of the season. "I don't mind admitting here and now that the reason is: I am losing my grip!" Busby said. "That is the honest reason after months of heart searching. I have not had enough time with the players, and yet, in soccer, players are the all-essential beings. Therefore a manager must be with them and must live with them and know them.

"As things have happened over the last few months this has not been possible. Therefore it is time to go. The decision, which is my decision and my decision only, was inevitable. Manchester United need new blood, a new supply of ideas from which they will progress and do better if it is possible."

The timing and the seismic nature of the event meant it was a shock to most. Paddy Crerand suggests, though, that some saw it coming. "You think of what Matt had been through in his life… we all knew he was going to retire in 1969, we were disappointed of course. But he was like a father to everybody," Crerand says. "Once Matt retired it wasn't the same for George. It wasn't the same team. I did have sympathy for him that he was approaching his peak and most of the rest of us were coming towards the end of our careers. I would think that affected him more than anything. He was a 17-year old lad growing up with us."

The "lost my grip" element of Busby's statement has been interpreted as a shifting of the guard; a moment where the change in eras can be traced. George is therefore seen as a figurehead of that and the idea of Busby being unable to truly comprehend his star player's celebrity was inevitably suggested as a significant factor. But there are a couple of elements to consider which rebuff that. The first is that Busby was a straight-talker. The second is that you didn't need to look too far to consider the literal interpretation of his explanation; since being knighted, there was a greater demand on his time, and having reached an age where it was time for him to consider stepping aside, taking the decision as he did and announcing it in that way might actually have a galvanising impact on United's flagging season.

"Matt would train with us sometimes, and you would think he was a young man, but then he'd be in the showers with us afterwards… you would see the scars on his body from the accident," Stepney recalls. "After Wembley in 1968, when he was knighted, he suddenly seemed to have all of these things going on that it became too much for him. I think his wife had an influence in him stepping back. Yes, the game was changing, but I don't think it was true that he'd lost his grip.

"His influence with the players was as great as it ever had been.

If you were getting a telling off by him it still carried the same weight. He certainly never lost control. But I think George lost his mentor when Matt retired. They were generations apart but shared the same dreams about how football should be played. George could see how things would go at United after Matt left. It was natural that when there was something negative happening, like it was at United, he would seek solace in the positive things in his life, and the feeling that he got from all the ventures away from the pitch, and so it's understandable that maybe for a time he enjoyed that more. He wanted United to be at the top all the time."

Manchester United were in 16th position in the league table at the time of Busby's revelation, with greater prospects of relegation than title glory. Their form would improve but the hopes of a glorious hurrah were all placed on the cup competitions – the FA Cup, and the European Cup in which United had progressed to the quarter final following comfortable ties against Waterford and Anderlecht.

The FA Cup campaign involved lower league opposition in the early rounds. Exeter City took the Estudiantes approach of hobbling; Best was forced to come off with a twisted ankle. United went through and Best was back to face Watford in the next round. The Hornets earned a draw at Old Trafford. "My one big worry was the United crowd and the effect they can have on their players," their boss Ken Furphy said. "When I saw them play Estudiantes, the crowd were willing the ball to go to George Best and Bobby Charlton, and their game was lifted by the crowd's encouragement. I felt that if we could keep Best and Charlton quiet we were halfway there."

Or maybe even two-thirds. The problem was that third element – Law. He equalised at Old Trafford and then scored both goals in the replay. United's FA Cup journey was ended abruptly by Everton at Old Trafford; Best was booked for arguing with the referee on a tough afternoon.

It had been a mixed few weeks for George since Busby announced his intentions. You might even trace it back to the bloodlust against Estudiantes and the general feeling of things being more wayward and uncertain than at any point before. Against Birmingham in the league, George appeared to have given his team a late 2-1 win when he scored in the 80th minute. Three minutes later he handled in his own box and gave away a penalty. He remonstrated for so long that he had to be pulled away from the referee by his team-mates. Finally, Brum took the kick and equalised to take a point.

Better fortune, and mood, awaited in Europe; Rapid Vienna were beaten in clinical fashion with Best proving to be the difference. The Austrian side put up stubborn resistance until just before the break. Best played a one-two with Charlton and broke behind the back-line; the last defender threw himself into a two-footed challenge and actually won the ball.

But, on the turf just inside the six-yard box, Best was able to pinch it off him. The defender took another swing; the goalkeeper dived forward to snatch the ball. George extraordinarily decided to pull the ball back, leaving the goalkeeper in a muddy heap. By now, another defender arrived on the scene and two more positioned themselves in front of the goal. George maintained his composure and lashed a thunderous left-footer into the roof of the net. In the second half, he added another, and Morgan grabbed the third in a 3-0 win.

"George Best and Willie Morgan, Manchester United's two 'Beatle Boys' virtually shot Rapid Vienna out of the European Cup last night," reported the *Mirror*'s Derek Wallis. He was right. A 0-0 draw in the second leg set up a potential classic semi-final against AC Milan. The bad mood of the winter seemed to be behind United. Best and Morgan looked to have established a genuine double act on the flanks with a run where the former struck seven goals in seven games and the latter five in the same spell – this included a remarkable game against QPR where Morgan scored a hat-trick and George got two. Poor QPR looked set to suffer a relatively respectable 4-1 loss in the 84th minute but United ran riot, scoring four more – including one for the recently returned John Aston.

Try as they might, even on occasions where they scored themselves, neither Aston or Morgan could take top billing from Best. Against Sheffield Wednesday in late March George scored the only goal but was in particularly devilish mood. This was one afternoon where he was not in the mood for sharing the ball and at one stage, having already inflicted torment on the Owls defence, he received a pass; and, as the ball was still bouncing to him, he put both of his hands up to invite players to tackle him. The Old Trafford crowd roared with appreciation of the showmanship.

"I know at times people would have a go at him because he was a little bit greedy on the pitch but George thought, and felt, he could beat everybody," Crerand says. "It wasn't that he couldn't pass. It wasn't that he didn't want to pass. He was an intelligent player and he had the confidence and self-belief to take on any player and beat them. He usually did.

"He was fantastic in training. It was sometimes impossible to get the ball off him. It's one thing when you have got that much ability, to take people on all the time. Plenty of players might overdo it. Most aren't good enough to do that and get the ball in the net. You knew George could do it all."

Nobby Stiles, like Crerand, simply felt that Best's tendency to be selfish had to be tolerated and accommodated. "There was never any doubt about George's contribution," he said. "His awareness of his team-mates on the field wasn't always the best – when the ball was passed to him there was never any guarantee that it would be returned, however well a position had been taken up – but there was never much delay in forgiveness. That was because you always had to believe in George's capacity to do anything he wanted on the field."

With Aston's natural width on the left adding to Morgan's on the right, and Best's trickery in the middle, Busby had a vibrant front line which had accidentally fallen into his lap with a knee ligament injury to Charlton. But Charlton was always going to be recalled for the games that mattered once fit and Law, with his own injury record, was also protected as much as Busby could ahead of the tie against Milan.

Speculation had been increasing week-by-week about who Matt Busby would pick as his successor. It was an indication of the power and status he yielded at the club in terms of the football operations and yet also an indication of the issues which were to follow. Busby had courted Jock Stein of Celtic. The move would have made a lot of sense – Stein had the pedigree to walk onto the Old Trafford stage and not feel daunted. Ultimately Busby made a judgement call which would have short and long-term repercussions – he promoted reserve-team manager Wilf McGuinness to take control of the first team, with the idea that hiring from within would see a continuation of the standards and practices Busby, Murphy and others had put in place.

"There was an after the Lord Mayor's parade feeling at United that Matt wouldn't have been oblivious to," Paddy Barclay says. "He knew the game was becoming more about coaching and less about stardust. He saw how Leeds were coached under Revie. He saw the Boot Room brains at Liverpool. I think history has been a little harsh in terms of the succession. Choosing Wilf McGuinness wasn't as bad or as inept a choice as is made out. Wilf had already marked himself out as one of the outstanding coaches in the English game. He was in Alf Ramsey's set-up for the World Cup win.

"Matt had no wish to see Wilf fulfil his promise at a club other than Manchester United. What he didn't perhaps factor in was that the ageing players might not take kindly to receiving instructions from a former player who was perhaps not quite in their class. But he was loyal to people who'd grown up within the club and Wilf was one of them. Matt's loyalty was a big reason the club never got Jock Stein. Jock's wife famously didn't want to move to Manchester, but Jock had also said he wanted to bring some of his backroom boys from Celtic, and that would obviously have meant men at United would have to go. Matt couldn't have that."

The emotional pressure of how the club's greatest custodian wished it would be run would cast a heavy shadow for years. In the newspaper columns announcing McGuinness' promotion – which would be effective at season's end – more inches were dedicated to Busby's announcement of the news than to McGuinness' own statements. A sign of things to come. "I don't know who was more surprised, the players or Wilf," Best recalled. "One of his first problems was that, at age 32, he was younger than some of the players he would be picking. That would make it hard for him to win the players' respect, although I, for one, was willing to give him a chance."

United's penultimate game of the league campaign came

against Burnley at Old Trafford. Before the match, Best was presented with his Ballon d'Or trophy, the golden ball – and he continued to show that he was worth his weight in the aforementioned material when he smashed home his 21st goal of the season. The 2-0 win in that match meant little for the league – Busby's tenure as United manager was going to end with a mid-table finish – but it was a shot in the arm ahead of the trip to Milan for the first leg of their tie.

Milan, though, were good. They won 2-0 at San Siro, controlling the game when John Fitzpatrick was sent off, but United saw enough to feel confident in their ability to turn it around at Old Trafford three weeks later (even if Pat Crerand did say: "Two goals might as well be four against Milan"). Milan coach Nereo Rocco explained that he would instruct the legendary Roberto Rosato to follow the best player in the world in order to minimise United's chances of getting back into the tie. "We have prepared two tactical plans… we shall begin by using Rosato to mark George Best," he said.

For their final appearance under Busby in this competition, United wore all white at home. They gave it everything. Best – up against Rosato and a wonderful defender in Angelo Anquilletti – was in thrilling form. Nominally starting from the left, George showed that nous to move central, giving Anquilletti a choice to make. He stayed put and trusted in his team-mate. For a while Rosato held firm but he was only one man; in the 70th minute, George finally broke free of the constraint, seizing on a defensive clearance and playing a one-two with Kidd to take out two defenders.

The Milan defenders rushed to challenge him; Best jinked to the left, catching one off-balance, and floated past two more to move wondrously in the box. The last got enough of his body in the way to stop the momentum of the player but not the ball; Charlton was arriving like a locomotive and absolutely drilled the ball into the goal to send the Stretford End crazy. It was United's 100th goal in the European Cup and there could not have been a more fitting combination to create it.

Sitting behind the goal was a young boy who had just signed for United by the name of Brian Greenhoff. He would go on to play almost 300 times for the club – some with George – but said he never experienced a noise quite like that inside Old Trafford for those last 20 minutes.

The atmosphere didn't only come close to boiling over, though. It repeatedly crossed the line. Milan goalkeeper Fabio Cudicini had been struck by missiles from the supporters behind him and the game had to be stopped on more than one occasion; the United fans were, in their mind, responding to the rockets and smoke bombs some of them had experienced in Italy in the first leg.

The home team had considerable momentum after breaking the deadlock and were certain they had equalised eight minutes later when Law's effort appeared to go in. "I know a goal when I've scored one and it was certainly in," Law later said. "Pictures and the television play-back only confirm something I was convinced of at the time. The ball was six inches over the line when it was cleared." French referee Roger Machin judged that it wasn't; but this was no case of sour grapes, as even the Italian press conceded that their side had been fortunate.

"The English now maintain they scored a second goal in the second half and that the referee did not notice the ball had crossed the white line of Cudicini's goal," Gino Palumbo wrote in *Corriere Della Sera*. "The impression from the press seats is that the English were right. It was a goal and the referee was mistaken in not giving it." This time, in contrast to the controversy at the end of the Estudiantes game, there was some considerable distress that there would no replay. United's efforts were more than valiant.

Two days later, United finally concluded their Division One campaign against Leicester City. The Foxes, coached by Frank O'Farrell, came to Old Trafford needing a win to stay up. They took a first minute lead but George levelled two minutes later, and within 60 seconds of the equaliser, Morgan had turned it around completely.

Law settled the result in Busby's favour before a late consolation goal for the team who were going down. It was an underwhelming end for the most significant reign in United history, with only 45,860 in attendance.

United finished in 11th but the final day victory did at least mean they finished above neighbours City for a smidgeon of pride. Compared to what was to follow, this was a heady achievement indeed, but the halcyon days at Manchester United were well and truly over.

ROAD
TO HELL

T he road to hell is paved with good intentions. Though some of the senior Manchester United players had reservations about Wilf McGuinness becoming manager, most were willing to give him a chance. But McGuinness' cause was not helped by Sir Matt Busby staying on at the club in an administrative role; Busby even kept the word 'manager' in his title – general manager.

There are facets of McGuinness' era which do not reflect favourably on how well it went. The first is the length of it. He was in charge for 18 months and this bare fact suggests that it was catastrophic. That is not true. But what is, is that he was fighting the tide helplessly from day one, doing a number of things as any successor of Busby ought to – and yet, whenever he required the support of the structure which was ostensibly there only to help him, McGuinness found himself in a position where he was almost exclusively undermined.

This was nobody's fault. Of course, that opinion is disputable, but what is meant by it is that nobody went in to the scenario with the intent to make it go as badly as it did. Busby did truly want to see McGuinness succeed and have a dynasty in the same way he had. The truth is that everything went as horribly as it could have been feared and everyone was culpable; though, in time-honoured human fashion, because so much went wrong, it meant the blame was so plentiful that many of the protagonists were able to point elsewhere.

The first problem was the chain of command. Busby had made it clear to McGuinness that he didn't want to interfere. So McGuinness interpreted that as both a freedom to do things as he wanted and also an indication that Busby shouldn't be relied upon. Busby's method as a manager had always been to observe whether his players could sink or swim before assessing how helpful his advice and influence could be. McGuinness was mindful of this. Where this became a problem was in how the players still perceived Busby, and his continuing presence at the club. They got there first, in other words, complaining to Busby when they didn't like what McGuinness did, and the former manager became a middle-man and a mediator; rather than the person to stand behind McGuinness when he needed it. This was complicated further by Busby's continuing loyalty to those men.

United hadn't fallen down to mid-table by accident. Improvement was desperately needed and McGuinness was going to have to bruise the egos of men his own age, men of greater playing achievement, as soon as he walked through the door. That was a fundamental necessity for United if they wanted to have greater fortune in the short-term. Those players were not ready for such a wake-up call. McGuinness had a similar approach to Jimmy Murphy as he did Matt Busby. Murphy was left without a clear role following Busby's retirement and although he was retained at the club and did plenty of scouting, McGuinness was again caught in a difficult position as he did not want to be seen as deferential to the erstwhile assistant. And so all of the valuable experience Murphy – who was more than willing to champion McGuinness' cause – possessed, was sadly lost as a coach.

But McGuinness' own loyalty to both his reserve team and the United way of doing things meant he was caught in a deadly trap. United's need for reinforcement was rather more serious and urgent than promoting reserve-team players and the quality of those players was reflected in the fact that Murphy's 1964 FA Youth Cup team had not been followed with another winning side. Graduates of that side included George Best and Dave Sadler who most certainly were good enough to build around, but also John Fitzpatrick, for example, who was a capable squad player and could effortlessly slide in if, say, Shay Brennan was injured.

The issue was that Steve James, Carlo Sartori, Paul Edwards and Tommy O'Neil were all capable squad players but were being asked to fill bigger shoes. Because McGuinness knew them and had coached them he was keen to see them make good. He was not afraid of making a difficult and unpopular call, but naturally, he would prefer not to have to make it so early. Unfortunately, time was not his friend.

The McGuinness era started with a draw at Crystal Palace. Twice United came from behind, with Willie Morgan getting the goal that earned them a point. "We were all devastated when the manager retired, but hiring Wilf seemed like a great idea. Revolutionary, even," Morgan – who has gone on record with much stronger, negative terms – says. "Unfortunately it didn't work. That was the start of the discontent and things falling apart. Jimmy Murphy didn't want the job, but he would have been perfect for it. If Bobby or Paddy had been named manager it would have worked out fine. George's relationship with Wilf was non-existent, just as it was with the rest of us. Two things should have happened when the manager was still in charge. We should have signed Alan Ball when he was leaving Blackpool, and also Mike England. I think those two signings would have carried us through."

Ball scored for Everton in a 2-0 win for the Toffees that ruined Wilf's first home game. In that match, Bill Foulkes had to be substituted, and against Southampton three days later he wished he was brought off when Ron Davies scored four times at Old Trafford. Foulkes was seen as the fall guy and never played for the club again. When Paul Edwards was tried as his replacement in the early return at Goodison, and United shipped another three goals, McGuinness was forced to make some bold calls.

The first was to sign Ian Ure of Arsenal, but that deal was infamous due to the nature of Busby's close involvement in it. McGuinness had wanted Colin Todd of Sunderland, but was told it would be too costly. So Ure was signed and it was seen as a transfer made by the former manager rather than the current one and the perception was not incorrect; though Busby's judgement for once was.

"I certainly wouldn't have signed myself," Ure told Paddy Barclay in *Sir Matt Busby – The Man Who Made A Football Club*, referring to a chronic knee injury he had. "They must have been bloody blind... apparently Busby had been impressed when I'd got sent off with Denis Law. I think the fight we had that day might have convinced him I was what they needed when Bill Foulkes was finished. But almost a whole team was going over the hill at the same time… after the European Cup he should have got rid of not only Bill but Bobby. And Denis. There was terrible wear and tear on Nobby too. They were all past their best. Even George should have gone. It would have caused a sensation, but by the time I got there he was drinking heavily three or four nights a week. He was a great player and the nicest guy but he'd become a bad influence on the club."

Ure's comments are blockbuster. We'll get to them in a moment, because they still weren't as stunning as the bold move McGuinness made of his own accord in just his fourth game. At Goodison, it was not only Foulkes dropped, but also Charlton and Law. The result went so badly that both were recalled into the team for the following game at Wolves, in which Ure made his debut. It brought some stability. United went ten games unbeaten after winning none and losing three of their first six. Nobody could accuse Best of not pulling his weight – 12 goals in 12 games underlined his contribution.

Furthermore, despite Ure's claim – and a little later George himself would concede the new player wasn't completely wrong – all the signs in the early days were that Best had decided to take some personal responsibility in this transitional period. Urged by everyone to settle down, George had fallen for Eva Haraldsted over the summer and they agreed to get married in the winter. The speed of their romance was met with a dubious reception, but again, the genuine intent was there.

Best's performance levels were just as impressive as his goals tally. The first big moment of the campaign came at Elland Road; previously so often a vacuum when it came to great George Best moments, it could now boast a volume of at least two. Leeds had grown wise to the Morgan and Best switch so instructed Paul Reaney to follow the Northern Irishman. With George now possessing the freedom to go either way in the middle of the pitch, Reaney for once suffered like so many of his peers. Best was able to find space to snatch United's equaliser following a Sadler own goal, and then again from a Charlton pass soon after. This time he was much further out – at least 30 yards – but had escaped Reaney's attention.

Jack Charlton did not want to commit but left the space in front of Best; George unleashed a remarkable drive from outside of the area that impossibly bent right, to the left-hand side of goalkeeper Gary Sprake, smashing the inside of the post and going into the net. George thrust his hand in the air with the conviction of a man who had finally proved his worth against a stubborn opponent. Billy Bremner's late overhead kick for the hosts ensured he would share the headlines and his team would share the points.

There was another brace on the road at Sheffield Wednesday with two late goals in a 3-1 win. Three days later, United were 2-0 down at Arsenal on September 20 before George led the fightback, scoring just before half-time and laying on the late equaliser for Sadler after twisting Gunners defender Frank McLintock inside and out. "McLintock knew exactly which way George Best would go. He knew exactly what had to be done to stop him. But Best's talent for fashioning something magical out of the most predictable of his skills left Arsenal's captain stranded, without hope or argument," reported the *Mirror*'s Ken Jones.

"There was nothing surprising about what he did, because he's done it so many times before," McLintock explained afterwards. "But the speed with which he leaves you puts him in a class of his own."

Next up in the league was West Ham and Best was once more head and shoulders above everyone, orchestrating a 5-2 win with two goals of his own. He began in blistering fashion, scoring and creating a goal in the first quarter hour. His second suggested United could enjoy much more prosperity with the speed of their play. He flicked a backwards header to Kidd, who then played it to Morgan, and Morgan's cross was headed home by Best, who had raced into the area.

"George Best was behind the crushing power of Manchester," reported Paul Doherty of the *People*. "The shattering spell for the Hammers came early, long before [Bobby] Howe had discovered he had the most thankless task in soccer – dousing the flames that the Irishman's inspiration ignite... Wee Georgie still had not finished. His impudence and immaculate timing cleared the way for Kidd to strike the last goal."

Best seemed in positive spirits when he spoke to Jimmy Hill for *Match Of The Day*. "Wilf's young, he trains with us, he's behind us all the time shouting and screaming so you feel as if you've got to do it for him," George said. "I've learned how to train harder [under Wilf]! We've tightened up defensively which helps a hell of a lot, it takes a lot of weight off your shoulders, you feel a lot more comfortable. I think we'll win something this year. I wouldn't like to say what."

Southampton did not have a McLintock, Reaney or Howe, so stuck two men on George at the Dell. The plan worked for 35 minutes. George indicated for Kidd to play the ball over the top – and knowing he was quicker than both of his markers, he took the lofted pass and thrashed the ball into the goal. United were able to grab two more goals in the second half.

Three days later United faced Ipswich at home. Best scored within two minutes; Mick Mills levelled in the 15th, but Kidd's goal after half an hour gave McGuinness' side the points. Mills was man-marking Best and felt he had done well in the first period. "In the second half, he really turned it on," the Ipswich defender said. "I fouled him, and the referee booked me. The crowd went wild. They slung paper cups at me and booed me every time I touched the ball. Best is the greatest player in the world. Playing against him is an experience and an education. It's stopping him that is the problem."

The result moved United to eighth in the table, obviously a much healthier position than fourth from bottom as they had been in August, but still an imposing – and as it would turn out, unassailable – nine points behind leaders Everton.

So there was no realistic likelihood of league success or even European football for George – but Northern Ireland did have a decent chance of qualifying for the 1970 World Cup. A September game against the USSR had finished 0-0. George had been followed everywhere by Revaz Dzodzuashvili who had been told by his coach: "There will be a match going on but it is none of your concern. If Best is kept out of it too, then your job is done." Dzodzuashvili was good on the instruction but found himself an unwilling partner in a slow dance for 90 minutes (and a fitting name for it, wouldn't you say?).

Best's evisceration of him was as masterful and complete as one footballer could inflict on another. Feints, step-overs, dribbles. You could stick on the tape of the game at half speed and then relax to the soundtrack of *O Fortuna* and ice knocking against itself in your whiskey and you would never tire of watching the art of football, expertly performed by the poetic and balletic George Best.

Direct from kick-off he had showed his intent, beating three players, playing a one-two, and, as the ball bounced on return to him, deliberating for long enough so that Dzodzuashvili – less than ten seconds in to the match – was forced to make a commitment of a sliding tackle that was nowhere near Best.

It was artistry. Years later, the great commentator Barry Davies likened Best's performances at Windsor Park as those of a "butterfly, stopping only to brighten the scene before flitting away'. Never was that description more apt than when the USSR came to Belfast.

Northern Ireland went into the return game in October knowing that with a repeat scoreline, they would be going to Mexico. But these were days where the relationship between club and international football was not simpatico – and United were scheduled to play a League Cup replay against Burnley 48 hours before that crucial World Cup qualifier.

Best was not released, and so would have to play the game and then catch a flight that would hopefully get him to Moscow 12 hours before kick-off. He scored a penalty for United – the game's only goal – but suffered a heavy kick to the shin that made it doubtful that he could travel. It was confirmed the following morning. "It's a real sickener. I was praying I would come through," he told press. "You have no idea how I feel about missing this match in Moscow. But the way my shin feels I know it's hopeless. There's no chance at all. I can't even see myself playing on Saturday."

Northern Irish officials were furious, even though Billy Brennan, the FA secretary, had not only been at the game, he'd been invited into the dressing room afterwards to see for himself the extent of the injury. "It was pretty bad," he'd admitted, but Harry Cavan, the Irish FA president, said from Moscow: "It is scandalous that we are here, playing a vital World Cup match, without one of our best players."

The national team selectors weighed in. Sammy Walker: "It is disgraceful that United did not release Best." Harry McNeilly: "I don't think Manchester United care tuppence about Northern Ireland."

The USSR, free of concern about facing the best player in the world, won comfortably. Best later admitted: "I wasn't all that keen to go after my Albania experiences. I knew it would cause uproar because whenever I missed games for Ireland, I got stick from the fans and a lot of bad publicity back home. Some people would blame the club, some would blame me and it made for some nasty reading for my family... in fact, it was starting to have a disastrous effect on my mother."

The USSR would be drawn in a group with hosts Mexico, Belgium and El Salvador in the World Cup – qualifying from the group only to be eliminated by Uruguay in the quarter-final. There would be more talk about George being part of a Northern Ireland team in a World Cup but never would it be on the same terms as it ought to have been in 1969.

"It always made me sad, and a little angry, that we never saw George at a World Cup," António Simões says. "A player of that talent should have been there. His club career saw him reach the pinnacle, he achieved the very top. The World Cup missed out on seeing something wonderful."

Best's legacy at international level would instead have to come in individual matches, just as against Scotland at Windsor Park. Another would come – but by then, almost everything in his life had changed. As privately relieved as he had been to miss the trip to Russia, it is undeniable that the disappointment of missing out on playing at a World Cup contributed to a tumultuous period in his life, disrupting the positive momentum he had and perhaps pulling the rug from underneath him with sharp enough force that it forced him to face up to some other realities. It was reported that his romance with Haraldsted had ended a few weeks later.

It was no coincidence that as Best's goalscoring form came to an end, United's positive run of results suffered the same fate. One win in five included an embarrassing 4-0 loss at Maine Road. United were back there a couple of weeks later when they competed in the first leg of their League Cup semi-final.

Compounding the poor form was the physical attention Best was getting on a weekly basis. He was leaving the field with cuts and bruises and was developing such a growing feeling of being persecuted by the officials that his responses often seemed to greater crimes than the fouls which provoked them.

And so it was against City with Best remonstrating with referee Jack Taylor and going in the book after Taylor deemed Best guilty of wasting time towards the end of a game that was petering out 1-1 (the pair had previous after Best felt Taylor had offered him little protection at Elland Road). City scored a late penalty that gave them a 2-1 win to take into the next leg, and as the teams left the pitch, Best – still arguing with the official – knocked the match ball out of Taylor's hands. George insisted he had done it in a playful manner, but Taylor did not view it as such, and included it in his official report. A 2-2 draw in the second leg meant semi-final heartache for McGuinness – who desperately needed a silver lining.

Best was handed a remarkably tough punishment – a four-week suspension, effective from early 1970, and a £100 fine. In his last game before the ban United went to Ipswich on January 3 in the FA Cup third round. Best was a man possessed, denied a hat-trick only by the exceptional form of his namesake, David Best, in the Portman Road goals. A late own goal sent United through. Portman Road would have been the venue for George's return, if his team-mates were unable to exact cup revenge on City with the neighbours drawn together for the fourth round. United won handsomely to set up a tie with Northampton Town, by which time George's suspension would have expired.

* * *

Having been gently moved into semi-retirement, Bill Foulkes was given the responsibility of fitness conditioning. Foulkes was old-fashioned in every sense of the word and it could be said that some of his practices were archaic. George confessed he was no longer of the same enthusiasm for training as he had previously been. He even admitted he felt the games were almost punishment rather than reward. But he was desperate to win the FA Cup. The final was one day of the year where the eyes of the nation were guaranteed to be on you.

Yes, television coverage was increasing, and Best's talents meant he was more often than not the man the broadcasters and viewers wanted to see, but live games were few and far between, let alone games at Wembley. These were the days when only one team from each country could play in the European Cup and the objectives were a little more clearly defined. The FA Cup final at Wembley was as big as any day in football and it was one that had already escaped George Best's grasp on a few occasions. It gave him a personal incentive to be at optimum condition when he returned.

"The management was fearful that he might let himself go physically during the ensuing lay-off," Foulkes said. "Now I would never have presumed to talk to George about football, but I knew something about fitness and could see that although he was a tremendous natural athlete, he was in need of a concentrated tune-up."

Foulkes considered George's attitude and felt he had been deeply affected by Busby's retirement and the way the club had been allowed to drift without serious investment since the start of the season. "I am convinced that things would have been much better if he [Busby] could have maintained much more control," Foulkes said. "For a start it would have sent a positive signal to George Best that the club's ambitions matched his own; then he might have retained his enthusiasm and deter-mination and, perhaps, would not have gone downhill."

Foulkes took him to a gym in Stretford run by his friend Tommy Hamilton. The legendary defender admitted to George it might have looked more like a torture chamber. "George's face was a picture when he walked in, but I explained it wasn't a punishment, merely a means to get him into top condition," he said. "My regime consisted of a morning's training at the Cliff, followed by weights at Tommy's in the afternoon, finishing off with a jog – and George did it! I'm not saying he enjoyed it, but he was in the best shape he'd been in his life."

Northampton were grateful the added attraction of Best would be part of the proceedings on their big day, but after the 90 minutes were through they were glad to see the back of him. In the 20th minute he grabbed the first goal, taking advantage of the goalkeeper Kim Book's flapping at a Morgan cross to head in. It was two a minute later. Crerand hit a long pass over the pitch which resembled a farmer's field and Best anticipated the flight of the ball to the embarrassment of the goalkeeper, who raced out of his box, and ended up ten yards away from the United man as he rapped the ball into the net again. 2-0 at half-time. From kick-off, Best dribbled across the defence and almost created a goal for Carlo Sartori. "At the moment this is a game that is certainly going to be remembered as almost a George Best birthday," remarked the commentator.

That was scarcely the opening act. Kidd crossed from the left and the ball squirmed through to George as Book and one of his defenders dived in vain. Best's first shot was blocked, but at the second attempt he fired through a number of bodies to grab his hat-trick. The second half started as it continued – Northampton missed a penalty (well, Stepney saved it) before Best made it four for him and his team with a glancing header across goal from a Kidd cross. Kidd finally got the goal he deserved and Best got another when Francis Burns played a defence-splitting pass. This time, George's finish was across the goalkeeper, hit with pace but slowed down by the muddy pitch as it bobbled into the corner.

The man given the job of marking him was enduring a living nightmare. "Why, oh why, did it have to happen to me?" Ray Fairfax, the Northampton defender, later said. "The only time I got close to him was when we went off at half-time and full-time. On top of his baffling skill, Best had all the pent-up energy and frustration of four weeks out of football. And he unloaded the lot on to poor me. What can you do about such a man? Long before he had finished running us into the ground I felt physically sick. If I had to play against such a man every week I would hang up my boots and quit the game."

Best, Burns and Morgan combined for Kidd to get another – 7-0. Dixie McNeil pulled one back for the Fourth Division team but Northampton scarcely had time to celebrate before they were kicking off again themselves. Best received a pass from Crerand on the edge of the box, moved with ease past one defender and then feinted to shoot so that Book collapsed on the floor. George walked the ball in for his sixth goal.

"I remember thinking George was going to go one way, but he dropped his shoulder and went the other, and by then I was already on the deck. He was just too good for me," Book told the *Telegraph*. "It's been a joke on the circuit ever since. You know, I'm on one side of the street, George Best is on the other. He nods to me and I dive under a bus."

Northampton grabbed another 'consolation' for a final score of 8-2; the last say but hardly the last laugh. "I am not being detrimental to my own team here, but as Fourth Division footballers they are used to getting away with errors," Northampton boss Dave Bowen said. "You don't make errors against a Best and get away with it. He'll punish you and smile when he's doing it. We thought we had a fair chance of keeping him in check if we went about it the right way.

"But there are so many things you cannot budget for. His amazing reflexes. His change of pace. The certainty of his finishing, and this enormous confidence he has in his ability to take people on. Defenders are always under a great strain even when they are keeping him comparatively quiet."

Ken Jones of the *Mirror* described what he had witnessed: "Best destroyed them as completely as one man can destroy others without inflicting physical damage. At the end they were almost queuing up for his autograph."

Reporters were queuing up for a quote. George told them that he "had been living with secret fears that we'd lose" and that he "treated it like a European Cup final". "While I've been suspended I've had letters from cranks saying that the team played better without me," he said. "I felt if we were beaten by Northampton, people would say it was my fault. People think just because I'm a bit of a showman and lose my temper occasionally I'm not trying but I do as much running as anyone. During the past week I drove myself harder than ever in training and when I went out yesterday I felt really great."

Matt Busby explained how he felt it was the nature of the challenge that provoked this sort of form and suggested that having something to prove meant, simply, that George would try and prove it – and so gave a summary with a challenge of his own. "I would think George is a fraction away from being the best player in the world and I am only holding back from putting him on top to keep him on his mettle," the former manager said. "The thing with George is you have to keep him going. If you can, then you will get this sort of performance."

It was difficult to recreate that sort of magic at Ipswich in the league in the next game. "Fans expecting to see a repeat of Best's six goals that flattened Northampton were disappointed," wrote the *Mirror's* Harry Miller. "He was kept in check by Eire international full-back Tommy Carroll."

United did win 1-0, and their good form continued into the middle of March. Middlesbrough were the opponents in the FA Cup quarter final and they were put away after a replay. The opponents in the semis were Leeds United; this by itself was enough to erode Best's enthusiasm, though he ought to have taken heart from his performance at Elland Road earlier in the season. He described the 0-0 at Hillsborough as "another punching and kicking match".

The tie went to a replay at Villa Park. United stayed overnight at a hotel in Droitwich. Half an hour before the team were due to leave for the game, George bumped into a married woman who he'd taken a shine to when he'd seen her in the hotel the previous evening. The woman said her husband was away a lot and George offered "to pop down and keep her company"; the pair went up to her room in order for the woman to pass on her number. When McGuinness gathered his team together and noted one significant absentee, he angrily tracked George down. "I didn't need to be Hercule Poirot for my little grey cells to start buzzing," McGuinness said. The United boss acquired the assistance of a hotel porter to take him to the girl's room, and when there was no answer, use his master key to get in. George and the woman were sitting fully clothed and as though butter wouldn't melt.

McGuinness admitted he was furious – not at the dalliance, but at the fact George had ignored him. "It seemed to be a blatant breach of club discipline and so, as that was his province according to the agreement when I took the job, I went to Matt Busby," McGuinness said. Although George claimed Wilf wanted to send him home without playing, Wilf rejected that and insisted as it was his biggest game as manager he would naturally want his best player.

Busby spoke to Best in private. McGuinness came away from it thinking George had been told he would be fined. George's recollection was: "Matt stood up for me as usual and told Wilf we'd sort it out when he got back to Manchester."

Paddy Crerand is naturally inclined to be defensive of all matters Busby and believes he stepped in with a disciplined arm. "Matt wasn't lenient with him," Crerand says. "He was one of the nicest men you could ever wish to meet but if you stepped out of line he wasn't very nice anymore. He was very strict. To be fair to Matt, nobody had ever dealt with or experienced anything like George before. The only time a footballer would be on the front page of the newspaper would be if they were going to court or jail. With George it was just because he was a footballer. And, obviously, because he was a good-looking fucker. He was front page news for these reasons."

Best claimed after his conversation he went back to the girl's room where they did more than just talk. "Realising what must have happened, Wilf just turned his back on me when I came down," George recalled.

Gossip spreads fast. In the tunnel before the game it was clear that the Leeds players had heard about what had been happening and were taking every opportunity to let George know. Nobby Stiles recalled one of them shouting at George: "Call yourself a professional?!"

"It was the kind of provocation that was regularly forthcoming during a game, but this time it had a particularly raw edge," Stiles said. "They played every card available to them. It might not have been nice, but it was the way it was."

Paul Reaney did his usual job, having grown wise to Morgan's attempt to switch. McGuinness' options to alleviate the on-pitch pressure on Best were limited. Law was on the bench but far from match-fit and Reaney was able to stifle the subdued number 11 with such effect that when George finally did get one chance in extra-time, it was as if – as one reporter put it – he was "astonished at finding freedom at last" and stumbled at the crucial moment. After the game, McGuinness was liberal with his criticism of Best to the press, and George admitted he was "cheesed off" with Reaney's man-marking.

Another goalless game meant a second replay, and the two United's tour of England took them to Burnden Park. Billy Bremner scored early on and Don Revie's side were able to concentrate for over 80 minutes with the same sort of miserly defending from the first two games. Manchester United were out of the FA Cup.

With little else to fight for in the season, McGuinness' greatest challenge was keeping George Best motivated. Both player and manager admitted George was regularly late to training. McGuinness strongly refuted this was down to drinking. "He was just late all the time, and so was Paddy Crerand," he says. "The way I saw it was they were the same as each other and they were disciplined and we would get on with it."

George could still look forward to playing at Wembley – Northern Ireland were scheduled to play there in the Home Championships on April 21 – but his journey there was still eventful even though there were only weeks of the campaign remaining. In United's penultimate league game they lost at White Hart Lane; Best was fouled by Alan Gilzean, but when referee John Hunting ignored the challenge, the United player grabbed Hunting by his shoulder and pulled him around to shout. Charlton, the team captain, immediately stepped in, apologetic on behalf of his younger colleague. Hunting was in forgiving mood and Best was immediately sorry. "It was in the heat of the moment and I regretted it as soon as I had done it," he told reporters. But his card was marked.

McGuinness' first season concluded with a 2-2 draw at home to Sheffield Wednesday. Best scored the opener after six minutes and Charlton made it two but the visitors staged a comeback – a fittingly underwhelming end to the year, although the new manager could claim marginal improvements from the last season under Busby, with an eighth-placed finish in the league to go with those domestic cup near-misses.

Three days later Northern Ireland welcomed Scotland to Windsor Park; a sequel to George's finest hour on the international stage (inbetween times, Best had played at Hampden against Scotland and had seen a winning goal chalked off after his incredible thigh control to set up his shot was deemed as handball by the referee who simply couldn't believe the player had the ability to cushion the ball so well). This outing rivalled Albania for his poorest.

Scotland, wary of what happened to them before, were more forthright in their approach with George, taking few chances and allowing little space. It was that sort of game. George was having a running conversation with the referee Eric Jennings about the attention he was getting. After the latest of his pleas fell on deaf ears, George – always ready to do the incredible – astounded everyone when he bent down to the grass and picked up handfuls of mud and turf, slinging them at the official to get his attention. This time it worked – but, as George had discovered with Jack Taylor, some referees took a dim view of such playfulness, and so it was on this occasion when Best was sent from the field by Jennings.

National team manager Billy Bingham blasted his player after watching his team lose 1-0. "I have no sympathy for what he did," he said. "In a way, he let the side down. But he is a boy who has taken a lot of stick because of his outstanding talent. He is still young but he must learn to live with these things." Still, Bingham said he intended to pick George for the game at Wembley a few days later: "I shall nominate Best to play against England on Tuesday, and don't expect any objection."

George, realising again that he was only doomed to get negative press, pleaded the Fifth. "I don't want to say anything. I daren't. All I want is to be picked against England at Wembley. If I am, I will do my best. I do that in every game."

Best did play on a proud night for Manchester United. Bobby Charlton made his 100th appearance for his country and was named captain to mark the occasion (though some later records listed Moore as captain in the sentimental pursuit of giving him more caps as skipper than the great Billy Wright). Brian Kidd made his international debut. And Nobby Stiles was given the task of marking his club-mate George.

England took a seventh-minute lead through Martin Peters. Early in the second half, George made a statement of his own. Stiles was as close to Best as he had been for most of the match. The club-mates chased for the ball into the right-hand side of the penalty area. Suddenly, George performed one of those bewitching drops of the shoulder, pulling the ball back to his left and taking Stiles out of the game. The move opened up the entire goal, and George drilled the ball into the near post past Gordon Banks.

"Seventy-five thousand fans who had an hour earlier booed and jeered the mere mention of his name filled the old stadium with cheers," Stiles said. "As I got to my feet I thought, 'What a player!' Afterwards I shook his hand and said, 'Well done, George – only you could have done that.' I'll never forget that goal."

England's response was instant and crushing. Geoff Hurst scored with a deflected effort in the 57th minute and neither Best nor his colleagues could come back a second time. With nine minutes left, Charlton – the main man of the night – gave the game the perfect crescendo in his and England's eyes when he capitalised on a goalkeeping error to tap the ball in inside the six-yard box. It was another hard lesson for George Best that you received no extra reward in a game for a goal that was more beautiful than another.

It was a week of tough learning curves to end a difficult 1969/70 season. Best had been succeeded by Gianni Rivera of Milan as European Footballer of the Year and his controversial brushes with the referees and frustrated reactions to aggressive challenges had transformed how some rival fans perceived him on domestic soil; as Northern Ireland played Wales four days after the England game, the Vetch Field crowd at Swansea booed George throughout. These days such events would be seen as mere pantomime, but Best's reputation was sincerely perceived as so much of a bad boy that it was beginning to impact on his earning power.

Ernest Garnett, speaking on behalf of Bellair – an aftershave lotion firm who had reportedly given George a £12,000 contract to advertise their product – threatened that they would reconsider the deal if there was further adverse publicity.

"I would say he'll have to keep his nose clean," Garnett said. "A lot of our dealers are a bit puritanical. Mr Best is very difficult to deal with. It's fair enough to say that if he goes on this way he would be more of a handicap to our publicity rather than an asset."

NEW TRICKS

W ith a fresh page, George approached the 1970/71 season with, if not optimism, then at least a positive attitude. That extended to taking personal responsibility and accountability. The fling with Eva Haraldsted the previous summer had invited even more press intrusion into the life of Mary Fullaway, still at this time George's landlady. The hundreds of letters every week now came with seemingly as many reporters and telephone calls to the house. George felt bad and wanted to take that pressure off Mrs Fullaway, so he decided it was time to find a place of his own.

The romance with Haraldsted had been genuine – and even though George had felt a little railroaded into the idea of getting married, he was coming around to the concept, whilst at the same time realising in his heart that this particular relationship wasn't working.

George commissioned the architect Frazer Crane to build a house for him in Bramhall and was still seeing Eva at that time; but the relationship broke down, and when he moved in to the distinctive residence in the summer of 1970, he was alone.

In one respect, anyway. As was the intention, the reporters found their new base camp outside of his new place, and at once George would learn how one of the most famous men in the country could also be one of the loneliest. He attempted to stave this off with a short-lived relationship with another Scandinavian blonde, Siv Hederby, but it was evident from the start that George was compensating for something when he proposed after a few weeks; it ended shortly after that.

There were more illusions at Old Trafford. Wilf McGuinness had been given a new job title – team manager – in an attempt to stabilise the perception of his authority. This did not hold any weight with those in the dressing room. For one thing, although Ian Ure had been a reasonable success in that he was more reliable than the veteran Foulkes, he had not been a tremendous example of money well spent.

Ure was effectively a Busby buy and McGuinness was not backed any more than that in the transfer market despite suggesting numerous players to the board and to Busby. That meant another year of attempting to inspire from within – and still, though McGuinness might have felt that he had answered strongly by bettering Busby's final domestic season, it was hardly glorious. There was even an argument – considering Busby's final act – that McGuinness had overachieved, but this was hardly likely to wash with a group of senior players who were not quite ready to accept that an eighth-place finish was solely their responsibility when the majority of them had won the European Cup two years earlier.

McGuinness' case hadn't been helped by the unsuccessful dropping of a number of players. Stepney, Crerand, Morgan, Dunne, Charlton, Law – all of these men were given highly publicised days off and over time McGuinness had been forced to bring them back into the team when the replacements had not convinced. It was probably an inevitable self-inflicted wound, but a necessary step McGuinness felt he had to take, when the manager decided the best course of action was to resort to discipline in the hope that it might force the players to realise who was boss. That ship had sailed. Best's late mornings became early afternoons after he moved to the new house. Living there by himself was a nightmare from day one. McGuinness felt that the move was the start of when "events in [George's] life spiralled out of control".

The manager recalled another late arrival and excuse: "George said he'd gone to bed at half past 10, but he couldn't sleep so he went downstairs to play snooker by himself. At midnight he still wasn't tired so he went into town and met a girl and by the time they got back home it was six in the morning. He told me that in the circumstances surely I didn't expect him to get up in time for training. I told him that of course I did and said he must go and speak to Sir Matt."

George was far from the only one taking McGuinness much less seriously than they would Busby. At the end of the prior season, following the FA Cup semi-final defeat, United were due to play Watford in a third placed play-off – a short-lived idea from the national body to pitch the losing semi-finalists against each other. With the game effectively meaningless, Alex Stepney asked if he could travel by himself so he could see his family; McGuinness said no, so Stepney went to Busby, who gave him permission.

George Best and Manchester United did make football history in the early weeks of the 1970/71 season but only as a footnote and asterisk; one of those oddities that end up in a pub quiz. The Watney Cup was another of these temporary additions to the football calendar – a pre-season competition where the top scoring teams of each division from the previous season would face each other. United scraped through against Reading to face Hull City in the semi-final. That game ended 1-1 and went to the first ever penalty shootout in English football. The first taker was George Best – he scored, as United won the shootout 5-4. In the final they met Derby County, who – as rams tend to do – battered McGuinness' team 4-1.

Worse still, Denis Law once again hurt his knee and that ruled him out of the opening league game against Leeds United at Old Trafford. With Willie Morgan missing, the job of Paul Reaney and co was more comfortable than usual. Best had a habit of starting the season well but never got going – neither did his team, as Leeds went away with a 1-0 win.

United's start to the season was poor. They managed only three league wins from their first 13 games, with George getting just three goals (two of them in two of the victories). One of those was against Coventry on September 12. George scored a fine header to seal the win but impressed the Old Trafford support more with his non-stop, tigerish persistence.

He was in fine form that afternoon and he created the other goal in the game after taking on two players – one of the City defenders thought they had won the ball, but Best slid a leg around and recovered it, dashing to the byline and crossing for Charlton to score the opening goal. It was thrilling. As was Best's remarkable back-flick goal in the home game against Blackpool two weeks later; the ball from Morgan's cross was beautifully kissed by George's right heel, which was behind his left leg. A pure snooker trick shot.

But these were rare flashes of positivity. Blackpool equalised to take a point. Then, in an October defeat at home to Crystal

Palace, away skipper Steve Kember praised defender David Payne who "was detailed to do a job on Best, and never gave him a kick." The 'stop him by any means necessary' approach crossed over into the illegal. George was relieved the annual battle with Leeds was over early – the return league game came on October 17. For once he had a different opponent in a white shirt, but the wily Jack Charlton (who, like his brother, had scored in the game) was not about to be caught out.

George knew he had the legs on the veteran and was pleading for balls over the top from the midfield. When that opening came with a bouncing ball that was definitely going to land in his favour, Best prepared for that famous burst of acceleration which would render him unstoppable. Unable to stop the ball legally, Charlton unapologetically raised his arm and bashed the ball away from Best's direction with his hand. He was booked, but taking one for the team was definitely worth it as it saved a point from a 2-2 draw.

The glory days seemed long gone. Even George's most impressive form had only helped United just about keep their self-respect and he was increasingly becoming a martyr, sacrificing himself on Saturday afternoons so that others could play with a little more freedom – and to what end?

Even the better players in the team were not capable of doing the things they once could and aside from his minder Pat Crerand, few players would put themselves on the line for George in atmospheres that were becoming increasingly hostile, especially with Busby's code of dignity at all costs. At Leeds, 44 supporters were arrested as tempers frayed on and off the pitch. When George invariably reacted – as any reasonable person would – he was cast as the villain of the piece, and so those light-hearted moments of harmless fun were seen as petulant reactions of a spoiled brat not getting his own way.

Any other player might have felt it a lost cause, and either requested a transfer or just given up. But there was still plenty of fire, magic, and a certain determination borne from that frustration – the competitive spirit within him that made George so keen to prove himself.

When Chelsea arrived at Old Trafford in late October for a League Cup fourth round tie, George was reunited with another aggressive competitor – Ron Harris. Harris, like others, had experienced some joy in encounters over the last 18 months as the support around United's main man had wavered. On this night, 47,000 supporters were treated to an episode of 'If Only'; a game that has gone down in legend, although there were possibly much deeper conclusions to be found if one paused to consider. Charlton had scored early and John Hollins levelled soon after. These two teams who knew each other so well were cancelling each other out, and once more, Blues boss Dave Sexton had Harris under strict instruction to follow Best.

With 20 minutes to go, John Aston, from the left, played a diagonal ball towards the area for George to run on to. Harris was in pursuit even though he knew he wouldn't catch him for the clean tackle. That scarcely mattered anymore – as long as you were quick enough to get contact on Best's ankles, the job was done. And thus, as was often the case, Harris was late.

Then came the extraordinary. George not only read the tackle – he read the foul. Only just, mind – he managed to manoeuvre his ankles away from the studs of Harris in the most marginal nick of time, the defender still managing to get some contact with the back of Best's leg to cause him a momentary loss of balance. It could only have been less than a moment. Peter Bonetti had seen the slightest of wobbles and was sufficiently encouraged to come out for the ball. He – like Gregg, like Stepney on the Cliff training pitches, like countless others when it came to the real thing – dived for the ball and was still in motion when he realised how helpless he was about to look.

The covering Chelsea defender had seen it so many times that he didn't even go for the tackle, instead racing behind Bonetti to try and act as a deterrent on the line. George, however, was not to be denied. Harris was on his knees as he saw the ball hit the back of the net.

"It was on *Grandstand* every Saturday for years after that," Harris says. "I watched it over and over again so many times through the years, each time convinced that this time I'd finally catch the bastard! But no… I remember that he went through, and it looked as if he'd overrun it. So I went in with a hard, high tackle. Somehow he was gone. By the time I looked up he's gone around Peter Bonetti and scored. I suffered reliving that nightmare for years, believe you me."

"I remember watching Harris trying to chop him down," said Jimmy Rimmer, who was watching from his goal at the other end. "He tried and he couldn't. Someone else went in at him, but they were too late even to foul him. George's bravery was such that he played knowing people were going to foul him. Not only was he too quick for their tackle, he became so good that he was even quicker than their late foul. The only way to stop George was to kick him and you had to get close enough for that. I think that was my favourite memory of George, watching him dance through in the rain to score that goal at the Stretford End. He was a genius."

Alex Stepney was sitting in the stands. "One thing that never really got mentioned was that George had really strong thighs, especially for someone of his size," Stepney says. "He had a six-pack nobody ever saw because his shirt was baggy.

"You could say it was a little like Mark Hughes, but it wasn't something many people commented on. He was like a rubber ball. If you tackled him hard, he'd bounce back up. Players stay down, they go down, to win penalties. George never did that. He just wanted to score, and if he was able to do that knowing he'd embarrassed you because you had tried but failed to foul him, that would be even better. He had become so used to the fouling and so frustrated with the aggressive tackling that he just seemed to decide he would find newer ways to beat people.

"You could see it with the Chelsea goal. He had gone through years of Ron Harris fouling him and now he had learned not only to beat him to draw the foul, but also, how to beat the foul. It really was quite something to watch. You have to remember the way the game was played in those days. You were expected to have to take a tackle. That's how people would see what you were made of. He became a master of timing; timing with his body and timing with his mind."

The goal was the winner. United were through. Sexton confessed Best had taken advantage of the only opportunity where there had been a space in his defence. Peter Bonetti knew he was well beaten. "A lot of players would have panicked – but Best kept moving towards me," he told reporters afterwards. "I had plenty of time to see him coming. But how do you stop a genius?"

Frank Taylor, the sportswriter who had been covering United since before Munich, wrote an impassioned reaction piece in the *Mirror*: "George Best has restored my faith in football.

He has reduced the robot men of soccer to the midget league where they belong and struck a blow for little men all over the world who are shackled by a system. With one flash of genius on an autumn evening at Old Trafford he has proved the game is not after all a soul-destroying system of geometric patterns. A man can still make mincemeat of machine."

It is Stepney's observation which is surely the most compelling. It adds an extra strand to the already considerable argument about how good George Best could have been. The goalkeeper had watched him at close quarters for four years. He had faced his shots and his methods every single day in training. He had been with him after regular training observing his intelligence and going through drills with him. The two most often mentioned lamentations attributed to George's career are what might have been if he had remained in peak condition from this point onwards and how he might have fared with better protection and on better pitches. The latter point received something of an answer the following year – more on that to come – but the first never would.

But what about a third point to introduce into the conversation – if he was capable of still finding new ways to overcome challenges at the age of 24 (and by new, we can say with some comfort revolutionary, as nobody else was doing it quite the same way), then what might he have come up with at the age of 27? At 29, when most outfield players could be said to be at their peak? Or 31, or 33, when the benefit of that intelligence would compensate for any physical decline?

It is something we're unable to comprehend because there is and was only George who could imagine the way he did. Of course it was a significant tragedy for George personally that his potential from this point would never be realised as many

Lap of honour: Best runs around a snow covered Old Trafford pitch with teammate David Sadler before a Division One game with Liverpool in April 1968

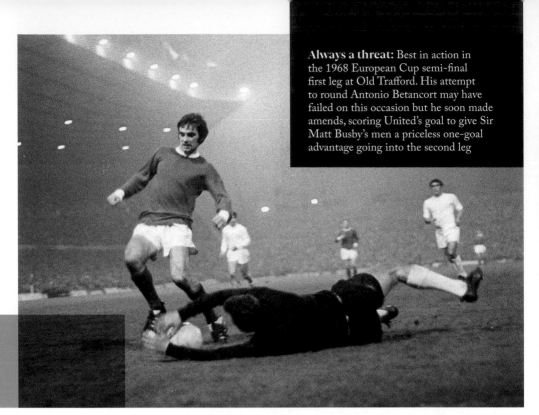

Always a threat: Best in action in the 1968 European Cup semi-final first leg at Old Trafford. His attempt to round Antonio Betancort may have failed on this occasion but he soon made amends, scoring United's goal to give Sir Matt Busby's men a priceless one-goal advantage going into the second leg

Real United: A fortnight later, glory was United's. A 3-3 draw at the Santiago Bernabeu saw United into the final of the 1968 European Cup, much to the soaked-through delight of Best and David Sadler

Happy Henrique: Benfica goalkeeper Jose Henrique races out of his goal to challenge Best during the 1968 European Cup final at Wembley. Best was to be denied, at least for the time being...

Unhappy Henrique: This time Best won't be stopped as he slips past the Benfica goalkeeper to score United's second and put them on the cusp of European glory

Let the celebrations begin (again): Sadler and Best again celebrating success - but this time after reaching the summit of club football

Simply magnificent: Arguably the two finest players in the club's history embrace after United's win. Sir Bobby Charlton and George Best - what would they be worth in the modern game?

The fun continues: Best and his United teammates enjoy a lap of the Wembley pitch with the European Cup. After the Munich disaster 10 years previously, what must Sir Matt Busby have thought when he saw his 'new' side fulfill his European dream?

A man fulfilling his destiny: Look at the sheer joy on Best's face. A wonderful man, at the peak of his wonderful powers, happy that he has brought joy to millions

Back to the grind: Best was always a good trainer and as this July 1969 photo shows, he worked hard in pre-season to maintain his fitness

The Best with The King: Best and Denis Law, pictured in November 1969, were a defender's worst nightmare. The two shared many glorious nights together, at Old Trafford and beyond

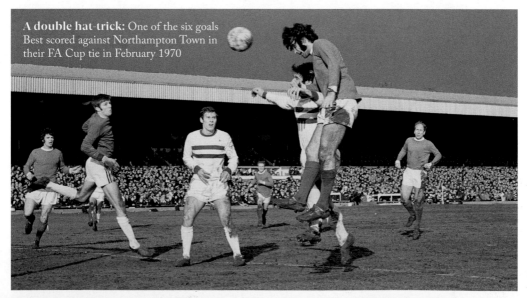

A double hat-trick: One of the six goals Best scored against Northampton Town in their FA Cup tie in February 1970

Friendship halted: Best and Manchester City legend Mike Summerbee were great mates off the pitch but this March 1970 picture shows that it was all strictly business when they were on opposite sides in the Manchester derby

Untouchable, unplayable, unbeatable: On certain days, the opposition must have wondered why they bothered showing up. Against West Ham United at Old Trafford in September 1971, Best was simply imperious, netting a hat-trick to help underline his footballing elegance and ruthlessness

believed it should, but it is arguably a far greater tragedy and loss for the sport because when it was lost, it was lost forever.

We can admire the great players that followed who did things quicker than their peers, who did things with more intelligence, who were better dribblers and goalscorers than any of their contemporaries. In the era of the publication of this book there have been two true greats, Cristiano Ronaldo and Lionel Messi, who have pushed each other to achieve in a way we have never seen, scoring goals at a rate we could scarcely believe. We've seen Zinedine Zidane and, before him, Diego Maradona and Johan Cruyff play with such imagination and majesty that they most certainly earned the title of 'King' of the game as António Simões declared.

Only Cruyff – and even then, it is arguable – played in such a fashion where he could make you believe that in a game of finite laws and boundaries, he had created something brand new. George Best was a magician – there is no other word for it. He took an idea, something he could not even explain, and made so what had seemed impossible.

Any professional footballer is somewhat dependant on what happens with the other 21 when it comes to their own fate but against Chelsea in October 1970, although it was probably not his greatest goal, George Best reached a personal landmark. The combination of his manipulation of balance, speed and time was so true that the only logical conclusion moving forward was that he could simply be unstoppable if only he chose to be. If he could still dodge the tackle of Ron Harris – who was often so late he'd arrive in the next game – and the foul, there was no limit to what George could achieve, just as there was no telling what he would come up with next.

THE OLD MAN

D espite the power possessed by George Best, he was still only one man.

The depressing reminder of what was going on at Manchester United came as they won just one of the next six games and they dropped to 16th place in the league. Pressure was mounting on manager Wilf McGuinness to turn it around. He was not helped by George's unpredictability. Before a game at Spurs, George had failed to report to Old Trafford and the team went without him. He caught a later train to London and after another dispute between Busby and McGuinness, he was allowed to play (and in fact scored in a 2-2 draw).

McGuinness' saving grace was the League Cup run – United had followed the Chelsea win with victory over Crystal Palace to qualify for the semi-final against Aston Villa.

Before the first leg, United welcomed Manchester City to Old Trafford in the league. City inflicted a devastating defeat on McGuinness' side, winning 4-1 and looking even better than their three-goal advantage suggested. Tempers were running high. Franny Lee – who scored a hat-trick – was booked for swinging punches and kicks with John Fitzpatrick. But the most horrendous incident from the afternoon was a complete accident; Best, in his competitive frustration, challenged Glyn Pardoe for the ball, but was late. The consequences were devastating. Pardoe suffered a broken leg.

Conciliatory tones were broadcast from both camps after the match. McGuinness told reporters George was "very upset" whilst City boss Joe Mercer confirmed that Best had asked if he could see Glyn to apologise again. "He desperately wanted to go and see him but I'm afraid that will have to wait," Mercer said. "He came to me after the match and was bitterly upset. It was not done intentionally, it was just one of those unfortunate things that happen in soccer."

Best was keen to stress it was not an act of malice. "Glyn and I went in for the ball together," he said. "Ninety-nine times out of a hundred nothing would have happened but this time the worst possible thing did happen and Glyn broke his leg. I feel sick to the bottom of my stomach. It was a complete accident."

The incident did not deflect any of the tension mounting at the club. United were eliminated by Villa in the League Cup and lost at Arsenal between the legs. The club were now 18th going into Christmas.

George – concerned about a personal hearing he was told he'd have to attend with the FA in the new year – admitted he got drunk on Christmas Eve and decided not to turn in to training on Christmas Day. When he reported to travel to Derby on Boxing Day, he was told he would be fined £50 – McGuinness now did want to send home the troubled star, but Busby overruled him again. Best played and scored in an entertaining 4-4 draw but it was merely a stay of execution for the manager.

The morning after, Busby was waiting for McGuinness at the Cliff, and told him Jack Crompton was taking training. The ominous news was confirmed, but in a strange fashion. Busby said the board had asked him to resume control, and for McGuinness to take his old job as reserve-team manager. Not sacked, then, but demoted. McGuinness considered his options. He was devastated by the decision, and did not want to leave Old Trafford, but had too much integrity and respect for Bill Foulkes – who had just been named reserve-team manager – to take his old pal's job.

With a heavy heart, McGuinness finally left United after many years of devoted service. Though his reign has unquestionably been categorised as a failure, over time there has been a greater appreciation for the struggles he endured and the scenario that played out suggested he was never fully in control and thus was never truly, fully, respected by the players.

Busby's return did not immediately inspire as hoped. United played Middlesbrough in the FA Cup in the first game of 1971. They drew 0-0 at Old Trafford and would have to play a replay three days later. On the day before the trip to the north-east, Busby and Best were due in the south-east for the FA hearing over the Pardoe incident.

George was struggling with his guilt on top of the loneliness and the struggles at the club. Guilt because he felt a sense of responsibility and had a stronger awareness than most about the fortune of staying injury-free; guilt because he had been on the receiving end of tackles that were far worse and executed with more negative intent than the sporting one he had performed. Exacerbating this was the dread of the negative press that he had already endured and the inevitable flurry that was still to follow. Windows of the boutique he owned in Manchester city centre had been smashed with bricks on the night of the derby. These were headaches none of his contemporaries had to endure.

On the morning of the hearing, George was scheduled to get an early train to London with Sir Matt. Suffering with a hangover, he didn't get out of bed in time to make it. He did get to London, two hours later than planned, relieved to find Busby had made excuses for him and managed to get the meeting delayed. "I felt sick when I woke up this morning," George told the press. "I telephoned Les Olive, the club secretary, to arrange a ticket for the 10.30am train. I got the ticket but then missed the train by two minutes. I tried to fly down to London, but all planes were cancelled because of fog."

The FA panel were lenient – giving George a suspended six-week ban and a fine of £250. "With the money I was earning, I didn't give it a second thought," said George, whose biggest headache had come from the hangover in the stuffy offices in London. Busby had arranged for them to reconvene at a local hotel before travelling back to Manchester. In the lift, Best threw up. "In any normal situation (it) would have been horribly embarrassing," he said. "But clearly I wasn't normal then because I didn't care... to be honest, I had reached the stage where I didn't care if they suspended me for two or three months or a year. I'd just lost interest in playing and when you start going through the motions, it's time to pack it in, which was an idea that grew more and more in my mind."

United – with Busby and Best in tow – made it to Middlesbrough only to lose in the replay despite a late goal from George. For the first time since Best broke into the first team, there would be nothing to play for in the second half of the season. Ordinary.

The following Friday the squad were due to report to the ground ahead of a trip to Chelsea. Again, one man was missing. "Before we'd go down to London for a game we'd arrive at Old Trafford, do a couple of laps and then get the bus to the train station," Willie Morgan recalls. "George slept in. He was by himself and slept in. He was never late for training. Never missed it. And he was a great trainer, too. His downfall started when he had that bloody house built. When he arrived at the ground the bus had gone. He missed the train by minutes, and got the next one which came in an hour later.

"We went to the Russell Hotel and he arrived literally an hour after we got there. There was no histrionics or anything – Matt just said to him, 'George, I'd like for you to take the weekend off, lad. I'll see you Monday.' That's all it was and then it blew up into this big media story, probably by an agent or something. And all he did was he slept in."

Morgan was one of the players aligned with George, with every right to feel as frustrated with how things had gone. Of course, one could read between the lines and note Morgan is being generous to George's memory by defending his training attendance record – and even gratuitously so, considering George himself had no problem conceding that his natural predilection for sleeping in was not helped by hangovers – but even Alex Stepney, a player of comparable pedigree to George considering they had shared the success of the First Division and European Cup triumphs, was not about to throw his colleague under the bus.

"We weren't upset with him," Stepney says. "Things were changing at the club. Lots of things were different. George and I were at similar stages of our career, when you consider the prime of a goalkeeper and of a forward. And so if I felt like I needed better defenders in front of me, I can understand why George felt he needed better support around him too."

The news of George being dropped made the front page of the Saturday newspapers on January 9, 1971; arguably the first time in history a regular football decision had commanded such attention. Perhaps it was as notable for the fact that the normally thoughtful Busby had taken such a hard line as it was for the identity of the player. It also suggested that the legendary manager was not going to simply go through the motions in his temporary return.

"George did not report for training this morning," Busby told press on Friday. "We were told that George would be arriving in London about 5pm. But on my instructions, the club told him not to bother – to stay home because he wouldn't be playing. I just don't know what's wrong with the lad. Something seems to have upset him. He has not been playing well for us lately, and didn't have much of a game in the cup replay at Middlesbrough. I spoke to his business partner, Malcolm Mooney, this morning and he suggested that George was upset about something. I don't know what."

Of course, Best did make it down to London to meet with the team after that statement had been given, but it was too late. Busby, again making the front page, told the *People* that he had not been there. "I understand he called at the team's London hotel last evening (Friday) but I wasn't in and I've no idea where he went," he said. "He certainly didn't stay with the team last night."

United won 2-1 at Chelsea. "Manchester United looked a far better TEAM at Stamford Bridge without the man who has won them many stirring victories and also grabbed too much of the ball through his selfishness," reported the *People*'s Steve Richards.

That weekend was the first time United and Busby were able to get a handle of what the fame for George Best looked like when he wasn't on a football pitch. After leaving the team, George went to the apartment of the actress Sinead Cusack in Islington, north London. By Sunday morning, the whole of Fleet Street knew where he was and the tiny flat was even more of a goldfish bowl than his garish Bramhall home.

"She had been expecting a quiet weekend but, thanks to me, spent four days with me as a prisoner in her own home," wrote a seemingly apologetic Best in his book *Blessed*. "Things were really getting on top of me now. To me, my life seemed to be in crisis. But to everyone else, it was just a bit of fun, something to give the nation a laugh."

As United despaired – and as Best failed to report for Monday's scheduled confrontation with the manager – George's friend Malcolm Mooney came to the rescue. It's a matter of interest only because George wrote that it was "always my friends outside football" that would help him in such situations. Within the football fraternity, these people were perceived as not only unhelpful but part of George's bigger issues which were starting to hurt his life.

The generational gap between George and some at the club was beginning to have a bigger impact than most appreciated. George described that Jimmy Murphy being "pushed into a scouting role" around this time "really did seem like the end of an era". Busby to him was more like a headmaster and although in some respects it was a good thing that he was still imposing enough to be fearful of, the great man's approach of allowing people to do as they wished was not the most suitable for this scenario. The trainers at the club were Jack Crompton and John Aston, both of whom had played under Busby in the early years and were loyal to his way of doing things, so – like Bill Foulkes – would not dream of advising George, as his situation was alien to what they had experienced.

"If I had poured my heart out to anyone at Old Trafford it would have been Matt's number two, Jimmy Murphy," George said – but Jimmy had been marginalised whether it was meant or not and was no longer involved directly in the day-to-day running of the first team.

There was one telling statement made by George which was heartbreaking. "If someone from the club had come and found me and spoken to me when I went missing, I would have listened," he said. "Although the fact that I was suffering from an illness called alcoholism meant that things might still have turned out the same, perhaps. But no one ever did come."

United were far from neglectful in their duty. It was just done in their own tried and trusted way, without a proper acknowledgement that maybe it was the way that needed a revision. It was not only George Best feeling the repercussions of that.

He went back to Old Trafford of his own accord – having required police to assist in his escape from his London trap – and pictures of him looking like a naughty schoolboy sitting alongside Busby at a hastily arranged press conference adorned the front and back pages of Wednesday's newspapers.

Player and manager had experienced an emotional confrontation – possibly the most emotional and frank conversation they ever shared. George, feeling his manager was now keen to hear his issues, unloaded all of them. He spoke tearfully of his loneliness, the criticism he was facing, the effect that the press intrusion and the political atmosphere was having on his family and his concern about the state of the team. He admitted that he was drinking too much to get away from thinking about it all and that it was that causing the later-than-usual mornings, as if Busby didn't know.

Busby informed him that he would have to serve a two-week suspension – it amounted to missing one game, which was, realistically, the most lenient punishment the boss could dole out in the circumstances. In a moment of admission, Busby told Best that he "needed to talk to someone". An arrangement was made to see a psychiatrist privately; remember, these were days when such extreme terms were used. There was no softer intermediary like a counsellor.

To the press, deliberately vague comments were made. "He has had this sort of problem inside him and it has been building up and building up," Busby said, conveying that message that he was a faithful confidante. "It is a private and personal matter. We have settled it amicably and we hope to start from scratch again."

George followed: "The only people who know about my problem are the boss and myself. The only person I can tell about it is the boss. I'm satisfied that I'm playing for the best club in the world. My future is still with United. I'll stay here until I finish playing."

Because the comments were ambiguous, they invited examination from cynical eyes. The suggestion subsequently made by many was that one, two or all three of the following happened: that Best had not been truthful to Busby; Busby had not fully comprehended what Best was saying; or neither of them had been truthful to the press. Of course, since their passing, whatever the truth was remains a matter of conjecture and speculation. It suits the salacious mind to feel that there was more to it than what was let on; there are reasonable and logical straightforward explanations.

The first was the statement made by Busby. "We have settled it amicably." He would not have stated with such certainty that the matter was resolved if he felt there was a realistic possibility of it coming back to undermine him; it would have been completely out of character for him to have done so. Best knew Busby's return was short-lived. But Busby did hear his concerns and made a club record offer of £125,000 for Luton Town's Malcolm McDonald. The Hatters rejected the offer, but the message seemed to be clear.

The next element is the disputed honesty of Best. But he had been quite candid about his issues beforehand, albeit with some retention of the old-school mentality he was brought up with. It wasn't a surprise that he was concerned about his family. He had previously spoken about hoping they would move to Manchester. It was not only true that the political discontent was growing, but the Best family would often be the recipients of unfavourable attention because of their most famous member. His sister Barbara had been at a disco when she was shot in the leg by an air rifle outside, simply because of who she – or rather, who her brother – was.

It wasn't a surprise that George would like the Manchester United team to be strengthened – and he wasn't the only one. The loneliness which was amplified by the press intrusion – well, that was played out in the newspapers every week. He was pretty much an open book – save for one thing, though it is impossible to know whether this was brought up in conversation in the manager's office at Old Trafford that January morning. Years later, in 2002, George confided to

Barbara that he had a daughter who was born in 1969. He had promised the mother and her husband that he would never try and get in touch. "Listening to him, I knew his heart was aching," Barbara wrote in her book *Our George*.

Phil Hughes, George's agent and long-time friend, also later said: "George once told me about his daughter and said he wasn't allowed to see her. He wouldn't want to do anything that would upset the girl, her mother and her husband."

Whether or not he told Busby about it, it seems pretty certain that he was still experiencing this sadness. Such a secret would have been an understandably horrendous thing to carry around – in trying to live with it, in attempting to be good to his word and also living with the anxiety that someone looking for a story might uncover the truth.

* * *

It could be said that in the months which followed this meeting, George Best and Matt Busby had a greater closeness than ever before – or at least a more open line of communication. George was reassured by Busby's signal of intent with the offer for MacDonald, even if it didn't come off. He agreed to his manager's request to speak to someone but it didn't go well. George didn't take it seriously and felt that he understood his problems and the cause of them – he just wanted them to end, and felt the approach of asking him about his upbringing and similarly invasive questions was counter-productive. He didn't go back to, as he described it, "the headshrinker", and was not pushed by the club to do so.

Instead, Best pushed Busby on other matters. He asked him once or twice to reconsider leaving. Busby insisted that he would be retiring for good in the summer as the job needed a younger man. If new blood was the plan then maybe George, as the central figure in all of that, could be team captain? George approached Busby with the idea, keen to demonstrate that he wanted the responsibility and could be trusted.

His form on the pitch had improved, coinciding with his new reliability in training. In his first home match after the suspension, Tottenham were the visitors, and only 15 minutes had been played when George struck one of the seminal goals of his career. A defensive scramble resulted in the ball dropping to him on the left-hand side of the box. Goalkeeper Pat Jennings – Best's compatriot (indeed, the two made their international debut together in the same game) was only six yards off his line. He had two defenders behind him.

Ray Evans, the Spurs right-back, challenged George, but the United forward had one thing on his mind with the ball bouncing as it was. Could he somehow loop the ball over all of them? It seemed improbable. To get the ball up and down such a short distance from goal was a feat that would require the perfect touch and weight. To get it over three players in the six-yard box was almost an impossibility. George was a player who thrived on exploiting such matters. Somehow the ball managed to get over them all into the net, and still far enough away from them that when you watch it again, you think he could have even got it over a fourth player.

In the fallout of the missed Chelsea trip, one "prominent First Division manager" told Ken Jones in the *Mirror*: "Frankly I wouldn't be interested… George seems to have lost his way. I don't think he's the player he was three years ago, and he seems to have got tremendous problems with himself. He's very much an individual who likes to go his own way."

Yet on this evidence there was not a manager in the world who would not dream of having a player like George in their ranks. United won 2-1 and George's own form stood up to scrutiny in the following weeks. The Spurs goal was the first of nine in 14 games. United's issues were still very much real and present – six of those games were lost – but there was a climb up the table which made things feel more stable for a platform on which Busby's successor, whoever that might be, could build. So Best felt emboldened to request the captaincy; and was hurt when the request was turned down.

Busby risked provoking a downward spiral when he told George he didn't think he was responsible enough, especially to succeed Charlton, who was still in the role. George felt that he could prove how responsible he was by becoming captain, instead of showing the responsibility to earn it.

Alex Stepney feels that Busby was right; but is keen to point out that it was far from a matter of saying George was unreliable. "I wouldn't class him as a leader on the pitch. But I don't mean that in a negative way," Stepney explains. "Nobby was a leader. Paddy was. Denis and Bobby obviously were. But George, I'm not sure. George was even told to just go out and do what he wanted to. He was a free spirit, and some of the things that were his positive qualities were also things that wouldn't have made him a good captain.

"We had our dressing room routines, some players would be in there for a full hour or more before the game. I'd take at least half an hour. George would always come in at a quarter to three. We'd all be ready and George's shirt would still be on his peg. He'd come in, put it on, put his shorts on, put the boots on, tie a little bow and say, 'Come on, let's go!' That was George. That was why he was such a great player. He wanted freedom on the pitch, he made and found freedom on the pitch. He had that fearlessness and that helped the entire team grow in confidence. But at the same time, that quality doesn't translate as an effective captain. I think Matt was trying to keep it as simple as he possibly could for George. To say don't worry about anything else, just go and what you did for me before. Go and enjoy yourself."

Best took Busby's decision badly – thinking it translated as being told he wasn't responsible, he would just play up to being irresponsible instead of proving the manager wrong or even just waiting it out until it was his turn. Charlton was 33. Busby couldn't demote him – but if George had been patient and proven himself then time may have taken its natural course.

Publicly, Busby couldn't have been more defensive of his player. He attended the hearing for the Pardoe incident when George's booking was wiped from the record. In late January, Busby was in Ireland and gave reporters one of the lines which has been quoted many times since: "Best is endowed with greater talent than any player I have ever seen."

He was the star of Busby's last ever match – for good, this time – as United boss. United won an entertaining Manchester derby at Maine Road – they were 3-0 up at half-time through, fittingly enough, Charlton, Law and Best. After a brief fightback to make it 3-1, Best secured the result with another in the 75th minute – his 21st goal of the season. City scored two more late on but still went away with a 4-3 defeat.

It did appear as if 1970 – and the first month of 1971 – was just a bad spell George had got over. There had been exceptional moments in the league following the lob against Spurs. A double at Stoke – the first an absolutely sublime left-footed piledriver on a bouncing pitch, and the second some classic 'he's behind you' ball-pinching (in the box) which was followed by some traditional rounding of the goalkeeper to roll the ball in – saw both points return to Manchester. Two more goals at Palace rounded off a 5-2 win – the first of these was wonderful, controlling a flicked ball from Gowling and then hitting it on the half-volley into the top corner.

He carried that momentum and contentment over into his international arena when he scored his first hat-trick for Northern Ireland against Cyprus in April 1971. The three came in a spell of 11 minutes either side of half-time, with the first the best of them all, a powerful shot in off the post. Jack Milligan of the *Mirror* concluded: "The incomparable George Best became the ringmaster of Windsor Park last night with a stunning performance that delighted the 20,000 gallery. Best, often criticised by the Belfast crowd, won them all over last night. They loved every second of his magical mystery tour."

George admitted he was in a better frame of mind to face England in the Home Championship than he had been a year earlier. "The last time I played against England, at Wembley last year, I was a very angry young man," he said. "The goal I scored that night was one of the happiest moments of my life… it was one of those nights when I could make things go my way – and this is exactly how I feel about the same against England tomorrow at Windsor Park."

Best was feeling the love from the home support and planned a special treat for them. World Cup-winning goalkeeper Gordon Banks was still in the England net. George's imagination studio included a scenario where he could intercept the ball as a goalkeeper attempted to kick it.

Banks was considered the best in the world – following not only the triumph in 1966, but the remarkable save he had made from Pele in the 1970 World Cup, a powerful palm to claw away a header that seemed destined for the goal. Banks had defied physics to make that save. And George wanted to make the player who denied Pele in such a way look a fool. Sure enough, as it does in every game of football, a situation occurred where the goalkeeper picked the ball up and sought to start an attack. He ran to throw the ball but George was there, standing in front to block him. Banks adopted the pose of a rugby player, crouching and feinting to throw twice, before changing his body shape and crouching left.

Having felt he'd thrown his opponent off, Banks tossed the ball into the air in preparation for the kick. Best knew from the angle that he couldn't steal in to nick the ball but thrust out a leg to see if it was strong enough anyway. It was. Banks needed a second to compute what had happened and that was enough time for George to move his body in front so he had the control of the ball.

Try as he might, Banks couldn't get back, and George headed the ball into the net. Banks appealed with both hands in the air but it was uncertain what for, unless he felt the referee could disallow goals on the premise of mercy. It turned out that this referee – Alistair MacKenzie – did. The official reason he gave George was that he had a raised foot – which seemed awfully timid considering the brutality which had been inflicted on Manchester United goalkeepers in successive FA Cup finals in the Fifties. England won 1-0, and the result was the difference between them and Northern Ireland winning the Championship.

THE QUIET MAN

F rank O'Farrell was not the runaway favourite to become the new manager of Manchester United but he was, according to George Best soon after the Leicester City manager was given the Old Trafford top job, the man most players were tipping for the role. "We've all been playing guessing games in the dressing room and Frank O'Farrell was the players' bet," Best told reporters. "So I'm not surprised. All I really know about the man is that he's Irish, like me. Whether that's good or bad, we'll have to wait and see!"

O'Farrell ticked certain criteria for Matt Busby. He was young, he had enjoyed some success – Leicester City, despite their relegation a couple of years earlier, were now promoted again and had got to the FA Cup final in 1969 too. Along with his coach Malcolm Musgrove, O'Farrell was seen as part of a new revolution in management. The task for the manager – proving himself worthy of the biggest club in the country. To do that he would need the best player in the country on his side and the first step on that road was an affirmation that O'Farrell believed that to be the case. It was ludicrous to many but there was nonetheless a growing community of people within football who thought George was not worth the hassle which came with the overall package.

The European Cup final that year had been contested at Wembley again, between Ajax and Panathinaikos. In the Ajax forward line was the 23-year-old Johan Cruyff, a player of such wonderful imagination that it was inevitable he would draw comparisons with Best. Asked who was better out of the pair ahead of the game, Cruyff dodged the question. "It would be better to ask him that," he said. "He might give the right answer. But to play alongside him? That would really be something. It would be marvellous. Magnificent. No team in the world would be able to beat us. We are different because I am married and he's not. It might be better if he were married. Then there is responsibility, a meaning to life. I think it has helped me to become a more certain player. I know now where I am going in the world."

Cruyff had a maverick streak that Best approved of even though he would go on record as saying he never felt inferior to another player. Earlier that season the Dutch schemer had been forced to wear the number 14 shirt after a mix up – when his team won the subsequent game against PSV, he super-stitiously decided to keep wearing that number, bucking the convention of the 1-11. He also underlined the importance of playing in a World Cup a few years later; it was during the 1974 competition when he beat Swedish defender Jan Olsson with what would become known as the 'Cruyff Turn'; a signature move for a player who had many more in his locker.

Individually there was plenty of evidence to say they were

closely matched in terms of talent. But George was seen as a more complete player, with the work-rate to help out his defence more than Cruyff. And O'Farrell – keen to get off on the right foot – quickly reminded everyone where he stood. "Some months ago I wrote that George Best was possibly the most complete player in Britain," he wrote in the *Mirror*. "He is certainly the most complete player since Tom Finney."

There was no doubting who the best in Britain was. And, although naturally biased, Manchester United supporters still firmly believed that too. George had emerged as a figurehead of a generation – adored by men and women alike. He was their representative on the pitch. A free-willed blazing spirit who did things others could not. One who would stand up for himself against authority. A personal champion against perceived persecution. He was liberation. He was wild and untamed. He was also the person leading that transition from the glory years at Old Trafford into a new era – nobody knew who would follow the likes of Charlton and Law, only that the time was coming soon, and George would be the leader of that group, whether or not he was made captain officially.

He was almost universally loved by journalists as well. Those who didn't know him were able to use his exploits as fodder for their work. Those who did quickly fell under his spell; George was charismatic but shy, and above all, enigmatic.

The reporter John Roberts was one such man. By chance, a compelling relationship developed. "I first knew George from Belfast working for the *Daily Express* over there," Roberts says. "I got to know his parents and when he won the European Cup I arranged the civic reception for him with the Lord Mayor. The *Express* asked me to go back to Manchester to work in 1969. I moved close to where George had moved into his new house around the time the newspaper signed him to do a column. The newspaper had done a lot of work on features around his image, his promotional contracts and so on.

"They wanted me to talk to him about the football and I was happy to do that. He was only a walk or short drive away. But even though he was so close, he was as elusive with me as he was with the full-backs marking him and the auxiliaries that would support them. If he wanted to, he could easily disappear, though in spite of that I would say that we got on as well as one could expect of a footballer and journalist.

"If George was with his friends, they had quite diverse interests. They'd talk about every subject under the sun. They'd watch *Parkinson* and talk about the subjects that came up from that. He was a genius as a footballer. He seemed to epitomise the Sixties. He was very much a part of that era; long hair, colourful shirts, flared trousers.

"After World War II there was a lot of austerity that gradually eased as we moved forward. He was a part of that first adult generation born after the war and it was very much a generation of youth, where younger people were getting ahead more quickly in all sorts of ways. They were getting into showbiz at a much younger age than before.

"When George did what he did against Benfica in 1966 it had the cosmopolitan aspect of being abroad and also broadcast on television around the world. He loved football once he was on the pitch. If he was playing well he didn't want the match to end. And if he wasn't, he still didn't want it to end until he started playing well again. You could tell he was a perfectionist although he didn't speak about it in those terms. He knew how good he was. There was no two ways about that."

From talking with his friends about *Parkinson* to appearing on the show himself, as he did in July 1971 – Best caused a commotion when he told the presenter about his dalliances with women: "It is always the same – when they are taking off their clothes, they say they hope I don't think they are doing it because I am George Best." The comment was received negatively, prompting many letters of complaint to newspapers.

Frank O'Farrell – who had literally only just spent time waxing lyrical about how George had surprised him with his professionalism in pre-season – was forced to discuss the matter, which would have been an alien experience for someone who thought he'd been hired to run a football club. O'Farrell was asked if he would ban George from appearing on any more talk shows. "No-one is talking about barring anyone," he said. "What a man like George Best must realise is that, if he is not careful, he is used by other people… Mike Parkinson is a good professional in his field. But I have pointed out to George that he doesn't need Parkinson or any TV producer to promote him. He can do that himself when he plays at Old Trafford – or on any other ground for that matter.

"I have a duty to perform, as manager of United. I don't want my only day off spoiled by people ringing up and asking what I think of a footballer's appearance on television. I have told George that when he appears on TV he has his own name to protect, and he should remember that the ripples of these types of interview can affect a lot of other people. I am sure he understands this. But I want to make it quite clear that there is no fitter or more dedicated player on my staff. His arena is the football field, not the TV studio."

There was a change in the rules of the game that summer which was sure to have an even greater positive effect on George's game than even the impact of a new manager. The

FA announced a clampdown on cynical tackles – a rule that seemed as if it had been personally introduced just for George. The United number 11 tried on his new power for size at Craven Cottage in the penultimate pre-season friendly, to the rage of the Fulham defenders. One of them, Fred Callaghan, was subjected to a new kind of ridicule after missing a tackle that George felt was too late. "Best swung round and mockingly pointed a finger at his own head," wrote Nigel Clarke of the *Mirror*. "Then, when he won the ball again, he turned his back on Callaghan and invited the tackle."

There was another incident late on between Callaghan and Best; this time, Callaghan's team-mate Reg Matthewson picked up the ball and threw it at Best, who threw a punch back in return. The referee was able to calm it down, but Callaghan warned the new rules were not likely to protect Best if he was so arrogant in future. "He was so clearly taking the mickey," he said. "I can't kick anybody and Fulham are not that sort of side. But if George starts doing that to some defenders he will be asking for trouble. He has such great ability, yet all he wants to do is fight everybody. The way he is going on he'll get barred."

* * *

The first league game of the new reign was at Derby County's Baseball Ground. O'Farrell's first United side read: Stepney – O'Neil, James, Sadler, Dunne – Morgan, Gowling, Charlton – Kidd, Law, Best. Alan Gowling was a converted centre-forward and so not a natural replacement for the veteran Crerand in the middle of the park – though his height did make him an asset on set plays. But Gowling, like Tommy O'Neil and Steve James, were obvious areas where a top replacement was needed, and that's before considering the ageing Charlton, problematic Law and want-away Brian Kidd.

But these were different days to the modern era where new signings would have been demanded instantly. More value was placed on coaching, development, improvement and patience. In the early weeks and months these qualities stood Frank O'Farrell in good stead. United's players responded very positively to a new way of doing things. There was nothing groundbreaking in the training – Musgrove was a fitness fanatic, and found the players receptive to his style. There was nothing groundbreaking in the formation – a 4-3-3 that could become a 4-2-4, a fluid interchangeable front line with a little extra responsibility placed on Morgan to play inside in order to compensate for Best's free role in the front three. It translated to good results – and fantastic performances – on the pitch.

There was an indication against Derby that there might be some bumpy times. United took a 2-0 first-half lead but the hosts responded to equalise. The 2-2 draw was a decent result but Derby had appeared keen to test the new laws and kicked Best from pillar to post so that he was unable to influence the game, other than to serve as the human piñata whilst the other United forwards found space.

The next game was Chelsea away. Despite what had happened in January, Stamford Bridge was traditionally one of George's favourite places to go, and despite carrying some significant knocks, he insisted he was good to play.

United started well and thought they had scored a good goal – it was disallowed by Norman Burtenshaw, who further frustrated the away side when deeming that a Chelsea goal six minutes before half-time was good, despite there being a clear and obvious foul on a United defender. "The referee was diabolical," Morgan recalls. "Peter Osgood flattened David Sadler and they put the ball in the net. The goal was given so naturally the lads surrounded the referee to complain, and naturally, the referee didn't change his mind. George was walking near him as they went back to the halfway line, he's giving the ref a mouthful and gets sent off."

Best responded in disbelief. What sort of madness was this? The rules had supposedly changed to protect him and others but it was starting to feel as if the entire world was conspiring against him. At first he sat down on the pitch before his team-mates convinced him he had to leave the field. One front page report claimed he "broke down in tears"as Malcolm Musgrove guided him down the tunnel. The lack of protection was one thing, but the reality of that suspended sentence coming into effect, with the likelihood of an even greater punishment to accompany it, started to dawn on him.

United recovered from the double setback to win after a thrilling second half. Next up was the first home game of the season, against Arsenal. But this was a home game with a twist – following some crowd trouble in the previous season's clash with Newcastle at Old Trafford where a knife was thrown on to the pitch, United were ordered to play their first two home matches of the following campaign at neutral grounds. So this game would be staged at Anfield of all places, followed by another 'home' game against West Brom at Stoke City's Victoria Ground.

With his red card, George had still been the headline act on what many newspapers described as a night of shame in the English game. Not only were there numerous bookings and red cards as teams became accustomed to the new way of life, the volatile atmosphere created by the dismissals (again, at the time, players would only be sent from the field in extreme cases, though in Best's case it often seemed over the top) resulted in many arrests at games around the country. Best faced a suspension but would be eligible until his hearing at least – United applied for a personal hearing and were told it would take place on Monday, September 13.

This was the player's first indiscretion under O'Farrell and the new manager was not going to take him out of the team until he was told to. "One of George Best's biggest assets – and problems – is that he is such a fiercely determined competitor," O'Farrell said. "I would have quite understood if he had pulled out of the team to play Chelsea... I'd seen the bruises and swellings on his ankles and feet. But George is no coward. He told me, 'If I can get my boots on, boss, I'll play.' And play he did, although now I wish he hadn't...

"There is no point in going into the rights and wrongs of this, but it underlines the problems facing football at the moment. So far as I am aware, the fellows who had given George those bumps and bruises were not booked. But it seems under soccer's current code of conduct the spoken word is considered a bigger crime than a kick on the leg. I've told George, 'I'm going to punish you. You're playing against Arsenal, and I want you out there for the full 90 minutes.'"

Best was good but couldn't play the full game – the swelling on his ankle getting the better of him, causing him to come off for Aston. But he was back in the first team days later for that match with West Brom. The Baggies players were cautious of recent controversies and did not apply the sort of personal touch others did to George. He ran riot with the freedom, scoring a tap-in on 10 minutes and then a dazzling solo goal in the 57th to make it 3-0 to his team. "Best, free from the vicious tackling which he endured last season, turned on one of the most skilful shows ever seen at Stoke," wrote journalist Bob Russell.

"Best held centre stage with a 90-minute solo spot that brought a standing ovation that even referee George Hartley and his linesmen joined in," Peter Hewitt wrote for the *Stoke Sentinel*. "As soccer's entertainers come into the own under the new disciplined regime, Best emerged as the top man. At times it was as though his colleagues were just making up the supporting cast. It takes more than one man to take a team to the top of the First Division but this was Best in the mood to tease and torment any defence and shattered Albion had no one to touch him… the anticipated night of terror from the fans never materialised. Instead it was Best running riot."

That game ended 3-1; Best scored again in a 1-1 draw at Wolves, and despite a setback with defeat at Everton, United were back to winning ways straight away by beating Ipswich. The setting was Old Trafford – the first game there under O'Farrell. Of course, George had something planned for the occasion. A poor first half was drifting from the memory of those supporters waiting for a pie at the break when United got a corner in the 43rd minute. "It just so happened George Best pulled off one of those remarkable strokes of sauciness that sinks all defensive plans," wrote Paul Doherty of the *People*. "Hammond conceded a left-wing corner as the subdued crowd yawningly awaited the interval. Best took it – a deceptively high inswinger. His namesake, the Ipswich 'keeper, advanced, realised he'd misjudged the flight, and could do little but claw backwards as the corner curled into the far netting."

The goal fittingly won the game. Maybe the only thing more staggering than the fact this was not the first time he had deliberately scored from a corner in top-level football, is the normal way in which Alex Stepney describes his recollection of it. "Yeah, I played in games where he scored corners," he says. "All he wanted to do was score goals, make goals, and beat people in the most imaginative way possible. Nobody expected that he would have the audacity to try it, and then to try it again. But he did."

Ipswich were put to the sword again in the League Cup three days later – Best scoring twice in a 3-1 win. But there was something arguably even more remarkable that took place. After the weekend game, Ipswich boss Bobby Robson had complained that his team had been beaten by a fluke. He said there was no way anyone could have meant to score from a corner. In the opening minutes at Portman Road, United won a corner. "I went across to take it and I looked over at him," recalled Best in 1985. "I took the corner, it curled over everybody's head and hit the far post. If it had gone in I think I would have retired then. And I looked across [at Robson] and he just shrugged and smiled. I did things like that for fun. I used to try things like that, do things a little different. I always felt like an entertainer and I knew I could get the crowd excited by doing little things like that."

United went to Crystal Palace and again won 3-1. George did not score but was in wonderful form, revelling in the fear felt by defenders who no longer had the questionable law on their side. United scored three (two from Law, one from Kidd) but had three more disallowed as George excelled. "Best had the lot – poise, balance, superb dribbles," wrote Frank Taylor of the *Mirror*, while Sam Bartram of the *People* went even further, giving the United star a 10/10 rating and declaring: "Fabulous Best. Tremendous Best. The Best I've ever seen."

There was an intriguing subplot developing in these early weeks of the season. With George in illuminating form, fans were flocking to grounds just to watch him. Palace's home gates that season were 25,281 against Newcastle, 28,488 against Liverpool and 17,699 against Nottingham Forest. Best's presence had attracted 44,020. Palace chairman Arthur Wait spoke for many when he felt the potential lengthy suspension for the player following the Chelsea incident would be a punishment to the game at large – despite how it had hurt his team – as much as it would be to Manchester United. "I'm all for the right sort of discipline, but we cannot afford to have great entertainers like Best sitting on the sidelines," Wait said. "We had 15,000 on the game today. Best put them there."

The problem was that George was bang to rights. There was no logical way he would avoid a suspension and the FA were not about to consider even the pleas of the opposition as a strong enough reason to disregard their disciplinary process. George, a master of manipulation on the pitch, became a master of that same trait off of it. It started with pleas of innocence to John Roberts, who could convey those same thoughts in the press.

"He was telling me with sincerity that he did not swear at the referee," Roberts says. "He was genuinely fearful that he would be banned for a long time. Perhaps it would have been better all round if he had been punished. I say that and consider the reality that he would probably have gone off to Majorca!"

The second part of George's plan was to find an accomplice. "He got the summons through for the hearing in London," Willie Morgan recalls. "We were lined up in training – there was George, Brian Kidd, Bobby, Denis and me. He went through each of the lads and asked if they would say that he was talking to them and not the referee. They all said no. He finally got to me and asked. 'I was 60 yards away from you!' I laughed, but I agreed to go along with it. We went down there and to be fair they treat you like a criminal. It was horrible. 'Morgan, where were you when Best was blah, blah blah?' and all that sort of stuff. They had a Subbuteo pitch with all the players marked out. 'You're trying to tell us that Best said this to you?' I insisted he did, and that I was very upset actually, because normally we get on very well."

Despite how preposterous it was, Best's sincerity accompanied with his alibi meant George was off the hook. "It's a very happy verdict for me, and it was a very fair hearing... now I can concentrate on playing my football," George told reporters afterwards, although it must have been hard to translate with his tongue stuck so firmly in his cheek. He maintained his innocence even after the event, never letting on to Roberts even though the journalist would quickly become a loyal aide.

Speaking the day after the hearing, Spurs striker Martin Chivers explained to journalists that he expected big things from the United player. "He is king of all the strikers and for the life of me I can't understand why he has not scored more goals since referees have cracked down on bad tackling," he said. "George is brave, with bewildering ability, and has two good feet. He's also good in the air, but it is his speed that impresses me the most. Against Tottenham he scored a goal of cool cheek and outrageous ability."

Those qualities were all present in some abundance when West Ham came to Manchester. When he was pitted against one of the game's best players, he saw it for the challenge that it was. He was not a ruiner of reputations. His greatness had ascended to a new plateau. Tommy Gemmell is still known as the man who won a European Cup for Celtic. Ron Harris is known as a Chelsea legend. Neither of them suffered any lasting reputational damage because it was acknowledged that George could do what he did against them to anyone in the game. George wanted to prove that he was better, but, as proven with the sombrero, these were scalps. Players might feel humiliated in the moment – insulted by the smile George wore as he went past them – but there was no malice, just that beautiful childlike enjoyment of the game.

Bobby Moore is regarded as the finest West Ham player of all time. That remains true regardless of the events of September 18, 1971. He was one of a number of central defenders who could consider themselves fortunate to rarely have any direct confrontations with Best because of the wide positions he normally operated in. Only if one was instructed to mark him – Harris, for example – would Best be accompanied by a defender who normally played in the middle. Moore was too pivotal to West Ham's needs to pin him on Best for 90 minutes. But in this new liberated era of the 1971/72 season, George was going anywhere and everywhere.

After a corner had been earned through a marvellous Best effort from 20 yards which was tipped over, George was there again at the back post to nod in Charlton's set-piece. West Ham soon levelled. Just before half-time Best got a second – another corner came in, the Hammers failed to clear, and the ball bounced in the congested six-yard box. Best made it look as if he had all the space in the world as he acrobatically fired a left foot shot through no fewer than nine players between himself and the goal into the top corner. As his body flew off the ground after connection, it was like a firecracker had gone off. Once more, he had bent the improbable actualities of the game to his own will.

That was good enough. But it was the third goal – his hat-trick – which became one of those fated to appear in highlights clips eternally. Charlton hit a long-range effort that was tipped wide by goalkeeper Bobby Ferguson. Ferguson complained that he didn't get a touch but Law quickly took the corner, tapping it to Best. From the left side of the box, George was jockeyed by John McDowell.

The United forward decided to move into the area and McDowell stuck a foot out; George shimmied to the left, and the West Ham defender tried to regain his balance, but was forced to do a 360 degree turn. In the midst of that movement, Best dropped his shoulder to the right. McDowell planted his foot into the ground just to ensure he remained upright – but that movement left him completely beaten and flat-footed.

George was around 12 yards from goal and had a clear shot. Moore, using his years of experience, rushed out to close that space off. He did his job well. But George kept moving, and kept hold of the ball, and now Moore – who had committed himself – had to keep going. He wasn't close enough. George shifted the ball away so that Moore couldn't even offer a challenge – and the space was clear. Best slammed the ball home with his right-foot. A perfect hat-trick in more ways than one. Not least because United won 4-2.

"I can't remember much about it. I just kept running until I saw space, and hit it," he said after the game. Bobby Moore was gracious in defeat. "George Best is playing exceptionally well," he said. "Possibly as well as at any time in his career."

Best admitted he was on a mission to break his personal record of 32 goals in a season – the hat-trick goal was his ninth already – but he also seemed desperate to do it with such style that would force those who had written him off to eat their words. Old Trafford was his church, the 50,000 plus in attendance his loyal congregation, and every time there was a gathering there seemed to be a seminal memory to take away.

Against Ipswich and West Ham he had contributed to the afternoon's proceedings in a way only he could. On October 2, Sheffield United were the visitors and had much more of a resolute attitude. They held out until seven minutes from time. Until George decided to take matters into his own hands.

In the late months of the year, when the sun goes in early, Old Trafford – the Theatre of Dreams – can become the Theatre of Sunblind for those sitting in the Scoreboard End, now the K Stand. One presumes that when the legendary architect Archibald Leitch had visited the area to map out his blueprints of the stadium, it had been a traditionally dour and cloudy day, one of those where you might question if the area had ever in fact been frequented by the sun. Well, on this day, it was. And George – no doubt like the thousands behind him – was facing the Stretford End and forced to squint as he received the ball and turned around. That he was able to do so effortlessly was almost a miracle in itself.

He turned, casting a Lowry-matchstalk shadow across the grass in front of him. The Sheffield defenders might for a second have been grateful that they could concentrate their eyes on the ground, following the ball. For that second, their vision might have been impacted enough to not know the identity of the opponent who had paused for a moment and was now accelerating towards them. But it would only have been a second; the feet moved with such speed and grace, they could not belong to anyone else. George, running through the middle, dropped his shoulder to the right. That was one defender beaten. And he knew he was, so he left George to his team-mate, in the sort of baton-passing defending they had partaken in all game.

Best's momentum carried him past another Blades defender, who knew he couldn't afford to challenge him. And then there were two left, one standing behind the other – anticipating that Best would have to cut in to score, the one behind stood his ground. But George continued to glide to the right, leaving this last defender both isolated and too distant to get close, even though he continued to jockey in vain. The angle was narrow. The goalkeeper came out to make it narrower. It would be a remarkable feat if George was able to get it past the 'keeper and on to the target. It would need to be perfect if it was to go in. And it was. The only way he could do it – with momentum moving him to the right and the narrowing of the gap – was to execute his shot in the style of a snooker player, using the rebound of the cushion, or in this case, the far post. The shot cannoned off the inside of the post and into the net.

George's celebration was akin to that of someone who had successfully scaled Everest – a mixture of delirium and relief, the distinctive feeling of euphoria that is released with a late winner in a football game regardless of whether the opponent is Barcelona or Braintree Town.

* * *

October continued in similarly glorious fashion. Best broke Huddersfield's stubborn resistance in the 65th minute at Leeds Road to open the floodgates – Law and Charlton, also enjoying a renaissance, netted after to give the score an emphatic 3-0 gloss, and Best then scored the only goal against Derby at Old Trafford to continue in his role as main man at home. In 16 games, he had scored 12 goals; Charlton had netted seven, and Law five. Even Gowling had netted four. O'Farrell's team were flying – eleven of those games had been won and only one lost.

What could derail United's momentum? One could come up with a hundred or more possible reasons. The last thing one would expect was a terrorist threat. But someone claiming to be from the IRA telephoned police, claiming that George would be shot if he played against Newcastle United at St James' Park. The police then contacted the club.

Paddy Crerand dismisses it as "a load of crap... paper talk... George wouldn't have believed it". But others saw it differently. Sammy McIlroy – a young player breaking through to the senior set-up – had taken that same journey from the Belfast streets to Old Trafford and took it seriously. "You would not dismiss anything like that out of hand," he says. "Threats were flying around. People were getting shot. People were dying.

"George was an international figure. If someone makes a threat you had to take it seriously. I think putting it into all of that perspective sums him up as a man, it sums up his bravery about playing. Some people wouldn't have even taken the chance. When I was manager of the country, a threat was put to Neil Lennon and we didn't take the chance. So when you look at how different life was in the early Seventies and how fresh these sort of threats were... you didn't see it as a hoax."

George himself didn't appear to leave anything open to inter-pretation. "I was under enormous pressure as it was and having enough problems just keeping my life together, without that," he said in his book *Blessed*. "And it wasn't just the threat that bothered me. It was the effect I knew it would have on my family." George called home and tried to put a brave face on it, attempting to reassure his father it was probably a prank. "You can't be sure," a worried Dickie replied.

John Roberts remembers George's dilemma at the time. "He didn't make a big deal about it," he said. "He took it seriously. It was a threat and it affected him. It wasn't something he took as an idle threat. And yet he still tried to go about his life as usual. George's friends were from across the spectrum. There was no bigotry within him whatsoever. I can't remember him ever speaking about being disagreeable with any individual, any race or way of life. He would be happy speaking to anybody."

O'Farrell and Best discussed the matter – the manager said he would understand if George didn't want to play. "I kept coming back to the feeling that I couldn't not play, otherwise, where would it all end?" the player said. "There could be death threats every week and I'd never play again."

So he decided to play, with some reticence about the pressure it would put on his team-mates. There was some extra anxiety on the morning of the game when the team coach was broken into and had to be checked for explosive devices.

Just after half-time, Best – typically – scored the only goal of the game. "I wish they had shot the little bugger!" Newcastle boss Joe Harvey told the press afterwards.

As it turned out, it was a hoax. But when there was another, the threat was sufficient for O'Farrell to intervene when Best was selected for Northern Ireland, who were due to play Spain in Belfast in a game that was dubbed 'The Fixture of Fear'. He decided he would withdraw his player. "George has been extremely worried since I told him of the first threat to his life," said the United boss on November 2. "Now the police have been informed by a person living close to George's home that there has been another threat to 'get him'… The value of human life is the thing that matters… It's something you cannot ignore, especially as he comes from Belfast and his family could be involved. It is very unfortunate that a brilliant footballer like Best should be involved in this sort of thing. If you study his performance closely in the last couple of games, you must accept that it has affected his play."

As it transpired, the game was postponed until February, when it would be played in Hull. By then, everything was different. Yet despite O'Farrell's observations, George's standard of performance continued to be the highlight for United in the following month. And, despite the distressing reminder of how things were at home, the presence of one young Belfast lad provided a nice fillip at just the right time.

Sammy McIlroy had followed the same path as George to Old Trafford. He was discovered by Bob Bishop. And, just as George had grown up watching the great players on television, he had been the player youngsters like Sammy were watching as they grew up.

"George was my hero," McIlroy says. "Everyone I played with when I was a kid wanted to be him. It was frightening to watch him in Benfica. I remember it clearly, on the black and white television, there was a boy from home playing in a way that everyone dreamed of doing. It was one of the best individual performances I ever saw, at such a young age.

"It was so inspirational. Everyone was talking about it. The whole world of course but for those few days at home it was all over the newspapers, it was on television every time you turned it on. There were some unbelievable players about and I want to stress how good they were. Eusebio was playing for Benfica and they had never been beaten at home. What George did was historic. So yes, I would agree with what Paddy [Crerand] says, he was the best at that time. His skill, his consistency, his ability to keep going after getting a kick... he was right up there. The Troubles were really bad at home and my dad would always drum it in to my head that there was nothing for me there, I had to go away to give it a real go. Then I was signed by United. Homesickness was a big thing for me – the club were really good, they would send me home at least once a month.

"George was one of the first I met at the club. He came over and wished me the best of luck. I noticed he paid a lot of attention to the lads who came over from Northern Ireland. He would come into the canteen at the Cliff after training and he'd watch how the young boys were getting on. He was very welcoming of my mum and dad and would reassure them about how I was doing. Does it get any better than that?"

Well, for McIlroy – who already thought he was in dreamland – it did. When Law was ruled out of the Manchester derby with injury, the 17-year-old was called up. His story is familiar. "I didn't find out until 11am Saturday morning that I was playing," he says. "Frank told me before we went to Davyhulme golf course. Before we even got on the coach, George approached me. 'Listen, just relax, enjoy yourself. And if you score today I'll give you a bottle of champagne.' I happened to score. Monday morning, true to his word, he brought in a bottle. It instantly made me feel a part of things."

United drew 3-3. McIlroy's introduction to the team went well – his first few games included a win over Spurs and then victory from a trip to Southampton. "George was fantastic to play with," McIlroy says. "Yes, sometimes people would get a wee bit frustrated with him keeping hold of the ball and beating man after man, beating the same one three times. I can remember Bobby and Denis throwing their arms up at times.

But the players understood him. Sometimes they'd be about to scream and he'd smash the ball in from 20 yards. Against Spurs in the next game I scored again and in the newspapers there was a picture of Bobby, Denis and George coming to celebrate with me. I wish I'd got a copy and framed it. Down at Southampton I scored again and George got a hat-trick."

Best's first came from a smart flicked header after just seven minutes. His second, two minutes into the second half, was classic George; Charlton fizzed a pass into the box and McIlroy showed fine intelligence to dummy. One Southampton defender threw himself at the ball, hoping the diving tackle would be enough to put off Best. It wasn't. When another defender rushed to block the space, George danced around him as if they were playing an exhibition. From there, he side-footed the ball into the corner as if the goalkeeper wasn't on the pitch. It was showboating time; Best thrilled everyone at The Dell with an array of tricks, stopping often, as he did, to tease players into tackling him.

Once again he was everywhere, all over the pitch, unable to be tracked by any individual foolish enough to try. Southampton's misery was complete when George nodded in his hat-trick goal in the 58th minute. Goals from Kidd and McIlroy not only made it worse on the day – United won 5-2 – but it sent an ominous sign to the rest of the First Division. Alan Gowling had been declared 'the most improved player in the league' before the game – it suggested that there was strength from within on that famous production line at Old Trafford.

United were top of the table with a three-point lead and playing the best and most consistent football since their last title win in 1967. In fact, one could argue it was even better, and could be compared to how good they were in 1965. With Best in imperious form – he was now on 17 goals for the season, before December – and, more pertinently, six years more mature than he was in those breakthrough days, the future once again seemed rosy for Manchester United. To illustrate just how wonderful George had been since 'mending his ways' at the start of the year, he was named in third place in the Ballon d'Or rankings – Johan Cruyff, with Ajax's European Cup to act as evidence, was number one.

O'Farrell was quizzed about the great start to the season. Up to this point, he was always happy to speak to reporters, especially when they were doing a very positive piece on him as Ken Jones of the *Mirror* did in mid-December. He said that he wasn't going to strengthen his squad for the sake of it. "You always have to be careful when spending other people's money," he told Jones, after dismissing the idea that his side were vulnerable at the back. "But I think I have learned the hard way... I know the spotlight will be on when I buy for United. But I can call on a lot of sound advice if I need it."

He also had his detractors. Malcolm Allison, the Manchester City boss, and Brian Clough, manager of Derby County, both went on record in December as saying they were certain United "would blow up". But that view wasn't only held outside Old Trafford. It was already a matter of concern among the players that they were having to play at their maximum just to get through games.

"From then Frank almost seemed to disappear," Alex Stepney remembers. "He'd been this happy-go-lucky guy and then all of a sudden, nothing. We never saw him. When we did he didn't speak. Frank came in at the same time the laws were changed to clamp down on the aggressive tackling. I don't think he could believe how well we started under him. The press had said how we had a lot of players who were close to the end and would soon retire but we started winning games handsomely and went to the top of the league. So he was blind to the cracks that were still there; yes, we were now winning more games because our attacking talent could play more freely, but we were letting a lot in. 3-2, 4-2, 5-2.

"We needed some centre-halves. Bill Foulkes played on for too long and after he retired we didn't replace him. When Frank eventually made the signing, it was one of the best the club ever made, Martin Buchan. But it was too late. If he'd done that before Christmas, we might have held on to fight for the title. Maybe he would have noticed the difference Martin made and been identified where else we needed strengthening. But he was too late. The momentum had turned.

"The whole ethos at the club had changed. Matt would come and talk to us about players he was interested in bringing to the club. Obviously new managers do different things. But Frank, for example, wouldn't come and ask senior players their advice. When we were winning he was all smiles and he would talk to us about other things. And then we started losing, and not playing well, and he didn't speak to us.

"There was a distance. Matt never did that. Win or lose he would talk to us. We could get beat, we could be defeated heavily, and he would always come and talk to us with the aim of reassuring us even if it came with criticism, because you know his aim was for Manchester United to win games. He would shake your hand in victory or defeat. That's just one example of how good a man-manager Matt was. And when you are used to that and you replace it with what we started to experience with Frank, it became a big hill to climb."

The numbers back up what Stepney claims. United conceded

two goals or more on nine separate occasions before Christmas. They were having to score goals at an unrealistic rate just to compensate. It wasn't a tactic that could hold out.

Best was going to need support. The last thing he needed at that time was even more personal attention. It was good-natured – television host Eamonn Andrews approached George to invite him to appear on *This is Your Life*, a biographical chat show where the subject would be greeted with notable people from his past and present. It was not a good time for George to be on the programme for numerous reasons – although he did participate with good humour.

The first reason was that, following the threats of October, he was struggling to comprehend why people would behave with such maliciousness. The second reason was that by his own admission he was starting to feel like two people; the man that he was and the celebrity and personality the public thought they knew. Another reason – the premise of the show was to reunite you with people you haven't seen for a while. The intention was often to surprise. You wouldn't know who Andrews was going to bring on to the stage next.

George already had a skeleton in his closet that he was struggling to deal with; one can only imagine the unsettling reaction a person could have when told they are going to be on a show where such things will be revealed in front of the nation. Andrews' show was far from malicious, but it's easy to consider George's potential anxiety over it. This was compounded by the fact he was treated like a child – the studio arranged a party in London the night before with limitless champagne and lots of women so that George didn't go anywhere else, while they also hired two men to follow him just in case he did.

In the late winter of 1971 it could be argued George was a

passenger in his own life, only able to assume control when on the pitch. Of course, he had not seen cause to change his lifestyle either. He was drinking more often – sometimes even breaking his own golden rule of not doing so on a Friday before a game. He was even being encouraged to do so, as exampled by the *This Is Your Life* episode.

As the festive season began and there were more parties, longer evenings and darker mornings, George's life of excess seemed to catch up with him. His performances grew lethargic. United drew three games in a row. It was increasingly obvious that it was his form compensating for the shortcomings in the team – and when he wasn't on song, United's own form plummeted. Of course, draws can be seen as a maintainer of consistency in a good or bad sense, and it's only at the other end when you're able to determine which way it went and why. O'Farrell's team weren't unlucky – their purple patch of goals had dried up, and now their defensive frailties were exposed.

On New Year's Day, West Ham recorded a comprehensive 3-0 win over United. Best was peripheral – and for once, not just because he was marked out of the game. "Manchester United are mystified by the almost total collapse of George Best's true form," Ken Jones wrote in the *Mirror*. "By his own mercurial standards, Best is struggling. He has lost his touch, his head is invariably down. The sneers were in evidence at West Ham, where his unbelievably clumsy ball-control was in shattering contradiction of the standards he has set himself. He no longer gets away from defenders when he has beaten them with the ball. He seems to be motivated into activity only by personal failure."

It did seem an alarming over-reaction – it had only been five games since the hat-trick at The Dell – but it was nonetheless true that George's form had nosedived. In addition to his physical excesses, he could look around and see the reality when he wasn't contributing as he had been. He was looking at Francis Burns and Paul Edwards in defence and realising that when he was dropping deep to tackle, it was more to do their job than to support. He was looking at Denis Law and Bobby Charlton and seeing a 31 (almost 32) and 34-year-old respectively. He was looking at the reasons for United's improvement and contemplating how sustainable it was. He was having to play some of the best football of his career just to keep United competitive.

The week after the West Ham game George, by his own admission, "didn't manage to get into the Cliff training ground once". He had grown to resent his home in Bramhall and even in the early days of a New Year there was always company or a party to be found if you were George Best.

Knowing his player was going through a difficult time, O'Farrell claimed that he went to visit Dickie and Ann, and appealed to them about moving over to Manchester.

"They said they were prepared to do that, they would do anything to help their son," he said. "So I was back at the club on the Thursday – we had a match with Wolves on the Saturday – and Malcolm Musgrove my first-team coach said, 'Oh George is over in Belfast visiting his family'. I said he's not in Belfast — I've been in Belfast, in his parents' house. Wherever he is, he's not in Belfast."

O'Farrell was particularly disappointed and made his first bold call, fining George two weeks wages and dropping him from the game against Wolves. When they talked, the manager advised George to return to his digs at Mary Fullaway's; the widow had vowed never to take another United player after

George, but still needed to work and was going to take a job until George, in an act of under-reported benevolence, intervened and said he would pay for the room anyway, even though United would no longer use it, effectively paying his former landlady's pension. He would often visit. She would often joke that he could return any time he liked. Neither thought it would happen, but when O'Farrell recommended it, Best thought it was a great idea.

"Loneliness is one of the reasons for George Best's problems at Manchester United, which I have tried to solve by returning him from his luxury home to his former digs," the United boss told the press. "It's difficult to adjust from a goldfish bowl to an echo chamber. After I had finished talking to George Best, the press and television last Monday, I was looking for quietness if not isolation. But I had forgotten about the post.

"Show me the size of your club's morning mail and I'll tell you how they are doing. When things aren't going well the number of letters increases, and we've had a lot at Old Trafford lately. There are two reasons: George Best and three points from five league matches. The older correspondents suggested George should be punished severely. No doubt they are influenced by memories of their youth, when they were deprived of what we now take for granted.

"The youngsters who wrote thought George should get off scot free, arguing that what he does in his spare time is his own business. But footballers need a high standard of fitness… He should have come to see me. I was hurt that he didn't. George has been fined and has to make up for the training he missed… He has been caught up by an accumulation of problems, though there was one particular one he discussed personally with me, which I would rather not disclose. But there is no dispute over his contract... and he will not be leaving Old Trafford."

O'Farrell might have hoped that dropping Best would send a message but if it did it was only to himself – Wolves won 3-1 at Old Trafford. He was, still, defensive of his decision. "If the club thought I'd done the wrong thing in dropping him, I would be prepared to leave the club in the morning," he said. "Sir Matt Busby, who built up United, has said many times that no-one is bigger than the club. I know I'm not. And I know Sir Matt thinks he is not. So how can George Best be? He's a great player, and it is my responsibility to get him on the rails and playing for the club at his best."

United could ill-afford to be without their most talented player, even if his replacement on the day, McIlroy, scored their goal. Things continued to deteriorate even when George was back in the team. The losses against West Ham and Wolves were the first and second of seven consecutive defeats – a run only ended by a goalless draw at Everton (their fifth blank of the run). There was the consolation of the FA Cup, which George was still desperate to win – and he had something to prove following his axing. As usual, he did, scoring two goals in the third-round replay against Southampton.

"He was getting a lot of stick in the press and a week later we're playing Southampton in an FA Cup replay at home," O'Farrell said. "George gets the ball, little jink, beats a couple of players and sticks the ball in the net. He goes straight over to the press box and sticks his two fingers up. That was the dilemma with George, the team wasn't good enough to win games without him."

There were sympathetic friends in the journalist area at Old Trafford. "It came over well on television and I don't think Best will be sorry for that," Alan Thompson wrote in the *Express*. "Because it is the public pressure when all is not going well for him that turns him into a rebellious truant." Thompson had enthused over Best's match-winning influence, and said: "Best will again grab the glory, but will be generous enough to share it with his colleagues."

* * *

In late February, another world soccer star arrived on the British Isles to take some of the headlines – temporarily – from the United star. Brazilian striker Pele was on a tour of the UK with his club Santos, to take on Aston Villa and Sheffield Wednesday before playing a game in Dublin.

After Third Division Villa won their encounter 1-0, Mike Langley wrote in the *Mirror*: "Not one saw the world's greatest footballer glittering in the showcase setting of Santos FC... what they saw was a fagged-out No.10 who needs a rest, treatment, training and the stimulus of more challenging opposition... George Best should live just a few days like Pele to understand real pressure. The demands, interviews, autograph-signing continue through every waking hour. He lives to the background rhythm of a camera click."

Langley was most certainly underestimating the personal pressure put on George over the last five months, let alone the last few years. But George was a lover of the game and would have been interested to know what Pele had to say about him, even if it might not have been what he wanted to hear. "I've grown up with this," the South American said. "Life's been like this since I was 16. For some with an aggressive nature, it's not easy to withstand such pressure, but I'm a calm man like my father, and naturally good-tempered. To me, football talent is a gift of God. Something to make the best use of. Not, as George Best seems to think, something to run away from. There are moments when every player needs ease and calm, but disappearing, as Best sometimes does, is not the right way to achieve it. The public made us and we must never forget it."

Presenting Best as someone who didn't understand what media attention was, in comparison to Pele, seemed an odd position to take. It may have been a case of familiarity breeding contempt and a case of the Brazilians still seeming cosmopolitan due to the lack of coverage and the amount of hype – justified though it was.

Although Pele's appearances on English shores seemed as much diplomat and politician as they were sportsman, his pristine image and cheerful persona was a contrast to the bad boy facade projected onto – and, admittedly, often welcomed by – Best. The Brazilian press has the propensity to be as vicious as their British counterpart, but Pele was the clean-cut poster boy with three World Cup winner's medals. He had played all of his career in his home country. He was theirs and protected as a son. George, on the other hand, had gone from similar adulation to constant speculation about his life off the pitch.

In January he was in a relationship with the model Carolyn Moore. It was suggested that this new development was the reason for George going wayward – something her father, Brian Moore, took offence to. "I know that the trouble is definitely nothing to do with his relationship with Carolyn," he told reporters. "The actual reason for his present trouble is his relationship with Manchester United."

There was some truth to this. George had been elusive, as usual, to John Roberts, but when Northern Ireland played their rescheduled game against Spain in Hull, the sportswriter knew where his occasional colleague would be, for once. And, having reconciled, George had a blockbuster of a story to share.

"That was when he first told me that he was sick of United," Roberts says. "He said it was bad enough for him to ask for a move. The problem was he didn't want to make it public because he didn't want the attention. He knew it would be a huge story. He didn't want to be a prisoner for nothing so asked even though he had a column, if he could have something more for it. It wasn't a king's ransom.

"I was told that the paper wouldn't pay for it because they didn't want to be seen to be encouraging it as he was already a paid columnist. I told George the newspaper's position and he just laughed and said they would take the story but wouldn't pay for it. I felt we were both in an invidious position.

"George was frustrated because he felt he couldn't do anything about it. He felt he was almost a one-man band after the team had broken up following 1968. He said in five years Sammy McIlroy could become a great player, but he didn't have five years to wait, and he could see that there wasn't much in the interim. I don't know if it was depression he felt. There was certainly a tremendous frustration.

"Consider that you're working in an environment with lots of talented colleagues. One by one they all leave and not only are you expected to perform to your own high standard, you are expected to keep the company afloat by compensating for all that lost work. And then you would have people saying that he wasn't doing it anymore. Yes there were 10 other players on the pitch but George had been a star among stars and this was no longer the case."

Maybe depression is the wrong term. Maybe it isn't – maybe

it's completely appropriate. It is important to remember the context and the era in which these discussions were held. That also presents a different perspective on George's drinking – or, to call it what it was, bluntly, alcoholism. Alcoholism had only been categorised as an illness by the American Medical Association in 1956. Sixteen years on, it was still a concept that people struggled to comprehend, in much the same way as it took discussions about mental health – just to name one example, considering its relevance to the subject – a long time to become mainstream. Alcohol was such a strong part of the British culture, and especially in football, that nobody ever contemplated the dangers of drinking to excess.

It was difficult for anyone within the sport to intervene because they would be seen as hypocritical. Even Bobby Charlton was known to have a drop of whiskey before a game. Only David Sadler had made a passing comment – "Think of your health", he had told his former room-mate, advice ignored partly because Sadler was fastidious in comparison and partly because, even at this stage, it was too late for it to be choice.

What started as drinking as part of having a good time became a habit and then became an escape. Where once football had been the escape from the pressures of his private life, it was now again something else to escape from itself, and after the year George had endured, it was as understandable as it was tragic that he retreated into a routine of solace.

There was an important sentence in Ken Jones' write-up after the game at West Ham on New Year's Day. "He no longer gets away from defenders when he has beaten them with the ball." Best attributed this to the boggy winter pitches and the general fatigue which came as the season reached its climax. Because there is always an indisputable element of truth in that, one can see why he would consider it the dominant factor, instead of fully appreciating what was happening.

There are innumerable tragedies in George Best's life and career and it is surely one that this affliction took hold in such a way at the time it did. George had not only conquered every professional challenge put in front of him – become the best player in the country, win the European Cup, become the best in the world – he was navigating unknown waters, pioneering change for the game in a way that could not be appreciated in the contemporary time.

His magic was one thing. But then there was the creative way he used his speed and intelligence to understand a player of his talent would be targeted, so he would need to be even quicker to beat late tackles instead of simply moving his body to win a free-kick. And now the rules had caught up to allow a player like him to flourish. Within months, all of that positivity was gone because of a horrendous set of circumstances which included his and Manchester United's malaise.

United had gone from top to eighth by mid-March. They had conceded 45 goals in 31 games. In a 2-0 defeat at Spurs in early March, one newspaper report described Best, Law and Charlton as "pale shadows of the men who carried United to the head of the table earlier in the season".

George never went on record as saying he had confided in O'Farrell as he had done to Busby about the weak squad. By all testimonies, the manager was so withdrawn that he would have had a job trying if he wanted to. Still, O'Farrell's response was to sign two players – though, as Stepney opined, it was a case of shutting the stable door after the horse had bolted.

Martin Buchan came from Aberdeen, captaincy material from the start in the backline with a presence and authority to match his significant defensive talent. And Ian Storey-Moore, the Nottingham Forest winger, was signed for a club record fee of £200,000. That took the spending to just over £330,000 in a week – one report suggested that outlay would be recuperated by the £300,000 sale of George to Derby. "It is ludicrous even to suppose that we would let Best go," O'Farrell retorted. "How could I sell such a player – and who could afford him? He is very much a part of my future plans."

In 1967, Best had named Storey-Moore as one of the top players of the previous season, describing his form as "amazing"; whilst it is not certain how much influence, if any, George had on this signing, it was one he probably gave the thumbs up to. And for the new man himself, the opportunity to play with George was a personal dream realised. "Everyone knew him as a wondrously gifted player so for myself to come from where I had and now share a dressing room with one of the icons of British football was a privilege, a real privilege," Storey-Moore says. "I had never heard of the praise he'd given me before... it was very kind, and the feeling was more than mutual.

"Part of the reason I went there was George. It was probably every player's ambition to play with him, quite aside from the club being fantastic. He was a very charming, very friendly, you couldn't wish to meet a nicer guy. Our partnership on the pitch took off a little bit. He was apparently known to be upset with the quality of the squad though I never saw him express that in training or in matches. George always seemed to enjoy his football and his training."

Storey-Moore's presence helped as hoped, in the short term, anyway. He scored on his debut and it seemed that another tricky forward player would again take some of the attention from George; he too scored against Huddersfield on March

11, his first goal in the league since the hat-trick at The Dell. "Yes, a great beginning for Storey-Moore," wrote Paul Doherty of the *People*. "But still the top billing must go to Best. All the familiar cheek, trickery and bounce was back as he tormented the Huddersfield defence."

Best did everything in his power to prolong United's stay in the FA Cup, but they were eliminated by Stoke City in the quarter-final after a replay, despite George scoring in both games. And with trophy aspirations gone for another year, it was another stagger towards the finish line, with United only able to win when Best and Storey-Moore turned it on. They both scored in wins against Palace, Southampton and Stoke, all at Old Trafford. Best's standout individual moment was at Highfield Road when Storey-Moore nodded down Buchan's long free-kick and Best followed the bounce of the ball, timing his half-volley with perfection. The 25-yard shot flew into the corner for the first goal in a 3-2 win.

Other than that, results were concerning – a 3-0 home reverse to Liverpool, a 3-1 home defeat to City, and a 3-0 loss at Arsenal in which Ken Jones described George as "almost anonymous", which was fitting, as by his own admission he was beginning to wish he wasn't there. George ended with 26 goals in all competitions – not quite the career high he had set as a target, though more than respectable in the circumstances – but in those last few months the same magic and wonder of the early autumn was notable by its absence.

Prior to the final game of the season – played in front of an Old Trafford low of 34,959 for the campaign – Hugh Ash of the *Mirror* asked some fans on the streets of Manchester what they would do with their troubled player. Their response, according to the headline – "SELL BEST, SAY FANS!"

Actions speak louder than words – George was reminded of the adoration the fans at large had for him when he scored in United's last game of the season – but the memory of the words remained, particularly for a person enduring such an emotional time. George was used to getting abuse from opposition players and rival supporters. His own, though? "When your own fans start turning on you and mocking you, that is hurtful," George recalled. "I began asking myself, 'Do I need all this?' and began answering that I didn't."

The worst thing that he could have at this moment was downtime – but that's precisely what he had, with a few weeks to kill before Northern Ireland's game with Scotland on May 20. He was due to join up with the squad on May 19.

George was going through an existential crisis. If his heart was not in football then what would he do with his life? It was a serious enough question to himself, so serious in fact that when the time was approaching to report for international duty, he went into fight or flight mode; and as was always the case, he chose flight.

MARBELLA

With time to wallow, George Best was able to allow all the pities to consume him. Now the season was over, he moved out of Mrs Fullaway's again and back into his house in Bramhall, having failed to convince Frank O'Farrell to get the club to buy it from him.

He told friends he planned to go to the Seychelles and not report for international duty. They talked him out of it. On the evening before he was due to join up with Northern Ireland, George was restless and couldn't sleep. He went out and came back home. Still awake at sunrise, he made an impulsive decision to go to Manchester Airport. The quickest way to get to Marbella, his favourite haunt, was to go via London, so he flew down there.

"When he arrived in Marbella I had a call from Eddie Hindle, one of his pals, who was at Manchester Airport," John Roberts recalls. "He said that I should come. This was before any of the news broke. I talked to our London office and they were sending a man from Madrid, but Eddie insisted it could be serious. I wasn't able to get there."

The press at large got wind of where George was and traced him to the Skol Hotel. On the eve of a big game, they put two and two together – one headline asked 'Has Best walked out of soccer?' Only one reporter got a line from him. "People can think what they like," he said on the evening of his arrival. "I have come here to relax for a few days and that's all I will say." He later said his intention was to stay there for a few months.

It was inevitable he would miss the Scotland game, but national team captain Derek Dougan appealed for George to come back for the following games against England and Wales. "There is no feeling among the players that George has let them down," he said. "He is a great player and there is no better sight in football than Best in full song. We need George."

The matter should also have rung alarm bells for Frank O'Farrell. Funnily enough, he was close enough to have possibly intervened. United were on a post-season tour, and had played in Majorca on May 18. They were moving on to Athens and then Israel, when George was due to report – and, bizarrely, the boss washed his hands of it, though he perhaps did not understand quite how serious it was. "I'm sorry this has happened," he said. "But it is the Irish FA's problem. We knew we would not have Best for our first two tour games. I expect to see him in Tel Aviv on May 28 for our third game."

It was most certainly his problem on the morning of Sunday May 21. With no John Roberts on the scene, it was the *Mirror* who claimed a world exclusive which rightfully took front page. "I QUIT BY GEORGE BEST" read the bold headline. There was no ambiguity.

"Tomorrow is my 26th birthday, the day I will always remember as the day I quit the game," he said. "It is finished. For good. I've made up my mind to get out before the game kills me. These last six to seven months have all gone sour on me. It became work instead of the sport I have always enjoyed and would play for nothing. Last year I began to wake up in the mornings dreading the thought of training."

More comments, all worthy of headlines all on their own – "matchdays became a nightmare", "going on for two years", "mentally and physically I am a bloody wreck".

"Visits to doctors and psychiatrists to try to help myself. Sleeping pills that proved useless. Not eating, not sleeping… I was in a void of despair, frightening of the telephone's ring, fearing the sound of the doorbell. I dreaded the cranks who rang me 24 hours a day threatening violence and death; of giggling girls who rang at 3am… I have not yet told Manchester United or the Irish selectors of my decision. It will come as a tremendous shock to them.

"It would be hateful to me for the fans to see me as a 'has-been'. It is right, I feel, that they should remember the real George Best. It might have all been different if I had married when I was 19. I have to get myself right. I hope to find myself again. When I can sleep eight hours at night I know I will be getting better. I want to eliminate forever the memory of the man I became. What I would like to do was to go home to my mother and father in Belfast… Unfortunately the state of things over there now is such that I dare not go home."

Carolyn Moore – still his girlfriend – admitted that he'd been depressed since the end of the season but that this had come as just as big a shock to her as everyone else.

And yet there were moments you could read between the

lines. His admission that he hadn't spoken to United seemed like a cry for help. He told Ken Graham of the *People*: "I just don't know where I'm going from here."

He confessed to another reporter, Bob Russell, that his decision had been inspired by United's downfall. "If my club had won just one thing last season… anything. I don't think I would have packed it in," he said. "I would have gone on for at least one more year. I hoped beyond hope that this was going to be one year in which United re-emerged as a winning team. We started so well. I had never felt so fresh, so stimulated for a new season. We were winning again. I was getting goals. I felt free… then, suddenly, it started to go badly for all of us."

On May 23, Sir Matt Busby told journalists he had "no intention" of meeting George and insisted he had "nothing to do with this matter". United played in Israel on May 30 and flew straight back to Manchester. George had also returned to put his house up for sale. Stories circulated that O'Farrell had met George to discuss it – but Best flew back to Spain, telling reporters he'd only returned to sell the house.

"I was told by one of his pals that he had already seen Frank and that he wasn't going to quit," John Roberts says. "I went to see George at an opening of a restaurant or a club and showed him the story I'd drafted. He said it was right but asked me not to quote him because Frank would go mad. George's agent asked me to call Frank, so I did. He was keen for me to help present it so it wouldn't look like a capitulation by the club. I went to see George again to try and get something more from him and it was obvious he was just fulfilling an obligation."

Without a quote, the story ran as speculation. George had given the bombshell story in the hope it would make reporters leave him alone for a while. After the furore of the first few days, they did. George admitted that a couple of weeks lounging around in the sun became boring. Distance and space gave him time to consider what had been on his mind in those days at home. He did want to play football. He felt that was his purpose. He also didn't want to play for anyone other than United, although he said nobody from the club had contacted him. In any event, it was on June 10 when he told the public of his intention, coming clean to say that he had seen O'Farrell (and later admitting it was he who had made the approach, and not the manager).

"It's amazing what a few weeks with the sun on your back can do," he said. "I've cut out most of the booze, it's not a case of not needing it anymore… simply not wanting it. I'm playing a lot of tennis and training on the beach as though it was the start of a new season. It's amazing the way it's all changed. Nobody influenced me. I saw Frank O'Farrell in Manchester, but my mind was already made up. I wanted to play again. He seemed to understand what had been eating into me."

O'Farrell's response was to treat it as a minor hiccup, which was probably for the best: "I never thought George would quit. Despite some unpredictable actions, I felt his great love for football would decide."

Those who had been through drama with George before were coming close to the end of their tether. Sir Matt Busby, who had said four weeks earlier that he was nothing to do with it, now suggested there were conditions in place for George if he was serious about playing again. "George's re-entry into soccer will be subject to certain reservations," he said. "Best is a genius. But we are no longer prepared to tolerate his wayward behaviour. The problem is that he has had as much adulation as Pele and he got it very young… if he got married and settled down, it would help somewhat, but his present behaviour has got to stop."

In his 1973 book *Soccer At The Top*, which was being written that summer, Busby went into more detail, conceding that he did not want George to leave the club. "George Best was a problem legacy," Busby said. "Many experts in the game would like such a problem. I did not believe his indiscretions would be cured by saying, 'You have finished with Manchester United.'

"He was still young, still in some ways immature. Some of the immense pressures, he brought on himself. He ran away from problems instead of facing them. But I set great store by patience. We had to hope that he would be cured, this the greatest entertainer, the world's most gifted player, who, man and boy, filled football grounds wherever he played and made people gasp and laugh by his sheer audacity… A man does not give up sons who love him as he loves them – unless they are determined to leave the nest. If the boy is sick, a father doesn't kick him out. He hopes for a cure."

His team-mates were nonplussed, going by their comments in the press. Willie Morgan: "I just don't care what George says he is going to do next. I can't believe what he says because he changes his mind so quickly, and so often." And Brian Kidd was even more annoyed. "There's one set of rules for George and one for the rest of us," he told David Meek.

Bobby Charlton went on holiday to Bermuda and seemed quite cross about it. "If it wasn't for him, we wouldn't be going on holiday to Bermuda," he said. "It's impossible to go anywhere in Europe because you get pounded by British tourists asking what's happening to George Best."

Norma Charlton – Bobby's wife – felt George had behaved without consideration for his team-mates: "All the people connected with the team have their phones ringing perpetually. Why doesn't George face the publicity himself? But no. He stays in Europe on holiday and attracts the publicity, so that it goes on and on."

The difficulty was almost certainly down to the generation gap between the players. They shared so many things in common – but Charlton despaired at Best's immaturity, and, in return, George would often mock his team-mate's ultra-professionalism. It was a shame that whilst at Old Trafford in these latter years, the pair did not make a more concerted effort to mend their professional differences so that they were on the same page. Especially considering George appeared to be taking a leaf out of Charlton's book when he reported back three days early for pre-season, and trained at the Ship Canal with the apprentices and goalkeepers Alex Stepney and Jimmy Rimmer. "I've lost five pounds in weight, I feel good, and I had my first cup of tea from the Old Trafford kitchen," he said triumphantly. "It tasted like champagne."

Stepney shared the disappointment of some of his fellow senior players but had a little more sympathy for George. "I was as upset as the supporters when he first announced he was giving up the game," he says. "But I want to explain how the mood at the club was changing. When Matt was there we'd have training with Jack Crompton from 10 to 12 and then we'd go across to the pub just to have a sandwich. We'd decide amongst ourselves to go back to the Cliff, four or five of us, just to keep training. But by the time Frank was there, that feeling had changed. Now when we left training we just went home.

"When George came back after the summer he'd obviously put on a bit of weight but he worked his socks off to get it off. The problem was that the mood around the club was still dark and once the initial buzz of coming back wore off it was the same old lack of enthusiasm... you could see in George's face that he didn't feel the same as he did when Matt was there. Maybe if he'd come back and Frank had brought in some players to do the job around him. But he didn't. So then you had a mixture of George trying to do his usual things while he was still trying to get back to full fitness, and then, George taking the responsibility to drop deeper and deeper to try and help his team out because we were struggling. He was trying. It was not through a lack of effort on George's part."

There were also more concerted efforts to change – George was going to take responsibility for his living arrangements. Sort of. He felt guilt for putting Mrs Fullaway back under the strain of the media attention and so was not going to return there. Sir Matt Busby offered George a room in his house; an arrangement the player felt completely impractical. Thankfully, Pat Crerand, now a coach at the club, stepped in to offer a room at his house. "I think I can help George," he told reporters. "If he settles down – and I think he will – he can become the best player in the world again." The arrangement lasted a week – Crerand's gesture had come without considering the impact it would have on his three young children, and as George's dedication to training did not include a self-prohibition on a social life, it was agreed that he would move back to Aycliffe Avenue with Mary Fullaway.

Still, George kept up a positive outlook. Despite the reservations of his peers, he insisted: "Since I came back they've been great. They understand me better than people outside the game. Now it's up to me to prove United made the right decision. The only way I can do that is on the football pitch. I feel great. I can't wait to play again... I know if I do anything wrong again, it will probably be the end. United could have thrown me out, put me on the transfer list. I think they have been very good."

His intent was genuine but it did not appear to be the rosy homecoming he'd hoped for. His apologies were followed by warning statements by the manager that seemed unnecessary.

On August 4, O'Farrell said: "George Best has a part to play that may be all-important to this team and he knows that if he doesn't knuckle down he will be away. Look at it from the point of view of the team. They train hard and they always try hard and George has got to be the same. Everybody had a great regard for his skills, but he has got to become far more professional in his general attitude. The onus is all on him... the challenge now facing him could make him as a man. Or it could go the other way."

Then, on August 7: "George Best's career is at the crossroads. He knows it. But I wonder if those who are so quick to criticise George know what it can mean to be pitchforked like him, into a glamorous life for which he wasn't equipped. Sometimes it is hard to live with fame. That, perhaps, has been George Best's biggest problem. The George Best I know has this great love of football. He would be lost without the game. All George has to do is keep fit. Last season he didn't lose his skills, he lost – or surrendered – those razor-sharp reflexes which put him among the aces. Without his speed and acceleration, he gets caught in possession and risks injury."

The authoritarian tone felt unknowingly detrimental. "Frank's nickname was the Reverend," Jimmy Rimmer recalls. "Nothing wrong with religion, and I know that George respected him and gave his best, especially at the start, but they didn't really get on that much and it was clear to see after a while that George was not enjoying it as much as he used to. It became more instructional. I think Frank tried to control him. There was no need to do that with George, and to try would be counter-productive. Obviously George had to behave, I just think they went about it in the wrong way."

That was especially so at the start of the season. Best played no pre-season games but was in the team for the opening day of the league campaign. Ipswich were the visitors to Old Trafford and claimed a 2-1 win which was a shock to anyone seeing the result but not the game. Ipswich planned for the reputation and not the ability of Manchester United – and it earned them a rich reward. Ian Collard had been tasked with man-marking Best, and said after the game: "I finished up feeling sorry for him. Bobby Robson, our manager, told me to do a tight-marking job on Best. The longer the game went on, the further back he dropped to try to lose me. He was swearing to himself and getting more and more upset. And I reckon it will get worse for him as the season goes on."

United lost 2-0 at Anfield. Then again at Everton, when O'Farrell dropped Bobby Charlton from the team, a decision so shocking that it caused Sir Matt Busby to intervene. O'Farrell was right to do it – Charlton was coming towards the end of his career and it was prime time to get new blood instead of relying on the old guard – but things were falling away from him so fast that he was alienating everyone. He later confessed that Best, for all his problems, had papered over many issues. "He was the key, really," O'Farrell said. "He was carrying the team. And once he stopped turning up, it complicated things."

O'Farrell's retreat from his players was accompanied by the relinquishing of his newspaper column. He even stayed away from Old Trafford for the game against Leicester City – and missed George's first goal and best performance of the season in a 1-1 draw. The manager admitted he was at another game scouting for players. One newspaper column had projected that it would cost O'Farrell at least £1m to get United challenging. David Nish, at £225,000, had become the most expensive player in the country in August when he moved to Derby.

Still, the manager deliberated his options. August had been a disaster. Three defeats and three draws, just two goals. In a goalless draw against Arsenal, Best had been praised for showing "leadership and a tremendous sense of responsibility". Positivity and entertainment were two more factors generally missing from United's season, although George did his utmost to inject some when they travelled to Upton Park.

Ten minutes in, wearing United's vibrant yellow away strip, he received a pass in the middle of the park and quickly shifted his feet to move past his marker, Bryan 'Pop' Robson. Robson got a touch to the tackle but Best displayed that tenacity to move away from his opponent. From 25 yards he struck a powerful shot that caught the keeper off guard and went in.

Unfortunately, in their vivid strip United looked more like Oxford than Brazil. O'Farrell's defence was weak – Sadler was suffering with inconsistency, but considering he was alongside O'Neil and James, one might appreciate why. Buchan, the silver lining, had been moved into the holding midfield role assumed by Gowling a year earlier. It wasn't working. The defence was porous. Best, despite his efforts, was unable to compensate for his team's shortcomings. It was his smart feet and fast thinking that created a second goal for his team – Storey-Moore netting – but West Ham scored two to draw.

"He's back in business as Britain's greatest footballer," Brian Hadley said in his report for the *People*. "And, after this performance United can have no doubt that whatever headaches he gives them, he's worth forgiving. For if ever one man kept a team alive, it was Best in this match. He didn't just give them the kiss of life. He performed a major operation."

The off-pitch surgery finally began later in the month when O'Farrell made his first signing of the season. That was Wyn Davies from Manchester City for £60,000; weeks later, Ted MacDougall signed for £220,000 from Bournemouth. It took nine winless games from the opening day to prompt him into action – and by that time, any positivity of a new season had completely evaporated, with George tempted back into the old routine of drowning his sorrows. The new signings were not going to inspire a turnaround in form. By the end of October United had won only three games and, just four years after winning the European Cup, were only saved from bottom place in the league by goal difference.

* * *

In October, Northern Ireland's qualifying campaign for the 1974 World Cup got under way with a trip to Sofia to face Bulgaria. George reported early for international duty for the flight from London, saying: "This could be my last chance in the World Cup. I want to make it count."

In Sofia he described it as "the game of my life". It didn't go well. Best – with his existing difficulty with officials in such games – found no protection. He was sent off eight minutes from the end of a 3-0 defeat in which Bulgaria were awarded two penalties. "They were at me right from the start," he said. "They were niggling, heel-tapping, jersey-pulling and elbowing. It was a disgrace. I was kicked by their No.10 as I was making a clearance. I fell to the ground and, as I got up, No.8 kicked me on the back of the leg. I kicked back but didn't actually hit him. I feel very low and I don't want to talk about it now. Maybe I'll have more to say in the morning."

"By now, I had already done enough damage to my body that training had become an effort," George later wrote in his book *Blessed*. "It had become like work, when before it had been more like fun, something that came entirely naturally to me. My good intentions didn't last long. We got off to a terrible start to the 1972/73 season and didn't even win until the tenth league match. I tried to tell myself that I couldn't go on the way I had been, that I had to stay fit and turn up for training every day… My life came completely off the rails in a real black November in 1972. Poor results had worn away my determination to stay on track and twice I just couldn't be bothered to get up for training and was dropped."

Those issues about being targeted became a bigger problem with Best's physical lethargy. O'Farrell was under pressure to play his new men – which in turn put greater pressure on the creative talent. Willie Morgan believes it was a complicated issue – of O'Farrell wanting his players to run through drills, and other teams being wise to it. "It was alright with Frank at first," Morgan says. "He had Malcolm Musgrove as coach and they would run through drills again and again. 'Alex, when you get the ball give it to Nobby, Nobby you give it to Paddy, Paddy you give it to Bobby. George you move there.' This sort of stuff. We would look at each other and wonder what the hell he was going on about. But I think the difficulty started with Wilf and it was difficult for Frank to turn it around…

"I'm not saying Frank was the right man, but it was much more difficult for him. The difference for me and George was that you would have three or four players around you. They didn't have to worry about the others because they were no bloody good. It made it more difficult. It was no fun. We spent more time getting back and helping the team defend. It was hard work, it was a hard slog and it wasn't very enjoyable.

"Players were coming to the end, and they were replaced by players who just weren't good enough. Nice lads, but it was bloody hard for them. I didn't feel let down by George. It was hard for him. When you played the way we did we relied on others getting the ball to us. That was happening less frequently. And even when we got the bloody thing it was frustrating because there was nobody to play with. With the greatest of respect for those lads, they just weren't good enough, and I could understand George's frustrations. I was having the same problems on the other side of the pitch. We would comment at half-time about how tough it was."

Sammy McIlroy – one of the few emerging players Best believed could come good – sympathised with both George and the club's plight. "George was getting a little disgruntled," he says. "It wasn't too long ago since we won the European Cup. He wanted the club to spend a few bob, get players in and build around him. It's very hard…

"When things started to go bad, Frank and Malcolm – who were nice people – were under enormous pressure. It would have been hard to even try because it's not so straightforward as money replacing the likes of Law, Charlton, Crerand. Even if those players were coming to the end it would still be difficult. I think George saw the European Cup as the start, something to move forward and build on. But so many key figures at the club started retiring and they weren't being replaced. The club was going through a transition off and on the pitch."

After another humbling by neighbours City, George missed training on Monday. When he went in on Tuesday, late, he claimed he had the flu, saying he "didn't understand what all the fuss was about". Malcolm Musgrove put him through a one-man session and told reporters, "George seems OK now, but it seems he has had a chill or something. And he's a bit depressed".

O'Farrell had said earlier that morning that he was waiting for George to contact the club before deciding what disciplinary action to take. He could ill-afford to drop him, so he was in the team for a crucial 2-1 win over Southampton. Crucial in another respect – Davies and MacDougall scored, giving the beleaguered manager much-needed vindication.

So when George was involved in a nightclub incident on November 29, where a girl accused him of hitting her – he claimed he was pushing her away softly in self-defence – O'Farrell felt emboldened to finally take a stand. It was rumoured that he would place George on the transfer list. In the meantime, he was dropped from the team for the trip to Norwich, with Storey-Moore and MacDougall, the manager's signings again, scoring in a 2-0 win.

George spent the weekend in Manchester. He was put through one of Bill Foulkes' fitness regimes. But once O'Farrell was back on Monday morning, George decided not to report, and went to London instead. When he didn't report on Tuesday, it was the straw that broke the camel's back as far as O'Farrell was concerned – he told the board, in Best's absence, that he was suspending the player for two weeks and instructed them to tell the press he was making him available for transfer for £300,000. "It is a thousand pities that we should have this problem at Old Trafford," he told the *Mirror*. "In my view it is a human problem as well as a football problem… we are losing a great footballer, but the decision is final."

As that news reverberated around the football world, a plethora of clubs were linked with him. Spanish football was set to enter a new era after a 10-year ban on signing foreign players – Real Madrid and Barcelona were both linked. So too were Manchester City, who had a lot of George's friends in their team. O'Farrell said nobody had been in touch in the first three days.

The manager's decision was final but his own long-term future at United was not guaranteed. He had Law on the bench for a 2-0 defeat at home to Stoke. Two days later, Best returned to Manchester to see Sir Matt and chairman Louis Edwards. Busby asked if he really wanted to leave United. George said he couldn't imagine playing for anyone else – and repeated the same concerns about the standard of player the club were signing. What followed was an embarrassing episode; at the same time as the meeting, O'Farrell was telling reporters he had no idea what was happening with George. And, no sooner had he said it, Edwards was announcing to the press that George had been taken off the transfer list because he "only wants to play for Manchester United".

O'Farrell was fuming. He had already been undermined by Busby stepping in to ensure Charlton was recalled to the team at the start of the season, and felt – probably fairly – that the same was happening again. He confronted George in the dressing room at the Cliff, complaining he went behind his back. George knew he had – so just shrugged. He was back again, it seemed, but still under the suspension imposed by the club, so wasn't considered for the game at Crystal Palace.

Palace won 5-0. Everything went as wrong as it possibly

could, and ominously, Louis Edwards spent more time talking to Scotland manager Tommy Docherty – present to watch some of his players – than he did his own manager. After the game, O'Farrell was keen to make everything look like a big misunderstanding.

"We had heard nothing from Best after the announcement that he had been suspended and placed on the transfer list," he said. "The chairman was anxious that stalemate should not develop and he said he thought it in the club's best interest to have a talk to Best and find out what was on his mind. When I arrived home on Thursday evening after that meeting had taken place I was told that the chairman had been trying to contact me, but when I rang him back the line was engaged. A few minutes later a reporter phoned me and I had to say that I didn't know what had taken place. It was unfortunate but the chairman had definitely tried to contact me."

There had been a meeting scheduled for the Tuesday after the Palace game to discuss what to do moving forward. "The meeting will be a long one," the manager said. "The position of George Best will be discussed, but that is only one of the items on the agenda."

Indeed it was.

The main item was O'Farrell's own position – and the club informed him that he was relieved of his duties. So too was Malcolm Musgrove, and somewhat surprisingly, John Aston Snr. The players were informed that Bill Foulkes and Paddy Crerand would take temporary charge until a successor was hired. George – taking responsibility, and feeling the shame which had been projected on to him – took decisive action. He also knew that Crerand and Foulkes wouldn't be leading things for very long, and whoever O'Farrell's successor was, it was bound to take time to turn things around. He wrote a letter to the board.

"I am afraid, through my somewhat unorthodox ways of trying to sort my own problems out, I have caused Manchester United even bigger problems," he wrote. "I came back hoping my appetite for the game would return and even though in every game I like to think I gave 100 per cent, there was something missing. Even now I am not sure what. Therefore I have decided not to play football again and this time no-one will change my mind.

"In conclusion I would like to wish the club the best of luck for the remainder of the season and for the future. Because even though I personally have tarnished the club's name in recent times, to me and thousands of others, Manchester United still means something special."

But this wasn't exclusively George's decision to make. Unbeknown to him, the decision had been taken to sack him too. "We've finally had enough of George," Sir Matt Busby told the press. "We've finally had to decide to get him out of our hair once and for all. All of us on the board were at the end of our tether."

It seemed as if there would be no going back this time.

DOCTOR'S ORDERS

Manchester United hired Tommy Docherty as successor to Frank O'Farrell. His task in 1973 was to save the club from relegation. He used his contact book from his time with Scotland to recruit a number of players to boost the team; Lou Macari, a diminutive forward, was added to the front line, Jim Holton, an imposing defender, was added to the defence, and George Graham, a hopefully calming presence in midfield, was also signed.

United were much better in the second half of the season, although the bar for improvement was set very low. A run of eight games unbeaten – featuring five wins – did the job although it was very clear to see that this was a club deep in transition. Docherty was going to have to make some tough decisions with regards the composition of his squad. He was not afraid to do so – Ted MacDougall, who had only just signed for a large fee, was instantly out of favour. Docherty also decided he wasn't going to renew Denis Law's contract as the striker was barely able to train due to his knee injuries.

Perhaps the biggest issue was the future of Bobby Charlton – the long-serving forward made it easy for the new manager by saying he would retire at the end of the season. But even Charlton's own career – by any definition a complete and fulfilled one, with the most appearances and goals of any player in the club's history – came with an observation, echoed by the man himself, that he might not and possibly even should not have had the opportunity to say 'when'.

The club had been stabilised, and nobody could really argue with the manager's decisions. However, his manner left a lot to be desired. Law claims he was told he would be receiving a new contract, and went home to Scotland for the off-season, only to learn watching the news the next day he had been released. Even Docherty's own lieutenants weren't safe. He named George Graham as his captain, but as Graham struggled to adapt to life at the club, that decision was soon reversed.

"I was called into the office by Doc who said George Graham had been struggling and wanted to relinquish the captaincy," Willie Morgan recalls. "Doc said he'd spoken to Matt Busby and Louis Edwards and they had suggested me as the successor. I accepted. A week later George complained I'd taken the captaincy from him. He said he hadn't spoken to Doc for months."

All was not completely rosy in the new era then. United were functional but most definitely missing the stardust of George Best – as, to be fair, they had been throughout most of 1972, even when he was playing. They were ordinary.

Docherty had even managed to annoy Best. Although club

and player had both agreed to part ways, United's decision to 'sack' George did not extend to releasing his registration. It was a constant feature as speculation raged in the months following his exit. He was not short of offers.

The first came from those who knew him. Noel Cantwell was manager of Peterborough. He had dinner with George and invited him to training; Cantwell left that night expecting his former team-mate to show the next morning. It never happened. Neither did a move to Swansea, now managed by Harry Gregg. Gregg claimed he was told personally by George that he would sign for him; but, as he tended to do, George was afraid of letting him down so got his friend Malcolm Wagner to call Harry to tell him he wouldn't be going there.

Docherty had branded the Swansea talk as "a sick joke", though when New York Cosmos of the NASL expressed an interest, United did confirm that they would not sue George for breach of contract if he wished to play in America. George flew out with Wagner to North America to discuss the offer with Clive Toye, general manager of the Cosmos.

"We needed to do things to attract the media and the people and burst soccer into view," Toye says. "George was not only good on the field but noticeable, shall we say, off the field. I'd known Tommy Docherty for years. Somehow or other I got permission to fly George to New York. It was chats and smiles all round and then George went home. I followed him after further chats with United. The deal was more or less done over the phone and when I arrived in Manchester I finished off all the negotiations with the club secretary.

"We were going to pay ten thousand dollars or pounds to United for each game where George turned up fit and ready to play. With the deal done we just needed to get George to sign it. So we set off around Manchester to find him, just so he could sign the contract and we could go. We looked all over and couldn't find him. He wasn't in any bar or club we were told he would be. Pat Crerand said he would help. He went looking and he couldn't find him. Eventually I left word that I would be at the airport at 11am the next day. He could come and find me to sign the contract, or he could forget about it."

George, of course, could be evasive in any environment. Ironically for someone who complained about being in a goldfish bowl, he had an uncanny knack of disappearing when the mood took him. Before he'd even left New York after agreeing with Toye that he'd go to the Cosmos, he had changed his mind, considering that the reality of living in the Big Apple would be far different from a break for a few days.

Months passed and George remained inactive. On March 27, Irish FA secretary Billy Drennan made a seemingly innocuous comment: "If Manchester United don't want Best, we certainly do." Best responded by saying he would be happy to consider it if it was a case of only playing a couple of matches – but, when it was put to Tommy Docherty, he indicated that he would only release George for international duty if he was at least training with United (he had said something similar when first quizzed about Swansea's interest).

It started a chain reaction. Best's response: "There's now no question of me making a comeback." United – realising there was no way they were likely to get a fee from any potential suitor with that condition – sent out word to reporters that they would no longer insist on George returning there first.

"I will consider any offers that come in," George responded. "It wouldn't matter where they came from… It was the obvious thing for United to do if they want to get a fee for me. They knew there was no question of me returning to Old Trafford to train."

Complications made that unlikely scenario happen, though. In late April, Brian Madley of the *People* reported George had been offered the "biggest commercial contract ever offered to a British sports star" – around £100,000 over five years – but it carried a stipulation that he must be active as a sportsman. New York Cosmos again made their offer to take George.

And, over Easter, Queens Park Rangers were promoted to the First Division and their manager Gordon Jago – an ambitious, forward-thinking coach who had spent time in America – expressed publicly that he would be interested in bringing George to Loftus Road. When it was hinted to George that he might be considered for selection to face England in May if he trained, he did indeed report to the Cliff to begin a one-person regime. It lasted all of four days – he was back on April 26, but when the squad was named on May 1 and he wasn't in it, George went to Majorca instead.

A few days passed and George started to feel a pain in his leg that was shooting down to his calf. On May 8 he was concerned enough to cut short his holiday and fly back home to Manchester, arranging to meet his doctor at the airport. From there he was rushed to hospital suffering from thrombosis. Doctors said that he had trained too hard after months away from the training pitch, and it had caused a painful blood clot. Any hard physical exercise would have to wait until early August on their recommendation.

While George was in the hospital, he was visited by Sir Matt Busby. After some general conversation, Busby said: "It's about time you were back playing, isn't it?" George didn't take the comment too seriously until he was later visited by Paddy

Crerand who suggested the same. Crerand was working as Docherty's assistant and said the manager would like to meet George to discuss a comeback. Docherty had observed a couple of comments George had made about returning to play for his country and noted how he reiterated that although he didn't have any intention of playing club football, he would only ever want to play for Manchester United anyway.

By then United's pre-season was under way and Docherty was less than enthralled by the creativity on his books. He'd also spent a lot of money upon arrival, and wasn't likely to be given much more. On the books was a player named George Best, a former European Footballer of the Year. A player who had all the qualities this team were crying out for. Docherty couldn't resist; in many ways, it would have been negligent of him to not at least try. In early September 1973 the pair agreed to meet and George agreed to give it another go. Considering George's history, they also agreed that if he did miss a morning session, he should make up for it with afternoon sessions.

On Monday September 10, George reported to training at the Cliff – he was an hour late, but this was one occasion where it was okay, as he was only scheduled to have tests and be put through his paces. He passed a medical check with a clean bill of health, and behind closed doors, took part in a training match of walking football where he played in goal for an hour.

It was done that way to avoid the eyes of the press who were camped outside. United were reluctant to put George in front of them straight away, but Docherty was never shy, and revelled in the public spotlight being Manchester United manager gave him. "The quicker you leave him alone the better chance he's got of making it," he told them. "The longer the press keep away from George Best the better for him. The comeback of George Best is the most controversial happening in my nine-month career at Old Trafford, but this time I believe he's not in the mood to embarrass anybody. And it's my job to make sure it doesn't…

"Considering he's been out for nine months, I was surprised to find George looking in such remarkable condition – only 10lb overweight. Except for Sir Matt Busby, my predecessors neglected George when he was going through troubled times. But I won't let this happen. I'm known as a players' manager and I'll strike up a relationship with George… I don't expect him to be an angel. In fact, I don't want him to become one. George will find a changed atmosphere at Old Trafford. He'll find the club is a family again."

Once more, intentions were positive. Docherty showed that he wasn't intending for it to be a quick fix by explaining he wanted to ease George back in gradually. It was fortunate that there were three friendlies in October to help bring him back up to speed. The first was a testimonial for Denis Law against Ajax on October 3. Law had reacted to Docherty's snub by agreeing a one-year deal with Manchester City that would take him up to the 1974 World Cup and retirement, but had still been granted his benefit match as a result of spending 10 years at Old Trafford.

As it was, a groin injury kept Denis out of the game, so all eyes were on George. He played the entire 90 minutes but was underwhelming simply because of the extra weight he was carrying. A couple of days later he played in a reserve game against Aston Villa at Old Trafford, suffering a minor injury to his leg. The energy levels were increasing, while reserve-team boss Bill Foulkes said: "His distribution was impeccable."

George worked hard for the next couple of weeks and was

picked to travel to Dublin for a friendly against Shamrock Rovers. He was more positionally disciplined than usual but still tried a few tricks, to the delight of all in attendance. Docherty described his performance as "scintillating". The game had to be abandoned 10 minutes from time due to supporters spilling on the pitch in an attempt to get close to George.

In the late September international break, some of the players not called up for their country were able to take advantage of the time to have a golfing break. George accompanied them to Majorca and, due to his friendships with many publicans on the island, he ensured his team-mates were given a more hospitable welcome than usual.

"We rarely saw him on that trip," Brian Greenhoff, a young defender breaking through, recalled. "It was probably the last thing he needed. It was arguably the least fit he'd ever been and he could have done with staying behind and having a mini pre-season." But George was using the warm weather to help him get back sharp. And, with a combination of his better-than-expected display against Shamrock Rovers, and United losing three games consecutively, George was told he would be in the squad to face Birmingham in the First Division.

He roomed with Greenhoff at Mottram Hall. Brian didn't know what to expect when he got to their room after he'd been playing snooker, but George was already there and ready to sleep. Brian asked if he should order breakfast for the morning, but George said he'd sorted that and the newspapers. The youngster was a little star-struck. He'd only been in the first-team set-up a matter of weeks. What was part of the old routine for George stuck with the impressionable Barnsley boy, appreciative of being treated as an equal.

"The young players loved him," Alex Stepney confirms.

"When they came through as apprentices or kids they grew up watching George at his best. They idolised him, adored him as an icon, that's what he was as a player and that's what he was to them."

Jimmy Rimmer's memory is similar – but felt that the positive impact of that could only go so far. "Those lads looked up to him," he says. "I know he would always talk to them and try and give them advice if he felt able to, if he was asked. There's a limit to that, though, because how could George teach what he was able to do, when sometimes he didn't even know? How do you pass that on? He would probably even do the opposite to what he was thinking at any given time."

Those unfamiliar with George were more generous and appreciative of what they still had, rather than carrying that nostalgic tone you can almost feel in the words of the players who had been alongside George earlier on. To be fair, even Stepney would still try and explain away what was happening to George physically as it seems he didn't want to accept it.

Lou Macari, for example, always speaks positively about having the opportunity to be at the club at the same time, so his memory in its absence of comparison to earlier days is more romantic. "When George did come back the thing that I did find out was how great of a player he was because when you were training with him, you couldn't get the ball off him, you couldn't get near him," Macari says.

"When he played on a Saturday it was the George Best that people that had talked about for years and years. Not much had deteriorated even though he had gone away for a while, he just seemed to be the type of player that could come back, walk through the front door, put his strip on. But of course that's never going to last if you're not training regularly... it didn't last, but I'm glad he did come back, because the memories of him training and playing against you on the training ground was enough that I could safely say that he was for me, the greatest Manchester United player ever. There's been lots of great players at Old Trafford but George was just an incredible, incredible footballer, incredible talent, and a character."

Sammy McIlroy, of course, idolised George, so his recollections of the early weeks of the return are all positive. "He loved training," McIlroy says. "Even when he came back, even when he was a wee bit overweight... he struggled, anyone would. But certainly before that he was one of the best trainers I've ever seen. He loved working out, he loved being with the ball."

The team to face Birmingham read: Stepney – Buchan, James, Holton, Young – Morgan, Greenhoff, Graham, Best – Macari, Kidd. It wasn't just Charlton and Law who had gone. Sadler, Dunne. Fitzpatrick. Ian Storey-Moore had suffered an ankle injury early into Docherty's reign. McIlroy was returning from a lung injury he'd sustained in a car crash.

Best did not think he was fit enough to play: "I'm quite a long way off the level I know I can reach, and, there's some way to go before I can fully build up my stamina. But the manager wants me to play, so I'll play and do my best... (but) it's marvellous to be back in the first-team squad so quickly."

However, he knew United's requirement for attacking firepower had become desperate. Even he didn't realise how desperate. In the second half United were awarded a penalty. Who would step up to take it? Lou Macari, the former Celtic goal-getter? No – he had been in Docherty's bad books after sulking when asked to play in the reserves. The man who stepped up to take the kick was Alex Stepney. He scored. It won the game. Because he had also scored one earlier in the season, Manchester United's goalkeeper was now joint-top scorer alongside McIlroy and Kidd with two.

As at Shamrock, there were a few nice touches for George, and a couple of moments where he dribbled past a couple of players. But the breakneck speed – the here-then-gone, that graceful flight – none of that was present. "Skill is something you never lose. I'll have it when I'm 100," George said after the game. "The question is whether I can use it. If I played like I did today, I would worry about staying in the team."

Docherty, listening, quipped: "He needn't. From now on George is in the first-team pool."

Ted Macauley of the *Sunday Mirror* had watched the big comeback and commented on the decision to bring George off with 15 minutes to go. "There was obviously not one single fan who supported manager Tommy Docherty's action as the comeback genius reluctantly jogged to the changing room," he wrote. "The jeers were, ironically, as much a salute and a thank you for George's smouldering magic as they were an echoing wave of derision aimed at Docherty… of course there were times when he looked sluggish, but his reactions, speed of thought and control were all that they used to be. And in the second half, when his confidence was surging, he shirked no challenge and rolled back that gap of months."

Best – conqueror of the best teams the world, the man who was so casual he sometimes had to be called into the dressing room from the hotdog stand before kick-off – admitted to Macauley: "I was very nervous at the beginning and terrified of touching the ball in case I made a mess of things."

Frank McGhee wrote in his *Mirror* column: "Sterile testimonials are not the settings for a George Best. The deep end is where he belongs, where he must live and flourish or drown and die, where he must find out – or be found out. Twice he was whacked with tackles that a couple of years ago would have inflamed him with berserk dedication to vengeance. This time he did what he must go on doing, choked back his curses, massaged his wounds, got up and got on with it."

* * *

The Seventies were feeling increasingly dour in comparison to the technicolour blaze of the previous decade that George had so personified. The politics, the strikes, the blackouts, the recession – people were desperate for life, personality and excitement where they could find it. In football, his talent was notable by its absence. There was Rodney Marsh across town at Manchester City but even he admitted he wasn't as serious as George; that George could do what he did, and do it to win.

So when George was making this latest comeback, the cynical doubt had subsided to a certain degree and people were hoping that he would illuminate as he did before. Even Birmingham captain John Roberts gave a definitely generous embellishment of George's display. "He wasn't taking people on, but his distribution was first-class and he's still got fantastic balance," he said. "There was one instance when he got the ball out wide and was faced with two of our lads. He looked as if he was going to cross. Instead, he dummied brilliantly. The crowd were going 'Ole'."

Damning George Best v3.0 with faint praise – so soon into his latest comeback – was to disrespect what George Best v1.0 was. Hopefully with increased fitness he could reach a close standard. But that was going to not only take internal discipline but also the external factors to be just right. That meant the team needed to perform but also to show the togetherness it was famed for earlier in George's career. It was clear there was still some resentment from Willie Morgan, who'd made a couple of choice comments about George getting another chance. "Until right at the end, he got away with it when he missed training or ran away," Morgan complained in 1973. "All kinds of people covered up for him, even the press, and he was lucky to get away with it for so long."

In more recent years Morgan – as he did for this book – spoke in nothing but glowing terms for his former colleague.

"No matter what I did, and I had a fantastic career, George's publicity was ridiculous," he says. "No matter how well anyone played, they'd write about him. If he had a bad game, it would be about how bad he played. After George left I became captain. And suddenly they started writing about me again.

"Doc talked to me about George coming back. 'You know what it'll be like,' he said. I said it would be fine. Of course it was – he was my pal. It would be great to have him back. And he was. It was just like old times. It was bullshit that he was only there every few days. He was there all the time. For a while it was great, and then, when it was obvious some of the players weren't good enough, it became difficult again. When he was playing he wasn't drinking. That was garbage. You can train for 10 years and not be match-fit. The only way to get match-fit is to play matches. He was fine."

It's possible to detect a hint of Morgan's old frustrations and even though Best's own comments suggest the pair weren't particularly close – ("It's true that Willie and I were never good friends and I always thought he was a bit jealous of me," Best wrote in *Blessed*) – it seems time brought a new appreciation from Morgan considering he did have some idea of what it was like to walk in George's shoes, even if only a percentage. But even Morgan in October 1973 would have wanted and needed George in full-flight, if only to help take the pressure off him in just the same way as he'd been brought in to do five years earlier. Storey-Moore's comments suggest that George's mere presence helped alleviate the weight of expectation on the creative players. "It was certainly better to have George Best in the team than to not have him, because teams would have had more to think about with Willie on one side, me on the other and George playing where he liked," he says.

United faced Chelsea at Old Trafford in November. The visitors went 2-0 up. In need of inspiration, George provided it with a rasping drive that smashed against the crossbar, behind Bonetti in goal, and seemingly over the line. Best celebrated – but the referee didn't give it. In the past, that might have invited the red mist. After the game, George was diplomatic. "The ball was over the line, but it all happened so quickly I can't blame the ref," he said, though his sporting response might have had something to do with the euphoria of United's late comeback to rescue a point with two goals in the last two minutes.

"Each game George has played has brought a two to three per cent improvement," Docherty said a few days later. "That's what I want. I didn't want him to be a sensation. People would have been looking for it from him every game. But frankly, I have been delighted by his attitude as well as his performances."

So too had the selectors for the Northern Ireland team. He was called back into the squad for the final World Cup qualifier against Portugal. After citing that 1974 could have been his last chance to play in the tournament, he could only have observed with some frustration as his countrymen drew home games with Portugal and Bulgaria. They finished third in the group; with Best on the pitch, they could well have won both, and that would have been enough to qualify. As it was, they gained a creditable draw in Lisbon, though it was not quite so memorable as George's visit there in 1966.

George's return to the first team at Old Trafford had brought a positive change in results – a win and two draws – and United went to Spurs looking to build on it. It was here for the first time where Best, though he was growing fitter by the week, suffered familiar difficulty. Yes, everyone wanted to see the old George. But an opponent as wise as Spurs boss Bill Nicholson was going to prepare for him as if he was still the same player.

"When he came back, he was still a fantastic player," Mike England recalls. "Yes, he'd been out of the game for a bit, but this was George Best, and whenever you played against him you took special precautions. The manager would always make a special plan for George. Because he was older and some of the other players who had previously been with him had retired, the job of dealing with him became a little easier."

Only a little – after Martin Chivers had given the hosts an early lead, George picked the ball up on the left. He moved past one challenge and evaded another tackle on the edge of the area before hitting a hopeful right-footed effort from 25 yards. It was on target, and though it appeared to take a deflection, it was Best's goal; a slice of luck, though all at United were desperate for it to be an indication of prosperity.

Greenhoff, Graham and Young all crowded around him in celebration, almost like boys at a youth club surrounding the best player on the team. The problem was the expectation against the reality. The reality for this Manchester United team was that Spurs had an experienced defence who didn't give George enough space to catch them by surprise again. They also had a team too good – and scored soon after to secure the win. A familiar pattern followed. United lost at Newcastle before welcoming Norwich to Old Trafford. The Canaries earned a 0-0 draw. Best, though, was brilliant. Ted Macauley, in the *Sunday Mirror,* described George as the "one lifeline" but said United were "engulfed in mediocrity... with players who once would not have earned a reserve place".

That weekend, George had announced that he was opening a nightclub in central Manchester and named it Slack Alice; Docherty had given permission, sure that it would not impact on the football. That was in the showbiz columns of the *Mirror*. In the sports section the same day was a seemingly innocuous line from Harry Miller. He wrote that United's board were keen to "balance their books" after Docherty's "massive outlay".

Two weeks later Southampton came to Manchester and they too got a goalless draw – it was almost a re-run, with Macauley again writing that Best was "the only United man on view with star quality".

It still felt like a battle between dreams and reality. Docherty had to perform a balancing act between the two – but couldn't afford for his team to think they could rely on George alone to pull them out of the mess they were in, especially after he had been told he could not strengthen his squad. In early December he fired the sort of missive through the press one would expect of a manager trying to boost the morale of his squad. "George Best has had a lot of richly deserved publicity recently for what he has done, but I think the whole Manchester United team deserve more praise," he said. "They have accepted George back and they have helped him generously."

Luck was not smiling on them. Coventry were the next visitors to Old Trafford on December 15. Martin Buchan tried to get in the way of a shot and it flew into his own net. In the opening moments of the second half, there was a flash of the old routine – get it to George as quickly as possible. Morgan ran down the right and played it into Greenhoff. He played it to George on the edge of the area. Best dummied the tackle and, even though the shift had put him in a more difficult position, he took his chances with a shot that managed to go through two defenders. The unlikely success of the technique caught the goalkeeper completely off guard, and he flung himself comically at the ball as it bobbled into the corner. It was George's second goal of the season – he was now level with Stepney, Kidd and McIlroy as top scorer.

Two years earlier, Best's contributions could compensate for his side's shortcomings. They were enough to move United to the top of the table. But not anymore. Sides like Coventry were not only now unafraid, they were confident in their ability to get a result. And they did, scoring twice more to get a 3-2 win.

It was a scalp for the Sky Blues but when United went to Anfield for their next game, they were playing against an opponent with ambitions of chasing Leeds at the top of the table. This was a professional job from a top team more concentrated on their own honours. United were defeated more comprehensively than the 2-0 scoreline suggested and Best was given plenty of time to ponder the standard he'd once contributed to and the memories he had on this ground, as he was marked out of the game. Before the match, George had claimed: "If I hadn't come back to football, I'd have been in the gutter right now… I'm settled. Calmer than I have ever been. I'm so relaxed I can hardly believe it."

But these were different times. And more change was on the way.

GOODBYE

A s with everything associated with George Best, there is the story and there is the legend. This book has attempted to tell just the story, in hope that the legend is brilliant enough that it needs no embellishment.

There are four threads tied to his final exit from Manchester United. There is the account of how it happened at the time. There are the accounts of how it has been explained by individuals since. There is the unknown truth of what happened between George Best and Tommy Docherty. And finally there is the truth unknown to even George Best.

The first two of those threads are on record and we'll revisit them briefly here. The third appears almost inconsequential because it amounts to the same thing. The fourth, revealed for the first time ever on these pages, was hitherto one of the most significant missing pieces from the story, and thus, one of the biggest stories in Manchester United history.

First, let us begin with the bare facts.

Manchester United entered 1974 with only goal difference keeping them out of the relegation zone. A 3-0 defeat at QPR on New Year's Day – a Tuesday – put them in it. George was peripheral, to put it politely. "There were a few grounds around in those days where you were close to the supporters," Alex Stepney recalls. "Everyone wants to beat Manchester United and every player is up for it. They absolutely battered us and there's nothing more you can say about it. If you couldn't get the ball to George, what chance has he got?

"When he came back under Tommy you could probably put that down as a bit of a publicity stunt for Docherty. Tommy could see that things weren't as they should be. Players were coming into the club for short spells, players you would never think would be at Old Trafford, with all due respect. Some of those were still there when George came back, so George didn't have the right blend with them anyway.

"I spent a long time with George. We developed a respect and affinity with each other. But towards the end, we didn't have that happy-go-lucky feeling between us… we might stay behind after a game for a good chat. Now he was gone as soon as he could be. By then it was only us two left from 1968.

"George was there all the time. He really did try. But I still felt it was a publicity stunt to bring him back. I think by then, George's enthusiasm had gone. I don't doubt his intention. He wanted to get it back. He was desperate for it to come back but he was hoping for something to magically happen around him and the club were hoping that would come from him.

"I still had my own career to think of. I was desperate for United to get back to where they should be, I was desperate to win things for the club, and it was sad to see that George had drifted so drastically. I think in his final spell at the club it was a mixture of things being as bad as they'd ever been, and the people around him having such an influence in his life away from football… people just wanted to be seen with him. They were hangers-on. George had gone past that stage of his brilliance now where it was obvious that he still had the talent to turn it on, but not for nine months of the year at the level we were going to need it."

David Lacey in *The Guardian* wrote of Best's QPR display: "Seldom can he have been caught in possession so often."

Sammy McIlroy had been concentrating on his own game but remembered the scathing criticism for his hero. "I can remember the press absolutely hammering him and saying he was a shadow of what he used to be," he says. "I found it very sad reading those headlines… He lost a bit of pace. He could go by players but they could get back at him. Everything he had was still there. His vision and his brain remained perfect.

"His touch was still there but physically people were catching him up. I could see what he wanted to do but he didn't have the same speed as before. It was so sad. When one player went it was one less for them to concentrate on, one more they could afford to have looking at George. So when you consider that they were still looking at him as the danger he had once been but he wasn't physically capable of doing what he used to, you can imagine how much more frustrating that would have been for him. He was frustrated with them and with himself. There were players looking at the name George Best and thinking they could now sort him out. They were kicking him and clattering into him and he just couldn't get away from it."

George's nightclub, Slack Alice, had opened over Christmas and was the place to be in Manchester. The club were running their New Year's Eve party all the way into January 2, so when

George returned home after the QPR game, he went straight to the club and inevitably missed training on Thursday, when the team were due to report back at the Cliff.

"I don't know where he's got to," Docherty told journalists. "He has not bothered to get in touch with me… All the players had yesterday off. He should have reported back with everyone else this morning but did not show up. I cannot really comment until I have heard some word from him, but it looks as if I will have to report the situation to the directors."

Manchester United's next game was against Plymouth Argyle in the FA Cup.

Here is where the story begins to take diversions in the 'Choose Your Own Adventure' subplot of George's exit from Manchester United. He turned up for training on Friday where he was put through his paces by Bill Foulkes and Pat Crerand. Docherty told his coach Tommy Cavanagh to concentrate on the rest of the first team, and he would manage George himself. As per the normal process, George saw that he was named in the team for the following day and reported for duty.

When?

According to Best: He reported first thing, was there with the team at their pre-match meal at Davyhulme golf course, and, 75 minutes before kick-off, was taken into the referee's room at Old Trafford where Docherty informed him he was not playing him because Best had missed training.

According to Docherty: He intended to select George to play, but the player didn't turn up on time. Tommy had to name his team by 2:15pm so was forced to leave Best out – only for George to turn up at 2.35pm. "I remember at 2:30pm we got the team sheet done and ready to go into the referee's room," Docherty said. "Who walks through the door at twenty five to three… Besty! He said, 'I've come to play!' There was a big bang on the door, I said, 'Hold on, hold on', I opened the door, I saw Besty with a very attractive young lady, he was stoned out of his mind, he said he wanted to play and I said, 'Well you can play, but you're not playing here, I'll see you on Monday, on you go'… I shut the door, and that was the last I saw of him."

The witnesses have different recollections but most of them corroborate Best's side. Crerand would later spectacularly fall out with Docherty, so much so that each of them would say the sky was black if the other said it was blue, so his defence of George is to be expected. "That was a total lie," Crerand said of Docherty's account. "George was at the pre-match meal at Davyhulme golf course and he was fine. George was physically gone, then, so Docherty was quite right not to pick him, but he should not have lied. George just left and never came back."

McIlroy and Stepney are two who have gone on record to deny George was drunk and Stepney, in particular, rejects that George would have ever been so unprofessional as to turn up just before a game, let alone in that state.

Willie Morgan was another whose relationship with Docherty would become irreparable but he presents a different take. "Bullshit. Garbage," Morgan says. "Because at that point he wanted to cut ties, he had to come up with a story that sounded plausible enough that would make George look bad. It was a story he made up to justify what he was doing."

To justify what he was doing would suggest a motive and an end game. But that is where the grey area has always been with this story. Tommy and George both went on record as acknowledging the manager had said it was the player's 'last chance' but the interpretation of that did not extend – at least in George's mind – to missed training sessions, as they had an arrangement in place. In any event, this was the first time. But Docherty needed Best and the potential incentive for bringing him back was obvious. It hadn't been a roaring success but there was plenty of goodwill and also a lot of positive reception to both George's attitude and his performances.

The above accounts are part of the established narrative. Best, enraged by the accusation, described Docherty as a "bullshitter". One can understand why – because the contemporary reports of the time paint a completely different picture. In Dublin, the *Sunday Independent* the day after the Plymouth game reported Docherty "dropped George Best a couple of hours before the start of the tie" and carried this quote from the United boss: "George has worked hard since coming back into football but has not done too well in two or three games recently. He would have been out anyway regardless of his failure to report for training this week."

*The Belfast Telegrap*h that was printed on the afternoon of the game – the edition that carried half-time scores – also, crucially, carried the news that George had been dropped, with a slightly different Doc quote. "This is not a disciplinary measure. I have chosen the team I think is the best. Even if he had not absented himself from training on Wednesday, I would still not have selected him."

In the 1991 book *Docherty* by Brian Clarke, the then-former United boss told the author: "I had picked George in the team and wasn't too worried when he didn't arrive for lunch." In response to the allegation from Best that the meeting was in the referee's room: "Why would I want to do that? It would have been a foolish place to hold such a private meeting… George apparently claimed I did not meet him early enough to tell him he was being dropped. That is nonsense because I fully intended playing him and had named him on my team sheet. I scratched his name out when he had not turned up."

The last time managers spoke to journalists before a game would have been Friday morning. In order for newspapers to be able to carry not only the news that George had been dropped, but a quote from Docherty to go along with it, it would have had to have taken place at the very latest by the time the team was announced. But the reports of the time clearly state that it was known around two hours before the game that George would not be playing.

It is not just that the contradictions in Docherty's various stories unravel one of the other versions. It's that with each contradiction, it becomes more confusing. On the day of the game Docherty said it wasn't a disciplinary measure. In accounts since he said he intended to play him, even though on the day he cited George's recent form (which, whilst poor, was not noticeably worse than anyone else's).

In the interest of full balance, George's own version of the events is that he sat in the stands after the Plymouth game – United won 1-0 – and reminisced about the glory days gone by, then rode off into the sunset; the sort of anti-climatic ending that would become popular with avant-garde movies in years to come.

That's not strictly true. George was reported to have been the first in for training on Monday January 7, and he was also there on Tuesday and Wednesday, but when he failed to turn up on Thursday, Docherty was speaking to the newspapers and his board.

"Somebody phoned to say that Best would not be in for training," Docherty told journalists. "The phone message was passed on to me, but there was no explanation. After failing to turn up twice the situation will be discussed by the directors at the next meeting."

Martin Edwards, the board member and son of owner Louis, remembered: "Tommy came with a recommendation that he didn't want George in the side anymore. It's very difficult as a director, no matter what you think about a former player, or whatever else, if the manager feels like he's got to discipline that player, then you have to support the manager really. Otherwise, where does it end? I think by then, maybe even some of the other players were beginning to think, 'Well what's all this about?', that there was one rule for George and one for another... so the board had to support the manager and once Tommy Doc said that he'd really come to the end of the line with George, we had no option but to support him."

It seemed an extreme line of action to take. Of course, Docherty had taken a radical decision before when he was Chelsea manager. But even if he was angry at Best for missing training, it seemed an over-reaction to completely get rid of him, especially considering he had been the one to bring him back to the club.

Here is where the missing piece finally falls into place.

We know that George being dropped from the team was pre-conceived and it was not a case of Docherty innocently waiting and being let down. That much more or less completely disproves the version of George turning up late, drunk, and with a girl, and this is supported not only by the testimonies of the day but also by the fact it would likely have been front page news if it were true. It's also supported by the relatively dignified responses afterwards from contemporaneous newspaper reports and interviews.

Best missed training – he understood it was his last

chance – and even though he felt Docherty had been harsh considering what they had agreed upon with his schedule, he took responsibility as he did before and accepted his time was up. The way both of them spoke in the weeks and months afterwards suggested that the story about turning up drunk didn't even exist at that point. How else could you explain George's comments to David Meek soon after? "I am very grateful to Matt Busby and Tommy Docherty for giving me another chance and I am sorry for them – and for Manchester United fans – that things didn't work out."

Docherty spoke to Meek too. And he echoed the tone. "On reflection it was worth all the effort and time we put in," he said. "I'd never have been satisfied if I hadn't made the effort or had the chance to work with him."

It all suggested that even though the end had come, it had been somewhat amicable. That was before George realised Tommy had a different version of events – and so he naturally sought to defend himself. Still, there remains a disconnect between simply dropping your best player and getting rid of him altogether. "There must have been something going on behind the scenes," Alex Stepney says. And he was right.

Docherty had received the message loud and clear that there were no transfer funds, even though he remained keen to bring in new players to fight off relegation. The dream of George as the player he had been even in the early weeks of the 1971/72 season had not come into fruition and even though he was doing a good job, the old magic wasn't there.

Docherty knew it was not working. Maybe it had been a publicity stunt – with the controversy over Law's exit, he needed to curry favour with the fans, and how better to do that than to bring back the club's best ever player? But even if it was to get some positivity, it was also done with the genuine hope George could save them.

United's trip to Loftus Road was significant. Tommy Docherty was a popular man in football, particularly in this part of London, where he knew everybody. He was the sort of man you would see at a football game and, if you were the owner or influential figure at a football club – let's say you were Louis Edwards or Matt Busby – then you could strike up a conversation and suggest that there could be a job available in a few days. Frank O'Farrell had discovered that to his cost in December 1972. Docherty was, then, the sort of affable fellow who enjoyed good relationships with owners of different clubs.

One of those was Queens Park Rangers owner Jim Gregory.

Before the game, Gregory and his manager Gordon Jago welcomed Docherty into Jago's office, where the trio exchanged pleasantries.

"I can't remember how the subject was raised, but we began speaking about our interest in George from a few months earlier," Jago recalls. "But I had only said that we would be interested then because George wasn't playing for anybody. Now he was back at United. So it was rather unexpected when Tommy suggested George might be available if the price was right. Jim was excited about it because of the potential numbers it would bring through the gate. We would get crowds of around 18,000 and for United we were expecting over 30,000. They were there to see George. So Jim made an offer.

"I can't remember how much it was – but we were talking tens of thousands, not hundreds, because Jim was excited that he was getting a bargain. We were amazed when Tommy accepted the offer there and then. I couldn't believe it. The deal was done in the office before the game. We shook hands and he agreed that he would get the paperwork done back in Manchester. I was excited about getting to coach a player of George's calibre and Jim was excited about the future potential. It was a big boost for us. We had a good team – it was proven by our 3-0 win – and we were keen to get to the next level."

QPR were certainly a team who were going places. They were in eighth place after their win, a tremendous performance for a promoted side. Jago was a conscientious manager. He had confessed to sleepless nights when he spent over £100,000 of the chairman's money on new players. That situation had arisen after a difficult period where Rodney Marsh had requested a transfer to Manchester City; QPR's good form became unstable after the disruptive influence Jago felt Marsh had been in the dressing room. Although he was sad to lose the talent, he was pleased to restore harmony, and yet still felt guilt when spending the proceeds of the sale on new players.

George was a gamble presented with a deal too good to turn down. That was until the newspapers of the next couple of days which pictured George in his nightclub and had Docherty confessing that he didn't know what was happening. Jago was concerned. Having re-established a fantastic balance in his dressing room, he did not want anything to ruin it, and, with that extra element of the transfer fee, he told Gregory that he would like to withdraw the offer.

Docherty did not even have the opportunity to present it to the board, or discuss it with George – a matter that would surely have been as complicated as it would be unpopular. He felt he had been given both a convenient out – as with Charlton – for ending a legendary tenure at the club, and also a potential transfer kitty. Now he had neither, and to boot, he had George's old problems back again. Maybe it wasn't

Docherty's intention to completely end George's career, but it was obvious that it influenced his decision to drop him from the Plymouth game. That much is clear by the instruction given to his coach to not include George in the first-team training even if he did turn up.

Everything spiralled out of control when Best missed training after that; Docherty, by now realising it would be difficult to command even a modest fee for the troubled star, made the choice to sever the relationship before George did, for the benefit of his control over the dressing room. "We're better off now without him and I don't mean that disrespectfully," Docherty told David Meek shortly afterwards. "With Best in the side United were attractive but not as well organised."

Ultimately you could make an argument that Best missing training was of his own accord and unrelated to the transfer deal that had been struck without his knowledge, and, as this was the start of the usual pattern which always culminated with him taking a leave of absence from United, it was doomed to end that way anyway.

But of course being dropped to face Plymouth accelerated matters. Best admitted he felt "utterly humiliated" by the decision and that he told Crerand: "If I'm not good enough to play against Plymouth Argyle, I ain't playing again." The decision to axe him from the side had brought the matter to a head immediately. And although it is difficult to say for sure, it is improbable – considering the actual sequence of events – that such a decision would not have been taken if George had not ruined a transfer deal he knew nothing about.

There is a truth within the dramatic liberty taken in George's account of leaving United. He did stay at the ground after the game (again – why would he have done this if he was with a girl?) and he did sit on the terrace, soaking in the atmosphere of years gone by, feeling – but not knowing for certain – he wasn't to play again for Manchester United on the hallowed turf of Old Trafford.

On Crerand's implore, Best did at least show his face at training. There was something remaining – his love for Manchester United. His impossible dream that what once was would soon return. But Docherty was in no mood to indulge George's melancholic nostalgia. He was suspended for two weeks. When he did report to training that week, it was with Bill Foulkes and the juniors. On Thursday and Friday he didn't bother turning up. "We have not heard a word from him," Docherty told the press. "And even if he does apologise, it would be too late. The damage has been done."

The domestic press waited with bated breath to see if George would show his face after his suspension. He didn't. On January 26, there was no letter on headed paper, no press conference, just a few words to the regular journalists who followed him around. "I cannot face being just an average First Division player," he said. "I know I have lost forever that certain spark that set me apart. I said that if I could not recapture my previous form I would call it a day. I am just sticking to that promise."

They'd heard it all before.

LOST

After some close calls, the official end of an era for Manchester United finally came at the end of the 1973/74 season when they were relegated from the First Division. They would keep faith in Tommy Docherty and together they would enjoy some fruitful times. George Best, however, was now a name of their past.

As for his own future?

Well, even by that point, it was not clear what George Best was going to do next. It had always been a suspicion of those around him that what he really wanted was for someone at Manchester United to put their arm around him and bring him back into the fold. That could have happened forever, with the cycle continuing as it always did. At the level Manchester United operated – or at least the level they felt they ought to be operating – there was just no room for sentiment, no room for accommodating and tolerating.

"George Best, I would say [was] the most talented, naturally gifted British player that I've ever seen," former chairman Martin Edwards says. "But he couldn't really handle the fame, he never really developed fully as a footballer, which is a strange thing to say. Basically the complications in his life prevented him from becoming a good influence on the club. He was a bad influence on the club. Because the other players became fed up with his absences, some longer than others.

"They liked him as a person, he was a lovely human being. Lovely companion and a really charming, generous person when he was sober. People were willing him to do well and Matt gave him chance after chance after chance and even O'Farrell sort of said, 'He carries us in some games, we've got to give him a bit of leeway'. But he became such a bad influence on the team ethic that he had to go."

The truth was that the damage already caused by the illness George was suffering with had taken such a physical and mental toll that persevering in that routine would have done more harm than good. The cycle could never be broken at Old Trafford because the hype machine would always be present. It would have done him no favours to pander to him – to embarrass him by pretending he was better than he was.

Still, it would have been nice for George to have known the truth. That he was seen as a player to offload and that had been the intention. If he had known, then perhaps he could have come to terms with it. It is impossible to know for sure, but George's propensity to accept responsibility for his own role in things was coupled by his tendency to blame himself.

It seemed as though he carried this with him for the rest of his career – that he had sabotaged his last chance at his club, and now was damaged goods. If he had known the truth, then there is a better than even chance that he would have used the incident as motivation to prove Docherty wrong – that he could still be a top player at a top club. That he wasn't a liability. It was the path he always took when he felt persecuted. However, the path he always took when he felt his own guilt was to self-destruct even further until help came. So it was.

George needed a clean break, the harshness and reality of a fresh page to reset. It was a difficult personal time. The press continued to hound him and there was no escape of training or a football match. It was continuous. The Troubles back home were unrelenting. He learned that his cousin had been killed. As he discussed the matter with his siblings he learned just how ill their mum had become through drink. It compounded the guilt. He continued to dwell and to wallow; in May he gave an interview to the *People* where he spoke publicly for the first time about his estranged daughter. "I would never make any attempt to see the child," he said. "I would probably feel worse myself if I did."

A strange opportunity presented itself to George at precisely the moment he was trying to work out what to do outside of the sport that had made his name. South Africa played their football season through the British off-season, and clubs backed by wealthy owners tried to attract players from the Football League to come over and play for a few games. It was also an attempt to get some attention on their domestic game with the World Cup being played at the same time.

Hellenic FC of Cape Town had convinced Bobby Moore to play for the summer. Jewish Guild, in Johannesburg, were even more ambitious, and their directors Abe and Solly Krok made an offer of £11,000 to George to play three games. After some deliberation he agreed – and was greeted like the prodigal son in South Africa, despite having never set foot in the country before. His time there got off to a bumpy start. He watched his new team lose 3-0 against Rangers, with locals claiming that the Guild players suffered from stage-fright in front of their soon to be new team-mate. He was due to report for his first training session the day after – but suffered from sunstroke after sunbathing for too long. He did attend training the following day, pink as salmon; while amusingly a local stripper by the stage name of 'Ultra Violet' was also watching.

"A beetroot-burnt George Best had Ultra Violet focused on him when he resumed training at Balfour Park yesterday afternoon," Sy Lerman wrote in the *Rand Daily Mail*. "No publicity hound could have dreamed up this gimmick. It had to be coincidence. Yet here was Best, the day after he was prevented from taking part in his first official practice because of sunburn, face-to-face with the slinky stripper who has burnt a few fellows in her time."

He also got face-to-face with locals who were keen to talk football with him. George spoke interestingly to former United player Eddie Lewis – now coaching Wits University – about coaching, saying that if he were a manager, he would bring back the 2-3-5 formation which emphasised the use of wingers. He also gave his opinion on events at Old Trafford. "In my first years at Manchester, Matt Busby never knew what the word defensive meant," he said. "Today, the only great player at Old Trafford is a defender, Martin Buchan."

There was some cynicism among local reporters. Lerman was one, suggesting George's reputation "surpassed his sporting prowess". Best did much to try and placate the inhabitants of his temporary home. He left the Guild's defeat to Rangers five minutes early – he insisted that it was to beat the crowds. He said he was not a has-been – he was here to train five hours a day. He also said he wanted to make a political point in the wake of the controversial and violent British Lions rugby tour of previous weeks.

"My family still live in Belfast, and I have had all the pressures possible over the tragic situation in Northern Ireland," he said, and referred to the Newcastle game in 1971: "Their manager said jokingly that he wished I had been shot. But it was terrifying at the time. I am a Protestant, and my best friend and room-mate in the Ireland team is Pat Jennings; the greatest goalkeeper in the world. He is a Catholic. That's all there is to be said: people matter, not politics."

In a practice game against Wits University to get him match ready, Wits defender Stewie Taylor launched into a crunching tackle which left Best reeling and rolling on the floor, holding his knee. "I told my players not to tackle him from behind," sighed a helpless Lewis.

George was fit enough to start against Hellenic, where he came up against Bobby Moore. The *Reading Evening Post* said neither were "able to impose their authority on the game", though George was happy with his contribution. "I feel great and hope to put up a better show in my next game," he said. "I lasted out better than I thought I would."

That 1-1 draw was followed by a 2-0 win over Durban City, in which he created the second goal. That was as good as it got – a heavy 5-1 defeat in the return game with Hellenic was followed by a 2-1 loss at home to Durban United. At least George was able to net his team's goal in that final game; giving those Jewish Guild fans an opportunity to say they once watched the great George Best play and score for their club.

This was a trend which continued over the next two years or so of George's life. The description of 'great' applied more to the legend than the experience. He was in desperate need of inspiration, but, in the time where that was missing, he followed the money instead. It meant that the decisions he made were not always the most credible. One couldn't imagine David Beckham, for example, making the same choices once he was left out in the Old Trafford wilderness. But George wasn't struggling for money, even by the financial standards of the game at that time. He was simply lost.

United still held his playing registration so the Guild had to pay them a loan fee of £6,400 – they were happy for George to play outside of England but were reluctant to give him away to a rival in the Football League. This stand-off led to non-league Dunstable Town making an offer. Their owner, entrepreneur Keith Cheeseman, was encouraged by his manager, former United trainee and publicity hound Barry Fry, and made a public offer of a £10,000 signing-on fee and £200 match fee. They were willing to bend to George's will just to be considered. "We are not making any rules about training and he can just play in home games if he feels like it," Fry said. "He will be playing for us for peanuts."

After discussions, United said they would not sanction a transfer, but allowed George to play in two friendly games – the first of those was against a United reserve side on August 5, 1974, meaning his old club would be his first opponent on British soil since leaving them. In front of 3,866 supporters, United took a 2-0 lead, but inspired by George, the home team turned it around to win 3-2. "I enjoyed it," George told reporters afterwards. "I look forward to the next match on Monday. But as for playing for them on a regular basis, we'll just see how it goes."

Cheeseman, on behalf of Dunstable, made an offer

of £40,000. United again turned it down. The club owner had brought George to the first game to make sure he was there. He was wishing he did it for the second – Best's car broke down on the motorway and kick-off against Cork Celtic had to be delayed by 20 minutes. He arrived and played in a 0-0 draw, but was in a foul mood and argued with one of the fans. Barry Fry said afterwards that there would be "far too many complications" pursuing a permanent deal and – probably relieved to be free of the potential media headache – was happy to just be known as the man who convinced George to turn out for Dunstable before wishing him on his merry way.

In the Dunstable crowd that day was the Luton Town team, who included Jim Ryan, George's former pal from their childhood days at United. "He was a little out of shape at this point," Ryan recalls. "He was still capable of pleasing the crowd – juggling the ball and doing a trick. I didn't like to see him like that. It wasn't something I particularly enjoyed watching when I knew what he was capable of. It was an exhibition. He was much better than that. The George I knew was a killer. He would embarrass you but he was doing it to win, not for show. It was difficult for me to put the player I'd watched blossom next to this one. I couldn't enjoy it very much."

And, for a long while, it really did seem as though that was it for George in football. The new season started without him. It was the game's loss.

"Hooliganism, I am sure, is not the reason for people staying away from football grounds. I think the public have become disillusioned with the type of football every side is playing. It is so defensive," Arsenal chairman Dennis Hill-Wood said in September 1974. "And I am afraid, in that respect, Arsenal are as guilty as anyone. But what can you do? Results have become all-important. Since George Best quit the game you wouldn't even need the fingers of one hand to count the number of players capable of pulling in a few extra spectators."

George admitted that he too found the current game boring in an interview the following March. "My problems all started with Manchester United," he said. "You can pick any player in the world, I don't care who, and you'll never find anyone who loves the game more than I did. All I wanted was for Manchester to be the top club in the country as long as I was there, and I couldn't see that happening. I went and told Matt Busby what I thought was wrong and he just said I was making excuses for myself. So I started losing interest.

"I began to miss training and to stay out later. Instead of having six or seven drinks, I'd have 10 drinks, then a dozen drinks. And then my other problems came... but I could have stood for all of that if we had been winning matches. If someone had given me the choice of having the most beautiful women in the world or winning the European Cup every couple of years, I would never have looked at another woman.

"But I'm missing nothing in the game because there's nothing to miss. It's boring and there's not a player in the country that I would travel 50 miles to watch. Since I left Belfast I've had two sisters and a little brother born, so I've missed their growing up. And I've worried my parents. I haven't any [friends], in that there is no-one I would phone up and ask for advice. Not one. I think people basically are hard, two-faced hypocrites. I've been two-faced myself in the past, but no more..."

He also said to the interviewer with a hint of finality and perhaps even resignation: "I was better than anyone else in the world." With enough time and distance from football he'd been able to evaluate that last two-year spell. The comedian and director Mel Brooks once recalled his colleague Andreas Voutsinas telling him: "Or you got it, or you ain't." It, in George's case, was that initial burst. He spent his first return to United desperately trying to reclaim it. He spent his second comeback knowing within his heart he would probably not be able to, but if he got as fit as he could be, he could do other things. He was almost curious to see how good he could be without it. He could have been good enough for Manchester United, though how good is one of the hypotheticals, and barely even worth dwelling upon because it would not be how it was before.

"If we were able to get him fit and in the best shape that version of George could have been – and understanding it still wouldn't have been the same as before – things maybe could have been different," Sammy McIlroy says. "It's very difficult to say. The situation we were in, we would have needed him to be really at it, and that's moving into ifs and buts."

* * *

With George's final acceptance that he would not be able to represent Manchester United again came a somewhat implicit understanding that it meant the top level of football, too. The last thing he wanted was to become another run-of-the-mill player, struggling to keep up or doing tricks and not going anywhere. He was competitive by nature. He wanted to be the best. It was a difficult thing for him to reconcile.

He had been tempted by another offer from Clive Toye and the New York Cosmos in January 1975. Gordon Bradley, coach of the Cosmos, told the *New York Times* that Best had initiated contact so he expected the move to finally happen.

"His [Best's] last words to me on Saturday were 'I'll see you Wednesday' and I believed him," Bradley said. "I believe he will be here Wednesday because he was the one who originated this thing. He called us first to tell us that he was interested in coming to play for the Cosmos."

Sir Matt Busby had even travelled to America to discuss the move. "Sir Matt told us he'd seen Georgie play in exhibitions and he was as good as ever," said Bradley. "We need a darn good player. If we bring Georgie to the United States, this is the city he belongs in. Nothing has been settled yet. We have to talk with him first and see how sincere he is about playing for us. But I know that he wants to get back into football."

And George, who had expressed some reluctance regarding the Big Apple, seemed to be coming around to the idea. "As long as I stay in training and play well, I don't see what objection there can be to what I do off the field," Best said. "I like a drink now and then and I enjoy being with women. Another reason I want to play in New York is because people here help athletes stay on top. In England when an athlete gets to the top we do our best to destroy him. I have really been disillusioned with soccer in England. We are very close, as far as I am concerned, there will be no problem."

Clive Toye had pulled out all the stops. He matched his previous offer and told the press: "We've talked about philosophies and things but nothing constructive at this point. We want George permanently here. This is where he belongs. We told George by the time he is in his early thirties he would be a multimillionaire. It will be cash from us and other benefits that come with playing in New York."

Best said he would be back in New York in two weeks. But on February 7, Toye told the *New York Times*: "We have hit a few snags. We were fully expecting George to arrive within a day or so. But early this morning we were contacted by George's lawyer and he told me that George was still interested but was having second thoughts about a number of things. I have arranged to phone George's attorney again on Monday and set up a meeting either here or in England. We'll have to get together with George again and find out what the true situation is. The prognosis is what it has always been. If George wants to play, we'll have a deal.

"He told the media people here he was extremely positive about playing for us. I hope that when I get to him again he feels the same way. I am a general manager. When I have a player like George Best telling me he wants to play for me, I am going to do my best to get him. The value of him playing for us is worth going to all lengths and exhausting all possibilities."

Toye had told reporters his chances of signing Best were 50/50 and if forced, he'd amend that to 60/40 in the favour of the Cosmos getting their man. But again, Best eventually declined. Snubbed for a third time, Toye decided to invest in Pele. This was a move that went swimmingly – though Toye would insist the Brazilian was always his first choice.

For a while George considered playing for Marbella. As he spent so much time there, he felt it might be good for him, but they were in the third division in Spain and only clubs in the top two divisions could sign foreign players.

So the 1975/76 season commenced without him. Bored, he played another friendly with Dunstable in October – and joked that he was off to a health farm afterwards. It also re-ignited his desire to play. New York Cosmos were reported to have made another offer of over £40,000 that never quite worked out. But there was a rumbling that something could be in the offing in

1976 if George could get himself in shape. In order to do that he would have to play competitive football again. United still held his registration. He asked them to release it – Docherty agreed, realising there was nothing to gain by retaining him. It was a double-edged sword for Best – he had agreed to play in Paddy Crerand's testimonial, but now, because he wasn't registered as a player with the FA, he wasn't eligible.

He set about finding a club. It seemed as if Stoke were set to get him, but they were in a fight with Stockport, whose owner Freddie Pye was a friend of George. Pye convinced George to play in a friendly for his club – ironically against Stoke – and he scored a fantastic free-kick from 20 yards. "I have three hard months ahead of me to get fit – but if I play for any English club I would prefer it to be Stoke City," George admitted – and Potters boss Tony Waddington had been impressed. "No-one expected George to run like a deer after 20 months out of the game," he said. "But when he had to do something spontaneously, the inspiration and skill was all there."

After scoring two goals as a guest in a Chelsea past v present team, George was feeling optimistic. "Now I know I can do it," he said. "I felt it all there again and it's getting easier. I'm only 5lb over my playing weight and will lose that this week. So far I've lost a stone in 12 days. I'll go to America after Christmas to open negotiations about playing there. As there's so much money involved I'd be a fool not to."

He was able to participate in Crerand's testimonial – another past v present affair with the European Cup winners reuniting. Docherty's team had transformed in confidence with Steve Coppell and new signing Gordon Hill on the wing in George's old shirt. Hill scored in the first minute, setting the tone for a 7-2 win, but it was George who got the biggest cheer when he received a Charlton pass and dummied goalkeeper Paddy Roche in the same way as all of his former United goalkeeper mates used to fall for before tapping the ball in.

After all of these cameos, George finally made his long-awaited return to English football in late November 1975 as he agreed to play in home games for Stockport County until Christmas. So it was the decidedly unglamorous setting of Edgeley Park for a lower mid-table clash against Swansea, with over 9,000 fans – three times their usual attendance – packed in to see the most famous footballer in the country.

They were not disappointed, even if they were not quite sure what to expect. In the 22nd minute George took a corner, and tried to do as he had done before for United against Wolves and Ipswich. It did catch Swansea goalkeeper Steve Potter out, but it went down rightly as an own goal as Potter fumbled and pushed it into his own net. In the 56th minute, there was a brief flash of brilliance through those quick feet when George set up a goal for Lee Bradley.

And in the 71st minute, the coup de grace – a bouncing ball fell kindly to him. An ordinary Fourth Division player might have found it a difficult shot to execute, but George was far from that, and made quite an awkward chance look fairly comfortable by catching it sweetly on his left foot. It was the winning goal.

"I think he's done a great job for us tonight," said Stockport manager Roy Chapman. "He's turned the game for us." Asked if he would select him again, Chapman smiled: "Yes, I think so!" He did – Best turned out in Stockport's next two home games, first against Watford (he scored in a 2-2 draw, a fantastic goal where he killed a high ball, then turned and fired in) and finally in a 1-0 win over Southport on Boxing Day.

That was the end of his arrangement and it was expected he would fly to the US to negotiate a transfer. San Antonio Thunder had expressed an interest, but on December 3, Los Angeles Aztecs announced they had made a deal. "The best description I can come up with is magic," said Aztecs general manager John Chaffetz. "I hope the sports fans in Los Angeles will be as excited as I am about the arrival of the premier soccer player to come out of the United Kingdom."

Best was moved to say the announcement was premature – he was considering an offer from Chelsea to play for £1,000 a game. However, his next move wasn't Chelsea or Los Angeles. It was, somewhat bizarrely, to Dublin, to sign a very short-term deal with Cork Celtic. The connection was made by Bobby Tambling, the Chelsea legend who was player-coach at Cork and had recently spent time with George at the charity game at Stamford Bridge and made a chance enquiry.

"Our chairman wanted to bring in someone to swell the crowds so who better to bring in than George Best?" Tambling told *The Irish Times*. "I knew him from playing against him, I didn't know him well but he always seemed like a nice guy. A friend of mine got in touch with him and set it up. So I flew over and we met up and had a good talk and he seemed keen to get back and have a game, I didn't really have to do much talking. He was going through his fight to get over the problem he had but he just wanted to play."

Two days after turning out for Stockport he was running out on to the Flower Lodge pitch (Cork had to switch venue from their usual Turner's Cross ground to accommodate a crowd of 12,000) as a 'home' player. They lost 2-0 against Drogheda. Club secretary Donie Forde estimated that the club made around 10 times the £600 match fee paid to George, but said:

"We played a load of rubbish. I believe our players were simply overawed by the occasion."

There was better luck for Cork in their following match as they won against Bohemians, but George was not impressing anybody with his performance. "Generally he was no more than an agitated onlooker," Peter Byrne wrote in *The Irish Times*. "Gone was the flair and willingness to run at defenders and, on this performance, the way back to the Olympian heights of the Sixties is now vertical."

The assessment of George's display in his final game – a 2-1 defeat at Shelbourne – by Byrne's colleague Derek Jones was even more cutting: "As far as I am concerned I never want to set eyes on him again. I would prefer just to remember him as he was during his Manchester United days."

Clearly the Cork manager agreed – and George was sacked the day after that last game for a "lack of enthusiasm". "We brought him to the club without knowing what he was capable of at the time," Paul Donovan said. "He was a success to a limited extent from a financial point of view and was very important to us because of that. He was not, however, a success from a playing point of view."

In 2019, Tambling preferred to look at the positives: "The marvellous thing when you think back on it is that thousands of people in Ireland can turn and say to their mates or whoever: 'I saw George Best play'. He obviously wasn't at his full fitness but just to see him on the field and see what he could do was marvellous and we thoroughly enjoyed his company."

At the time, many supporters felt cheated and requested their money back. They thought George was going through the motions and there was certainly none of the nostalgic romance Tambling refers to; just an ire that the club had sought to take advantage of a temporary financial boost when there was a serious element to their competition and existence. George's fleeting appearances as he moved from club to club were beginning to elicit derision.

In early January 1976, East Ham – yes, East Ham, you read that right – offered George £500 per game to turn out for them. "Perhaps Best can laugh himself silly all the way to the bank at £500 for every custard pie in the face," John Gibson wrote of the rumour in the *Newcastle Evening Chronicle*. "But if he has an ounce of pride left, surely he will quit this ridiculous merry-go-round and leave us all the memories of 'El Beatle'."

He was only 28.

The Cork episode had been baffling – George later admitted "the games didn't mean anything to me" – but they helped to "fill the time" before he went to America, where he had now agreed to go to play for the Aztecs. After much soul-searching, George decided that America could be a genuine fresh start. It was a wise decision in just about every aspect. It was far enough away from home that he wouldn't be harassed by the press. Los Angeles also always had the sun, which was another factor to George's liking.

But he was steeled by the competitive element of it. The NASL was an ambitious league. Yes, there was a quality gap between the American players and the world stars who shared dressing rooms, but in a way that added to the spectacle and there was most definitely an emphasis on providing entertaining football, or soccer. Pele was now there playing for the New York Cosmos and his strike partner was the legendary Italian Giorgio Chinaglia.

Up the coast from Los Angeles, George's old wing-mate Willie Anderson had spent time with Portland Timbers and enjoyed it so much he wanted to go back. Yes, it was mostly a collection of players past their peak, but there was a genuine competitive element of some of the most illustrious names in the sport wanting to test themselves at club level where they might not have had the chance before. Given the increasingly drab perception of the sport in the UK, the US scene seemed animated, dynamic and serious; qualities George believed he once represented, and hopefully, could once again.

WHO THE HELL'S GEORGE?

There is a fine line between reality and illusion.

In professional sport, particularly at its most dramatic and entertaining, that line is blurry. Live crowds, television audiences and media coverage – all of these factors combine to make it feel like football occasionally qualifies as a performing art. But football itself is insular. It doesn't automatically transcend or unite; at its root is physical competition.

It is intended to divide. It is the division and the competition that creates the tension and drama. The bigger the occasion, the greater the stakes. The identity of the master performer on these occasions therefore benefits from a certain elevation – still, within the boundaries of the sport. And competitive sport is not something enjoyed or understood by all. Without wishing to burrow away into a pit of existentialism, all sport and all football exists for its own audience. It doesn't exist for the good of mankind.

Profile depends on exposure. And within those parameters the sportsman or woman – who has chosen this as their profession – has one of four things as their objective. The first is the enjoyment of the game. The second is an acknowledged capability that the individual can play the game at a professional standard, and so it therefore becomes a career, means by which food can be put on a table and a roof over one's head. The third is the thrill of competing and testing yourself against others, wherever that might lead. The fourth is a desire to be the best.

After George left Manchester United in 1974 he was at a personal crossroads between reality and illusion. He could no longer carry on the charade of hoping he would return to the levels of that time between 1965 and 1971. It is a point we'll return to later, but the period of time is mentioned for a specific reason. United were no longer able to indulge that hope or invest in it. They had a practical reality to consider. So too, now, did George, and it was after this period of wallowing and realising nobody was going to offer an olive branch that he took responsibility for that which he already understood.

He was not going to play for Manchester United again and although he was sincere in that he didn't want to play for anyone else, he knew in football that sometimes you must, and even eventually named Chelsea as "the only other English side I would have signed for on a permanent basis". He knew that his time at United would have put off anyone in England with serious ambitions of their own, including Chelsea. He was genuinely disillusioned with the quality of the domestic game. And – after that brief period of acting out and playing the travelling showman, almost an act of self-sabotage to prove the doubters right, as he felt like doing when Sir Matt Busby said he wasn't mature enough to be captain – George was now left to reconcile the reality with his future.

America had started to appeal throughout 1974 and 1975. New York Cosmos had responded to their snub from George by signing Pele. The Brazilian legend had always been followed by just one criticism – nobody had seen him play club football outside of Brazil, and even though those World Cup winners' medals were a fairly conclusive response to any doubts, many were keen to see how he would do away from what was deemed his comfort zone.

Of course, the NASL was not perceived as the most competitive league in the world. But the authority figures and financiers were keen to change that. They had lured many coaches from the UK – Bill Foulkes left his reserve-team role in Manchester to coach Chicago Sting. There, Foulkes used his contacts back home to arrange loan spells for promising players during the English off-season (Gordon Hill from Millwall being one of these in 1975). But it wasn't just rookies making the move. Pele's arrival caused a lot of turned heads.

In fact, some prominent names to already feature in George's story followed the Brazilian and made immediate impacts of their own – Willie Anderson as already mentioned, but Peter Bonetti, Mike England and António Simões were there too, and all three (along with Hill) were named alongside Pele in the NASL All-Stars team for 1975. Giorgio Chinaglia, Bobby Moore and Rodney Marsh were among the big names set to move across the Atlantic for the 1976 season.

When John Chaffetz, general manager of the Los Angeles Aztecs, got in touch with George, everything seemed to fall into place. LA was the perfect stage for a player of George's profile, ego and sensibilities. After all, where better for an individual with an identity crisis over what was real and what was fantasy? Here, it could be both. Chaffetz made no secret that his interest in George was to rival what the Cosmos had done with Pele (the Brazilian had brought a global interest and spotlight on the US game) and even one-up them by getting the player the Cosmos couldn't.

Finally, there was the sporting objective. The American game was taking itself seriously and the investment suggested everyone else ought to. George was a visionary on and off the pitch – in 1967 he had discussed an idea of the top European clubs facing each other more regularly; the modern-day Champions League – and could see the credible value in a league where many of the world's greatest players were on show. It was difficult for George to accept that he would not be competing for the Division One title or the European Cup, but moving to America was choosing a different challenge and not necessarily conceding defeat in another.

Maybe that was not how it would be perceived back in England, and maybe it would not work out that way in the US, but the fresh page was alluring enough to capture George's imagination. There was slight hesitance in his commitment – he asked for a one-year deal after he was offered two – but Chaffetz told the press in early February 1976: "Best said he wanted to start working out with the team immediately."

George spoke about his future ambitions before leaving the UK. "If I get six or seven months' football in the USA with no other commitments, then I may return here and play for an English club next season," he said. "I must prove myself, however. Those games for Cork Celtic were a real shambles.

I did not get sufficient time for preparation because of my business. If I'm fit then I'm available [for Northern Ireland] and Aztecs would release me for the British championships."

He arrived in Los Angeles to all the fanfare of a movie star. Wearing a t-shirt with the self-deprecating but ironic phrase 'Who the hell's George?', a smiling Best walked through the terminal to the sort of reception he was used to. So far, so familiar. He had plenty of bitesize quotes for the local reporters to lap up.

"I'm better than Pele. I can kick with both feet. In fact I think I'm better right now than Pele was in his prime. It'll take a while to adjust, but I think I'll play all right. I'm better than Joe Namath in both sports he participates in."

Then, perhaps sensing he might be coming across as obnoxious, a counter: "I do not expect to play on a losing side. You'll find I have a nice personality when we start winning."

Chaffetz was there to greet him at the airport and staged a mini-press conference – complete with the gimmick of a young model handcuffed to George and wearing a t-shirt saying 'George does it best'. "This is our attempt to get some insurance for our heavy investment," Chaffetz said. "And to make sure he doesn't go anywhere."

There was no worry about that. As he had been in the initial stages of his United returns, George was 100 percent committed. "America offered a fresh start," George said in his book *Blessed*. "It took me out of the goldfish bowl at home and the drinking, gambling routine which I knew I had to stop… I was training like a lunatic at the beginning, working hard and playing racket ball every day as well, sometimes for three or four hours. I drastically cut down on my drinking too and for a time, at least, I kept the demons at bay."

Two exhibition matches were arranged to take advantage of George's arrival – inevitably against Pele's Cosmos, with the first in New York on April 4, 1976 and the return in Los Angeles a week later. But when the two players billed as the greatest ever came face-to-face for the first time it was drab to say the least; a 0–0 draw in front of 15,500 fans was not what the promoters had in mind.

The stars did their best – Pele hit an early free-kick and George responded with a mazy dribble and shot in the 31st minute and another effort just before half-time. In LA, a more serious football game was played in front of 29,232 supporters (the second largest crowd ever for a soccer game at the Coliseum) – and Cosmos controlled the midfield. Stifling the game worked – Pele netted the game's only goal just after half-time. Aztecs manager Terry Fisher defended George's performance: "You've got to be able to get the ball to these players if you expect them to score goals."

Before the second match, Clive Toye finally got his hands on George, who had evaded him back in Manchester in January 1973 and rejected his advances again in February 1975. "There he was, lining up with LA for the national anthem," Toye says. "So I walked up behind him, grabbed him round the neck and said, 'So that's where you got to, you little bugger!' He turned round, smiled and said, 'Hello, Clive.' I had got my revenge when I signed Pele and was asked if I was going after Best again, now that I had Pele. 'No,' I said, 'Why sign George Best when you've just signed the best'."

Toye insists that it was George who had been the back-up choice and not Pele. "I went for Pele long before George and after much trying I needed to look elsewhere – partly to show Pele that life, and the Cosmos, could go on without him when

I was not making progress," he said. Given the players the Cosmos would go on to sign – Franz Beckenbauer and Carlos Alberto – it's not difficult to envisage a scenario where Pele and Best might have even lined up alongside each other. It was not to be. Still, considering the numerous times the Cosmos attempted to convince George to move to the US, one might consider Toye was protesting too much.

* * *

When the regular NASL season got under way the reality of the sporting situation hit home. The star names alongside George were Ron Davies – a journeyman footballer who had played a few games for United in their season in Division Two, and Bobby McAlinden, a former Manchester City youngster who George knew from back home.

"There was a buzz about him when he was 15," McAlinden recalled to *the42*. "We were playing them in the FA Youth Cup in 1964 and he ran fucking rings around us. They were just too good and only because George played. The kids from United and City tended to socialise in the same places. We'd go to the Stretford Bowling Alley and places like that. So we were around each other quite a bit. And then we found out this huge coincidence: me and George were born on the exact same day – May 22, 1946."

McAlinden had dropped out of the sport, only taking part in local Stockport five-a-sides which a few pros arranged throughout 1975. "We were friends – not the greatest of friends – but friends nonetheless," McAlinden said. "There was a bunch of us that used to go to the YMCA and we'd play a lot of five-a-sides. After he left United, George used to show up and play with us alongside some other guys he knew from the club scene in Manchester. It was great and I even think Rodney Marsh played with us once or twice."

It ought to be noted here that George had a strong affinity with players who had an allegiance to Manchester City. Marsh would become one of his closest friends, whilst it would be negligent to not mention Mike Summerbee again – Best and Summerbee were tremendously close, with the former being the latter's best man at his wedding.

When the LA offer came in, George arranged for McAlinden to go along and get his second shot at the game. He also arranged for Charlie Cooke, the Scottish international midfielder, to join.

Results were mixed in the first couple of months. After a few close games to start the season, it was Best and Pele at the Yankee Stadium in real competition. Pele's side ran riot, inflicting a 6-0 scoreline on their visitors. There was less excuse for an embarrassing performance against Toronto Metros-Croatia a couple of weeks later. "We were playing up in Toronto, getting our asses kicked in the first half," Fisher told *The Athletic* in 2020. "I was giving the team talk at half-time and I said, 'Hey George, don't hang onto the ball so much — they'll just put numbers on you. Spread the ball around'."

Fisher alleges that Best responded angrily, much to the embarrassment of the other players: "Seriously? Who would you rather have the ball – me or any of these guys?"

There was a recovery in June with consecutive wins by one goal over Portland Timbers, Vancouver Whitecaps and Tampa Bay Rowdies. All of the winning goals that season, save for one match, had been scored by George. On June 20, the Aztecs took a trip to Texas to face off against Dallas Tornado.

In the Tornado ranks was Jim Ryan, the former youth-team colleague of George's at United. "I had read he was starting to get himself fit again," Jim says. "When we played in LA it was a close game, but when we played in Dallas,we were winning quite heavily. I think he'd stopped drinking, but his team-mates had been out the night before. I was curious about this new George. I didn't want to hear that he'd been drinking – I just wanted to see him play in the way I knew he could.

"I didn't want him to be a pop star, I wanted him to be the best footballer, the terrific player I knew he was. We were up by about five or six and then, with about 20 minutes to go, George suddenly jumped up out of nowhere and scored two goals. They were great goals – the wonderful magic, the individual solo goals that he was capable of and which were far beyond my capability, or the capability of anyone else I knew.

"The goals were similar to the one he scored for the Earthquakes a few years later. I was quite pleased. We had a number of American lads in the team and I'd been talking about George before the games, saying how good he was. They'd asked about playing with him and I enjoyed telling them all about how fantastic he was. I talked about the player I had known, not the one who had this bad reputation.

"I wanted them to see him the way he was and I didn't want anything to mar that memory. After the game they were all asking me to introduce them to him. As we were coming off the pitch, the lads were running up to me. 'Did you see that? It was unbelievable!' I felt proud. It made me very emotional.

"We'd won the game – quite convincingly – and all the talk was about George. I just felt so happy. 'Well, I told you before about him, didn't I?' I'd built him up as the George I knew and he lived up to it… I didn't spend so much time with him, but

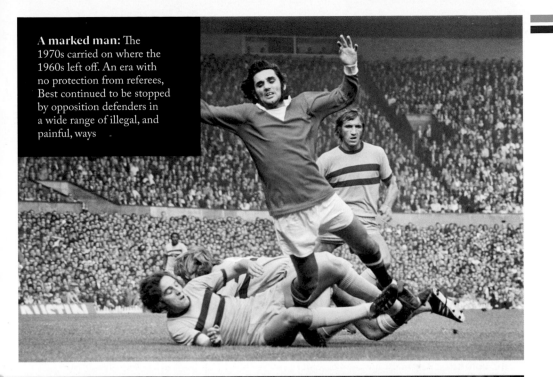

A marked man: The 1970s carried on where the 1960s left off. An era with no protection from referees, Best continued to be stopped by opposition defenders in a wide range of illegal, and painful, ways

Poetry in motion: The bend at the hip, the dip of the shoulder, the perfect balance and poise, Best with a football at his feet looked like the most natural thing in the world

Home comforts: Best tucks into another meal cooked for him by his landlady, the redoubtable Mary Fullaway, in her home at Aycliffe Avenue, Chorlton-cum-Hardy, Manchester in January 1972

An unlikely star in an unlikely fixture: Best in action for Dunstable Town versus Cork Celtic in August 1974

What's up, Doc?: Best with United manager Tommy Docherty at Heathrow Airport in September 1974. Docherty was desperately keen to harness Best's skills in a United shirt

Back in boots: Best is the box-office star as he returns to league football after 20 months out in November 1975. In a friendly for Stockport County v Stoke City, Best scored a 25-yard free-kick to show that his skills were as sharp as ever

Old pals: Best and Denis Law are full of smiles at a Bury FC testimonial game in November 1975

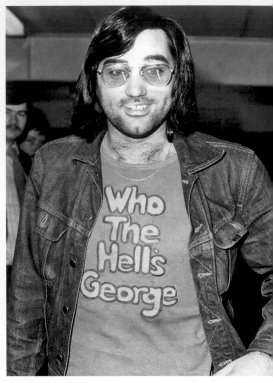

A sense of humour: Best answers his American critics with aplomb ahead of a move to the States

Fulham finery: Best and fellow footballing maverick Rodney Marsh enchanted Fulham when they played for the Cottagers. This January 1976 shows how at home they were in each other's company off the pitch as well

Still got it: Best starring for Fulham in September 1976

Aztec bound: Best joined the Los Angeles Aztecs in 1976 and scored 15 goals in 24 matches in his first season

Stateside: In action for the Aztecs in April 1978. As well as spells with the Los Angeles based side, Best also featured for Fort Lauderdale Strikers and San Jose Earthquakes while on the other side of the Atlantic

North of the border: Best celebrates signing for Hibernian in November 1979 in the most traditional away imaginable and is also pictured in action against St. Mirren on his debut later that month

Best plays for Borough: In March 1983, Best featured for Nuneaton Borough, answering a plea from Noel Cantwell to play in order to help the club pay a tax bill

They loved each other: Sir Matt Busby and Best take a trip down memory lane at Old Trafford in 1990

Overcome: Best gets emotional at Old Trafford in 1994 as the Old Trafford crowd salute the recent passing of Sir Matt Busby

Back together: Denis Law, Sir Bobby Charlton and Best at a Sky Sports promotion

Where do the years go?: Eusebio reunited with Charlton, Law and Best at Old Trafford in 2000

Pompey fan: Best looking healthy and happy as he watches Portsmouth take on Tottenham Hotspur in August 2005

Heartbroken: When Best passed away on November 25, 2005 Old Trafford immediately became a shrine to the greatest of all the club's No.7s. Fans flocked to United's home to leave shirts, flowers, signed messages and to comfort each other in their collective grief. It was a spontaneous showing of love for a footballer who had spent his career entertaining football fans across the world

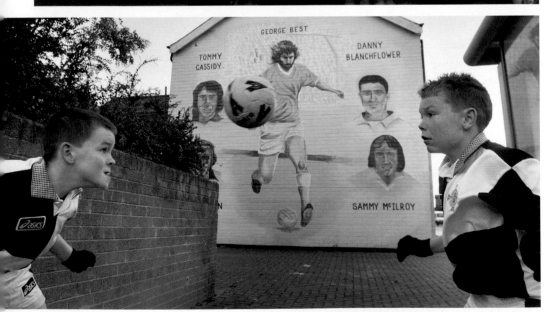

An inspiration: Two young footballers kick a ball around in the shadow of a mural to Best and other Northern Ireland greats. How many youngsters across the world were inspired to take up football after watching Best with the ball at his feet? Perhaps that is the greatest compliment, and legacy, of all

to me it didn't seem to be a different George. He just seemed the same lad I always knew in terms of personality."

That 6-3 loss to Dallas was followed by defeats to Minnesota Kicks and San Antonio Thunder. And then a couple of weeks after that, George scored a hat-trick in an 8-0 win over Boston Minutemen. Despite the indifferent results, the new way of life had proven revelatory. "George is not an asset, he's a necessity," Terry Fisher said. "Seven goals scored by him have been game winners. With him, if we are within two goals, we can still win the game. Of course, getting George was the easy part; building a supporting cast around him is the hard part. He is improving in every game, gaining lost time. But sometimes he forgets how gifted he is and gets frustrated when other players don't match up. He can do it all."

Fisher was only 26. But this was no repeat of the Wilf McGuinness episode, where senior players could not respect him due to a relative lack of experience. George was accommodated as a special talent, someone to be treated differently. Everyone in Los Angeles had prepared for that, but had been pleasantly surprised. They'd prepared for him to not show at the airport and had drafted excuses just in case. Chaffetz had found a house in Beverly Hills for George; he turned it down, saying it was too far from training, and he shared a house with McAlinden in Hermosa Beach instead.

"He calls and asks if there is anything he can do," Chaffetz said. "And to date, he's never missed practice. There are no pretensions. He has no limo, no special food. At the first pre-game meal, the team ordered steak while Best ordered cornflakes and bananas. Sixty-four cents instead of six bucks. Now the rest of the team orders cornflakes."

By July, George had dropped so much weight he was at his

lightest since he was 21. "I realised I had only three or four good seasons left," he told *Sports Illustrated*. "I couldn't live like I had been living the past few years. It was terrible at first. I could barely keep up with the others. I have this picture taken of me about two years ago. I really should get that thing blown up so I could look at it every day. The way I looked then and the way I look now are so different. If I had kept on that path, well, I just don't know where I would have ended up. I think I'm happier about myself. I've gotten my head together."

George spoke to the magazine about the possibility of moving his family out to LA. He had recently found a new girlfriend, the British model Angela Macdonald James. He discussed the state of the game at both his new and old homes. "The game that I loved playing had gone a bit sour," he said. "The team that had been so good was running on its past reputation and wasn't bringing in any new players. I was bored and upset with the whole situation.

"It used to be that anybody from England could get on a US team. That's not so anymore. In 10 years at the very most, America will be in competition for the World Cup. And the American style of play will be identical to the European, because so many of the players on the teams are European. Our biggest differences are primarily limited to terminology and have little to do with playing style."

Well, there were some differences. The American version of the game came with a particular aversion to tied matches, so every drawn game finished with a shoot-out. Then, the practicalities of playing a sport over a country the size of America came into play, with conferences and divisions separated by regions, and winners of those regional conferences pitted against each other in play-offs. The Aztecs qualified for the play-offs but were eliminated by Dallas Tornado. The end was anti-climatic but it had been a hugely successful first few months in America for George – he'd missed only a couple of games and ended with 15 goals and seven assists, earning him a place in the All-Stars team for 1976 alongside Pele, Simões, Chinaglia, Moore, England and Rodney Marsh.

Marsh and Best shared an agent in America, Ken Adam, who also had Bobby Moore on his books. Moore had been playing at San Antonio Thunder on loan from Fulham. Through his contacts there, Adam set up deals with the London club. The Cottagers were in Division Two but, with Moore in tow to elevate them, had reached the FA Cup final in 1975. When Adam put the suggestion to George – who had committed to play on with Los Angeles in 1977 – the forward was enticed by the prospect of Wembley and also the opportunity to play in West London.

Moore, incidentally, had passed comment on George before he knew he'd be sharing a dressing room with him that summer, saying: "George should have been the best player in the world. For a time he probably was. All the skill, goals, courage. Complete. He was right at times when he said he was Manchester United. There were times I saw him dominate a whole game from start to finish. Other times he did enough in 20-minute bursts to win matches outright, even for Northern Ireland. He played teams on his own... What I can't understand is why he just threw it all away... he's not only abusing himself but abusing other people's respect for him."

The *People* reported that George would be the highest paid player in Britain on a fee of £500 per match and a potential three-year deal. Fulham in fact offered £1000 a game but George turned that down to prove he wasn't in it for the money, although there were clauses written into a short-term deal to make it lucrative.

"Ken Adam was looking after our contracts and did the negotiating with Fulham for both of us," Marsh recalls. "We had bonuses on for appearances and attendances and so on. The first game I played in, the attendance went up from seven or eight thousand to around 11,000. George played his first game a week later. The crowd was about 21,000. I remember looking at my first pay packet and thinking, 'Christ almighty!'"

George's debut was delayed by a hold-up with the Football League. Because the Aztecs deal still stood, the American club wanted compensation. The Football League were aghast at this, with Alan Hardaker – infamous for his closed-mind-edness that some felt bordered on xenophobia – enraged at the mere thought of the English league being considered as inferior so as to owe the Americans anything. "As far as we are concerned, George Best doesn't exist in this country," he said, threatening that he would only consider official applications at the next management committee which was due to take place on September 19. There was one suggestion that the league wouldn't even make a decision until December 31!

Eventually common sense prevailed and George was free to make his debut against Bristol Rovers on September 4 – and Fulham coach Bobby Campbell insisted he would have no hesitation about playing him. "George has looked sharp in training and I have no doubts about his fitness to go straight into a match," he said. "He is dying to play and really excited about getting back into things… George has done everything asked of him in training. Sure, he has lost the ability to explode suddenly. But his skills are as sharp as ever and we are going out to play football the way it should be played."

The day before the game there was a buzz around Craven Cottage unlike anything the club had ever experienced. One hundred extra season tickets were sold with assistant secretary Nigel Williams saying: "It's been just like a cup final here. The rush for tickets started at 9am and it hasn't stopped all day. We have never known anything like this for a normal league game. It's all very exciting."

George was just as keen as everyone else. "I'm as excited as when I played my first match for Manchester United," he said. "Entertain? Just watch us. They are going to need three balls out there. One for me, one for Rodney Marsh and another for the rest of the lads."

The Bristol Rovers player marking the former European Footballer of the Year was 30-year old Lindsay Parsons, who claimed he had more important things on his mind. "Right now the problem of looking after George Best is secondary to sorting out my contract," he said. "This is just another game and I know what to expect from George Best. I have played against him before against Manchester United. I have never had a complex about him and I am not going to start now at my age. Rovers can rely on me. I shall mark him out of the game. There will be no dream debut for George Best."

At 3pm, fans were still trying to get in to the tiny ground by the Thames. Many of them missed George making a mockery of Parson's promise. Within two minutes, a free-kick was teed up for George on the edge of the box, and he bent it around the corner of the wall and into the net. The stunning shot was the only goal of the game.

"By George, he's done it," Mike Langley wrote in the *People*. "Doubled the gate, scored the winner and convinced 21,000 supporters that there's a bit of the Best yet to come. Go and see him while it lasts. No-one else today spins a long ball to a team-mate like a giant leg-break. Or tantalises them with a ball dragged under the sole – after wrong-footing them by stopping dead... Don't go to Fulham hunting the old Best. Go and be pleased by the present version. He's the Best around."

More followed. Against Peterborough in the League Cup a few days later, he scored a goal described by Jack Steggles of the *Mirror* as worth "every penny of the £500 a week Fulham are paying him": "Receiving a pass 25 yards out, the Irish genius stood stock-still as though daring defenders to come at him. Before they could move he flicked the ball arrogantly into the air and drove a sweeping volley into the top corner."

Best admitted it was "the most satisfying goal I've scored for a long time". Danny Blanchflower, the new Northern Ireland coach, said he would be ending an international exile by calling George up for the game against Holland in Rotterdam the following month.

Even in a 0-0 draw against Wolves, George was in entertaining mood. Wolves defender Bobby Gould admitted he had brought his sons to the game to get autographs. "Up until now George has only been a name to them," Gould said. "I wanted them to see the greatest player the game has ever produced. Were they disappointed? No. This fellow still devastates a defence... he does things that make you weep for the lost years."

The Fulham circus travelled to Luton and took a 2-0 win; the entire crowd of 19,997 stayed behind to applaud Best and Marsh off the pitch. "Marsh and Best were world class, magic – and what about their work rate?" purred Bobby Campbell.

Best scored early again in an entertaining League Cup game with Bolton before September's schedule concluded with the visit of Hereford to Craven Cottage. The cameras were in town for the highlights to be broadcast so that the nation could see if the hype was justified. Just who was this new George Best?

In the first half, it was more like: who are these new Fulham players? It was like the 1970 Brazil side had rolled into town and changed their yellow shirts for white ones – and that's not an exaggeration. It was easy to see the confidence pumping through the veins of these Second Division players, and easy to see they were doing things that were so extraordinary from what you might expect to see not only in a game of this standard but probably, at this time, in a game anywhere in England.

Alan Slough and John Mitchell were the personification of decent professionals at this level but today they were Gérson and Jairzinho; Slough playing the ball forward, Mitchell doing an elaborate dummy to set up the through ball for Slough to finish. The home fans responded by singing "Que sera sera… whatever will be will be… we're going to Wembley…"; it summed up the high spirits, lofty ambitions and the inspiration to dream that had been given to the fans.

This was the glittering period. The swelling of the crowd and the noise of the support were reflective of that. And it wasn't just the hardcore devotees here; there were many more in attendance due to the curiosity of seeing George Best and if he really was as good as they remembered, and as everyone was saying. There were moments in the first half where he strode like a lion out of an enclosure at a zoo, roaring into life; such as the mazy dribble past two defenders which brought a foul – from the resultant Marsh free-kick, the ball was crossed for John Evanson to make it two.

With the result comfortable, it was the second-half display which really lingered long in the memory as possibly the greatest 45 minutes of football you're ever likely to see in the second tier of English football. There was Best in the opening moments, prowling on the halfway line before surging forward 20 yards and shooting from outside of the area; the effort cannoned off a post. There was George just after, puffing out his cheeks at the exertion of energy where before it might have been effortless.

There was Best, creating an opening for Marsh who narrowly fired wide. There was Best, receiving the ball after an elaborate Marsh dummy, teasing his own full-back before finally providing the cross from which Marsh would score a header. It was not George's assist, but Marsh and Best celebrated together with high-fives in recognition of the elaborate and perhaps even over-the-top skill for this level. There was Best, winning the ball back at 3-0 with a tackle so ferocious you might have mistaken the game for the World Cup final; the retrieval starting the move from which Marsh claimed a magnificent second goal from long range. There was Best, put through by Marsh and giving his poor marker a nightmare by deliberating his move until right at the last, a crude blocking tackle from another Hereford defender knocking the ball away.

That was the problem with football at this level. If you were going to embarrass an opponent, it would reach a threshold where it would just not be tolerated anymore. And Hereford were not happy to be made clowns of. When Best received another pass on the halfway line, he had to use all the nimbleness of his peak to flick the ball up and away from the dangerous sliding tackle of his opponent. The speed with which the skill was executed was beautiful and left the defender some 10 yards away. Now, another tackle came in – but this time it was the white shirt of his good friend, Rodney Marsh.

Best's momentum helped him dodge the collision. The crowd roared as they felt it was more showmanship than entertaining accident; Marsh responded playfully by going back at George to try and tackle him again – only for Best to switch the ball between his feet, tricking his team-mate and leaving him laughing in his shadow. Fulham won a free-kick on the edge of the box; when Marsh caught up with the play, Best was still laughing about the previous incident. The mischievous pair stood over the ball ready for their final party piece. Best bent down as if to shift the ball with his hands, but instead, scooped it up with his right-foot for Marsh to strike on the volley. The connection this time was wild and wide, but the home crowd were appreciative of the brilliant imagination nonetheless.

Afterwards Marsh said it was the most fun he'd ever had in a game. "When I said it was the most enjoyable game I've ever played in I didn't mean it was the most productive or the most meaningful… it was just a beautiful game of football the way it should be played," Marsh explains. "All of the other lads raised their own game and they were trying tricks. It was like we were the Harlem Globetrotters. We did plenty of things that were planned but the tackle wasn't one of them! It wasn't strictly a tackle, we both went for the ball and he got there a split second before me… so I went back at him for the ball, and he beat me the second time too!"

Ah, there it is – the inevitable line. The Harlem Globetrotters. The backhanded compliment given to a team who are good but have no substance. This was the fine line walked by Bobby Campbell as far as Fulham were concerned. It was something he had to tentatively encourage – that's what came with signing a player like George Best.

"As I was becoming a professional there was Bobby Moore

and Alan Mullery at the club," recalls Tony Gale, a youngster breaking through at the time. "Alan retired, but then in my first full season as a pro I've got George Best and Rodney Marsh arriving on the scene. I was 17. I didn't get the opportunity to play alongside Bobby, because he retired, and I didn't get the chance to play with Rodney because he'd gone by that time.

"But spending that time with them was brilliant, and they were brilliant to me, considering they were world stars. When you're that age it's something you think will happen for the rest of your life and then nothing's quite the same after that! It was surreal. We had celebrities coming to watch us every week. Raquel Welch in the stands. Jimmy Tarbuck. Sean Connery. Kenny Lynch. Anyone and everyone coming to watch Fulham Football Club play in the Second Division.

"Obviously Rodney and Mooro brought a certain glamour but then we signed George, the man I still regard as the best I played with or against even when he was at that level... so goodness knows what he was like in is pomp. To watch him in training every day, we were watching him do things with the ball that I never saw anyone do again throughout my career.

"I don't want to talk about his drinking, it was obvious he was drinking quite a lot but he was a freak of nature because he was still at the front of every running session. No matter what coaches put on, he was the best at it. The normal drills. Tackling drills. Obviously he could dribble and he could spot a pass brilliantly. I was a young lad watching that Hereford game in the stand. Football is meant to make people smile and they certainly did when George was there. People talk about that game but that's because the cameras were there. There were other games like that which weren't televised. The boys were at that stage in their career... it was a strange blend. You could say that the rest of the Fulham lads would ordinarily have been struggling to stay in the division. And you knew the stars we had were not going to win the First Division. But boy, was that mixture going to be fun. Not just for the crowd."

Fun was fine. It was part of the reason for George doing this – he wanted to enjoy his football again. He also, though, wanted to be taken seriously. He wanted to be recalled to the national team. He wanted to show that now he had dropped the weight, even though that natural spring had gone from his game, there were now other strings to his bow, and there was still a player capable of shining on the big stage.

"Fulham did light a fire with him," Marsh says. "I want to make a point about George. I don't want to discount other writers, but whenever anyone is asked about anything, it's very easy for the interviewee to get carried away with their own importance and for the writer to indulge it. But I want to make this point. People said at the time it was George Best and Rodney Marsh. They spoke about us and how great it was. No. That's not true. It was George Best. They said it was great that the entertainment was back at Fulham and it was. But George was an entertainer and a truly great player. I was a great entertainer. There is a huge difference. A massive difference.

"When you have George, and then in his supporting cast you can have a World Cup winner in Bobby Moore and then someone who likes to entertain like I did, of course it helped to bring that quality out of the other lads as well. My attitude to football was that people paid their money to watch people dribbling, shooting and scoring goals. So that's what I tried to do. But George did it all. A fabulous player, the greatest player in the world. Scored goals, made goals, did it winning league titles and European Cups. On top of that, he entertained. He was the full package. He was still determined to win football matches wherever he went. He was a ruthless winner in every aspect. Even after we retired.

"We were invited to speak at a golf day for charity. There were two beautiful British Airways girls greeting everybody on the putting green. They were running a putting competition – you had three chances and if you made it you won a trip to New York for two. I don't care what anyone says, I never saw him play golf. He wasn't a golfer. The putt was downhill – started left, went down right into a valley and was 30ft down. George stepped up and gave it a tap. One shot, one try, straight in the hole. I couldn't believe it. I had 20 goes and couldn't do it!"

That mentality extended to training. George had returned to London with his partner Angela with every positive intention but was quickly consumed by the culture of the British game and started drinking again. But even if he turned up for training late, he would still turn up. "He might come in one day at 3pm and Bobby Campbell would give him a rollicking then take him and Perry Digweed, our apprentice 'keeper, down in to Bishop Park," Gale says. "It was jumpers for goalposts. George would be there dodging kids and women with prams on the park… Bobby was bringing through some young players and having legends of the game like that with us gave us an insight into what it was to be the best. George was a good influence on the young lads. He'd bring in free boots and bags for us."

The missed sessions were down to his illness, not – as it was at United – a lethargy and disconnect with the standard of the team's performance. In training, George was a popular character and had settled in well. "He'd always be betting you he could do something in training," Marsh recalls. "I remember him saying he could score three consecutive goals from the corner flag and he did it. No keeper, but still." There was also the time where there was a keeper – Peter Mellor – who George bet he could score a penalty against without looking. George back-heeled the ball past Mellor into the net.

"It's more than just saying he had imagination," Marsh says. "Because there were many players who had that. But the reason George was so unique was that his imagination could be spontaneous. He could think of it on the spot and do it – you never knew how and I'm sure he wouldn't have been able to explain it. As a player it's impossible to truly plan. You might think before of scenarios that might happen in a game and you can imagine how things would go in the moment. I certainly did that myself. But at the point of time of it happening, a lot of players fall down because they freeze, they can't think of it.

"George would do things… he would do a new thing in the middle of the thing he was doing. He'd be taking on one player and one would become two or three… or he'd just stop and go the other way. There was a moment in the game at Northampton [the six-goal game for United] where he sold the goalkeeper a dummy without touching the ball. He just left it and then walked it in to the goal."

* * *

To Rodney Marsh – and George Best – Fulham was only a temporary stop before a return to America. The other players at Craven Cottage had careers to think of. This was one season in a finite number of campaigns. Tony Gale was lucky – he had more than 20. Included in that cross-generational 20 were games against some of the best players the UK has ever seen. Kevin Keegan, Kenny Dalglish, Bryan Robson, Graeme

Souness, Paul Gascoigne, Gary Lineker, Alan Shearer, Eric Cantona, Ryan Giggs. In 1995, as a veteran nearing the end of his career, Gale tasted Premier League glory with Blackburn Rovers. In the 1976/77 season, he played in midfield alongside George Best, and for him it was not a only very serious business indeed, it was one of the most precious times of his career.

"You could say that the period wasn't really sustainable and in terms of a long-term plan it wasn't the best," he admits. "Those players were only there for a short time. There's the inconsistency that comes from when those players weren't available or after they left… but it put Fulham on the map.

"It wasn't just Fulham who loved it. Opponents did too. They were rammed. The atmospheres were incredible. Everyone looked at the comical side of George and Rodney tackling each other and that apparently summed us up at Fulham. They saw it as a carnival. I played eight games with George in midfield and then for the rest of my career I played centre-back. Those eight games… what an experience. He was so intelligent.

"He would constantly tell me to make sure I could find space, and if I could find myself space when he had the ball, he would find me. There were situations it should have been impossible. I did as he said and I'd still be surprised when he passed me the ball because either the angle should have been against him or there were too many players. I'd literally think, 'Fuck me, how've I got the ball here from where he was?' It wasn't for show. He had lost that burst of pace but he was compensating with trickery. His passing improved. He didn't get the credit, but his intelligence of passing and his range became incredible."

The honeymoon period ended after Hereford. It was down to earth with a bump when Fulham lost 4-1 at Southampton on October 2 and Best was sent off; another piece of history for George even with this mishap, as it was the first day in English football history where actual red and yellow cards were shown. Referee Lester Shapter was only too happy to show a red to the most famous player in the country after some "foul and abusive language". It was something even Saints boss Lawrie McMenemy felt was harsh, and indeed, he said he would personally appeal on Best's behalf to get the card rescinded. "Swearing is industrial language – it's part of the game," McMenemy said, but to little avail – George was suspended for one game.

He was still in positive spirits as he joined up with the Northern Ireland team to travel to Holland. "Obviously I've matured – off the pitch anyhow – but living in London helps," George told reporters. "Perhaps if I had moved to London earlier, with the right team of course, I would never have gone out of the game. Manchester was much too claustrophobic… don't get me wrong, I love Manchester and have some great friends there. It's a great place – if you're not a footballer. There are so many places in London you can lose yourself. I know Chelsea wanted me some years back… if I had gone to them a lot of things may have been different for both of us."

That wasn't the only talking he did. Bill Elliott, reporter for the *Express*, was keen to ask George what he thought about coming head to head with Johan Cruyff, acknowledged by most as the number one player in the world. A couple of hours before the game, travelling to the stadium (reporters were allowed on the team bus), Elliott asked George if he thought Cruyff was better than him. "You're kidding aren't you?" Best laughed. "I tell you what I'll do tonight… I'll nutmeg Cruyff first chance I get."

Nutmegging had been the talk of the squad since a practice

match against Luton on the Monday. Best had told team-mate Derek Spence to count how many he did in the game. "Not being funny, I lost count," Spence told *The Irish Times* (although he also told the *Belfast Telegraph* it was "at least 20"). "He was unbelievable, to see him in action like that."

At De Kuip there was a sense of dramatic occasion even when the teams were announced; a pause for "Number seven, Georgie... Best!" As he made his way out of the tunnel, a blonde girl reached out to hand him a red rose. He ran past her but then noticed, ran back to take the rose and kiss the girl's hand to a rapturous reception.

The game was five minutes old when George received the ball in a menacing position. He dodged the tackles of three Dutch players and seemed to be making a beeline for Cruyff on the opposite side. Their paths collided. Best versus Cruyff. George dropped his shoulder once. Twice. Cruyff was drawn in. Best slipped it through the stationed feet of his legendary foe, and ran round to get the ball. He raised his fist, pumping it towards the press box, though in the heat of the moment it looked like a personal celebration. "Only a few of us in the press box knew what this bravado act really meant," Elliott recalled. "Johan Cruyff the best in the world? Are you kidding? Only an idiot would have thought that on this evening."

Another in the press box was Paddy Barclay. He had not enjoyed the same conversations with Best as Elliot, but even to him it was obvious the motivation of coming up against Cruyff was irresistible. "It was almost like a red rag to a bull," Barclay recalls. "That's exactly how it looked. All I can remember from that game, all I can see is George. I remember nothing of Cruyff or anyone else. Best single-handedly took them on. He was unbelievable. Sometimes it seemed as if he was taking them on all by himself, and I say that without wanting to do anyone from the Northern Ireland team a disservice. He was running the Dutch players all over the park. It was an incredible performance and you don't do that with just talent. You need mental and physical strength. It didn't get heralded like his performance at Benfica but it was one of the most remarkable things I saw in that whole period of covering football."

It was a triumphant night, without victory, for Northern Ireland. Their 2-2 draw was a famous result. Best was magnificent throughout. Having got the taste for it, Johan Neeskens fell victim to another nutmeg later in the first half.

"I remember standing back and watching him nutmegging Cruyff and then nutmegging Neeskens," Jimmy Nicholl, the then-Man Utd full-back, told the BBC. "It gave us a lift. There was one of the best players in the world, if not the best, playing for us. I remember standing back thinking, 'This is great'. I honestly felt, 'Come on then – we deserve to be here.'"

Nicholl recalled that at the hotel afterwards, Best was fielding phone calls all night from potential suitors enquiring about his availability – teams from all over Europe – to the extent that the hotel staff had to bring the telephone to the dinner table.

"It's amazing he did it to players of that calibre," Sammy McIlroy recalled. "They didn't like it and it rattled the crowd."

According to Spence, the evening lingered as long in the memory for the Dutch players as it did the Irish – and even though Neeskens himself had been a victim, he couldn't resist poking fun at Cruyff. "Jimmy Nicholl says that when he met Neeskens and Krol years later they remembered because they were delighted," Spence recalled. "They were finally able to take the piss out of Cruyff."

There is a difference between playing in the Second Division on the back of a long sabbatical from English football and a spell in America, and then playing in the Second Division on the back of an international game against another of the all-time greats when everyone is talking about you. Especially when the novelty had worn off and the true disparity between Best, Marsh and Moore and the rest of the team was revealed.

Bolton Wanderers stopped one route to Wembley by winning in the League Cup after a replay in which Moore was sent off. The winless streak continued for eight games and included a defeat to Cardiff where George scored his team's consolation goal and then blasted his team-mates for "playing like a bunch of schoolboys in the first half".

That was nothing compared to the 5-1 defeat by Notts County at Craven Cottage; although County manager Ron Fenton appeared to be more starstruck than his players had been. "I hope my lads took note," he said. "George's work-rate was unbelievable in a situation where his attitude was probably put to the test in a manner he had never previously experienced. He might have been forgiven for drifting out to the wing to sulk, but did exactly the opposite. He ran and chased in that last half-hour with the same conviction as he had early on and was a credit to himself and the game.

"I have never known a crowd behave like Fulham's did that day. They were watching their team being thrashed yet got behind them with tremendous enthusiasm. I felt that much of this was due to Best. The fans could see the effort he was putting in and responded to it... I always thought my most fond memories of George Best would be of him turning defences inside out and scoring spectacular goals at Old Trafford. But now, I shall never forget the way he applied himself when there was nothing to be gained but self-respect."

Fulham were desperate for a boost but had to find it without Marsh, who was now back in America. His replacement for the visit of Oldham in early December was Teddy Maybank, whose coiffured blond locks were just about the only thing they shared. In midfield were Slough and Evanson, partnered by Best who was dropping back to conduct the play.

If George needed any inspiration to perform on top of the fact it was a professional game, and televised for *The Big Match* again, he had it in the presence of a few hundred Manchester United fans who had made their way to Craven Cottage following the postponement of their own game at nearby Loftus Road. The second half was Best's; after first showing fine defensive work, some of the old tricks came out. A fine flick to beat a man in his own half brought the crowd to their feet, and soon after, a tremendous dummy and pass on the right started the move for his team's third goal.

Best scored the fourth; without doubt his best moment in a Fulham shirt, even though the Hereford performance gets the greater exposure. The Oldham defence failed to clear a cross and George picked up the ball 25 yards out. Yes, the old speed of body had gone, but the speed of thought and ability to move the ball deceptively remained. He hurdled one tackle and, with two defenders in front of him, feinted to shoot. The Oldham players were not fooled enough to fall but not brave enough to commit, leaving a good space for George to get his shot away. He clipped a chipped effort and the goalkeeper, expecting something else entirely, slipped. All that was left was to see if the accuracy of the shot was good – and it was perfect, caressing the bottom of the crossbar on its way in for extra visual effect. A fifth goal followed, but everyone was – as always – talking about George.

"What a funny old club they must be to support," commentator Barry Davies exclaimed. Ten days later, Best was starring again, this time at Ewood Park in a 2-0 win. "George Best confirmed last night that scoring great goals has become a habit again," Nigel Clarke wrote in the *Mirror*. "He received the ball on the edge of the area, then coolly bent a beautiful shot that left England's new Under-21 goalkeeper, Paul Bradshaw, shaking his head in astonishment."

"It wasn't one of George's best games, but what a goal," Bobby Campbell said. "It was worth the fans coming just to see that. We have to encourage George to be selfish now because he so badly wants to fit into a team pattern."

On December 27, Fulham made a short trip for a local derby. "I was on the bench as a 17-year-old at Stamford Bridge where 55,000 people turned up to watch George Best and Bobby Moore play against Chelsea," Gale remembers. "Chelsea beat us 2-0. But George and Bobby were always demanding the ball. That showed their bravery and responsibility. To want the ball in any situation to try to win the game."

George was not able to make a playing impression the way he once had at Stamford Bridge, but did experience a familiar feeling from trips there in the past when he made a gesture at the referee John Homewood and was charged with disrepute. "The referee was disgraceful," he said. "I have been whacked a lot this season, and never seem to get enough protection. Obviously I get upset and frustrated. Now it seems I am not only playing the opposition every week, but taking on all the country's football administrators as well."

Indeed. Alan Hardaker was at his meddling best when the issue of George's return to America was brought up, due to the NASL season starting before the Football League season ended. Hardaker said Best had been "dumped on Fulham for the winter", threatened to investigate the transfer and involvement of agents, and finally said the league wouldn't approve his return to America until Fulham's fixtures were completed. Bemused, Best and John Chaffetz simply agreed he would see out the campaign in London.

It was a disastrous winter for Fulham, whose 10 losses in 13 games starting with defeat at Chelsea included an unceremonious thrashing at Swindon in the FA Cup. No Wembley, and no promotion hopes either. But Best was doing his utmost to turn it around. He was praised particularly for performances against Burnley and Bristol Rovers when he was clearly of a higher standard.

But those on-pitch problems inevitably resulted in George returning to familiar ways to cope off the pitch. That meant more appearances in the newspaper gossip columns. Where he could keep it separate he was still able to function but when the two collided – quite literally, as it did when the car he was driving hit a lamppost shortly after 4am on February 24, 1977 – then he was unable to do anything to help on the pitch either. He was originally scheduled to miss the rest of the season with a minor shoulder fracture but rushed himself back after just five games, that keen he was to help his team.

He was back for the loss at Hull on April 2 where one journalist described him showing "lots of class without making much impression"; but his return attracted the biggest crowd of the season to Craven Cottage the following week for the visit of Chelsea, and Best turned on the style in a 3-1 win which was ultimately the difference between survival and relegation.

He flew back to Los Angeles on May 8, promising that he would come back and play some more games for Fulham the following season. Later that month, Manchester United finally returned to a position of certifiable health when they defeated Liverpool in the FA Cup final. Tommy Docherty was soon to be sacked for having an extra-marital affair with the wife of the club's physio, but had transformed United into a vibrant team playing the best football seen at the club in years.

George was a part of the club's past, now, but even as Alex Stepney celebrated winning the one medal he had so coveted, he could not help but feel a slight tinge of regret. "George should have been with us in May 1977," Stepney says. "Instead he was at Fulham with Marsh and Moore. He could have been with us, still young enough to have been the main man on the day, still young enough to be part of the team moving forward. It is tremendously sad for everyone that he wasn't."

HOLLYWOOD SEQUEL

T he mid-1970s saw the boom in popularity of the movie sequel. *The Godfather: Part II* was released in 1974. Many reckoned it to be even better than the original. Blockbuster movies of the decade like *Jaws* and *Rocky* followed the trend, to mixed receptions.

George Best had already tried his hand at starting a new chapter of the same story. It hadn't ended well. Now he was hoping he could follow the narrative of Sylvester Stallone's titular character following the vindication arc of his first spell in Los Angeles. Now came the glory – or so he hoped. The problem is real life does not always play along with the dream, even in Tinseltown or the convenient landscape of sport, which allows you to pick and choose your own beginnings and ends.

Still, it must be said that there was a time in Los Angeles where it seemed like it might continue perfectly. George took his spell there seriously and returned with proper ambition. Though he was joining up with his Aztecs team-mates after the season had started, this time he was able to hit the ground running due to the match fitness routine he'd put himself back into over the last year.

Aztecs had started their season well, with four wins (two through shootouts) but were stumbling by the time George returned. They lost against Dallas Tornado and Minnesota Kicks, and on George's comeback match, lost against Portland Timbers. It was only 1-0 – but on the Timbers team was Willie Anderson and he watched his former colleague with a certain sadness. Whilst America waited for George to show flashes of what he'd displayed the previous year, Anderson watched an imitation of the greatest player he'd ever seen – and wished for what might have been.

"He was done, really, at 27 or 28, and he hadn't even hit his peak…he was the greatest player of his kind and we still never saw the best of him," he says. "What a terrible waste of a magical talent. Imagine him 28, 29 or 30 with even greater maturity. We missed all that, he missed all that. God… we missed it.

"The way he could make fools of opponents, that was something that came as he matured, got stronger and became more confident. In the youth team and in his early days in the first team his raw talent helped him stand out. Once he realised how good he was and grew into it he became even better. What could have been? I know Pat Crerand tried but George went from being one of the lads to being a superstar, his family were far away in Belfast but they might as well have been a thousand miles away. His family were the guys at the club and his landlady, but then he bought that bloody house and became very lonely, so never stayed in. I felt [his social circle] were the wrong people for him, they didn't care that he had a game on Saturday and they didn't have his best interests in mind. We cared. We would have at least stood up to him. But at that time, everyone just wanted a piece of him."

Despite his sadness, Anderson is keen to point out how good George was. "Nobody came close. The greatest players today who have the best of everything in terms of facilities, pitches and diet, are still in his shadow," he says. "He was the greatest ever, playing on mud heaps with cannonballs in heavy boots and people throwing themselves at him on and off the pitch…"

Anderson pauses. He knows he has to make the modern comparison: "Messi is the best around today. There are similarities, perhaps he's the closest. He has a similar feistiness, and he goes at players…" Again, he drifts mid-sentence. There's a tone of regret. It's almost as if he's apologetic to Messi.

"…But not like George. George was like the Rolling Stones, everyone else was and is a middle-of-the-road band, and he just loved being on stage."

Just like the Rolling Stones, and keeping with the sequel theme, George's latest comeback tour did have its moments. But in his earnest approach he'd also brought back some of the baggage he'd left behind on his first trip to LA. He was drinking again – part of a routine at first, something he felt able to carry with him whilst still being better than just about everyone else, just like in the Second Division back in England.

He had settled with his partner – although there had been a brief split following the accident in London, as George had been driving the car of the chairman's daughter – and had also settled into the scene in Los Angeles. He was of enough importance that he would be invited to celebrity social events – such as the one he met Angela at – but of enough insignificance to the California public that he could walk around the streets with his top off without being stopped once.

But there were issues. The drinking, yes, although that didn't impact on his performance in an obvious way. After starring in a win over Vancouver, he went on to score in five consecutive games, all won. Instead it was other ailments that begin to play a part in hampering what George could do on the pitch. He had complained about ankle problems all year following some agricultural tackling from the second tier players in England and was now suffering from a flare up of the knee problems he'd encountered early in his career. Years of being physically targeted had caught up with George, who had just turned 31.

Still he continued. Though the goals dried up over the summer, George remained productive. His only goal in eight games came in a 5-2 defeat against the Cosmos. Pele got a hat-trick. Some revenge over the Brazilian, Toye and co was exacted a week later in LA when the Aztecs won 4-1. It was a very different George Best to what the English audience were used to seeing. He was still the best player on the pitch but he was a deeper schemer, operating from the middle or inside left positions with two lines of the play in front of him.

Though no longer able to accelerate off the shoulder, it almost appeared – especially in games against the Cosmos and Pele – as if George would drop deeper deliberately to keep the attention on him, so that people would observe in a head-to-head that he was the one showing all the skill. That in a demonstration of their all-round capability, George was the one who could do everything.

The Aztecs had invested in that very hope. They moved grounds from El Camino College to the Romanesque, column-surrounded Coliseum, hoping for bigger attendances that never materialised because George alone wasn't able to capture the mainstream attention of the non-soccer public in Los Angeles. Best told the press he wanted the team's backers to provide more big-name signings. He'd seen Franz Beckenbauer make the move to New York and was keen to see someone of similar ilk alongside him. It didn't materialise.

Through it all there were no disappearing acts. George played in 25 successive games, contributed 18 assists and then scored in the last five successive games to help the Aztecs claim a play-off place. The first of those five was a true rarity – at the Aloha Stadium of Team Hawaii in their sole year of existence.

The swing in the scorelines against the Cosmos had created the impression that these would be the two teams facing off in the SoccerBowl; this was the impression that those in charge of the game would have liked to present too, considering it would pitch Best v Pele on the big stage. Best would have liked that too – but the Aztecs were eliminated in the 'Conference Championships' stage, the semi-final, and Cosmos went on to defeat the Seattle Sounders in the final.

Eight days later, George was lining up for Fulham in London against Blackburn Rovers, having stayed good to his word about returning there. This was a short-term agreement – arranged almost as an apology for missing those games after his accident. This time, there was no Moore, no Marsh. Nothing to hide the difficult world of the Second Division, nobody else to take the kicks, and George was not only going through the motions, he was being flogged at the same time, subject again to the same over-the-top treatment from defenders. The rule changes had helped him when he had the speed to get away. Now he was often embroiled in the thick of it. "After 10 games, I decided I'd had enough and went back to LA," he said. (He actually played 11 times – including an Anglo-Scottish Cup game against St Mirren – and scored three times, twice in the league.)

Despite this decidedly underwhelming return to Craven Cottage, the shine was not taken off his overall spell in London, according to Tony Gale. "Some of the lads went on to have decent careers. We'll often meet up and we'll always talk fondly of those early days with George," he says. "I know George went elsewhere but I always thought Fulham was the only place apart from United where people got to see what he really was capable of. Yes, he was good in America but in the competitive element of British football he thrived again."

Gale insists the performances for Fulham were even a rubber-stamp on his greatness for anyone who might have doubted him. "George could play anywhere," he says. "He came down to the Second Division after people had written him off. People ask if a player like that could really be as good today and he would be the best today. There's no doubt. He'd be even better than we thought he could be because there were still people trying to kick the shit out of him on bad pitches."

George went back to Los Angeles again, ostensibly to prepare for the new campaign, but found himself caught in one of those cycles. His drinking routine had become worse. Sometimes he was skipping training altogether to start drinking at 10.30am. He confessed that he would often not go home for days but had proposed to Angela – Angie, as she is more popularly known to readers – in a show of commitment to pretend the reality wasn't occurring. The behaviour was accommodated by his team-mates. McAlinden would accompany him on his benders although he didn't have the tolerance George had developed. "It didn't matter at all [to us] because he did the business on the field," goalkeeper Bob Rigby told *The Athletic*. "Why would we really care?"

Well, Best had cared. He'd cared enough for the Aztecs to succeed. He wanted them to act like a proper football club. But now they were, he was becoming a problem for them. In came the investment George had pleaded for from Larry Friend, Rudy LaRusso and Alan Rothenberg. Friend and LaRusso had played in the NBA so felt they could help the Aztecs connect with the domestic audience. Rothenburg had a serious ambition to transform the American game. His fingerprints would be all over the US hosting the 1994 World Cup and then launching the MLS. He was, in effect, the person George had been crying out for, but now George was stuck in the cycle of unprofessional behaviour which had undermined various points of his career before.

In January 1978 George married Angie in Las Vegas. He phoned his parents to tell them the news – forgetting that he was the news, and they'd already heard rumours that it was going to happen in the papers. He invited some of his family to Los Angeles for the first couple of weeks of the NASL season, as the first two games were at home. The second was against the Cosmos. Before the game George presented the recently retired Pele with an award for 'The Greatest Soccer Player in the World' on 'Pele Appreciation Day'.

Members of the Best family were present. Ann was not well, so Carol stayed in Belfast to look after her, but Grace, Julie, Ian and Dickie all went to Los Angeles. George was keen to show them his new way of living. They took a trip to Disneyland. Ian remembered the laid-back lifestyle of George's Hermosa Beach apartment – and the mess one might associate with someone trying to get out of their bachelor lifestyle – and also how relaxed George had seemed in those weeks. Ian had just turned 12 and idolised his older brother. They played darts – George bet Ian he could beat him playing with his feet. "He did, as well," Ian says. "It seemed like there was no sport he wouldn't be the best at."

The family had been used to traveling to Old Trafford. They were part of the fixtures and fittings there, welcomed as part of the club by the players and Sir Matt Busby. Ian, whose middle name was Busby in a nod of respect from Dickie for all Sir Matt had done, recalled Busby often slipping him a £20 note to "buy some sweets". But things were decidedly more manic in the Rose Bowl. Dickie decided that they would not stay in the player's lounge and instead escape for the anonymity of life outside the stadium, but not before watching some of the game, where Grace remembered seeing George dribble around a number of players to the thrill of the crowd, and realised "for the first time just how good he was". Still, the tourists had become homesick.

Even without Pele, Cosmos won that game 1-0. The Aztecs needed George at his best just to compete. When he was struggling – which he started to do once his family were back home – they struggled even more. In 1978, they lost eight of the 12 games he played. George scored a solitary goal against Portland Timbers in a 4-1 defeat. He complained to the owners that they needed to buy players. They did – George disagreed with the standard. The new owners, for their part, disagreed with George's approach to life as a professional player. They told Ken Adam they wanted to trade him. "It kind of blew me away," Adam said. George, though, agreed that his time was up in LA, and said he didn't want to play there anymore.

There was no acrimonious, drawn-out affair this time. The

speed with which everything moved was enough to spin your head. Four days after making his final appearance for the Aztecs in a disappointing 4-0 defeat to Washington Diplomats, George was on the other side of the country, making his debut for Fort Lauderdale Strikers against New York Cosmos.

The Strikers had endured a rough start to the season themselves. They had a traditionally abysmal record against the Cosmos and added to that with a 7-0 loss on the opening day. They lost their next two matches. Their next game was, conveniently for them, against Best's Aztecs. George had watched in bemusement as before the game, there was a funeral procession where a hearse was driven on to the field. Then a coffin was taken out. Out of the box popped Strikers coach Ron Newman, who jumped in front of a microphone and declared: "We're not dead yet!" Fort Lauderdale duly recorded a 2-0 victory against the Aztecs to kickstart their season.

When the chance came to sign George, Miami Dolphins owner Joe Robbie pounced to bring him to Florida. George didn't take much convincing, but was happy to see Gordon Banks, Ian Callaghan and Ray Hudson as established British players in the team. Robbie also spoke of his ambition to bring Gerd Muller, the legendary German striker, to the US.

In the short term, Best would have to sprinkle the stardust to compensate. He was motivated to begin well. He always was. That much was familiar, though the long-haired man in the garish red and yellow horizontally-striped jersey wearing a number three on his back would have passed for an impostor before people would have believed he was George Best. He would have to win his new crowd over.

But when George was as able as he was willing, that part of the deal was never in question. Within the first 60 seconds of his debut, the ball dropped kindly to him in the box, and Best showed that instinct he was renowned for, smelling the chance and lashing it into the net with his left foot. An avalanche of goals followed. Strikers, Strikers, Cosmos, Strikers, Cosmos. Late in the second half George received a pass from the right wing, took a touch, and then – with a defender either side of him – struck an effort that slipped under the goalkeeper and into the net. Cosmos scored again, but it was Best's night.

"We felt on top of the world," Ray Hudson says. "Bestie was tremendous. He was spellbinding. He was everywhere… cutting across the field, beating one player after another."

Speaking to *The Athletic* in 2020, Hudson continued: "To have that sort of ingenuity and brilliance – in the most profound sense of the word – and to be that sort of person amongst his team-mates, it was beautiful. It was truly beautiful."

The honeymoon periods, however, were getting shorter. Best had been brilliant and influential but he was pumped on adrenaline and, once again, the incentive to prove people wrong. It wasn't a sustainable mindset to carry him through a season. The coach in Florida was Ron Newman, a former professional at Portsmouth and Gillingham among others who had made America his home since 1967. He was one of those trailblazers keen to introduce the English culture to the American game. What was theoretically a match made in heaven became a nightmare due to the fact that Newman was of that older generation to Best. George described Newman as an "Alf Ramsey" of coaches and it was meant as a slight regarding his old-fashioned values.

Hudson recalled how he and his team-mates had been shocked by George Best the person – how he was "beautiful and charming", and had settled right into life with his new colleagues, generously offering them lifts to their hotels even though it would be a journey in the opposite direction to where he was residing.

The Strikers qualified for the play-offs, but were eliminated by local rivals Tampa Bay Rowdies, who had a British coach of their own who once courted Best in Gordon Jago. But on the pitch they also had Rodney Marsh, and old acquaintances were renewed over the summer.

"He was maybe 10lbs overweight, he'd lost that yard – in his case, three yards of speed – but he still had that innate skill," Marsh recalls. "He could still do incredibly brilliant things, and because some of the players we were with were obviously nowhere near his level, he most definitely enjoyed an Indian summer in America. I saw him a few times a season. When he was at Fort Lauderdale we would see each other often through the summer. We continued that through the rest of his life."

Marsh recalls Best being in reminiscent mood. "I always found George to be incredibly self-reflective," he said. "We'd go out for dinner and have a drink and he'd always be reflecting on things that he'd said and done. It all boiled down to the fact that football was the true love of his life, and everything else was a distraction. We could go out for a coffee and talk about football for five hours. He could be an anorak, talking about who scored this goal or that goal…

"He talked about United. George told me that when Frank O'Farrell went back into the transfer market and signed Ted MacDougall and Ron Davies, and invested all this time in players like Alan Gowling, he said that was when he knew it was all over for him at United. He hated Docherty. He used to say that when Tommy said 'Good morning', he would go and check the weather. But he took responsibility himself.

And George was right to take responsibility. He was on the downward slope from 26... the downward slope for George Best was still much higher than for other players. When you're the best player in the world and unstoppable... but he lost his edge and you can't recapture that.

"When you've been idolised in front of 100,000 people, they are moments you don't forget. I have said before to anyone who loves football, I wish that they could be able to transport into my body to experience what you feel... the veins in your neck get so white, the blood rushes so intensely... it's something you can't translate. I wish it could be neurolinguistic. I had it for moments. George had it for nearly all of his life."

When the two competed in the play-offs, Marsh recalls one incident which summed up everything: "I think the problem was that George was so great... now this is just an opinion, it's nothing that he ever told me, but I think because he was so great, he had a problem dumbing down to play at a lower level. That might offend a few people but that's just how I saw it.

"We were contesting the play-offs. They won the first game, we won the second, so it went to a mini-game. George was on one of his dribbles. He was going left, going right. Suddenly he clipped a ball out right. Even I thought, 'Where's that going?!' but when I looked up, I saw there was a player clean through on goal. The only problem was even that player hadn't anticipated the ball, and he just let it roll past him out for a throw in. George was furious. In fairness, nobody knew what to expect – nobody did the things George did, apart from the truly great, so what came next sometimes was difficult to anticipate, as that poor lad found out."

The Strikers lost on penalties. Best had been substituted towards the end of the match, as well as Hudson and David

Irving, the former Everton forward. Newman had withdrawn them to discuss the impending penalty shoot-out, not realising that only the players on the pitch at the end of the game were eligible to take the kicks. Best admitted he was "fuming" that Newman didn't know.

Further professional complications which seemed needless to George continued to frustrate him. He'd agreed to play for Detroit Express as a guest player on their European tour in September 1978. Fulham complained to the FA, insisting they held his registration. The FA went to FIFA, who issued a suspension on October 11 to stop George playing in any country under their jurisdiction.

The day after, he received a shocking phone call from his father. Of all the difficulties to face George, the greatest tragedy of his life surely came when his mother Ann passed away at the age of just 54 in October of that year. She suffered from the same illness as George – something he often felt guilty for. She had also survived two heart attacks. After the second, George had gone to see her. He had lied and told her she looked fine. In many respects, that act of pretence summed up a tremendously sad situation all round.

George was told by his siblings that their mother had given up drinking for a year before she died. "I felt guilt over my mum's death, but like any alcoholic, (which I was, though unaware of it) I didn't relate it to my own drinking," he said. "That might sound incredible but I hadn't admitted to myself that I had any sort of drink problem at that stage… If I had related her situation to mine, I would have tried to sort out my own drinking then. But I drank even more heavily after her death, partly because of that guilt, I suppose."

Where once football had been his escape, it was now part of

his living hell. A legal battle rumbled on until March. When it got to court, the judge ruled against Best, but FIFA lifted the ban right before the NASL season was about to resume. George had not treated this pre-season as seriously as his others. He was nonetheless selected to play against the New England Tea Men. The Strikers were winning 2-0 but George was frustrated. Newman felt Best was annoyed with himself and was lashing out at opponents, so, fearing he was going to get sent off, substituted him with half an hour still to play. That fury Newman had been concerned of came back to hit him, literally, when Best threw his shirt at the manager as he made his way to the bench.

"How can I get fit if I'm taken out 29 minutes before the game is over?" Best said to *Soccer Digest*. Newman attempted to diffuse the row. "It's fine," he told the press, "I've always wanted a George Best shirt."

It was not a happy camp. Two weeks later the Strikers were playing Cosmos at the Giants Stadium in front of 72,342 supporters. With 20 minutes left, Best and his team-mates had a 2-0 lead. Newman took off Irving and Hudson and in their place came on a rookie American and an Australian trialist. Cosmos staged a late comeback and won 3-2. Newman congratulated his players for their effort – Best was furious and blamed the coach in front of the other players.

If there was anything remarkable to take from Best's 1979 season, it was that he managed 19 games for the Strikers, considering that he missed training as often as he did. In fact, on four occasions he was said to have done a 'vanishing act' and those disappearances would consist of three or four days in a row where he didn't turn up, nor did he tell anyone of his whereabouts.

"It was like, 'Where would he even go?' He was with his friends and he just disappeared," Guy Newman, defender at the Strikers and also son of the manager, told *The Athletic*. "Obviously all the players, we all loved him. Everyone loved him. But he just kept letting people down. People would keep sticking up for him and he'd let them down. He'd let himself down. It was a shame. He was a fabulous player and he was just a great person. It was tragic really."

The dispute became public – thanks to George telling the press. Newspapers ran a poll asking who the club should get rid of – Newman or Best. Newman was the landslide choice – but he still had the backing of Joe Robbie, and in late July, George was once more looking for a new club.

EASTER ROAD

I n November 1979, George Best was 33.

Though there were undoubtedly years of his prime that were consumed by the anxiety of not being able to perform to the standard he had once achieved, now various other personal issues – his illness, the death of his mother, the temporary breakdown of his marriage to Angie – were at the forefront of his mind, rather than whether or not he would win another European Cup or whether he could be perceived the same as Johan Cruyff or Pele.

Angie had flown back to Los Angeles and George followed her. She told him that if he promised to sort himself out, she'd give the marriage another go. He agreed and said he'd find a club back home to prove himself.

The truth is that George Best's time at any football club was eventful enough for a supporter of that team to fill a book should they wish to write it (and, indeed, the author John Neil Munro wrote *When George Came to Edinburgh* on this very period). Team-mates have stories of him off and on the pitch. Managers and owners have tales of the experience of dealing with him. There was usually at least one magic moment on the pitch, one incredible occasion of legend on the training ground, and more than a handful of stories about convincing him to join the club, convincing him to train, and then the implosion of his departure. Hibernian Football Club are no different, though before November 1979 they would have probably considered themselves one of the last places on the planet George would end up.

That he did was thanks to the ambition of chairman Tom Hart and the idea of *Edinburgh Evening News* reporter Stewart Brown. Brown and Hart were friends; the journalist suggested George might be the tonic when a defeat at Dundee left Hibs bottom of the league. "Can someone like George Best save Hibs in their present plight?" Brown asked.

"Best is, or was, a footballer of the highest pedigree and he is a personality – the like of whom does not exist in Scottish football. Best does not need to rush around madly to display the skill that oozed from every kick in his great days with Manchester United. Somehow I think he might pull in the fans too. Hibs' present predicament is perilous and it will take a feat of some magnitude if they avoid the drop."

Brown also attended a testimonial at Ipswich where Best played – before the match, he was drinking orange juice instead of the offered champagne, insisting he was keen to show "the old magic is still there".

Hart promptly paid Fulham £50,000 for his registration. His team were struggling in the league, but quite aside from anything else, he knew that bringing Best to Scottish football would guarantee money on the gate. Hibs manager Eddie

Turnbull was reticent, but Hart could not resist and reportedly not only agreed to pay Best £2000 per week out of his own pocket (a matter of concern for the Hibs players who were on an average of £110 per week) but also told the player he didn't even have to live in Scotland. He could fly in on Thursday, turn up to training on Friday and fly back to London on Saturday after the game.

George agreed, although even this commitment was beyond him at this stage. It began as it always did, however, after the inconvenience of an ankle injury was overcome. Some 13,670 packed into St Mirren's Love Street for Hibernian's visit with their new player. "I remember going there for his first game and it was a sell-out," Turnbull recalled. "He was a great lad with the others... never said much, a bit of a quiet guy in the dressing room."

But an immediate impact on the pitch came. Best scored in a 1-1 draw. A week later was his home debut against Partick Thistle. The regular attendance at Easter Road was around 4,000 – this time 20,622 were there to watch George, and the huge attendance inspired his colleagues to record a desperately needed 2-1 win. George looked good. Not as good as his pomp, of course. Not even as good as his first year with the Aztecs. But a definite improvement on the heavy player who had cut a uninterested figure for Fort Lauderdale.

Just as it seemed there was a positive momentum shift, George skipped training in mid-December. He turned up on the morning of the game against Morton. Hart claimed Best was drunk; he said when he suggested that Best could feign injury but at least sit on the bench to save face, George told him: "I could try to sit on the bench, Mr Hart, but I might fall off." He wasn't included in the squad.

He was also accused of being drunk for the following week's game against Rangers. But this time he played, and played well; starting the move for his team's first goal and generally showing some of the skill he was known for. The frosty December pitch added to the spectacle; if Best was inebriated, then perhaps he ought to have played under the influence more often considering how wonderful his balance was.

One hapless Rangers player got the Bilardo treatment; a late challenge by Derek Johnstone, made to look worse by the icy surface but most definitely still a red card by modern standards, came in from behind on George. He picked up the ball, turned around and offered it to Johnstone. Hibs scored again to secure another 2-1 victory. No, it wasn't quite the Stadium of Light, or Windsor Park and Scotland, or even Rotterdam and Holland, but Rangers at Easter Road on that surface was a game forever known in this corner of the world as the George Best game. The away fans were wound up at George's showmanship but even they saw the funny side.

"I remember playing Rangers," Tony Higgins, the Hibs midfielder, said. "In a very contentious game, George goes to take a corner. He had a can thrown at him. Rather than remonstrate with the police, he picked the can up, took a sip and took the corner. The Rangers fans laughed, it completely diffused the situation."

In mid-January, 21,932 were at Easter Road for the visit of Celtic. In the 26th minute George netted his second goal for his new club, latching on to a heavy touch from a team-mate and cutting inside to fire in a quick shot which caught the goalkeeper off-guard at the near post. The 1-1 score was another good result.

"There were moments of genius from George and sometimes

he was a move ahead of his colleagues but that only confirmed my fears that he was out of step with the rest of the team," Turnbull said. "And all the time I had that deep-down feeling that you know something is going to go badly wrong.

"Watching George was like being witness to a car accident taking place in slow motion. And it was only a matter of time before the head-on crash occurred. In February 1980, George simply went absent from training sessions. Nobody knew where he was until he was photographed coming out of a nightclub in London."

First, George failed to turn up for the home game with Morton on February 9. Tom Hart told the press he had "no alternative but to suspend him until he reappears". On Monday, George travelled to see Hart and apologised. He agreed to stay in Edinburgh for two weeks. The following week, before a Scottish Cup game against Ayr United on the Sunday, George was at the North British Hotel with the French rugby team who had played against Scotland that afternoon. He got drunk with them and Hart had to go and see if George could play. He couldn't. The Hibs owner decided to sack George.

For the first time in the press, George made an admission. The *Mirror* carried the front page headline "DON'T BUY GEORGE A DRINK!" – a plea from Angie. "I have a big alcohol problem and I must get it sorted out," George told the newspaper, saying he was "disgusted" with himself. "Now I stand to lose everything. Even Angela is disgusted with me."

On Saturday February 23, he appeared on ITV's football show *On The Ball* where he openly admitted he had a problem, but he explained he was seeking therapy and that he felt it was a issue within the sport, not just him. "I walk into a room and 60 people want to buy me a drink," he said. "But I know it is my problem. I've just got to learn to say no. I've been running away and hiding in a bar behind a bottle when I should have been standing up and facing things."

Hart, on seeing Best's contrition, had a change of heart and presented an olive branch. "I am offering George the chance to come back once he has sorted himself out," he said. "His suspension will be lifted if he reports to Easter Road and conforms to club discipline." Hart said he would be happy to fly Angie in to keep him company, and claimed George could play for another three years, but warned: "He has let me down three times since he joined the club… this is his last chance."

"He was just like Sir Matt, always giving me another chance, which again made me think it was fine to carry on the same way," George said. It was this routine that saw his peaks and troughs continue. Whilst one couldn't doubt the affection Hart already had for George, his suggestion that this affliction could be solved so easily was naive at best.

The fact remained that even as damaged goods, there was pretty much always something to be seen from a player whose primary goal was now to entertain fans. San Jose Earthquakes offered George a chance for the 1980 NASL season and so he got himself into some sort of fitness – though already noticeably heavier in just this brief spell – by playing in Hib's last few matches of the season.

There was one slight reward for Hart's faith. One final mesmerising display against Dundee on March 25, now played in front of a low crowd who didn't know what to expect or whether to even expect George any more.

"George Best chose this occasion to turn on his finest performance for Hibs," read the match report in the *Aberdeen Press and Journal*. "He scored one goal and laid on the other…

for most of the first half it was virtually a one-man show. Best's distribution was a treat for the 5,000 to watch. Everything revolved around him… There was no keeping Best out of the picture. Schaedler was booked in 20 minutes for scything him on the right touchline, before he opened the scoring five minutes later. He dummied four defenders in the box, and sent a beautifully judged left footer low past Donaldson."

It wasn't enough to save them from relegation. His entire deal with Hart had been based on a handshake and he gave the Hibs owner his word that he would come back and play more games at the end of the NASL season, though even he didn't know if that was from a sense of duty or an acknowledgement that he would probably be indulged once more.

In his penultimate game in this first stint for Hibs, George played against Aberdeen – who were managed by Alex Ferguson, and were challenging for the league title. Best had an infamous argument with Dons midfielder Willie Miller; Miller making some disparaging comments about George's performance, and George jibing back that the 1-1 draw would cost Ferguson's side the title. It didn't – Aberdeen actually sealed the league with a 5-0 win at Easter Road – but by then George was back in California, too far for any salt to be rubbed into the wound.

REMEMBERING THE BALL

M ilan Mandaric was a Yugoslavian immigrant chasing the American dream. He succeeded, becoming very wealthy through the manufacturing of computer components, and used his money to invest in football, where he became a part of the circle of financiers involved in the negotiations to bring the top players in the world to the NASL.

With George Best known to reside in Los Angeles for many months of the year, and with the bridges to and from the Aztecs already burned, there was an opportunity for Mandaric if he could convince the player to move a little further up the Californian coast to play for San Jose Earthquakes. But Mandaric himself needed a little convincing after Best's previous spells in the NASL. Fortunately, in George's corner was Bill Foulkes, who was the head coach at San Jose. "Although Mandaric was sceptical, he left it to me," Foulkes said in his autobiography. "Pretty soon George was training in a magnificent climate. Suddenly, this was more like the player I knew. There was a sparkle in his eyes, some colour in his face and before long the old confidence flooded back. As the season went on, George looked better and better."

Mandaric was soon won over. "He came to my club, in two years we forged close ties and became great friends," Mandaric told Slovenian website SiolNET. "George was a great footballer and a man. He was good to everyone, just not to himself. Only those who know him know how big his heart was. Of course he was also a fantastic player who knew everything about football. I remember one Monday, training after the games was getting more and more relaxing, asking him to teach me to play. He told me he couldn't teach me. 'How can you not?' I asked him. He replied that he still doesn't know how he does it. 'I get the ball and then it runs by itself,' he said.

"He was a genius. A football genius. I also hung out with Pele. Of course the Brazilian was a great footballer, but he was also a man who knew exactly what he had to do and how he had to behave. He was a great professional. George was in my opinion even more talented than Pele. He was a man of the people who behaved the way he felt. He was like a child. No matter where he was, he played football as if he were playing with his peers from childhood. He played for pure pleasure."

It was this quality Mandaric and Foulkes were hoping to bring to San Jose. But the 34-year-old George had mostly lost that childlike charm when it came to the sport, and had been overcome with the weary cynicism of the business aspect of it. He was not in the right frame of mind, as he conceded in his book *Blessed*, when he described it as "the worst place ever for me, in just about every aspect of my life".

Still, he gave it a professional shot, playing against Edmonton Drillers on April 27 1980, just eight days after his last game for Hibs. George also played in the next six games over the space of a month. The results had started poorly – Best's first four games were lost – but two of the next three were won as the team got used to George playing a central role in the middle of the park, dictating the play in front of him.

There were signs of positional intelligence which had been adapted with the new skill-set – or limitations, to be cruel – that George found himself with. But he was still a positive contributor, measuring up an opponent before deciding what he could and couldn't do. If there was an athletic midfielder against him, he wouldn't try and beat him in a standing sprint. But he would still see it as a challenge, an opportunity to outwit the opposite number and get the edge of him over two yards before running. His use of the ball and the intelligence of his passing was far greater than anyone else on the pitch.

When he had the ball he was rarely caught in possession in the same way as he had been in his final outing for United in 1974. In a certain way, there was a maturity to his play he did not have when he was 10 years younger. It was enough to make you yearn – as Willie Anderson obviously did – for what might have been if this version of George had the physical capabilities of that player Anderson had broken through with.

For the first time in a while it seemed as though there was a set-up designed to help George and not just take advantage of what he had left. Foulkes had protected the financial risk of the deal by proposing to Mandaric that George would be paid on the Monday after the game to incentivise him showing up for training and matches.

It wasn't just Foulkes that George was reunited with. António

Simões, the former Benfica winger, was coaching at the Earthquakes. Simões was given the task of chauffeuring the man he had quietly idolised. "I would pick him up from the hotel to take him to training. He was a quiet guy outside of the field – and he was not very good in the morning!" he laughs. "But when training started and a ball was put in front of him, he was alive. He became the artist. There was the smile. There was the fun. When I remember George I remember the ball, and when I remember the ball, I remember George Best."

Despite being at an age to wind down, there were still times George displayed the familiar competitive frustration. "America was relaxed compared to Europe," says Simões. "He knew he was near the end of his career. He played in a more casual way. There was not the same intensity. Training was not the best for him. In games he still had the same fire because it was still competition, but in training, it was difficult for him to keep that standard. His frustration seemed to come from the standard in training rather than the opponents.

"Every morning I watched him still capable of the magic, the frankly unbelievable. One morning he decided he was going to dribble everybody. So he did. He took the ball around everybody and then he dived to the grass and started laughing. He said to me, 'Please, can you just get me somebody who will at least try and challenge me?!' At times when I picked him up or we would be at the club away from the pitch, that handsome face would often be frowning. I did not know why he was sad. But as soon as he was with a ball he was enjoying himself and we were all full of enjoyment just to watch him.

"It was truly fantastic. It seemed like football was the only thing that made him happy. One morning when I asked him if that was the case. He smiled and said, 'You're right, but I don't want to talk about it.' It was so interesting to me. I wish I could have talked more. The way he expressed himself on the pitch, with his heart and with his passion, … and then when he was away from the pitch, 'Don't talk to me about football!' I was fascinated by his personality. I really miss him. This kind of personality should live forever. In a sense it will, of course."

Best was attempting to hit reset whilst searching for some stability in his life. For once that took precedence over his desire to truly prove himself on the pitch. Even when he was reunited with Johan Cruyff, who had signed for the Vancouver Whitecaps, on June 22, the intensity that had been present less than four years earlier, that desire to prove himself as the better player, was no longer in evidence. That was partly due to the problems in George's right knee, which were growing worse. He was now having to have fluid drained from the joint before and after a game, as well as at half-time.

For this period in his life it seemed that George was trying to take a greater sense of responsibility. He knew that time now had a greater grasp than he did over how long was left of his football career. He was there at training. He was present for games. He even continued through the pain barrier for charity events. In one – a fundraiser for underprivileged children – he stayed behind afterwards with the children and bet them each $10 that they couldn't score a penalty kick past him. This was one wager he didn't mind losing. He'd attended the event with Rodney Marsh. "In the car afterwards, he took my hand and put it on his knee," Marsh says. "It was twice the size of what it should be. My fingers literally sunk into his skin because of all the fluid. No-one ever talks about him doing things like that. He was so kind. So generous."

At the end of the NASL season, George had agreed to go

back to Hibs for a few extra games – and to make "easy money, too, since I was not expected to be the George Best of old". Before he departed, Angie told him that she was pregnant.

"I'm just hoping I can continue where I left off," George told reporters upon his return to Scotland. "I'm trying to pretend nothing's happened in between and I hope they accept me back. When I was here originally the response was tremendous and I just hope it continues."

Cameras were present to watch George's taxi arrive at Easter Road from the airport. Only one supporter with an autograph book was waiting – perhaps the others didn't expect him to show. It was difficult to find Hibs as enthused for the second spell, with their recent relegation meaning there were no more glamour games. He played six matches – none of them were lost, although none quite had the sparkle of his performances against Rangers, Celtic and Dundee. The last was against Falkirk in front of 6,947 – higher than average, but still only a third or so compared to what they had pulled in at the start of the year. Obligation fulfilled, George went back to California.

* * *

As much as the American game could claim George was not the same as when he first arrived in the country, he was able to level the same accusation right back at the authorities. The NASL's 'speculate to accumulate' philosophy hadn't worked. Crowds came to watch the star players but when the likes of Pele and Beckenbauer left, attendances and interest dropped and there was no succession plan on which to build.

The American game wasn't as strong. The money was no longer there. No-one was willing to throw good money after bad. It meant making the most of what you had while you had it and hoping what was left would be enough to create a league. For a while this new approach included an indoor competition over the winter – which prompted George's early return from Scotland.

Having failed to penetrate the outdoor sport market that was saturated by baseball and American football, it was thought that soccer's similarity to hockey might bring in some interest and also even provide a solution for stadium sharing. The idea had temporary success – but it was the worst possible thing for George's knee issues due to the harder surface, smaller pitch and unrelenting pace. He agreed to have cortisone injections just to alleviate the pain but even then had to play in a fashion where he favoured his left foot and shifted his body weight over to that side whenever he could.

"The indoor league was created, which was a lot of fun to play in," recalls Chris Dangerfield, who had just arrived at the Earthquakes. "George wasn't meant to play in those games, but he came to watch us training and then, when he felt like it, decided he was going to join in the games too. He hadn't even played indoors before. He scored five goals and laid on three assists in the first game. It wasn't massively different to the outdoor game but most of us took some time to get used to it. You had the rebounds from the boards around the pitch, the rolling substitution system that was sometimes so fluid a player would run on and off the pitch depending on if the team had possession or not. George refused to come off! Even with the bad knee, he was brilliant, as you would expect because of his ability to control the ball in tight spaces."

The indoor season was unrelenting as George and Angela prepared for the birth of their child. George was still drinking but was desperate to change. In his 1968 book *Best of Both Worlds*, George had mentioned "an uneasy desire to die peacefully in my sleep around the 40 mark. Old age? Ugh!" Now, with more than a decade having passed, time and mortality were put into a new perspective. Having gone through counselling, rehab didn't appeal initially, and he tried taking Antabuse tablets that would make him violently ill if he tried to drink. It didn't stop him – his excuse was that he was testing the pills. He pledged to change after the birth, telling himself that this should be the moment; and for a while, it was.

Dangerfield, who later married Angela's sister Lindy, stayed with them around the time that Calum was born on February 6, 1981 (the anniversary of the Munich Air Disaster, a coincidence that took George some time to comprehend). He recalls George's efforts to stay sober included filling the void of boredom with other activities. "George wanted to get his act together," Dangerfield says. "We used to go to movies, read, play darts, have cups of tea… He was such a lovely guy when he wasn't on the booze. I always try and stress that. He could talk to you about anything. He was so intelligent. Angela went out and bought him the most expensive set of golf clubs. God knows why. He was the worst golfer you have ever seen in your life! He could only hit with a three iron so used it for everything. Tried all the clubs but only used the three iron."

Dangerfield's background in football was similar to Bobby McAlinden's and it was through him that he became acquainted with George. "Everybody wanted to be George Best if you were a footballer," he says. "He was a game changer in so many ways. On the pitch, yes, but also with his style… his shirt was untucked, his socks were down. Anyone growing up playing the game in that era wanted to be him. It was a working man's game, everyone was cut from the same cloth. But there was nobody else like George in the '68 team, so it made him stand out even more that he could do things nobody else did, too... they could be so much more expansive and unpredictable with him. He brought colour into a black and white game.

"It is always awkward when you first meet someone you have a high regard for. We met through Bobby McAlinden, a mutual friend. It was terrific to meet him on a personal basis. The first thing you recognised was that he was just a lovely guy to be around. I didn't know him before that time but I was always under the impression that he was more relaxed than he had been earlier in his life. He enjoyed the idea that nobody knew him in LA. He was super famous and able to enjoy an easy-going life where he wasn't being harassed.

"He wasn't the character he was perceived to be. He seemed very focussed on settling down and being good for his family. I ended up in San Jose because George wanted me there. I was leaving the Aztecs and I actually had a more lucrative offer elsewhere but George insisted that I join the Earthquakes and convinced Milan Mandaric to make an offer. I have no regrets, they made it right, I made it into their Hall of Fame!"

Despite his own initial reluctance, Best had found San Jose a place conducive to his recovery in some aspects. Before Calum was born, Chris remembers George spending evenings painting Disney characters for a mural on the nursery walls. "He was doing everything he could to be better," Lindy says. "He really wanted to get over it, but it took him over. He was one of the nicest people you could meet. He wasn't a partier, he wasn't a person who sought the headlines – that just happened to him.

"He just loved football, that's all he lived for until Calum came along. Nobody would go to the lengths George did if he didn't want to beat his disease. He was a genuine and nice person. We'd sit and have quiet nights in watching television, Ange would cook – or try to, bless her! George wanted to be better. In California he had people around him who were genuine. He wanted to get past the illness, but it just sadly wasn't his direction. It was so very sad."

The day after Calum arrived, George turned up to play against Dallas Tornado for the indoor Earthquakes side. He remained reliable and responsible. He tried to abstain himself. The physical effects of George's withdrawal concerned him so much that he agreed to take Milan Mandaric's offer of rehab a few weeks after Calum was born. He was checked into the Vesper Hospital for 30 days, but left after two weeks. One doctor told him that he must abstain from drinking for 12 months or he would either die or be back in the hospital. To the best of his knowledge, George did abstain for that period. But it didn't always work out.

"The area suited him for what he wanted to do – but he couldn't do it because he had a disease which followed him everywhere he went," Dangerfield recalls. "We'd play darts at the local pub…we'd only be drinking tea, but the bartender would say, 'Hey, should I put a shot of vodka in George's tea?' I'd go, 'Are you crazy? He's trying not to drink. Take it away, that's not what we're here for.' What the fuck were they thinking? I guess these were people who were trying to be his friend, they just wanted to talk to him, but didn't realise what harm they were doing."

Mandaric asked counsellors to visit the club to talk through what was happening so George's team-mates could help him stay sober and spot the warning signs. "We had AA meetings in the locker room sometimes, so yeah, it became a bit of a distraction," Tony Crescitelli, forward for the Earthquakes, told *The Athletic*. "They'd tell us what to do if George got offered a beer, or if he asked for one. They'd tell us how to deal with George if he was drunk; it was all a little crazy."

These concerted efforts had George in the best mental and physical condition he'd been in for some time. He gave Calum the middle name 'Milan', following the Best family tradition in such matters. And, with things in his personal life feeling so settled, he was able to adopt a healthier mindset to his football. No longer was it just a means to an end, a ritual of eking out what money he could in what little career he had left. "I wanted to prove that I could still play, to myself as much as anyone else," he said.

The only issue was the Earthquakes team did not have enough quality. Earlier in his career George had been demotivated by such a scenario but in these latter years, accepting his own place and reputation, this was now a challenge.

"What got him out of the bed in the morning was the love of the game," Dangerfield says. "You could say that he needed to maintain an income but I felt he just enjoyed playing. Once it's taken away from you, you miss it. The football dressing room is a unique place for a player. And although the San Jose locker room was a small one, and it had a strange mix of American, English and Yugoslavian players together – it certainly wasn't Old Trafford, preparing for a European Cup game – it was a locker room nonetheless and he enjoyed everything about it.

"There was a time when I felt the NASL was the most exciting league in the world. It was so much fun. You could get on a plane and go to a different climate to play against stars like Ray Hudson, Pele or Chinaglia, Rodney Marsh, George… you bring players like that over then the quality improves.

"The assistant was a guy called Peter Short. He'd coached under Rinus Michels. They used to love a drill where they'd have a 30-yard square, big goals, three on three with goalkeepers. You'd play for hours, the idea was repetition through triangle shapes, always having two options when you were on the ball. As soon as one team let a goal in, another team of three came on. It was great. Our little three was me, George and an American kid called Mike Hunter. George bet us $20 that he would be able to get all of the opposing team on the ground before scoring. He sat them all down and rolled the ball into the net. 'That's it,' he said, 'That's me done!' He laughed, took his shirt off and strolled off the pitch. He was still that good."

* * *

On the opening day of the NASL season on March 29, New York Cosmos visited California. Nobody knew what to expect – whether George would show or not, and what condition he would be in if so. Mandaric tells the story: "Two hours before the game, the coach came to me and said George wasn't there. 'Put him on the list, he'll come,' I told him. The clock was running, but he was not there. He didn't show up 15 minutes before the match, so we had to take him from the team.

"I went to the parking lot in front of the stadium and saw him. He was just slowly getting out of the car, he was all messy and sleepless. He hadn't slept all night. I thought I was going to kill him. 'Boss, I'm going to win this game for you!' he told me. I quickly intervened with the referees – back then in the US the rules were looser – but it was clear that half of the stadium came because of him and Best was allowed to play."

Cosmos won 3-0. The season started as well as could have

been hoped. Eight of the first 16 games were won with George scoring six goals. But the next seven games in a row were lost, pretty much guaranteeing bottom place in the Western Conference. There was only pride to play for when Fort Lauderdale Strikers travelled to Spartan Stadium on July 22.

For a moment in time on that night in California everything seemed to align perfectly. Many things had changed but one thing remained true – George Best, with something to prove and fuelled by some feeling of injustice, was still capable of producing magic.

There were always two facets to this.

There was the showman – the one who planned what he was going to do. The one who practised scoring corner-kicks. Who dreamed of dancing around everyone at Wembley. And then there was the pure footballer. The athlete. The competitor. The one who did what he did out of instinct and succeeded just because he was better – moments where even he didn't appear to realise what he was doing. The great unplanned. Benfica away. Chelsea in the League Cup. The ruthless killer. The breathtaking moments nobody could quite explain. There was no innate desire in the moment to provide something that nobody had ever seen before. But, because he had the talent, the moment duly arrived anyway.

Why was there no great plan anymore? The mental and physical frustrations of the last few years had taken their toll. George wanted to prove himself but proving himself these days meant different things. It meant being reliable. It meant competing without people saying he was embarrassing himself. It meant proving in a one-on-one against any opponent, he retained the trickery and intelligence to beat anyone.

He had won the European Cup. He'd scored the most

important goal in Manchester United history to do so. He'd scored some of the best goals in Manchester United history. He could not win the SoccerBowl like Pele. He was not going to have anyone making the pre-game song and dance that was made of Pele. He was not planning on scoring the greatest goal in NASL history, but, because he had the talent, the moment duly arrived anyway.

Fort Lauderdale were a goal up. George, already frustrated with the referee, Ian Foote, after feeling he wasn't being properly protected, was simultaneously annoyed that the official would not play advantage when he had beaten players and been fouled. He felt the referee was too hasty; too condescending, almost, as if he was doubting George's ability to do damage. He was fuming when his former team were awarded a soft foul. He was incensed further still when they took the free-kick and scored whilst he was still remonstrating.

Best received the ball from the kick-off. He was still arguing with Foote in the centre-circle as he played it out wide to his team-mate Gary Etherington. Etherington advanced and did well to evade a defender. George jogged forward with Foote, before noting a corridor of space, and yelled at Etherington to "give me the fucking ball".

Then comes George Best's final act.

Two Fort Lauderdale players come at him. One is Ray Hudson. He jogs and comes to a stop, acting as a brick wall. George drops his shoulder to approach the other player, Thomas Rongen, who is coming in from the left. Rongen's momentum means he has to turn his entire body around. He can't – he's in a tangle – all he can do is throw himself into a slide tackle with the sort of brute force Best has faced all night. He does, but he's too late.

George Best is 35. No, he's not at his prime. But he's had more than 15 years of knowing how to deal with the threat of two defenders. He has reached the stage of unconscious competence – he can do this on auto-pilot. It's not done with the 'what just happened' grace or speed of the teenage years. But it's no less mesmerising. Perhaps it's even more mesmerising, because now we know George. We know his fallibilities.

"I made an attempt, and after that I had the best seat in the house," Hudson says. "He was using the players as just slalom gates. The ball was velcroed to his foot. Our players were just diving at him desperately, trying to get a touch to the ball."

Two more defenders – Bob Bolitho and Ken Fogarty – are in the box. One stands behind the other, the standard and accepted practice to serve as a roadblock. Again, George has been here before. He just has to show tricks and balance until one loses their cool. They always do.

In the space of three seconds and six yards – which seems like a lifetime for the eviscerated defenders, and proved to be considering the endless times this was subsequently shown on repeat – Best pulls the ball to his left with his right foot, drops his right shoulder after feinting to move the ball to his left, drops his left shoulder and pushes the ball to his right, and immediately uses his right foot again to pull the ball to his left.

In the switch of the ball, Bolitho has lunged. He's committed. He's nowhere near. Fogarty is off-balance. He's wobbly-legged, too spellbound by the path of the ball to even attempt to throw at a leg at it. Fogarty is still watching the ghost of the ball as Best moves past him into the middle, free of all challenges – somehow – eight yards from goal. At the last, Colin Fowles steams in from the left like a kamikaze pilot, and though he is much too late, simply adds himself to the list of Strikers players who would forever be linked to this moment as those who tried and failed to stop George Best. By the time Fowles is on the scene, Best has already wrapped his left foot around the ball and fired it into the bottom corner. Hudson described it as "like watching van Gogh paint *Starry Night* live."

"He was just so good," Fogarty recalled, telling the story to *the42* in 2015, becoming the final name on the long list of opponents keen to share the story of how they were beaten by the magnificent Best. "He was supposed to be washed up... If you look at the goal, initially, some of the defending is very poor – we had guys who weren't goal-side and weren't in a good start position but having said that, it was brilliant... It was the greatest goal in NASL history, but before that goal, he had made an even better run and he went past about seven of us and just as he was about to stick the ball in the back of the net, somebody brought him down for a penalty. It would've been a better goal than the one he'd scored."

The other run was actually after the first – and Best scored the penalty. Earthquakes staged an impressive turnaround to win 3-2. Later, George would explain how it "felt like watching someone else score" when he saw the goal. "It didn't mean anything in terms of the table," he said. "But it meant everything to me in terms of personal pride."

It was also a one-up on the referee. "When you are at that level you need something to motivate you," says Dangerfield. "George was actually trying to prove a point, to the referee of all people. The referee had blown for a foul on someone pulling George's shirt, and George had turned to the referee and said he was going to score, he should have played advantage. 'Nah, you wouldn't have scored,' the referee said. The first thing he did after scoring was to let the referee know."

George was a fan of Western movies. He envisaged himself as the hero in his own story. Here he was in the Wild West of America, resembling Gene Wilder's Waco Kid in *Blazing Saddles*, the gunslinger everyone thought was past it who stuns everyone with one more act of bewildering brilliance.

But life isn't a movie. It was not quite his last moment in American soccer. There were encores there and elsewhere. He played five more games and scored two more goals for the Earthquakes. As usual with George Best, the sight of him doing something only he was capable of raised hopes that it could happen again. Suddenly eyebrows were raised. It just so happened that at this time, Northern Ireland were enjoying their best qualifying campaign in years and would eventually reach the 1982 World Cup in Spain.

"We all saw that goal when he beat five defenders in the box," Sammy McIlroy says. "Bestie was in unbelievable nick then. I remember being asked for my opinion, Pat Jennings too…all the Northern Ireland players were clamouring to get him in the squad. With George playing that way, we thought it would give us a right lift. We all wanted him in, but Billy Bingham, the manager, said he couldn't really trust George to be away for five or six weeks. It is a crying shame for a country like Northern Ireland that the best player we ever had never played in a World Cup Finals."

For a while his future was up in the air. San Jose took a four-game tour of the UK in England. The first of those was at Hibernian, where the hosts won 3-1. George felt he played poorly but was surprised when Bingham called him up for the crucial qualifier against Scotland. On watching him again a couple of days later, Bingham reconsidered, feeling he had been too hasty and that Best wasn't fit enough for international football.

But George had seen that, again, as a challenge. It was briefly rumoured that Ron Atkinson, now manager of Manchester United, might offer George a chance to end his career where it had all started. Prior to the San Jose tour, George went to Highbury to watch United's game in September 1981.

"If you told me there was a game tonight, I'd just put my boots on and go and play," George had told a reporter soon after landing in England. "I still regard them as my club, Manchester United, and obviously if I had to pick a club that I wanted to play for in this country they would be the team. It's early days and I don't want to put too much pressure on myself or people connected with the club. If it happens I'll be over the moon about it. I'll just sit down and talk with Ron and see where it goes from there. If it doesn't work out we haven't lost anything… I'd love to do it."

Atkinson was not long in the job and was busy trying to sign Bryan Robson to wear the number seven shirt at Old Trafford when he was suddenly inundated by local press. "The radio station rung me and I said that if he was serious I'd have a look at it," Atkinson says. "So we were playing Arsenal on the Saturday. He was at the game and I told him I'd meet him at the Royal Garden hotel after the match, at 8pm that evening. I heard that he'd left the match early and he wasn't there later. We gave him five minutes to show and he didn't."

United chairman Martin Edwards was quizzed by television reporters as he made his way into the ground before the game. "The position is that George Best has expressed a wish to come back to Manchester United," he said. "Ron Atkinson is sufficiently interested to want to talk to him. I've spoken to the manager about him and I've said that obviously the club would want to be satisfied on one or two things and of course so would the manager. One would be his fitness and whether he would be up to the rigours of First Division football at the age of 35. If he is and he proves his fitness then he can obviously take a chance with the other players in the squad."

Atkinson insists the offer was more out of ceremonial obligation than a serious proposition to get back into the Manchester United first team. "No, it wasn't really serious," he says. "I mean, he could have come and trained with us and I would have had a look at him. But it was a long time since his peak. It was more of a courtesy because he was a legend and I'd only just got to the club and I didn't want to be disrespectful.

"It would have been a million to one chance of it happening to the point where he would have played for United. Maybe even two million to one. Mind you, the game with Arsenal was awful. It ended goalless – he might have thought there was no way he wanted to play for us!"

George's version of events was that he didn't want to ruin the memory for the fans if he couldn't do himself justice. The move didn't happen. The idea of a romantic farewell remained only in the dreams of every Manchester United supporter.

The idea of a serious return to competitive football in England, however, was still very much on the table. Middlesbrough, struggling in Division One, made an offer to sign him, with manager Bobby Murdoch explaining that it could be just the place for George to prove his fitness if that was the key.

Best, again, was not put off by the idea of playing in a team that were poor. He did, however, pause to consider that with a young baby, it would not be the best thing for his marriage to return to play in England, even if there was a significant carrot dangling. Murdoch had fully expected that incentive to be enough to convince George, and was devastated when he learned of the refusal. George had contemplated and felt that even though it was a World Cup, just as the idea of going back to United, he would not do himself justice, and said: "I never wanted to go to any tournament just to make up the numbers."

George returned to San Jose but the Earthquakes had been taken over by new owners and when he dropped back into the routine of drinking and womanising again, his life was once more at a crossroads. He completed a stint at the Vesper but it did no long-term good.

"There was a dinner where George was awarded with the best goal of the year for the strike where he went around everybody," Dangerfield remembers. "He wanted to go out and celebrate. He was asking us all and we were telling him to just go to bed. He didn't – and that was basically the end of that at San Jose. It was just more that he was feeling so good that his natural reaction to that was to go out and have a drink to celebrate. He had such a good relationship with Milan but the new owners came in and they were not as tolerant."

Angie said she was leaving to go back to England and live with her parents. She issued George an ultimatum to try and fix their marriage. He followed. Back in England, George was faced with a bill from the Inland Revenue and was declared bankrupt in November 1982. He was taking work as a television analyst following the World Cup where he'd appear for ITV, but was also looking for a new club.

"The nomad had started again, I was flying here, there and everywhere," George said of his exit to Michael Parkinson in an interview on his 50th birthday in 1996. "All the top players started to leave the States. The crowds were dying down, the best players were leaving. All the reasons I'd gone there for the buzz were disappearing."

George's marriage eventually broke up for good soon after, when Angie discovered George's affair with the model Mary Stavin. He began to look for offers to play down south. One came from Reading in mid-October. "I've no problems any more. I can go out until four in the morning and there's no-one to stop me. That's why I don't want a long-term commitment to one particular club – not even three months," George said, which naturally put a stop to most clubs making an offer in the short term.

Plenty were prepared to make the case on his behalf. In late September, Denis Law had told the *Daily Star* that his former team-mate's genius was "too precious to leave on [the] sidelines". "His kind of brilliance happens only once in a generation," Law said. "Even after his prime, George could guarantee to fill any ground from Hartlepool to Hong Kong...

"I have been delighted to see he is over his drinking troubles and back to fitness. But can he make it back to the First Division at the age of 35? Football may need him, but does he need the kind of pressure that will mean? The pace of the game keeps on increasing. If only the men who run it would realise how precious are the skills of a man like Bestie and how much his example – the right kind of example, now, I am sure – could mean to the young players of today. There ought to be a place for Bestie and I only hope he finds the right one."

In mid-December, one club took the chance. David Webb, manager of Bournemouth, initiated a conversation, but was sacked before a deal could be agreed. "He had worked out a way for me to play in English football again which is something I have been dreaming about for ages," a despondent George said. "I am shattered."

Webb, however, was succeeded by Don Megson. Megson had

been coach at Portland Timbers, and needed no convincing from managing director Brian Tiler, who was keen to bring in some extra match-day revenue. Tiler had reportedly agreed a deal to pay George just £20 a week, though it was suggested the player would receive a percentage of the gate receipts.

Nigel Spackman, the young midfielder, had been so used to rumours about George signing for his club that he had almost gone past taking it seriously. "There had been a lot of speculation in the local press," he told the official Bournemouth website. "It would all die down and then raise its head again. One day, we turned up for training and Don Megson, who had taken over as manager, told us we had a new signing.

"We were in the dressing room getting changed and Don asked us to give him a warm welcome when we went outside to meet him. To my recollection, Don didn't say it was George. I think it was a surprise when we got out there. I might be wrong but that's how I remember it, it was a long time ago!

"As we walked across the field, you could see this guy volleying balls and warming up. As you got closer, you could see the beard and you could see it was George Best. Everybody got together and welcomed him. In the session, you could see George wasn't as fit as he needed to be but it was amazing to be on the same training pitch as an absolute icon of the game.

"The thing I remember most is a woman in a tracksuit watching the training. I was 21 at the time and admit I had taken my eye off the ball, looking at this rather attractive young lady in a tracksuit. That young lady turned out to be Mary Stavin, the former Miss World! It was a double whammy for me – George Best and Miss World both at the same time!"

"This is not a gimmick," George said on the eve of his debut on March 25. "Bournemouth have done me a favour and I have not come here as a showpiece. I am going to be part of a team. I am still ambitious. In the last 12 months I have had about 20 offers from English clubs, including Manchester United, but there have always been problems with my registration."

Best played in a 1-0 defeat to Newport where 9,121 were in attendance – more than double Bournemouth's previous home game. "When he played for us, he looked quite frail and certainly wasn't at his physical best," Spackman recalled. "His touch wasn't as good as it normally was but, technically, he still had it. His vision was good but he couldn't execute what he used to do. George wasn't at the level of fitness he needed to be to play but he had to because of the whole bandwagon and he doubled the gate, which is what he had been brought in to do.

"Losing the first game was a bit of a downer but, for me as a young player, it was great to play in front of such a big crowd. I played in midfield and George floated around. He was never going to run back and tackle. You had to get the ball to him and that's what we tried to do. As you get older, you realise players can't do it all on their own and certainly not at that age. It was a physical league and a physical game. When you got the ball and gave it to George, you would try to give him an outlet. If you made the right move, he'd find you. But he was used to playing with far better players than me."

Harry Redknapp – himself a veteran, close to retirement – has fonder recollections of the time. "George was great," he said. "He came to training; he was just fantastic. I still don't think I've seen a better player in this country. He was one of the lads. Came in, trained every day. The lads couldn't believe they had got him here to play. I think he absolutely loved it here. George was enjoying his life, still playing. Obviously he'd lost that pace and everything that he had which was a shame.

He was nowhere near the George that we knew in his prime, but it was great just to have him around for that spell. I think any way the club could make a few quid at the time they would do it. George came in, gates went up home and away so I think commercially it was quite a good move for the club."

When he didn't show for the next game against Orient, it was speculated that he had once more gone missing, but it transpired that Mary Fullaway had passed away and George took the time to grieve. His deal had been to play in home games at Dean Court, but Southend chairman Mark Rubin – whose club were to face the Cherries on April 16 – offered to pay Bournemouth to guarantee George's attendance. George did play, though the 0-0 result summed up the flat mood around his last spell as a professional in English football.

His appearances were unpredictable. After Orient, he also didn't turn up for the game against Chesterfield on April 9. He had agreed to see out the season and played the next home game against Lincoln, but was injured ahead of the match against Doncaster. Signs were put up outside Dean Court – 'GEORGE BEST WILL NOT BE PLAYING TODAY' – so supporters knew before paying for their tickets.

The next week, George made it on to the pitch to face Wigan for his final game – the Latics, funnily enough, were under the caretaker management of Bobby Charlton. The game finished 2-2. Fourteenth place in the Third Division was how Bournemouth finished the 1982/83 campaign, and five games without a goal was how George Best – the greatest to ever play the game – completed his professional career in England.

And his professional career altogether concluded shortly after with spells best marked as addendums; remarkable to those who were able to witness George play, but insignificant in all but pay-packet to George himself. He played four times for Brisbane Lions and agreed to another after Ed Marconi, the Lions owner, said he would split the gate receipts with him. That was some 9,500 miles away from home.

George – who had wanted to end his career at home, citing Old Trafford – actually finished literally five miles from the Best family home on the Cregagh Estate when he turned out for Tobermore United in an Irish Cup game on February 9, 1984. He was wearing number seven – but that number was lucky for Tobermore's opponents, Ballymena, who won 7-0 – the joint heaviest defeat of his career.

He racked up the appearances in testimonial and benefit matches after he retired. More than 50 of them going all the way into 1995. On that 1983 tour of Australia, after he'd finished with the Brisbane Lions, he guested for Osborne Park Galeb, a local club in Perth. They normally had 30 people watching them – when it was announced George was playing, over 2,000 people crammed around the pitch. Best scored one and made the other in a 2-1 win. There was a myth that he grew so frustrated with his team-mates that he literally took the ball off one and dribbled the length of the pitch to score his goal. "I don't believe that actually occurred," then-Galeb player Bert Kirkpatrick told ABC News. "To me he was very humble, he didn't big-note himself in the dressing room. It was a vivid memory. He was one of my heroes."

He had played on, but it was fitting in the extreme that the last goals of his career came in that victory for San Jose against Fort Lauderdale – and that it was George Best at his very best to boot. Making history with the greatest moment in the NASL.

Just as he would have liked to have been remembered.

SOMBRERO

T here was a greater emotional connection between George Best and Manchester United than the average player.

That connection, that bond, was forged between everything Sir Matt Busby and Jimmy Murphy had sought to create when they took over at Old Trafford, and George's own liberation. He personified and embodied all of the positive characteristics of those players who tragically died in Munich and the scores of players who came through afterwards and struggled to deal with the pressure.

It seemed he would be granted the fortune of fulfilled potential when he danced on the Wembley pitch in May 1968. In some ways you could argue he was, although it is by far the prevailing thought that he was not. If one is to consider that he was able to enjoy more success from his talents than most of the Munich team and still not reach his own potential then you're able to peek into the nuanced and complex situation that was George Best's relationship with Manchester United, and ultimately with himself.

Timing is everything. It is timing that ensured George's relationship with the Old Trafford support was a little bit different. The generation he was a part of – the liberal personality that was encouraged in the post-war era. The way in which he seemed to revel in the mere opportunity to play for United six years after the disaster – close enough to it for those who saw their heroes die to now have someone else to worship. And then his age, which seemed to count both for and against him.

Was George's path in football and in life avoidable? Was it fated? Could we change the narrative so that instead of there being an undertone of regret, there is less talk of things being 'avoidable' and more acceptance of a human being with human flaws and an extraordinary gift he gave to the world?

You can trace each of his 'explosions', consider the actions of him and others, and wonder what might have been. That is part of the nostalgic journey we take – a part of the reason you're reading this. But every action does indeed have a consequence.

Let's take one of those explosions and consider that there was an intervention for George's benefit. Benfica away, and the fateful decision to wear a sombrero coming off the plane. George was a teenager with limited exposure to the press. That relationship was still being developed between those of his generation who marvelled over his personality and those of the older generation who were still getting used to it.

He wasn't a seasoned traveller like Harry Gregg and Bobby Charlton. Where Charlton despaired, Gregg felt a greater sense of burden and tried to get George to remove the hat. He could see a simple gesture for how it would be taken – an invitation to the dance. A gesture that said, 'Use me, because I want to use you too'. George himself confessed it was a mistake. But was it? The point, of course, is one of maturity. That deciding not to wear it would have been seen as more professional, more dignified.

There is another side to it. Suppression. If George had decided at this crucial moment that he ought not to wear the hat because it was crass, he was conceding that he shouldn't do something based on the advice of his elders because of how it would look. It would be denying his natural urge. It would be admitting that others knew better than he did and so, when it came to subsequent matters of impulse, he would have cause to check and ask for guidance. Who knows how that would have manifested itself?

Would he have thought to take Pat Crerand and Alex Stepney out on to the training pitch because he had an idea of what he could do at Anfield? Would he have felt confident enough to take the ball around the goalkeeper at Wembley with such individual style? Would he have been brave enough to face Carlos Bilardo in the lion's den and offer him the ball after a vicious foul? In modern years people have pondered how Roy Keane, Eric Cantona and Wayne Rooney might have been without their temper. Sometimes what can be lost is forgotten in the hypothetical scenario of what could be gained.

Certainly, suggesting the decision to not wear a sombrero could have prevented Manchester United's decline after 1968 is ludicrous. For that, George could not be blamed, and it was indeed his wonderful form which prevented the decline from being much harsher, much earlier. Ultimately, having been a victim of that downward spiral, George himself contributed to it. But he was every supporter on the pitch. Trying in vain to make it better. Drowning his sorrows off the pitch to try and forget about it. And then, when it came to George in particular, everything was about the blame game. Was it the managers? Was it a lack of discipline? George himself? His friends? His team-mates? The media? A lack of investment into the playing staff at United? The illness?

Just as circumstances came together perfectly to create the star, so they aligned to make it fade.

Yes, Sir Matt Busby's retirement contributed. Wilf McGuinness' inexperience contributed. Frank O'Farrell's inability to deal with the spotlight on George or himself contributed. Tommy Docherty's decisions, unbeknown to George, contributed. It was a lack of discipline for which George admitted he was accountable. There were occasions before the illness took a firm hold when George could have not skipped training. He could have made the decision to not go out the night before.

His friends – well of course there were some who only wanted to be seen by others as knowing George. Those who didn't have his best interests at heart. So they would encourage him to go out with them and feed his ego with the consolation of his own greatness when things were not going well on the pitch. Perhaps his team-mates could have done more to appreciate that fame was a different animal than it had been just five years earlier – it was not George's fault that he was so much better than his peers that he graduated into an older team. He needed support and not just from one or two.

The press knew he was good for a story. Better when that story was controversial. George Best in the London flat of an actress made more engaging front page copy than George Best being despondent over his team's decline.

No football team should ever really be held ransom to one player's demand for greater talent around him but United made half-hearted belated responses because they knew it was for their own good. Busby made offers but was reluctant to spend lots of money when a successor was due to be appointed. O'Farrell didn't do it until it was too late and even then his success rate was mixed. Docherty spent but by then George was more valuable to the club as an asset – for someone else to speculate on a turnaround in fortunes – than he was on the pitch due to his illness now having taken hold.

Then you look at it the other way – Busby, McGuinness, O'Farrell. All of them tried to reason with George. They knew they would have to make concessions because he was so gifted and they tried where they could to accommodate him and also reach out to him. They were unable to empathise. Who could? Even his team-mates, used to the attention that came with playing for Manchester United, could not comprehend the extra that came with just being George. Their personal lives had been the subject of interest, but never really speculation.

His old youth team-mates, the ones who had known George personally, were now mostly at other clubs concentrating on their own careers, or out of the game altogether. The true friends he did make out of the game were good for him. That much is proven by the fact that many of them were lifelong. In fact if it weren't for some of them, George might not have made it back into the United fold when he did on occasion.

It is a tremendously complex scenario with moving pieces. The simplest answer is that if United had been more proactive than reactive when it came to their squad strengthening then George may have been more professionally engaged and less likely to stray, or at least not as frequently. Asking for that to happen under Busby would not have been practical. In fact, showing such ruthlessness at such a stage of his managership would have been counter-productive to the family atmosphere he had built at the club. Yes, he'd done it before, but asking him to axe Bill Foulkes or Bobby Charlton would have been like asking him to put down the family dog when it turned 10 years old just because it might die soon. No, it was someone else's job. And we know who tried and didn't succeed.

What about the names who didn't get the job? Perhaps the most famous who gets brought up in these conversations is Brian Clough, who was both linked with the United job and with Best when he was Derby County manager. But Clough's outspoken personality had already seen him ruled out by the Old Trafford hierarchy – and his ill-fated spell at Leeds in 1974 gave them vindication. According to Paddy Crerand, Clough was desperate for the United job; according to Martin Edwards, he was never even a consideration at any of the five stages where the club were looking for a new leader between 1969 and 1981.

Clough went on record as saying that he could have had Best sorted "within a month" at Derby. In his book *Hard Tackles and Dirty Baths*, George himself said: "I simply adored Brian Clough's management style, and perhaps it is one of my regrets that I was never a player under his leadership; I feel sure I would have enjoyed it immensely. I can imagine there being many people thinking I was such a rebel there was no chance of me and Cloughie hitting it off. How wrong they would be. I had no time for liars and cheats, but Brian Clough was the genuine article and I wish he had been my manager because I know, under the right guidance, I could have stayed on and played at the highest level for longer than I did."

Best, though, did also confess in his role as a television pundit before one Nottingham Forest match when Clough was in charge at the City Ground: "I like him as a manager, I'm not too sure [if I like him] as a person."

When there is an unexplored avenue it is only natural to wonder that it would have been the right one. Sure, Clough could have indulged George a while, and Derby were more successful than United over that period so it would have served as a fine incentive. But one looks at such a scenario and tends only to deliberate over the positives.

By then, George was suffering from alcoholism. Clough did too, despite also having a reputation for being strict with players over their own drinking habits. It would not have been the romantic happy ending, even if it's plausible to consider that the moments at Fulham and San Jose could have been replicated in a Derby shirt instead, and so they would have been the club to celebrate the connection.

The only other reasonable suggestion might be Dave Sexton, who was manager of Chelsea at the time the player and club were often paired together in press speculation. Sexton, however, was almost the antithesis of everything George represented. He was a great coach, but pernickety on instruction, as Manchester United's players would later all find out in Sexton's spell there.

It seems that Alex Stepney's consideration that O'Farrell should have strengthened before Christmas 1971 is probably the most on the money when it comes to the fork in the road of what was inevitable and where it might have had a real tangible difference. First of all, United needed someone in charge from outside of the club – they needed to acknowledge that McGuinness as led by Busby was never going to work.

So that part had happened with O'Farrell. It's easy to see O'Farrell's point of view. You don't just walk into a club like Manchester United and start wielding the axe to club legends. It's part of the process to give them the opportunity to succeed or fail. One could even say it's good management to not make major changes straight away.

So even if he did have the foresight to see that the concession of goals was becoming a major concern, he might have reckoned he was better placed giving those players enough time to prove him wrong than to just replace them. Even if it was wrong, maybe it was still right. Falling out of favour with star names accelerated O'Farrell's departure. Doing so earlier in his reign might have rendered his tenure shorter still.

He probably did the logical thing that most people would have done. Still, it does seem right to say that if Martin Buchan and Ian Storey-Moore had arrived in October 1971 rather than March 1972, the entire story of United in the 1970s – and consequentially, George Best, who was in red-hot form – might have been different.

"I definitely agree with that theory," Paddy Barclay says. "They were terrific signings, players who were obviously O'Farrell's choices. And they were obviously United standard. Buchan in particular was probably the captain or at least the natural leader of every team he ever played for. Storey-Moore, as goalscoring wingers go, wasn't far off George Best. The sooner they could have signed, the better."

Everything that followed felt like an anti-climax to those who knew how good George truly was at his peak and how much better he could have been. But it didn't feel that way to most of the players and supporters who experienced time with him wherever he went after he left Old Trafford. They were the glory days of the Los Angeles Aztecs. Of Fulham. Of the San Jose Earthquakes. That was the case because of who George was and what he did, not what he might have done. There was no decrying and bemoaning the same fate which meant he was at those clubs.

You could even present an alternative argument. If we accept that Manchester United's fate was unavoidable, and that even with George, there were no more First Divisions or European Cups to be won, then there were two options. One is that George stayed at United – progressively becoming more ill, at best reaching the same infrequencies of brilliance as the football world saw elsewhere. There is most certainly a large percentage of United supporters who would have been happy with that, because in their minds George should have stayed at Old Trafford forever and if he could have given them just one golden memory a year, it would have been enough.

The other is what actually happened and simply requires a change of thinking – that having spent their glory years together, George went away and thrilled supporters around the world. The circus went global. The Rolling Stones, as Willie Anderson put it, went on tour. In 1899, the German poet Ludwig Jacobowski wrote his sonnet *Leuchtende Tage* which included the lines: "Nicht weinen, weil sie vorüber! Lächeln, weil sie gewesen!" This is translated as: "Do not cry because they are past! Smile, because they once were!" and the lines have often been reimagined into other variations. This is a philosophy almost universally shared by supporters of the other teams George played for. There are no lamentations. They were the glory days.

No, we can't pretend that the reality compensated for what we knew should have been different. But we can find beauty and acceptance in what was. We can look at the story of a football career that was the way it was and still come to the conclusion that George Best entertained like nobody else from the first moment to the last.

These are the footballing factors. There are a multitude of extra-curricular components to take into consideration. Some George could control. Many that he could not. For example, it's one thing to say someone should find a partner and settle down. How do you instruct someone to fall in love? If only it could be so easy. A difficult thing to achieve in life becomes even more so when you are George Best. He finally married for the first time only when he left United. That was probably in itself no coincidence.

It is also worth considering the newness of certain elements. Media and travel were becoming more prominent features of everyday life. The world was getting smaller. The landscape was changing. There was no example to follow. When you are living your life in the public eye, and you're being judged based on the perception of how someone else thinks you should behave, that situation is almost always negative. It wouldn't be news to print 'Man behaves well'. George, for his part, understood that and took it on his shoulders.

But what about when it went beyond the grain? Because it was not common, when Dickie and Ann Best were growing up, to see sportspeople receive personal criticism in the newspapers, it became difficult to handle when their son became the target. George's success bred contempt and jealousy.

The better he was, the greater the contempt and jealousy. The more often that George's relatives would find themselves receiving criticism. They too had to learn to deal with it without guidance. George had to let them get on with it. Many times they wouldn't tell him about it. It was part of their everyday life now too.

In October 1971 the Troubles from back home were present in a very real way when the news of an alleged threat on his life was leaked. These were things that nobody should ever have to go through. Ordinary people didn't go through it. Unfortunately for George, there were no extraordinary solutions for people in extraordinary positions. It was only natural he would need to find an escape. A release. And so, where do you go from there? If someone is in trouble they need help. By the time anyone noticed George's trouble – by the time anyone was able to even identify that it was trouble – it was already too late.

It could not be said that George didn't take responsibility. He took practical steps. He moved across to the other side of the world to try and break the cycle and rediscover a positive outlook on life away from those vices. Time and again his illness returned. He sought intervention. He undertook rehabilitation. This doesn't absolve him of his actions and indiscretions. This book doesn't seek to excuse them or pretend they didn't happen. It doesn't point the finger at anyone else, or pretend that alcoholism wasn't one of the biggest contributing factors for his 'fall'. It's just that there is more to it.

He wasn't perfect. But he wanted to be better. He said and thought and hoped all of the same things that anyone with an addiction would. He hoped that some lifestyle changes would be enough. That finding love would be enough. That becoming a father and actually being present would be enough.

Again, this is a book about George's football career, and not a psychological dissection. And there was much more of a career, a full career, than the tired trope of wasted potential. There was a genuine greatness that does not bind itself to conventional storytelling. The point is that all of these factors were bound to weigh heavy on the mind; for a football player at the level of George, and for a man of his intelligence, his mental health needed to be just as strong as his physical health in order for him to truly succeed. One fed the other. It was a cycle. A spiral. One that nobody could impact, once they were too late. All a matter of timing and circumstance.

***

In January 1994, Sir Matt Busby died. George's reunions with his 1968 team-mates had been few and far between but there had been a poignant one in August 1991, when Old Trafford hosted a testimonial for Sir Matt with the present Manchester United side against the Republic of Ireland. Some 33,412 turned up to watch a 1-1 draw, but most of them arrived several hours earlier for what they considered the true highlight of the day – a seven-a-side game between a few players from the 1968 side and a veteran City team.

Nobody was entertained more than the man who was being honoured. Busby told the *Manchester Evening News*: "My mind was somewhere out in space, waltzing with my heart." A 3-3 draw entertained the crowd, with George sporting a full, thick beard with flickers of grey. Those first signs of age had appeared only over the past year.

In September 1990, George had returned to Old Trafford for a meeting with Sir Matt, the purpose of which was a painting by artist Ralph Sweeney from a photograph by Robert Aylott. Busby and Best sat in the stands, deep in conversation, and Aylott captured an emotionally-charged moment between protege and mentor when Busby began to cry, and George put his arm around his shoulder. The bond between the two was deep and the rekindling of these feelings made the news of Busby's death much harder to comprehend when it arrived, even though he had been ill for a while. There was a service for the funeral at Chorlton-cum-Hardy and George was one of a few who had been invited to the burial at Manchester's Southern Cemetery later in the day.

The funeral cortège was a literal journey down memory lane for George, a genuine 'this was your life' moment in time as it passed his old haunts; Mrs Fullaway's, and the bus stop where he would wait in a morning and sometimes hide behind if he saw Busby's car passing, so scared was he to even accept a lift. "My whole life flashed before me," George recalled, and though he had just about overcome the tears when the journey concluded at the cemetery, he was helpless to stop them when Sandy Busby, Matt's son, said to him at graveside: "You know he loved you."

There had been a reconnection to some extent. He had become fonder of Bobby Charlton and remained good friends with Denis Law. He wrote a foreword for Harry Gregg's autobiography, describing his compatriot as his "hero", a compliment Gregg was incredibly emotional about.

"Everyone climbed on the Georgie Best bandwagon," Gregg told this writer in 2013. "They didn't know him. When my autobiography was released, it was suggested that George write a foreword for it. But as far as I knew he might charge £15,000, and I didn't have fifteen thousand pence! But out of the blue, I was contacted by my ghostwriter who said George was going to do it, provided he could write it himself. It brought tears to my eyes.

"He came to me the day after the Benfica game in March

1966 and said, 'H, do you think I could ask for a rise?' In those days the contracts were binding. I said, 'Aye son, but be nice about it. Don't be cheeky.' George sought further advice and he was put off asking for a rise by another player. I heard no more about it for a while until we played Partizan Belgrade, and George was badly hurt in a tackle.

"A couple of days later I was sitting with my new wife and two little girls across from George's boutique. In he came on a pair of crutches, and he said to me, 'H, can I talk to you?' Me being the pleasant fella I am, I refused because I was with the family, but he insisted. 'What do you think I should do now?!'

"When George had his testimonial match in Belfast in 1988 he called me and asked me to come to the dinner the night before. I got my dickie bow on and drove there; all the world's great players were there. He had to make a speech. 'Before I attempt to make a speech,' he says, 'There's one man I want to stand up so I can thank him for being here. Harry Gregg.' I nearly died. But that was the true George."

It had been a matter of some consternation for George that he was not awarded a testimonial from the club. He was told he had not given 10 years of continuous service as a senior player – effectively, it meant that his sabbatical after O'Farrell's sacking had counted against him. He was upset that the same technicalities were not applied to his friend Paddy Crerand, who had been awarded a testimonial with eight-and-a-half years' playing service. It remained one of the crying shames in United history that a testimonial was never played in his honour or name, and although he was given some recognition with a game in Northern Ireland in 1988 against an international XI that included his old foe Johan Neeskens.

George's greatest emotional pull in football was his

relationship with Manchester United, beyond any considerable doubt. He would confess that leaving Old Trafford was the primary thing he would change in his life. When he got a dog towards the end of his life, it was inevitably called Red.

Best reckoned that from the European Cup winning-side, despite being one of the youngest, he would have been "odds-on favourite" to die first due to his lifestyle. He was heartbroken again when Shay Brennan – by George's odds, the "rank outsider" – passed away first in June 2000. Sadly, his personal prediction was a little too close to the bone.

George made the transition from footballer to personality. His appearances on television talk shows were frequent and especially so after controversial incidents. There were two notable appearances on *Wogan*. The first was after a stint in Pentonville prison. Terry Wogan played for gags; George confessed on air that he was an alcoholic and struggled daily. The host asked why he didn't just reach out for help.

A few years later he was back on the same show and left in the green room with lots of alcohol. George took responsibility for the spectacle which followed and refused to blame the host or the backroom staff. Responsibility, in this circumstance, was something that should have been shared. Subsequently, Wogan had no problem retelling the story of a drunk George appearing on his show in the countless 'top 20 television moments' shows which aired over the following years, as if it were an exercise in how to remain professional on his own part. As if it was one of the hazards of live television. Something to share with a smile and a laugh instead of acknowledging the part that was played in worsening an already tragic situation. What passes for entertainment in one era often ages badly.

There's something most definitely uncomfortable about

watching such shows with a modern eye; Wogan, who confessed he himself drank too much but insisted he wasn't an alcoholic, was just representative of a nation of many who did the same and yet almost needed to see George's illness to make them feel better about themselves. Wogan was a national treasure. He would not have appreciated being put in the same position as George.

There were other television talk show hosts who had George's best interests at heart. "I wasn't bothered if I woke up or not. Sometimes I wished I didn't," George said in an interview with Michael Parkinson. "I think you do [feel suicidal], when your brain is that muddled and scrambled with what you're taking. Especially when you don't know where you're going with your life. It can be very depressing."

George was reflecting on his years after football. He spoke about how the boredom of not having training in the morning had consumed him for a while and this had increased his consumption of alcohol. He spoke with an acceptance of his illness and felt sometimes it was under control and sometimes it was not – still with the tone of someone who probably never really appreciated this was not always within his power. He was faced with the questions as if he could pull himself together, if only he chose to. Parkinson adored Best. He was compelled by him. They'd known each other for many years. There was one telling moment in their interview in May 1996.

"You mentioned your career was finished at 27," Parkinson said. "In a sense, we hadn't seen the best of you, had we?"

"No," George conceded. "I hadn't peaked."

"It's a thought, isn't it?" Parkinson replied. "Do you ever think about it?"

"I do," George replied. "I actually enjoy watching myself play.

That was the best part of it. I've often wondered what… the problem would have been, if we could have kept that great side together for three, four more years, what would it have been like, or if I'd stayed with a side as good as that for three or four years, or even longer… if I'd have kept fit, I could have kept playing. There's still players today at 36 or 37. I could have been playing sweeper until I was the age I am today!"

The last line was delivered with a smile, self-deprecating. It was almost a grimace that said this was cutting close to the bone. He chuckled and looked away.

"The famous line," Parkinson responded with a laugh, whilst also searching for the right note to wrap up on. "Where did it all go wrong, George?"

"People still say that to me," George smiled. "Where did it all go wrong?"

"For the few people who've not heard, tell us the story," Parkinson said.

Well, where do you begin? Life after football for George Best was a life remembering football.

Every conversation about the good old days was followed by another. Where did it all go wrong, George? Sometimes those words formed a punchline. Other times they formed a genuine question. It was all part of the same act. He was never allowed to separate the agony and the ecstasy because to most, it was like a Shakespearian tragedy and the story had to be told whole. It was, to be fair. George never appeared to be the most naturally confident talker; there was a buzzing nervousness that probably had something to do with the fact he knew every conversation would lead to the inevitable.

"For the people who've not heard, tell us the story."

George told the anecdote.

Mary Stavin, the casino, the champagne, £25,000 on the bed and the hotel porter. Then came the punchline. Parkinson, a close friend of George's, laughed despite having heard the story many times. Where did it all go wrong?

"…And people still ask me today. People say what happened? Would you change this, would you change that? Where did it all go wrong, you coulda done this, you coulda did that, and I say that I've done it all. I'm still enjoying my life. So, that's the bottom line," he concluded, smiling hopefully and looking away, just for a moment, but for long enough to betray his projected demeanour.

In his book *Blessed*, George admitted he sometimes thought "the first 27 years were sheer bliss and the last 27 have been a disaster". He wrote: "Of course, it did all go wrong. And I can tell you where it went wrong. It went wrong with the thing I loved most of all, my football, and from there the rest of my life unravelled."

Self-deprecating to the end; as well as his peak years, there were thousands of people grateful for the years which followed.

BEYOND IMAGINATION

Watching George Best play football had always been a spectacle, although you might have had to be creative with the description when it came to what you were expecting. An exhibition – much the same. Observing George Best in the halcyon days before 1971 and those terms meant you were witnessing history.

After? Well, it usually meant something more anecdotal. The sort of event you would expect to attend with thousands of others just to be entertained without anything being at stake. Fun for everyone, everyone that was except for George, who was desperate to prove himself or recapture something. It was no pity mission. The occasions where he did recapture what he had – however brief – did become historic moments in their own right. Rotterdam. Fulham. San Jose. Three random parts of the world, forever associated with George Best, forever attached to him, ready to evoke memories for those who worshipped him. Three random parts of the world that, when attached to his name, instantly bring a picture.

When that picture materialises, the feeling of sadness doesn't exist. Nor does the feeling of lost potential. What prevails is majesty and brilliance.

It's nutmegging one of the greatest players of all time.

It's beating an opponent and then his own team-mate.

It's beating an entire opposition defence to score one of the greatest goals ever.

What, in football, could be more beautiful? Of course, though, we have to consider things in perspective. Where there is beauty there is often tragedy.

There was tragedy in the lost potential on the pitch.

There was tragedy in his life, lost when George Best died on November 25, 2005 after a long battle with alcoholism.

A potted history of life after football for George Best: He was charged with drink-driving in November 1983. After failing to appear in court, he was arrested; during the arrest he assaulted a policeman and was sentenced to three months in jail in December. He was released in February 1984. In July 1986 he divorced Angie. Nine years later he married Alex Pursey and they divorced 20 months before he passed away. He lived in London and also Northern Ireland for a time.

He took the time to reconnect with his family. For most of their lives, George had belonged to the world more than he had to them, even though he missed them. The idea of having his family around was certainly in his mind when it came to what being settled represented. There were years that such a relationship might have been impossible. The time where he was so famous that resentment factored high. So people would be critical of George to Ann. They were – as Barbara found out – capable of violence. George's younger brother Ian played football. He was promising, and even though he didn't play in the same position, the comparisons were inescapable. "I got fed up of people telling me that I didn't play like my brother," Ian recalls. "I never intended to, I played my own game and he played his. People used to tell me George didn't do that or do this... I don't know what people were expecting. As I got older, it became a pain in the backside."

Ian was so good he played in a cup final for his local team, which attracted the attention of the press. He was only 15 – when he saw reporters and photographers at the game, Ian told his coach he wasn't going to play. He was talked around, and even put in a man-of-the-match performance with two goals, but afterwards he insisted he was going to stop playing. George felt guilty, saying he was sure Dickie was heartbroken and that he felt his fame had stopped Ian "getting the professional career he deserved". He did, however, admire his brother's strong-mindedness on the matter.

There seemed to be concerted efforts to atone although most of his family never saw it as necessary. Of course, for some of his family and his past relationships, friction was unavoidable as their relationships had been played out in the press. This was particularly difficult for Calum, who still hero-worshipped his dad despite a relationship that was not quite the idyllic one either of them had hoped it would be.

For his own father and siblings, George had been our George before he was anything else. That's all he wanted to be to them. He had been close to desperate throughout his life to have them with him. He had asked them to move to Manchester and Los Angeles.

On one occasion, Ian recalls George making an incredibly grand gesture on one trip to Manchester. Dickie had remarked how nice the hotel they were staying in was. George offered to buy it. His siblings were excited. Dickie couldn't do it. It was almost as if the extravagance of the offer only highlighted the difference between the definition of 'normal' for George and the rest of his family. But he never stopped trying.

So George and Ian were able to put their individual difficulties with football behind them and talk about the game, where the elder brother would talk about the best days of his life at Manchester United. They shared a similar sense of humour.

Ian moved to the south-west of England and would often travel up to London to see his brother. "If I was nearby an area where he was doing one of his after-dinner events, he'd always make sure we got in and that he had time for us," Ian said.

George also became close again with his sisters. Barbara remembered a time when people were more kind about her relationship with her brother, and were keen to have a signed copy of one his books. She had been embarrassed to ask but George obliged without even a second thought. Barbara and her husband Norman assisted George in buying a house just outside Portavogie, the fishing village where Carol and her husband Allen lived.

Despite the best of intentions for a quieter life, the journalists were never far away and the intrusion became greater for his family. He reconnected with the twins Grace and Julie. Julie would remark how like Dickie George was starting to look. He adored Grace's daughter Ashleigh, who had been born with hydrocephalus. He was devastated when she died. The funeral was set for May 22, 1996 – George's 50th birthday. The BBC had dedicated their entire schedule that night to him. George recalled that Grace and the family had been quite relieved the funeral could proceed with dignity and without the press intrusion his presence would have attracted.

The two opponents even he could never evade were controversy and tabloid newspapers. The two he could never defeat – alcoholism and time.

"A year in the life of George Best was like seven or eight years of a human being," Terry Fisher, George's coach at the Los Angeles Aztecs, told *The Athletic* in 2020. "So in eight years, George would live 70 years if you talk about the wear, the tear, the strain, the stress of those on his mind and body."

George died at 59, which, by Fisher's calculation, is over 400 years, and that probably sounds about right.

There was certainly enough to fill the lifetimes of at least seven or eight ordinary men, and then some, and that much is proven by the many volumes written on his life both directly about George himself and then by those who knew him. The Shakespearean tragedy told by the Greek chorus.

The man who had once considered life without football such an unthinkable prospect that he spoke of dying peacefully in his sleep at the age of 40 had found a different contentment, but retained that love for the sport. The man who spoke in the most ambitious terms about the things he wished to do on a football pitch had but two simple wishes in his latter years. If just one person thought he had been the greatest footballer, he said, he would be happy. He hoped that his football would be all people remembered him for.

Of course, he never really left football. It was one of those urban legends that he even played for the HMP Ford open prison football team. What was certainly true was that he worked as a television pundit and after-dinner speaker. He was a commentator for radio. Doors opened to him from the footballing fraternity. But he was too big a name to have been a coach or manager; too individual to explain his inspiration. Too flawed to give guidance.

"He was a pure genius," Rodney Marsh says. "And geniuses straddle the line…sometimes they go one way, sometimes the other, sometimes everything is perfect. And that's why they are geniuses. He couldn't have been a good coach, his heart wasn't really in punditry, and he wouldn't have made a good counsellor for anyone who might have struggled… George couldn't have been anything other than the greatest player there has ever been, because that's what he was destined to be.

"I spoke to George 15 minutes before he died. I went to Cromwell Hospital and I was completely shocked. There were pipes and tubes coming out of him everywhere. He'd bled a lot overnight, there was blood around his face. He was in a coma. Just laying there. I cried. I went and put my hand on his hand and told him that he was the greatest player that ever played the game. He didn't hear it. But I thought it was right thing to do for him. And for me, come to that. Because I believed it."

In August 2002, George had a successful liver transplant at King's College Hospital in London. He was unable to overcome his illness. In October 2005, he was admitted to intensive care at Cromwell Hospital, suffering from a kidney infection due to the side effects of immuno-suppressive drugs. His family made regular trips to see him. In the early hours of November 25, treatment was stopped, and later that day George passed away.

George's funeral was on December 3, 2005. The event was broadcast on national television. Mourners in their thousands lined the Belfast streets his coffin passed down. Football shirts were thrown at the hearse. George's younger brother Ian, his brothers-in-law Norman McNarry and Alan McPherson, his agent and long-time friend Phil Hughes and his doctor, Dr Akeel Alisa, all served as pallbearers. So too did Denis Law and Harry Gregg, and some of George's former international team-mates. He was buried beside his mother at Roselawn Cemetery in Belfast. On April 16, 2008, Dickie would join them after a short illness.

Many from the world of football were at George's funeral. One of those was Sir Bobby Charlton, who spoke of his loss of a "dear friend and marvellous person", their relationship repaired in the latter years as George grew to appreciate why Bobby despaired at times, and Bobby, for his part, acknowledged that his younger colleague was not acting out of impetuosity.

Some have taken umbrage with the depiction of him as a marvellous person, citing actions taken when he was in the depths of his addiction. They see that as an excuse, not a reason. Some don't believe in the adage of not speaking ill of the dead and seek to demonise. Many of those who knew George closest have had stories of their relationship published. Because those relationships were different, and the experiences different, it has meant others who knew George have objected, and that has resulted in conflict.

One thing almost everyone agrees on is that away from his illness, George was quiet, funny, charming and, perhaps most importantly, he wanted to be good. There was an infamous story of his darker days in Los Angeles where, when drunk, he stole money from the purse of a woman who was drinking at the same bar and had gone to the toilet. Consumed with guilt, he returned a few days later, found the woman and returned the stolen money.

Almost every reference to George is accompanied with a reference to his lifestyle and his illness. It's rarely celebratory, usually melancholy, and always intrinsically linked to his decline. Since his passing those conversations have been morose. But the passing of Diego Maradona in 2020, 15 years to the day after George died, brought a different perspective. Maradona had his demons. But he was universally celebrated for his positive achievements. It was proclaimed as the passing of the greatest. His relatively underwhelming time at Barcelona wasn't held against him.

Nobody talked about him playing at Napoli instead of going on to star for Real Madrid or AC Milan. People chose to remember the glory of the 1986 World Cup rather than the cheating in the same tournament or the shame and scandal of USA 1994. His drug addiction was not viewed in the same way as George's relationship with alcohol. His faults were not put under the microscope in the same way that George's have been. They were not presented as evidence, as contributing factors to a career that should have been so much more. Why?

George was right about the press; in the UK, they loved to build a hero up and knock him down. There was a much greater protection for Maradona in his homeland; he was worshipped and canonised. That status of a national hero was emphasised by his contribution to the World Cup in 1986 but that doesn't mean that Northern Ireland loved Best any less. They are, however, just one part of the United Kingdom, and Best wasn't England's own. You might say that had something to do with it, if only the English press hadn't made a national pastime of knocking the likes of Paul Gascoigne, David Beckham and Wayne Rooney off the pedestals they'd been put on. Perhaps there just isn't the same loyalty.

Little separates Maradona and Best.

There are many similarities and interchangeable arguments – Maradona won the World Cup and elevated Napoli to unscaled heights. Best won the European Cup and was the best player in the best team in Europe that included two former European Footballers of the Year. It's a matter of preference. It could easily be argued that Best's achievement was the tougher to accomplish.

It could be the difference in perception is due to their personalities. Maradona, emboldened by how much he was worshipped and accommodated, was larger than life, often causing offence with his outrageous behaviour. Best was much more reserved, though this too had been influenced by how he had been portrayed in the press; he knew he had to be careful. He also cared about how he was perceived. In Maradona's autobiography, he described George as "a great player, but crazier than me" – it was surely only he who saw it that way.

But this record is – again – about his football. And in football, as in life, the last memories weren't always fond. In June 1989, George had been back in California. "The last time I saw George it was for a testimonial match where Portland Timbers took on the San Jose Earthquakes," Willie Anderson recalls. "It had been a big rivalry when we were playing so it was sort of like a reunion game. We were all put up in a hotel and we were sitting around the pool. George came out to the pool and everyone was suddenly in awe. All the lads were having beers and George sat with us not touching a drink.

"After a while he said he was going to his room ahead of the reunion dinner that evening. A couple of the lads actually thought they would follow his example and go back to get ready, but as they walked through the bar, they found him in there doing shots. He managed to get back to his room to pass out; we managed to get him to go out at night but he wasn't in a good way. We played the next day, including George, and he shouldn't have been out there. He was there to pull in people, but they didn't see the real George. That wasn't him."

Anderson's voice carries the same emotional tone as those who were lucky enough to have shared good times with him on the pitch. It is rare in football for individuals to be so wistful, melancholy and almost regretful over another, but when it comes to George Best it's almost unified. The only division exists between those who will confidently assert he was the greatest player ever and those who say he could have been and should have been if not for his demons. The split usually lies between those who knew him before and after 1971, with some notable exceptions.

Often, those last memories were more positively emotional. Tony Gale had played with George for a time at Fulham that ought to have been more memorable for one than the other. But George had an emotional attachment to the good moments in his career. Just as he remembered Eddie Harrop on Market Street in Manchester, one afternoon in London George spotted Tony from down the street.

"A couple of years before he died I bumped into him somewhere in London," Gale recalls. "He called me over for a chat, he wanted to ask what I was up to. I was working for Sky doing the punditry and told him so, and asked him what he'd been doing. 'I've just been in Monaco, getting a Hall of Fame thing with Pele and Maradona.' And there he was, just as casual as anything, asking me how I was doing.

"Bobby Campbell died around 10 years after George did. I was at his funeral and so was Jimmy Tarbuck, his best mate. Bobby played for Liverpool, he managed Chelsea, but according to Jimmy the best days of Bobby's life in football were the months he spent with George, Mooro and Rodney at Fulham. It was football for entertainment. People still talk about it now and that proves it was the right thing to do and also the best place and club for George to be at, at the time."

There was not much in his career that went to convention. But because he was only 27 when he left Manchester United, he has found himself pigeonholed in the category of players who did not reach their peak. That makes it easier to say we never saw the best of him. It makes it easier to conclude he misses out on being named the best player that ever lived.

So, turning the argument around, how long is long enough? And what must one accomplish within that defined timeframe? Some elements, as discussed, are interchangeable. Pele never played in Europe so he couldn't have won the European Cup. Diego Maradona never won the European Cup and though he accomplished great things with Napoli, didn't really with Barcelona. Neither were eligible for the Ballon d'Or at that time. But both won the World Cup. Johan Cruyff was quite clearly great with Ajax but didn't enjoy unqualified success with Barcelona as a player. This is just a selection of the 'Kings', as Simões put it, in the era George played.

In the modern day of course there has been Zinedine Zidane, following on from his countryman Michel Platini. Then, from Brazil again, Ronaldo and Ronaldinho. In long careers, there are definite periods where their talent was more pronounced and influential than at others. And then there's Lionel Messi and Cristiano Ronaldo, who had the fortune of starring in top teams from the start of their careers through to the twilight, and never really suffered a serious injury or illness.

There's a snobbishness in some circles that favours the players of today and the argument usually includes diet and conditioning attitudes, as if the players of 1975 would exist on a diet of six pints on a Friday night, steak and chips before the game and a few cigarettes at half-time if they were transplanted into the modern game.

There's a bias from players of the past when they all insist it would be much easier to compete in today's game and that the greats of yesteryear would be even better today. The pitches, the rules. The coverage. The easier route to play in the top competitions. The logical argument is the second and it's supported, in many cases, by the duration of a player's career at the top level. Messi and Ronaldo were still the best when they became cross-generational. At Manchester United, Ryan Giggs possibly spanned three generations and was one of the team's most influential attacking players when he retired at 40.

George Best, even in his relatively short spell, is also evidence of it. When the laws on tackling changed, his goal average in the months that followed jumped from one in three to two in three. What might that have been with the eminently less physical game of today? On pitches that didn't cut up from November to April? With lighter balls? You can't discount these points, because George himself had proven there was tangible evidence that it made a difference.

Reducing the discussion to numbers is to eliminate all of the beauty and essence of what George Best stood for. It is about impact and influence. It's about achievement. It's about memories. There is no argument than Cruyff isn't Ajax's best ever player. He played there from 1964 to 1973. Maradona was at Napoli from 1984 to 1991. Again, let's realign the parameters of the argument to Manchester United. Cristiano

Ronaldo was there from 2003 to 2009. Eric Cantona from 1992 to 1997. When you put it in such terms and consider the perspective, the argument changes slightly and becomes more about what you did in the time you did it than anything else.

In any event, the aim of this book isn't to persuade or convince. It's not even to legitimise. George Best doesn't need me or any other writer to state his case. He did that himself.

It's quite possible that George was even under-appreciated. The accolades almost sound unrealistic, especially when you go back to his very roots and then appreciate that there is nothing but reverence.

Take Willie Anderson's ultimate tribute: "I've never seen anything like it before or since. Maybe Diego Maradona, in the way he moved, and he was so stocky and feisty, but even then you could argue George's frame gave him a certain grace. But he also had everything. And it all came so naturally. He was good on both sides, he could head the ball, he could run with it and he would run after you all day to win it back, he could score goal after goal. He scored six goals in a cup tie and he wasn't even trying."

Maybe it's the "he could do everything" line or the straight-forward way in which others just describe him as superior to others. "I wouldn't like to make comparisons about other players on the continent, but having played with and trained with George, he was fantastic," Jim Ryan says. "You couldn't get the ball off him. You could compare him to other First Division players and know that he was better. It didn't matter who you cared to mention, you just knew that George was better than them. You know, I was at United when Cantona, Giggs, Ronaldo were all there… great players. I would probably say George is better than them. That he had more in terms of natural ability. In some ways it's probably true that I hero worshipped him. He played football the way I loved to watch it. I suppose I loved him, not just the way he played."

And then Jimmy Rimmer. "In that era, nobody was capable of doing the things George did. They can today, but that's because the rules on tackling have changed so much," he says. "He was that good he had two numbers. Everyone remembers Cruyff with 14, Pele with 10. It tells you how brilliant George was that you can wear number seven or 11 at Manchester United and you're following Best. He is the best of all time. I loved Cruyff, I have loved watching Messi, but George for me was every bit his family name."

Rodney Marsh's superlatives are similar. "He was quicker than everybody else. He could jump higher than everybody else. He was braver... there was just no weakness to him. His concentration as a player was just out of this world."

Then there is the summary of Chris Dangerfield, who had the rare privilege of sharing a training pitch and dressing room with both Best and Cruyff. "Whenever anyone ever does a poll of the greatest ever Earthquakes players, George's name is always mentioned," he says. "And he played for them for all of five minutes, in reality. He just made such an impact and a large part of it was because of that goal. As an individual, technically, he was the greatest.

"I played with Johan Cruyff for a couple of years. He had the technical knowledge to be what the coach wanted him to be at any given time. If we were winning 2-1, for example, Cruyff would assume a different role and give out instructions to the rest of us. If we were losing 2-1 he'd give out different instructions and move himself into centre-forward. George wouldn't do that – he would basically get the ball and do it himself. From an individual perspective, George was the best. The balance, the ability to change direction, the ability to use both feet and the internal desire he had to compete and win the ball against you. He would go in for the tackle and the headers… he was just complete."

Because the praise is so effusive, and our perception of footballers generally rests within our learned limitations, we apply it to how we understand it. If someone said a defender is a complete player we think of Franz Beckenbauer or Paolo Maldini. If they refer to Messi as a complete player we consider that the attacking side of his game didn't have a weakness and discount the fact he was not a player who could retrieve the ball. This is not a slight at one of the greatest, it's because we don't expect a player who plays in attack to be able to do that. This is the crucial difference with George Best and any other player. Limitations did not apply. Completion was absolute.

Paddy Barclay's conclusion brings to mind those earlier remarks from Bill Foulkes about how Best could have "excelled in any position".

"He was as naturally gifted as any player I've ever seen… I saw Maradona and Messi and George was the most naturally gifted player," Barclay says. "I am not saying he was better. But he had all of the ability that they had. Perhaps what he didn't have was the capability to harness that to a team. There was never a period of time where we saw him develop that attribute, that final piece of the jigsaw which would have removed the question of whether he would have been the greatest.

"And we'll never know that. Everybody knows about the dribbling and the great goals. One of my great memories of George came when I was standing in the Scoreboard End for a game between Manchester United and Liverpool. Liverpool won a corner. Up came Ron Yeats. Now, Ron was his middle name. His first name was Big. He was a 6ft 2in former slaughter man from Aberdeen. He had a tremendous physique. Upon his signing from Dundee United, Bill Shankly invited reporters to take a conducted tour around his new centre-half. That's how impressive a colossus he was.

"Peter Thompson's delivery was good, just where Yeats would have wanted it. I might be a little romantic with my memory but I'm sure I saw Yeats' neck muscles flex as he prepared to head the ball. Just as he was about to apply the finish, this red elfin took off, rose above Yeats – who must have been nine or 10 feet off the ground – and headed the ball away so confidently that it cleared the penalty area. He was of slight and elegant build but he was quite a physical specimen. George was complete in every aspect. If you told George he would have to play an entire season at right-back he would have been the best right-back in the league. There's no question about that."

Barclay has another personal memory of George away from the pitch. He explains: "As a young reporter in late 1968 I convinced *The Guardian* to give me a column for their Scottish edition. There was a player at Dundee called Billy Campbell who played on the other wing to George for Northern Ireland. They'd just defeated Turkey 4-0 in a brilliant vibrant performance at Windsor Park led by the wingers.

"As I was based in Manchester I thought what a great idea it would be to do a feature on Billy, and to interview George for it. George was the best player in the world at the time, just about to receive the award of European Footballer of the Year. I rang Manchester United and asked if I could interview him. They said they would pass the message on and I was welcome to wait at the Cliff for him after training.

"The players came out, the European champions, one by one. I was a little bit starstruck and then along came George wearing a fashionable roll-neck jumper and his hair beautifully styled. I introduced myself. He seemed quite keen to get out but as I said I was from *The Guardian* he stopped for a moment as something flickered in his memory. Although he seemed a little reluctant, he sat down to talk. I got out my pen and notepad, shaking with nerves. Imagine, you have the opportunity to interview the greatest player in the world. My first question: 'So, George, what do you think of Billy Campbell?'

"He paused. He obviously wasn't expecting that! But he answered it fairly, explaining how Billy could be a real asset to the team. I wrote it down. 'What do you think are Billy's best attributes?' Looking back I think what an opportunity it was to launch my career and all I'm doing is asking questions like these. 'Do you think he's got any drawbacks?' He must have thought I was taking the piss.

"The point is he had all the time in the world for somebody who was a nobody and he was the best in the world. He patiently answered everything. He was a lovely human being. A very nice young man. I saw the sunny side of his character."

It is important these personal recollections are put forward, whilst also remembering the purpose for them. Those reminders are plentiful today. In May 2006 Belfast City Airport was renamed George Best Belfast City Airport with a ceremony on what would have been George's 60th birthday. In 2008 – the day after United won their third European Cup – a statue was unveiled on the forecourt outside Old Trafford, where the figure of Best stands to the right of Denis Law and Bobby Charlton. In May 2019, on what would have been his 73rd birthday, another statue of George was unveiled, at Windsor

Park in Belfast. There are plenty of places to pay homage. The reason most people knew George was because he had moved to Manchester, became a professional footballer, and became one of the most famous footballers in the world. That's why Sir Matt Busby got to know him. When considering the most apt way to summarise Busby's fondness for George, there's perhaps no better quote than the statement he made on *This Is Your Life* in 1971.

"In any era there are geniuses come along, whatever phase of life you're in," Busby said. "Every century a super-genius comes along. And this is what George Best is in football today. If you just look at the two feet there. They pass the ball, they dribble the ball, they shoot the ball, and of course he's got this appetite for the game. He's got all the quality of balance which is phenomenal. He's very good in the air. A tremendous heart. Most important of all he's got a great temperament. There are periods of matches just before kick-off where players are kicking the ball and getting all excited. George will be in the corner reading the programme as if it's a Sunday school meeting. George Best is a football magician."

Jimmy Murphy was always even more liberal than Busby with his plaudits for the players he had helped develop. "George Best goes out on to the pitch to prove himself the best in the business," he said in 1968. "He stamps his authority on the game no matter where he plays. Tom [Finney] never forced his personality so strongly. If he was playing outside-right and the ball didn't get to him, he would often stay rigidly on the touchline until play reached his sector of the field. The essential difference is that George Best is always in the game. If he is beaten he chases back and tackles with the ferocity of a Nobby Stiles. I don't think Matt Busby's comment on Best can be bettered when he said, 'George Best is possibly the greatest player on the ball I have ever seen. You can think of Finney, Matthews… and all the great players of that era, but I cannot think of one that took the ball so close to an opponent to beat him with it as Best does.'

"This boy lives for his football. I think he would play a league match every day, and I have never known such a fantastically hard trainer. He has incredibly powerful legs and is well muscled. He has the facility to beat a player on the left or on the right with consummate ease. If a movement breaks down he is one of a few forwards who has a surge of annoyance, and comes racing back snapping for the ball like a terrier. He hates losing the ball. The boss says Bobby Charlton improved his game as he became more mature. I say wait five more years when Best has matured. The prospects for this boy are beyond imagination. I honestly don't think we have seen the best of Best by a long, long way."

Beyond imagination.

Within the realm of all the things impossible to even dream when it comes to what could or should have been, at least one thing is definite. In a perfect world George Best would have spent his entire career at Manchester United. There are the obvious thoughts which follow – more league titles, more European Cups, more European Footballer of the Year awards. Then all the memories which are impossible for us to imagine George would have left us with, because only he could provide them, and even he didn't know how those moments would arrive sometimes. Things changed over time. His enthusiasm for the game changed. But his love for the Old Trafford club never went away and it never weakened.

"I said that football was his one true love but that was

linked 100 per cent to Manchester United. George Best loved Manchester United," Rodney Marsh says."He lived and died for them. He told me many times how much he loved them, and how much everything afterwards was an anti-climax."

He was romantic when it came to his old club. He spoke glowingly of Ryan Giggs when the Welshman was breaking through the United ranks and was being compared due to his balance and natural dribbling style. When Cristiano Ronaldo arrived and was given the number seven shirt, Best remarked: "There have been a few players described as the new George Best over the years, but this is the first time it's been a compliment to me." He also once said: "I'd give all the champagne I've ever drunk to play in a European match at Old Trafford alongside Eric Cantona."

Cantona is interesting because there is only Best who has the same sort of cult status with Manchester United supporters. There are other greats, but those two stand alone, undoubtedly due to two factors – their unpredictability and their brilliance. One of the most profound reasons for Cantona's success at United was Sir Alex Ferguson's indulgence of him. It was clearly something George thought about. He wondered how he and Ferguson would have got on. "If he had been in charge of me, maybe he would have come and grabbed me when I went missing and things might not have turned out the way they did," he said.

Evidence, again, supports either side of that argument. Norman Whiteside, Paul McGrath and Bryan Robson are three of the most naturally gifted players Manchester United have ever had. One was indispensable to Ferguson. The other two were made examples of.

George himself placed so great an emphasis on what might

have been that he probably encouraged the narrative. That's because he yearned for what was lost – the competitor in him was not satisfied with what he had accomplished. Those reflections and recriminations for George always came back to Old Trafford. To the Cliff. And ultimately to Wembley, the night of his greatest triumph and arguably his greatest source of angst.

And it's only right that should be the case, because George is there. He is there, so much better than anyone else that it is beyond comprehension. It's so far beyond superlatives that the only thing to do is to relay the events in plain English and trust that you can believe.

He's there, at the Cliff, in the mind of Jimmy Rimmer playing a practice match against Oldham: "He scored seven or eight goals. I watched him take the ball past five or six players on a run, and then, he brought the ball back to the halfway line, took on two more, and then scored. There is no exaggeration there – that's exactly what he did."

He's there, at Old Trafford, in the memory of David Gaskell, lobbing the ball over Pat Jennings: "It was an impossible chip. He was unbelievable. The things he could do… I don't even think he knew he was doing them half the time. I don't ever remember him going to any extra effort in training to do this sort of thing, he was just one of the lads, and it came instinctively. George was the perfect player. The best I played with."

He's there at Wembley, scoring the most important goal in Manchester United history, beaming on television into the home of many Belfast boys, like Sammy McIlroy, giving them hope as well as the dream: "He's the best I ever played with. The history of Manchester United has seen some wonderful players, before my era and after my era. But I would argue

George is the greatest that there has been. The brilliance he had. The stick he used to take. The players he played against. He was a showman – he was still always talking about wanting to try different things. He wanted to show everyone what he was all about. Extra-time, European Cup final, Wembley, he still goes around the goalkeeper and puts it in with his left foot. You've got everything attached to it. The heat. The emotion. And he still does what George Best does naturally, fit as anything. It sums him up."

He's there.

Dropping his left shoulder.

Enticing the goalkeeper.

Making the goalkeeper think he's got a chance.

Scoring the goal.

Raising his right hand.

Wearing a smile of relief, delight and self-satisfaction.

There's George Best.

True genius.

Beyond imagination.

George Best career statistics

Manchester United Junior, Youth and Reserve Team Games

<u>61/62 A Team (* denotes supplementary competition)</u>

Date	Opponent	Comp	Score	Goals	Number
9/9/61	Stockport A (H)	A*	W2-1		8
17/2/62	Stockport A (H)	A	W7-0		8
3/3/62	Blackpool A (H)	A	L2-4		7
14/4/62	Everton A (A)	A	W3-1	2	8
17/4/62	Liverpool A (H)	A	L0-2		8

<u>61/62 B Team</u>

Date	Opponent	Comp	Score	Goals	Number
23/9/61	Oldham A (H)	B*	W2-0		8
30/9/61	Bury B (A)	B*	W5-1	1	8
7/10/61	Tranmere A (A)	B	W3-1		8
14/10/61	Bury B (H)	B	W1-0		7
28/10/61	Man City B (A)	B*	L1-2		8
11/11/61	Oldham A (A)	B	L1-4		8
18/11/61	Burnley B (H)	B	W2-0		8
25/11/61	Blackburn B (H)	B	D1-1		8
6/1/62	Man City B (A)	B	W4-2		7
13/1/62	Bury B (A)	B	W4-0		8
20/1/62	Rochdale A (A)	B	W10-1	2	8
27/1/62	Blackpool B (A)	B	L2-3	1	8
10/2/62	Oldham A (H)	B	L1-2	1	8
24/2/62	Liverpool B (A)	B	D1-1		7
10/3/62	Everton B (H)	B	L0-4		8
17/3/62	Rochdale A (H)	B	D3-3		8
24/3/62	Bolton B (H)	B	W2-0	1	8
31/3/62	Rochdale A (H)	B*	W5-0	2	10
7/4/62	Blackburn B (A)	B	W5-2		8
12/4/62	Man City B (H)	B	W2-1		8
28/4/62	Burnley B (A)	B	W4-0	1	7
30/4/62	Bolton B (H)	B	W2-0	1	8

<u>62/63 A Team</u>

Date	Opponent	Comp	Score	Goals	Number
24/11/62	Preston A (A)	A	W3-0	2	10
1/12/62	Man City A (H)	A*	W1-0		8
8/12/62	Liverpool A (A)	A	L0-1		8
15/12/62	Burnley A (H)	A*	W4-2		8
23/3/63	Burnley A (A)	A	L2-4	2	8
6/4/63	Preston A (H)	A	W8-2	1	7
11/4/63	Tranmere A (A)	A	W2-1		7
13/4/63	Blackpool A (A)	A	D1-1		7
18/4/63	Tranmere A (H)	A	W4-2	2	7
27/4/63	Liverpool A (H)	A	W6-4		11

STATISTICS

62/63 B team

Date	Opponent	Comp	Score	Goals	Number
18/8/62	Burnley B (H)	B*	L0-2		8
25/8/62	Burnley B (A)	B	L2-5	1	8
1/9/62	Man City B (A)	B*	W6-0		8
15/9/62	Burnley B (A)	B*	W4-3	1	8
29/9/62	Bury B (H)	B*	W5-0		8
6/10/62	Rochdale A (H)	B*	W4-1	2	8
13/10/62	Bolton B (A)	B	W3-1	2	8
20/10/62	Rochdale A (A)	B*	D1-1	1	8
3/11/62	Bury B (H)	B	W2-1		8
10/11/62	Everton B (A)	B	D2-2		8
26/12/62	Blackburn B (H)	B	W1-0	1	8
23/2/63	Oldham A (H)	B	D1-1		10
2/3/63	Bury B (A)	B	W8-2	2	8
9/3/63	Man City B (A)	B	W7-0	4	8
16/3/63	Bolton B (H)	B*	W3-0	2	7
30/3/63	Everton B (H)	B	D2-2	1	8
2/5/63	Man City B (H)	B	W4-0	2	8
21/5/63	Oldham A (A)	B	L0-2		8

FA YOUTH CUP 62/63

Date	Opponent	Comp	Score	Goals	Number
24/4/63	Newcastle (H)		W3-0		11
30/4/63	Sheff Wed (A)		L0-2		7

63/64 A Team

Date	Opponent	Comp	Score	Goals	Number
19/10/63	Preston A (A)	A	W2-1	1	7
26/10/63	Rochdale Reserves (H)	A	W5-1		10
2/11/63	Man City A (H)	A*	L2-3	1	7
30/11/63	Burnley A (A)	A	W6-2	3	7
7/12/63	Tranmere A (H)	A	W10-1	2	8

FA YOUTH CUP 63/64

Date	Opponent	Comp	Score	Goals	Number
18/12/63	Barrow (H)		W14-1	3	8
8/4/64	Man City (H)		W4-1		8
20/4/64	Man City (A)		W4-3	1	8
27/4/64	Swindon (A)		D1-1	1	8
30/4/64	Swindon (H)		W4-1		8

63/64 Reserve Team (CL - Central League)

Date	Opponent	Comp	Score	Goals	Number
24/8/63	Sheff Wed (H)	CL	W4-0		11
26/8/63	Chesterfield (A)	CL	D1-1		11
7/9/63	West Brom (H)	CL	D1-1	1	7
9/9/63	Blackpool (A)	CL	W2-0		11
21/9/63	Huddersfield (H)	CL	W3-1		7
2/10/63	Man City (H)	CL	D2-2	1	7
12/10/63	Blackburn (A)	CL	D1-1	1	11
9/11/63	Aston Villa (A)	CL	L1-2		7

Manchester United First Team Senior Games

63/64

Date	Opponent	Comp	Score	Goals	Number
14/9/63	West Brom (H)	Div 1	W1-0		7
28/12/63	Burnley (H)	Div 1	W5-1	1	11
4/1/64	Southampton (A)	FAC	W3-2		11
11/1/64	Birmingham (H)	Div 1	L1-2		11
18/1/64	West Brom (A)	Div 1	W4-1	1	11
25/1/64	Bristol City (H)	FAC	W4-1		11
1/2/64	Arsenal (H)	Div 1	W3-1		11
8/2/64	Leicester (A)	Div 1	L2-3		11
15/2/64	Barnsley (A)	FAC	W4-0	1	11
19/2/64	Bolton (H)	Div 1	W5-0	2	11
22/2/64	Blackburn (A)	Div 1	W3-1		11
26/2/64	Sporting Lisbon(H)	ECWC	W4-1		11
29/2/64	Sunderland (H)	FAC	D3-3	1	11
4/3/64	Sunderland (A)	FAC	D2-2		11
9/3/64	Sunderland (N)	FAC	W5-1		11
14/3/64	West Ham (N)	FAC	L1-3		11
18/3/64	Sporting Lisbon(A)	ECWC	L0-5		11
21/3/64	Spurs (A)	Div 1	W3-2		7
23/3/64	Chelsea (H)	Div 1	D1-1		7
27/3/64	Fulham (A)	Div 1	D2-2		7
28/3/64	Wolves (H)	Div 1	D2-2		7
4/4/64	Liverpool (A)	Div 1	L0-3		7
6/4/64	Aston Villa (H)	Div 1	W1-0		7
13/4/64	Sheff Utd (H)	Div 1	W2-1		7
18/4/64	Stoke City (A)	Div 1	L1-3		7
25/4/64	Nottm Forest(H)	Div 1	W3-1		7

64/65

Date	Opponent	Comp	Score	Goals	Number
22/8/64	West Brom (H)	Div 1	D2-2		11
24/8/64	West Ham (A)	Div 1	L1-3		11
29/8/64	Leicester (A)	Div 1	D2-2		11
2/9/64	West Ham (H)	Div 1	W3-1	1	11
5/9/64	Fulham (A)	Div 1	L1-2		11
8/9/64	Everton (A)	Div 1	D3-3		11
12/9/64	Nottm Forest (H)	Div 1	W3-0		11
16/9/64	Everton (H)	Div 1	W2-1	1	11
19/9/64	Stoke City (A)	Div 1	W2-1		11
23/9/64	Djurgardens (A)	IC FC	D1-1		11
26/9/64	Spurs (H)	Div 1	W4-1		11
30/9/64	Chelsea (A)	Div 1	W2-0	1	11
6/10/64	Burnley (A)	Div 1	D0-0		11
10/10/64	Sunderland (H)	Div 1	W1-0		11
17/10/64	Wolves (A)	Div 1	W4-2		11
24/10/64	Aston Villa (H)	Div 1	W7-0		11
27/10/64	Djurgardens (H)	IC FC	W6-1	1	11
31/10/64	Liverpool (A)	Div 1	W2-0		11
7/11/64	Sheff Wed (H)	Div 1	W1-0		11
11/11/64	Dortmund (A)	IC FC	W6-1	1	11
21/11/64	Blackburn (H)	Div 1	W3-0	1	11
28/11/64	Arsenal (A)	Div 1	W3-2		11
2/12/64	Dortmund (H)	IC FC	W4-0		11
5/12/64	Leeds (H)	Div 1	L0-1		11

12/12/64	West Brom (A)	Div 1	D1-1		11
16/12/64	Birmingham (H)	Div 1	D1-1		11
26/12/64	Sheff Utd (A)	Div 1	W1-0	1	11
28/12/64	Sheff Utd (H)	Div 1	D1-1		11
9/1/65	Chester (H)	FAC	W2-1	1	11
16/1/65	Nottm Forest (A)	Div 1	D2-2		11
20/1/65	Everton (H)	IC FC	D1-1		11
23/1/65	Stoke (H)	Div 1	D1-1		11
30/1/65	Stoke (A)	FAC	D0-0		11
3/2/65	Stoke (H)	FAC	W1-0		11
6/2/65	Spurs (A)	Div 1	L0-1		11
9/2/65	Everton (A)	IC FC	W2-1		11
13/2/65	Burnley (H)	Div 1	W3-2	1	11
20/2/65	Burnley (H)	FAC	W2-1		11
24/2/65	Sunderland (A)	Div 1	L0-1		11
27/2/65	Wolves (H)	Div 1	W3-0		11
10/3/65	Wolves (A)	FAC	W5-3	1	11
13/3/65	Chelsea (H)	Div 1	W4-0	1	11
15/3/65	Fulham (H)	Div 1	W4-1		11
20/3/65	Sheff Wed (A)	Div 1	L0-1		11
22/3/65	Blackpool (H)	Div 1	W2-0		11
27/3/65	Leeds (N)	FAC	D0-0		11
31/03/65	Leeds (N)	FAC	L0-1		11
3/4/65	Blackburn (A)	Div 1	W5-0		11
12/4/65	Leicester (H)	Div 1	W1-0		10
17/4/65	Leeds (H)	Div 1	W1-0		11
19/4/65	Birmingham (A)	Div 1	W4-2	2	11
24/4/65	Liverpool (H)	Div 1	W3-0		11
26/4/65	Arsenal (H)	Div 1	W3-1	1	11
28/4/65	Aston Villa (A)	Div 1	L1-2		11
12/5/65	Strasbourg (A)	IC FC	W5-0		11
19/5/65	Strasbourg (H)	IC FC	D0-0		11
31/5/65	Ferencvaros (H)	IC FC	W3-2		11
6/6/65	Ferencvaros (A)	IC FC	L0-1		11
16/6/65	Ferencvaros (A)	IC FC	L1-2		11

65/66

Date	Opponent	Comp	Score	Goals	Number
14/8/65	Liverpool (H)	CS	D2-2	1	7
21/8/65	Sheff Wed (H)	Div 1	W1-0		10
24/8/65	Nottm Forest (A)	Div 1	L2-4	1	10
28/8/65	Northampton (A)	Div 1	D1-1		11
1/9/65	Nottm Forest (H)	Div 1	D0-0		11
4/9/65	Stoke (H)	Div 1	D1-1		11
8/9/65	Newcastle (A)	Div 1	W2-1		11
11/9/65	Burnley (A)	Div 1	L0-3		11
15/9/65	Newcastle (H)	Div 1	D1-1		11
6/10/65	Helsinki (H)	EC	W6-0	2	8
9/10/65	Liverpool (H)	Div 1	W2-0	1	8
16/10/65	Spurs (A)	Div 1	L1-5		8
23/10/65	Fulham (H)	Div 1	W4-1		8
30/10/65	Blackpool (A)	Div 1	W2-1		8
6/11/65	Blackburn (H)	Div 1	D2-2		7
13/11/65	Leicester (A)	Div 1	W5-0	1	7
17/11/65	ASK Vorwarts (A)	EC	W2-0		7
20/11/65	Sheff Utd (H)	Div 1	W3-1	2	7

1/12/65	ASK Vorwarts (H)	EC	W3-1		7
4/12/65	West Ham (H)	Div 1	D0-0		7
11/12/65	Sunderland (A)	Div 1	W3-2	2	7
15/12/65	Everton (H)	Div 1	W3-0	1	7
18/12/65	Spurs (H)	Div 1	W5-1		7
27/12/65	West Brom (H)	Div 1	D1-1		7
1/1/66	Liverpool (A)	Div 1	L1-2		7
8/1/66	Sunderland (H)	Div 1	D1-1	1	7
12/1/66	Leeds (A)	Div 1	D1-1		7
15/1/66	Fulham (A)	Div 1	W1-0		7
22/1/66	Derby (A)	FAC	W5-2	2	7
29/1/66	Sheff Wed (A)	Div 1	D0-0		7
2/2/66	Benfica (H)	EC	W3-2		7
5/2/66	Northampton (H)	Div 1	W6-2		7
12/2/66	Rotherham (H)	FAC	D0-0		7
15/2/66	Rotherham (A)	FAC	W1-0		7
19/2/66	Stoke (A)	Div 1	D2-2		8
26/2/66	Burnley (H)	Div 1	W4-2		7
5/3/66	Wolves (A)	FAC	W4-2	1	7
9/3/66	Benfica (A)	EC	W5-1	2	7
12/3/66	Chelsea (A)	Div 1	L0-2		7
19/3/66	Arsenal (H)	Div 1	W2-1		7
26/3/66	Preston (A)	FAC	D1-1		7
9/4/66	Leicester (H)	Div 1	L1-2		7
13/4/66	Partizan (A)	EC	L0-2		7

66/67

Date	Opponent	Comp	Score	Goals	Number
20/8/66	West Brom (H)	Div 1	W5-3	1	7
23/8/66	Everton (A)	Div 1	W2-1		7
27/8/66	Leeds (A)	Div 1	L1-3	1	7
31/8/66	Everton (H)	Div 1	W3-0		11
3/9/66	Newcastle (H)	Div 1	W3-2		11
7/9/66	Stoke (A)	Div 1	L0-3		11
10/9/66	Spurs (A)	Div 1	L1-2		7
14/9/66	Blackpool (A)	LC	L1-5		8
17/9/66	Man City (H)	Div 1	W1-0		7
24/9/66	Burnley (H)	Div 1	W4-1		11
1/10/66	Nottm Forest (A)	Div 1	L1-4		7
8/10/66	Blackpool (A)	Div 1	W2-1		11
15/10/66	Chelsea (H)	Div 1	D1-1		11
29/10/66	Arsenal (H)	Div 1	W1-0		11
5/11/66	Chelsea (A)	Div 1	W3-1	1	11
12/11/66	Sheff Wed (H)	Div 1	W2-0		11
19/11/66	Southampton (A)	Div 1	W2-1		11
26/11/66	Sunderland (H)	Div 1	W5-0		7
30/11/66	Leicester (A)	Div 1	W2-1	1	7
3/12/66	Aston Villa (A)	Div 1	L1-2		7
10/12/66	Liverpool (H)	Div 1	D2-2	2	7
17/12/66	West Brom (A)	Div 1	W4-3		7
26/12/66	Sheff Utd (A)	Div 1	L1-2		7
27/12/66	Sheff Utd (H)	Div 1	W2-0		7
31/12/66	Leeds (H)	Div 1	D0-0		7
14/1/67	Spurs (H)	Div 1	W1-0		7
21/1/67	Man City (A)	Div 1	D1-1		11
28/1/67	Stoke (H)	FAC	W2-0		7

Date	Opponent	Comp	Score	Goals	Number
4/2/67	Burnley (A)	Div 1	D1-1		7
11/2/67	Nottm Forest (H)	Div 1	W1-0		7
18/2/67	Norwich (H)	FAC	L1-2		11
25/2/67	Blackpool (H)	Div 1	W4-0		7
3/3/67	Arsenal (A)	Div 1	D1-1		7
11/3/67	Newcastle (A)	Div 1	D0-0		7
18/3/67	Leicester (H)	Div 1	W5-2		7
25/3/67	Liverpool (A)	Div 1	D0-0		7
27/3/67	Fulham (A)	Div 1	D2-2	1	7
28/3/67	Fulham (H)	Div 1	W2-1		7
1/4/67	West Ham (H)	Div 1	W3-0	1	7
10/4/67	Sheff Wed (A)	Div 1	D2-2		7
18/4/67	Southampton (H)	Div 1	W3-0		7
22/4/67	Sunderland (A)	Div 1	D0-0		7
29/4/67	Aston Villa (H)	Div 1	W3-1	1	7
6/5/67	West Ham (A)	Div 1	W6-1	1	7
13/5/67	Stoke (H)	Div 1	D0-0		7

67/68

Date	Opponent	Comp	Score	Goals	Number
12/8/67	Spurs (H)	CS	D3-3		7
19/8/67	Everton (A)	Div 1	L1-3		7
26/8/67	Leicester (H)	Div 1	D1-1		7
2/9/67	West Ham (A)	Div 1	W3-1		11
6/9/67	Sunderland (A)	Div 1	D1-1		11
9/9/67	Burnley (H)	Div 1	D2-2		11
16/9/67	Sheff Wed (A)	Div 1	D1-1	1	7
20/9/67	Hibernians (H)	EC	W4-0		7
23/9/67	Spurs (H)	Div 1	W3-1	2	7
27/9/67	Hibernians (A)	EC	D0-0		7
30/9/67	Man City (A)	Div 1	W2-1		7
7/10/67	Arsenal (H)	Div 1	W1-0		7
14/10/67	Sheff Utd (A)	Div 1	W3-0		7
25/10/67	Coventry (H)	Div 1	W4-0	1	7
28/10/67	Nottm Forest (A)	Div 1	L1-3	1	7
4/11/67	Stoke (H)	Div 1	W1-0		10
8/11/67	Leeds (A)	Div 1	L0-1		10
11/11/67	Liverpool (A)	Div 1	W2-1	2	10
15/11/67	Sarajevo (A)	EC	D0-0		10
18/11/67	Southampton (H)	Div 1	W3-2		10
25/11/67	Chelsea (A)	Div 1	D1-1		10
29/11/67	Sarajevo (H)	EC	W2-1	1	10
2/12/67	West Brom (H)	Div 1	W2-1	2	10
9/12/67	Newcastle (A)	Div 1	D2-2		10
16/12/67	Everton (H)	Div 1	W3-1		7
23/12/67	Leicester (A)	Div 1	D2-2		7
26/12/67	Wolves (H)	Div 1	W4-0	2	7
30/12/67	Wolves (A)	Div 1	W3-2		7
6/1/68	West Ham (H)	Div 1	W3-1	1	7
20/1/68	Sheff Wed (H)	Div 1	W4-2	2	7
27/1/68	Spurs (H)	FAC	D2-2	1	7
31/1/68	Spurs (A)	FAC	L0-1		7
3/2/68	Spurs (A)	Div 1	W2-1	1	7
17/2/68	Burnley (A)	Div 1	L1-2	1	7
24/2/68	Arsenal (A)	Div 1	W2-0	1	7
28/2/68	Gornik Zabrze (H)	EC	W2-0		7

2/3/68	Chelsea (H)	Div 1	L1-3		7
13/3/68	Gornik Zabrze (A)	EC	L0-1		11
16/3/68	Coventry (A)	Div 1	L0-2		7
23/3/68	Nottm Forest (H)	Div 1	W3-0		10
27/3/68	Man City (H)	Div 1	L1-3	1	10
30/3/68	Stoke (A)	Div 1	W4-2	1	7
6/4/68	Liverpool (H)	Div 1	L1-2	1	7
12/4/68	Fulham (A)	Div 1	W4-0	2	7
13/4/68	Southampton (A)	Div 1	D2-2	1	7
15/4/68	Fulham (H)	Div 1	W3-0	1	7
20/4/68	Sheff Utd (H)	Div 1	W1-0		7
24/4/68	Real Madrid (H)	EC	W1-0	1	7
29/4/68	West Brom (A)	Div 1	L3-6		7
4/5/68	Newcastle (H)	Div 1	W6-0	3	7
11/5/68	Sunderland (H)	Div 1	L1-2	1	7
15/5/68	Real Madrid (A)	EC	D3-3		7
29/5/68	Benfica (N)	EC	W4-1	1	7

68/69

Date	Opponent	Comp	Score	Goals	Number
10/8/68	Everton (H)	Div 1	W2-1	1	7
14/8/68	West Brom (A)	Div 1	L1-3		7
17/8/68	Man City (A)	Div 1	D0-0		7
21/8/68	Coventry (H)	Div 1	W1-0		11
24/8/68	Chelsea (H)	Div 1	L0-4		11
28/8/68	Spurs (H)	Div 1	W3-1		11
31/8/68	Sheff Wed (A)	Div 1	L4-5	1	11
7/9/68	West Ham (H)	Div 1	D1-1		11
14/9/68	Burnley (A)	Div 1	L0-1		11
18/9/68	Waterford (A)	EC	W3-1		7
21/9/68	Newcastle (H)	Div 1	W3-1	2	11
25/9/68	Estudiantes (A)	IC	L0-1		11
2/10/68	Waterford (H)	EC	W7-1		7
5/10/68	Arsenal (H)	Div 1	D0-0		11
9/10/68	Spurs (A)	Div 1	D2-2		11
16/10/68	Estudiantes (H)	IC	D1-1		11
19/10/68	Southampton (H)	Div 1	L1-2	1	11
26/10/68	QPR (A)	Div 1	W3-2	2	11
2/11/68	Leeds (H)	Div 1	D0-0		11
9/11/68	Sunderland (A)	Div 1	D1-1		11
16/11/68	Ipswich (H)	Div 1	D0-0		11
23/11/68	Stoke (A)	Div 1	D0-0		8
30/11/68	Wolves (H)	Div 1	W2-0	1	11
7/12/68	Leicester (A)	Div 1	L1-2		11
14/12/68	Liverpool (H)	Div 1	W1-0		7
21/12/68	Southampton (A)	Div 1	L0-2		7
26/12/68	Arsenal (A)	Div 1	L0-3		7
4/1/69	Exeter (A)	FAC	W3-1		7
11/1/69	Leeds (A)	Div 1	L1-2		7
18/1/69	Sunderland (H)	Div 1	W4-1	1	11
25/1/69	Watford (H)	FAC	D1-1		8
1/2/69	Ipswich (A)	Div 1	L0-1		11
3/2/69	Watford (A)	FAC	W2-0		11
8/2/69	Birmingham (A)	FAC	D2-2	1	11
15/2/69	Wolves (A)	Div 1	D2-2	1	11
24/2/69	Birmingham (H)	FAC	W6-2		11

26/2/69	Rapid Vienna (H)	EC	W3-0	2	11
1/3/69	Everton (A)	FAC	L0-1		11
5/3/69	Rapid Vienna (A)	EC	D0-0		11
8/3/69	Man City (H)	Div 1	L0-1		11
10/3/69	Everton (A)	Div 1	D0-0		7
15/3/69	Chelsea (A)	Div 1	L2-3		11
19/3/69	QPR (H)	Div 1	W8-1	2	11
22/3/69	Sheff Wed (H)	Div 1	W1-0	1	9
24/3/69	Stoke (H)	Div 1	D1-1		11
29/3/69	West Ham (A)	Div 1	D0-0		11
31/3/69	Nottm Forest (A)	Div 1	W1-0	1	11
2/4/69	West Brom (H)	Div 1	W2-1	2	11
5/4/69	Nottm Forest (H)	Div 1	W3-1	1	11
8/4/69	Coventry (A)	Div 1	L1-2		11
12/4/69	Newcastle (A)	Div 1	L0-2		11
19/4/69	Burnley (H)	Div 1	W2-0		11
23/4/69	AC Milan (A)	EC	L0-2		11
15/5/69	AC Milan (H)	EC	W1-0		11
17/5/69	Leicester (H)	Div 1	W3-2	1	11

69/70

Date	Opponent	Comp	Score	Goals	Number
9/8/69	Crystal Palace (A)	Div 1	D2-2		11
13/8/69	Everton (H)	Div 1	L0-2		11
16/8/69	Southampton (H)	Div 1	L1-4		11
19/8/69	Everton (A)	Div 1	L0-3		10
23/8/69	Wolves (A)	Div 1	D0-0		11
27/8/69	Newcastle (H)	Div 1	D0-0		11
30/8/69	Sunderland (H)	Div 1	W3-1	1	11
3/9/69	Middlesbrough (H)	LC	W1-0		11
6/9/69	Leeds (A)	Div 1	D2-2	2	11
13/9/69	Liverpool (H)	Div 1	W1-0		11
17/9/69	Sheff Wed (A)	Div 1	W3-1	2	11
20/9/69	Arsenal (A)	Div 1	D2-2	1	11
23/9/69	Wrexham (H)	LC	W2-0	1	11
27/9/69	West Ham (H)	Div 1	W5-2	2	11
4/10/69	Derby (A)	Div 1	L0-2		11
8/10/69	Southampton (A)	Div 1	W3-0	1	11
11/10/69	Ipswich (H)	Div 1	W2-1	1	11
14/10/69	Burnley (A)	LC	D0-0		11
18/10/69	Nottm Forest (H)	Div 1	D1-1	1	11
20/10/69	Burnley (H)	LC	W1-0	1	11
25/10/69	West Brom (A)	Div 1	L1-2		11
1/11/69	Stoke (H)	Div 1	D1-1		11
8/11/69	Coventry (A)	Div 1	W2-1		8
12/11/69	Derby (A)	LC	D0-0		8
15/11/69	Man City (A)	Div 1	L0-4		8
19/11/69	Derby (H)	LC	W1-0		7
22/11/69	Spurs (H)	Div 1	W3-1		10
29/11/69	Burnley (A)	Div 1	D1-1	1	7
3/12/69	Man City (A)	LC	L1-2		7
6/12/69	Chelsea (H)	Div 1	L0-2		7
13/12/69	Liverpool (A)	Div 1	W4-1		8
17/12/69	Man City (H)	LC	D2-2		11
26/12/69	Wolves (H)	Div 1	D0-0		11
27/12/69	Sunderland (A)	Div 1	D1-1		11

Date	Opponent	Comp	Score	Goals	Number
3/1/70	Ipswich (A)	FAC	W1-0		11
7/2/70	Northampton (A)	FAC	W8-2	6	11
10/2/70	Ipswich (A)	Div 1	W1-0		11
14/2/70	Crystal Palace (H)	Div 1	D1-1		11
21/2/70	Middlesbrough (A)	FAC	D1-1		11
25/2/70	Middlesbrough (H)	FAC	W2-1		11
28/2/70	Stoke (A)	Div 1	D2-2		11
14/3/70	Leeds (N)	FAC	D0-0		11
17/3/70	Burnley (H)	Div 1	D3-3	1	11
21/3/70	Chelsea (A)	Div 1	L1-2		11
23/3/70	Leeds (N)	FAC	D0-0		11
26/3/70	Leeds (N)	FAC	L0-1		11
28/3/70	Man City (H)	Div 1	L1-2		11
30/3/70	Coventry (H)	Div 1	D1-1		8
31/3/70	Nottm Forest (A)	Div 1	W2-1		11
8/4/70	West Brom (H)	Div 1	W7-0	1	11
10/4/70	Watford (N)	FAC	W2-0		11
13/4/70	Spurs (A)	Div 1	L1-2		11
15/4/70	Sheff Wed (H)	Div 1	D2-2	1	11

70/71

Date	Opponent	Comp	Score	Goals	Number
1/8/70	Reading (A)	WC	W3-2		11
5/8/70	Hull City (A)	WC	D1-1		11
8/8/70	Derby (A)	WC	L1-4	1	11
15/8/70	Leeds (H)	Div 1	L0-1		11
19/8/70	Chelsea (H)	Div 1	D0-0		11
22/8/70	Arsenal (A)	Div 1	L0-4		11
25/8/70	Burnley (A)	Div 1	W2-0		11
29/8/70	West Ham (H)	Div 1	D1-1		11
2/9/70	Everton (H)	Div 1	W2-0	1	11
5/9/70	Liverpool (A)	Div 1	D1-1		11
9/9/70	Aldershot (A)	LC	W3-1	1	11
12/9/70	Coventry (H)	Div 1	W2-0	1	11
19/9/70	Ipswich (A)	Div 1	L0-4		11
26/9/70	Blackpool (H)	Div 1	D1-1	1	11
3/10/70	Wolves (A)	Div 1	L2-3		11
7/10/70	Portsmouth (H)	LC	W1-0		11
10/10/70	Crystal Palace (H)	Div 1	L0-1		8
17/10/70	Leeds (A)	Div 1	D2-2		8
24/10/70	West Brom (H)	Div 1	W2-1		8
28/10/70	Chelsea (H)	LC	W2-1	1	8
31/10/70	Newcastle (A)	Div 1	L0-1		8
7/11/70	Stoke (H)	Div 1	D2-2		8
14/11/70	Nottm Forest (A)	Div 1	W2-1		8
18/11/70	Crystal Palace (H)	LC	W4-2		8
21/11/70	Southampton (A)	Div 1	L0-1		8
28/11/70	Huddersfield (H)	Div 1	D1-1	1	8
5/12/70	Spurs (A)	Div 1	D2-2	1	8
12/12/70	Man City (H)	Div 1	L1-4		8
16/12/70	Aston Villa (H)	LC	D1-1		8
19/12/70	Arsenal (H)	Div 1	L1-3		8
23/12/70	Aston Villa (A)	LC	L1-2		8
26/12/70	Derby (A)	Div 1	D4-4	1	8
2/1/71	Middlesbrough (H)	FAC	D0-0		8
5/1/71	Middlesbrough (A)	FAC	L1-2	1	8

30/1/71	Huddersfield (A)	Div 1	W2-1		11
6/2/71	Spurs (H)	Div 1	W2-1	1	11
20/2/71	Southampton (H)	Div 1	W5-1		8
23/2/71	Everton (A)	Div 1	L0-1		8
27/2/71	Newcastle (H)	Div 1	W1-0		8
6/3/71	West Brom (A)	Div 1	L3-4	1	8
13/3/71	Nottm Forest (H)	Div 1	W2-0	1	8
20/3/71	Stoke (A)	Div 1	W2-1	2	8
3/4/71	West Ham (A)	Div 1	L1-2	1	8
10/4/71	Derby (H)	Div 1	L1-2		8
12/4/71	Wolves (H)	Div 1	W1-0		7
13/4/71	Coventry (A)	Div 1	L1-2	1	7
17/4/71	Crystal Palace (A)	Div 1	W5-3	2	7
19/4/71	Liverpool (H)	Div 1	L0-2		7
24/4/71	Ipswich (H)	Div 1	W3-2	1	11
1/5/71	Blackpool (A)	Div 1	D1-1		11
5/5/71	Man City (A)	Div 1	W4-3	2	11

_71/72_

Date	Opponent	Comp	Score	Goals	Number
31/7/71	Halifax (A)	WC	L1-2	1	11
14/8/71	Derby (A)	Div 1	D2-2		11
18/8/71	Chelsea (A)	Div 1	W3-2		11
20/8/71	Arsenal (H)*	Div 1	W3-1		11
23/8/71	West Brom (H)*	Div 1	W3-1	2	10
28/8/71	Wolves (A)	Div 1	D1-1	1	11
31/8/71	Everton (A)	Div 1	L0-1		11
4/9/71	Ipswich (H)	Div 1	W1-0	1	10
7/9/71	Ipswich (A)	LC	W3-1	2	10
11/9/71	Crystal Palace (A)	Div 1	W3-1		11
18/9/71	West Ham (H)	Div 1	W4-2	3	11
25/9/71	Liverpool (A)	Div 1	D2-2		11
2/10/71	Sheff Utd (H)	Div 1	W2-0	1	10
6/10/71	Burnley (H)	LC	D1-1		10
9/10/71	Huddersfield (A)	Div 1	W3-0	1	11
16/10/71	Derby (H)	Div 1	W1-0	1	11
18/10/71	Burnley (A)	LC	W1-0		11
23/10/71	Newcastle (A)	Div 1	W1-0	1	11
27/10/71	Stoke (H)	LC	D1-1		11
30/10/71	Leeds (H)	Div 1	L0-1		11
6/11/71	Man City (A)	Div 1	D3-3		11
8/11/71	Stoke (A)	LC	D0-0		11
13/11/71	Spurs (H)	Div 1	W3-1		11
15/11/71	Stoke (A)	LC	L1-2	1	11
20/11/71	Leicester (H)	Div 1	W3-2		11
27/11/71	Southampton (A)	Div 1	W5-2	3	11
4/12/71	Nottingham Forest (H)	Div 1	W3-2		11
11/12/71	Stoke (A)	Div 1	D1-1		11
18/12/71	Ipswich (A)	Div 1	D0-0		11
27/12/71	Coventry (H)	Div 1	D2-2		11
1/1/72	West Ham (A)	Div 1	L0-3		11
15/1/72	Southampton (A)	FAC	D1-1		11
19/1/72	Southampton (H)	FAC	W4-1	2	11
22/1/72	Chelsea (H)	Div 1	L0-1		11
29/1/72	West Brom (A)	Div 1	L1-2		11
5/2/72	Preston (A)	FAC	W2-0		11

12/2/72	Newcastle (H)	Div 1	L0-2		11
19/2/72	Leeds (A)	Div 1	L1-5		11
26/2/72	Middlesbrough (H)	FAC	D0-0		11
29/2/72	Middlesbrough (A)	FAC	W3-0	1	11
4/3/72	Spurs (A)	Div 1	L0-2		11
8/3/72	Everton (H)	Div 1	D0-0		11
11/3/72	Huddersfield (H)	Div 1	W2-0	1	10
18/3/72	Stoke (H)	FAC	D1-1	1	11
22/3/72	Stoke (A)	FAC	L1-2	1	11
25/3/72	Crystal Palace (H)	Div 1	W4-0		7
1/4/72	Coventry (H)	Div 1	W3-2	1	8
3/4/72	Liverpool (H)	Div 1	L0-3		8
4/4/72	Sheff Utd (A)	Div 1	D1-1		7
8/4/72	Leicester (A)	Div 1	L0-2		7
12/4/72	Man City (H)	Div 1	L1-3		7
15/4/72	Southampton (H)	Div 1	W3-2	1	7
25/4/72	Arsenal (A)	Div 1	L0-3		7
29/4/72	Stoke (H)	Div 1	W3-0	1	7

72/73

Date	Opponent	Comp	Score	Goals	Number
12/8/72	Ipswich (H)	Div 1	L1-2		7
15/8/72	Liverpool (A)	Div 1	L0-2		10
19/8/72	Everton (A)	Div 1	L0-2		10
23/8/72	Leicester (H)	Div 1	D1-1	1	10
26/8/72	Arsenal (H)	Div 1	D0-0		10
30/8/72	Chelsea (H)	Div 1	D0-0		10
2/9/72	West Ham (A)	Div 1	D2-2	1	10
6/9/72	Oxford (A)	LC	D2-2		10
9/9/72	Coventry (H)	Div 1	L0-1		10
12/9/72	Oxford (H)	LC	W3-1	2	10
16/9/72	Wolves (A)	Div 1	L0-2		10
23/9/72	Derby (H)	Div 1	W3-0		10
30/9/72	Sheff Utd (A)	Div 1	L0-1		10
3/10/72	Bristol Rovers (A)	LC	D1-1		10
7/10/72	WBA (A)	Div 1	D2-2	1	10
11/10/72	Bristol Rovers (H)	LC	L1-2		10
14/10/72	Birmingham (H)	Div 1	W1-0		10
21/10/72	Newcastle (A)	Div 1	L1-2		10
28/10/72	Spurs (H)	Div 1	L1-4		10
4/11/72	Leicester (A)	Div 1	D2-2	1		7
11/11/72	Liverpool (H)	Div 1	W2-0		7
18/11/72	Man City (A)	Div 1	L0-3		7
25/11/72	Southampton (H)	Div 1	W2-1		7

73/74 (Reserve Team - Central League

Date	Opponent	Comp	Score	Goals	Number
6/10/73	Aston Villa (H)	CL	L0-2		7

73/74 First Team

Date	Opponent	Comp	Score	Goals	Number
20/10/73	Birmingham (H)	Div 1	W1-0		11
27/10/73	Burnley (A)	Div 1	D0-0		11
3/11/73	Chelsea (H)	Div 1	D2-2		11
10/11/73	Spurs (A)	Div 1	L1-2	1	11
17/11/73	Newcastle (A)	Div 1	L2-3		11

24/11/73	Norwich (H)	Div 1	D0-0		11
8/12/73	Southampton (H)	Div 1	D0-0		11
15/12/73	Coventry (H)	Div 1	L2-3	1	11
22/12/73	Liverpool (A)	Div 1	L0-2		11
26/12/73	Sheff Utd (H)	Div 1	L1-2		11
29/12/73	Ipswich (H)	Div 1	W2-0		11
1/1/74	QPR (A)	Div 1	L0-3		11

Jewish Guild

Date	Opponent	Comp	Score	Goals	Number
31/5/74	Hellenic (H)	League	D1-1		11
2/6/74	Durban City (A)	League	W2-0		11
5/6/74	Hellenic (A)	League	L1-5		11
7/6/74	Durban Utd (H)	League	L1-2	1	11

Stockport County 75/76

Date	Opponent	Comp	Score	Goals	Number
28/11/75	Swansea (H)	Div 4	W3-2	1	7
12/12/75	Watford (H)	Div 4	D2-2	1	11
26/12/75	Southport (H)	Div 4	W1-0		11

Cork Celtic 75/76

Date	Opponent	Comp	Score	Goals	Number
28/12/75	Drogheda Utd (H)	BLI	L0-2		10
11/1/76	Bohemians (H)	BLI	W1-0		9
18/1/76	Shelbourne (A)	BLI	L1-2		7

LA Aztecs 1976 - NASL

Date	Opponent	Comp	Score	Goals	Number
17/4/76	San Jose Earthquakes (A)		L1-2		11
25/4/76	Rochester Lancers (H)		W1-0	1	11
2/5/76	San Diego Jaws (H)		W2-0	1	11
8/5/76	San Antonio Thunder (A)		L2-3		11
9/5/76	Seattle Sounders (H)		W4-3	1	11
14/5/76	Philadelphia Atoms (A)		W2-1		11
17/5/76	New York Cosmos (A)		L0-6		11
2/6/76	Toronto Metros-Croatia (A)		L0-2		11
5/6/76	Portland Timbers (H)		W1-0	1	11
12/6/76	Vancouver Whitecaps (H)		W2-1	1	11
19/6/76	Tampa Bay Rowdies (H)		W2-1	2	11
20/6/76	Dallas Tornado (A)		L6-3	2	11
26/6/76	Minnesota Kicks (H)		L0-1		11
3/7/76	San Antonio Thunder (A)		L1-2		11
5/7/76	Portland Timbers (A)		W2-1		11
10/7/76	St. Louis Stars (H)		W2-1	1	11
16/7/76	San Diego Jaws (A)		W2-1	1	11
18/7/76	Boston Minutemen (H)		W8-0	3	11
23/7/76	Vancouver Whitecaps (A)		L1-2		11
25/7/76	San Jose Earthquakes (H)		L0-1		11
31/7/76	Seattle Sounders (A)		L0-1		11
10/8/76	Minnesota Kicks (A)		L2-6		11
14/8/76	Dallas Tornado (H)		W4-1	1	11
18/8/76	Dallas Tornado (A)	(Play-off)	L0-2		11

Fulham 76/77

Date	Opponent	Comp	Score	Goals	Number
4/9/76	Bristol Rovers (H)	Div 2	W1-0	1	7

7/9/76	Peterborough (A)	LC	W2-1	1	7
11/9/76	Wolves (H)	Div 2	D0-0		7
18/9/76	Luton (A)	Div 2	W2-0		7
22/9/76	Bolton (H)	LC	D2-2	1	7
25/9/76	Hereford (H)	Div 2	W4-1		7
2/10/76	Southampton (A)	Div 2	L4-1		7
16/10/76	Sheff Utd (A)	Div 2	D1-1		7
18/10/76	Bolton (N)	LC	L1-2		7
23/10/76	Hull City (H)	Div 2	D0-0		7
30/10/76	Bolton (A)	Div 2	L1-2	1	7
6/11/76	Cardiff (H)	Div 2	L1-2	1	7
13/11/76	Plymouth (A)	Div 2	D2-2		7
16/11/76	Carlisle (H)	Div 2	W2-0		7
20/11/76	Notts County (H)	Div 2	L1-5		7
27/11/76	Blackpool (A)	Div 2	L2-3		7
4/12/76	Oldham (H)	Div 2	W5-0	1	7
11/12/76	Orient (A)	Div 2	D0-0		7
14/12/76	Blackburn (H)	Div 2	W2-0	1	7
27/12/76	Chelsea (A)	Div 2	L0-2		7
3/1/77	Bolton (H)	Div 2	L0-2		7
8/1/77	Swindon (H)	FAC	D3-3		7
11/1/77	Swindon (A)	FAC	L0-5		7
15/1/77	Burnley (H)	Div 2	D2-2		7
22/1/77	Nottm Forest (A)	Div 2	L0-3		7
5/2/77	Charlton (H)	Div 2	D1-1		7
12/2/77	Bristol Rovers (A)	Div 2	L1-2		7
19/2/77	Wolves (A)	Div 2	L1-5		7
2/4/77	Hull City (A)	Div 2	L0-1		7
8/4/77	Chelsea (H)	Div 2	W3-1	1	7
9/4/77	Millwall (A)	Div 2	D0-0		7
11/4/77	Plymouth (H)	Div 2	W2-0		7
16/4/77	Notts County (A)	Div 2	D0-0		7
23/4/77	Blackpool (H)	Div 2	D0-0		7
30/4/77	Oldham (A)	Div 2	L0-1		7
7/5/77	Orient (H)	Div 2	W6-1		7
14/5/77	Blackburn (A)	Div 2	L0-1		7

Fulham Reserves 76/77 (Football Combination League)

Date	Opponent	Comp	Score	Goals	Number
4/4/1977	Hereford (H)		L1-3		10

LA Aztecs 1977 - NASL

Date	Opponent	Comp	Score	Goals	Number
20/5/77	Portland Timbers (A)		L0-1		11
22/5/77	Vancouver Whitecaps (H)		W3-1		11
28/5/77	Seattle Sounders (A)		W2-1	1	11
30/5/77	St. Louis Stars (H)		W3-2	1	11
5/6/77	Dallas Tornado (H)		W4-3	1	11
12/6/77	Las Vegas Quicksilver (H)		W3-0	1	11
19/6/77	Minnesota Kicks (A)		W3-2	1	11
22/6/77	Rochester Lancers (A)		L3-4		11
26/6/77	New York Cosmos (A)		L2-5	1	11
29/6/77	Connecticut Bi-Centenn (A)		W3-2		11
2/7/77	New York Cosmos (H)		W4-1		11
4/7/77	Toronto Metros-Croatia (H)		L0-2		11
9/7/77	Washington Diplomats (A)		W4-2		11
13/7/77	Tampa Bay Rowdies (A)		L1-4		11

17/7/77	Fort Lauderdale Strikers (H)		L1-3		11
22/7/77	Team Hawaii (A)		L5-6	1	11
27/7/77	Las Vegas Quicksilver (A)		W3-2	1	11
30/7/77	San Jose Earthquakes (H)		L2-3	1	11
4/8/77	Vancouver Whitecaps (A)		W2-0	1	11
7/8/77	Seattle Sounders (H)		L2-4	1	11
10/8/77	San Jose Earthquakes (H)	(Play-off)	W2-1	1	11
14/8/77	Dallas Tornado (H)	(Play-off)	W3-1		11
17/8/77	Dallas Tornado (A)	(Play-off)	W5-1	1	11
21/8/77	Seattle Sounders (H)	(Play-off)	L1-3		11
25/8/77	Seattle Sounders (A)	(Play-off)	L0-1		11

Fulham 77/78

Date	Opponent	Comp	Score	Goals	Number
3/9/77	Blackburn (H)	Div 2	D0-0		7
24/9/77	Cardiff (A)	Div 2	L1-3		7
26/9/77	St. Mirren (A)	ASC	L3-5	1	7
1/10/77	Crystal Palace (A)	Div 2	W3-2		7
4/10/77	Burnley (H)	Div 2	W4-1	1	7
8/10/77	Blackpool (H)	Div 2	D1-1		7
15/10/77	Luton (A)	Div 2	L0-1		7
22/10/77	Orient (H)	Div 2	L1-2		7
29/10/77	Sheff Utd (A)	Div 2	L1-2		7
5/11/77	Sunderland (H)	Div 2	D3-3	1	7
12/11/77	Stoke (A)	Div 2	L0-2		7

LA Aztecs 1978 - NASL

Date	Opponent	Comp	Score	Goals	Number
2/4/78	Houston Hurricane (H)		L2-3		11
9/4/78	New York Cosmos (H)		L0-1		11
16/4/78	California Surf (A)		W4-1		11
22/4/78	Fort Lauderdale Strikers (A)		L0-2		11
30/4/78	Oakland Stompers (H)		L1-2		11
7/5/78	Seattle Sounders (H)		L0-2		11
18/5/78	Tulsa Roughnecks (A)		W1-0		11
27/5/78	Colorado Caribous (A)		W2-1		11
29/5/78	Portland Timbers (H)		L1-4	1	11
7/6/78	Portland Timbers (A)		L0-1		11
17/6/78	California Surf (H)		W2-1		11
20/6/78	Washington Diplomats (A)		L0-4		11

Fort Lauderdale Strikers 1978 - NASL

Date	Opponent	Comp	Score	Goals	Number
24/6/78	New York Cosmos (H)		W5-3	2	3
28/6/78	Memphis Rogues (A)		W2-1		3
1/7/78	San Jose Earthquakes (A)		W1-0		3
4/7/78	Toronto Metros-Croatia (H)		W4-0		3
9/7/78	Houston Hurricane (A)		W2-1		3
12/7/78	California Surf (A)		L0-5		3
19/7/78	New England Tea Men (A)		W2-0		3
30/7/78	Detroit Express (A)		L2-4	1	3
4/8/78	Rochester Lancers (H)		W2-1	1	3
9/8/78	New England Tea Men (A)	(Play-off)	W3-1		3
13/8/78	Detroit Express (H)	(Play-off)	W4-3		3
16/8/78	Detroit Express (A)	(Play-off)	L0-1		3
20/8/78	Tampa Bay Rowdies (H)	(Play-off)	W3-2	1	3
23/8/78	Tampa Bay Rowdies (A)	(Play-off)	L1-3		3

Ford Lauderdale Strikers 1979 - NASL

Date	Opponent	Comp	Score	Goals	Number
31/3/79	New England Tea Men (H)		W2-0		3
8/4/79	Toronto Blizzard (A)		W2-1		3
14/4/79	Washington Diplomats (H)		L0-4		3
22/4/79	New York Cosmos (A)		L2-3		3
28/4/79	Tampa Bay Rowdies (H)		L1-2		3
5/5/79	Philadelphia Fury (A)		L1-2		3
12/5/79	Toronto Blizzard (H)		W4-0		3
26/5/79	Memphis Rogues (H)		W3-1		3
16/6/79	San Jose Earthquakes (H)		W3-1		3
20/6/79	Tulsa Roughnecks (H)		W3-2	1	3
23/6/79	Tampa Bay Rowdies (A)		W2-1		3
27/6/79	Detroit Express (A)		L2-8		3
4/7/79	Chicago Sting (H)		L2-3		3
7/7/79	San Jose Earthquakes (A)		W2-1		3
11/7/79	San Diego Sockers (A)		W3-2		3
14/7/79	Rochester Lancers (A)		L1-2		3
18/7/79	New York Cosmos (H)		L3-4		3
21/7/79	Portland Timbers (A)		L1-4	1	3
25/7/79	California Surf (A)		W6-3		3

Hibernian 1979/80

Date	Opponent	Comp	Score	Goals	Number
24/11/79	St. Mirren (A)	SPD	L1-2	1	11
1/12/79	Patrick Thistle (H)	SPD	W2-1		11
22/12/79	Rangers (H)	SPD	W2-1		11
5/1/80	Kilmarnock (A)	SPD	L1-3		11
12/1/80	Celtic (H)	SPD	D1-1	1	11
26/1/80	Meadowbank Th (N)	SFAC	W1-0		11
1/3/80	Rangers (A)	SPD	L0-1		11
8/3/80	Berwick Rangers (A)	SFAC	D0-0		11
15/3/80	Dundee (A)	SPD	L0-3		11
25/3/80	Dundee (H)	SPD	W2-0	1	11
29/3/80	Celtic (A)	SPD	L0-4		11
2/4/80	Dundee Utd (H)	SPD	L0-2		11
5/4/80	St. Mirren (A)	SPD	L0-2		11
12/4/80	Celtic (N)	SFAC	L0-5		11
16/4/80	Aberdeen (A)	SPD	D1-1		11
19/4/80	Dundee Utd (H)	SPD	L0-2		11

San Jose Earthquakes 1980 - NASL

Date	Opponent	Comp	Score	Goals	Number
27/4/80	Edmonton Drillers (A)		L2-4		11
30/4/80	San Diego Sockers (H)		L2-3		11
3/5/80	Seattle Sounders (A)		L0-4		11
10/5/80	New England Tea Men (H)		L0-1		11
15/5/80	Edmonton Drillers (H)		W1-0		11
17/5/80	Houston Hurricane (H)		W3-0		11
24/5/80	Portland Timbers (A)		L1-2		11
7/6/80	Vancouver Whitecaps (H)		W2-0		11
11/6/80	Detroit Express (A)		W1-0		11
14/6/80	Philadelphia Fury (H)		W2-1	1	11
17/6/80	Fort Lauderdale Strikers (A)		L0-4		11
22/6/80	Washington Diplomats (A)		L4-5	1	11
26/6/80	Toronto Blizzard (A)		L2-3		11
29/6/80	California Surf (H)		W5-1	1	11

2/7/80	Dallas Tornado (H)		L1-2		11
5/7/80	New England Tea Men (A)		L1-3		11
9/7/80	Tampa Bay Rowdies (A)		L1-4		11
12/7/80	Atlanta Chiefs (A)		W2-1		11
16/7/80	Tampa Bay Rowdies (H)		L0-3		11
19/7/80	Vancouver Whitecaps (A)		L1-4		11
30/7/80	Memphis Rogues (H)		L0-1		11
9/8/80	Chicago Sting (A)		L1-4	1	11
12/8/80	Memphis Rogues (A)		L0-1		11
16/8/80	Portland Timbers (H)		L2-3	2	11
20/8/80	San Diego Sockers (A)		W3-2	1	11
23/8/80	Los Angeles Aztecs (H)		L1-2	1	11

Hibernian 1980/81

Date	Opponent	Comp	Score	Goals	Number
9/9/80	Dundee (A)	SD1	W2-1		11
20/9/80	Hamilton Acad (A)	SD1	D1-1		11
24/9/80	Clyde (H)	SLC	W2-1		11
4/10/80	Dunfermline (A)	SD1	W2-0		11
8/10/80	Ayr Utd (A)	SLC	D2-2		11
11/10/80	Falkirk (H)	SD1	W2-0		11

San Jose Earthquakes 1981 - NASL

Date	Opponent	Comp	Score	Goals	Number
29/3/81	New York Cosmos (H)		L0-3		11
5/4/81	Los Angeles Aztecs (A)		L0-1		11
12/4/81	Jacksonville Tea Men (H)		W3-0		11
19/4/81	San Diego Sockers (H)		W2-1	1	11
26/4/81	California Surf (H)		L0-1		11
2/5/81	San Diego Sockers (A)		L2-4	1	11
6/5/81	Portland Timbers (A)		L0-3		11
10/5/81	Edmonton Drillers (H)		W1-0		11
15/5/81	California Surf (A)		W2-1	1	11
19/5/81	Atlanta Chiefs (A)		L0-2		11
24/5/81	Calgary Boomers (A)		L0-1		11
27/5/81	Los Angeles Aztecs (H)		W3-2		11
31/5/81	Calgary Boomers (H)		W4-3	2	11
7/6/81	Tampa Bay Rowdies (H)		W2-1		11
14/6/81	Edmonton Drillers (A)		L2-6		11
17/6/81	Atlanta Chiefs (H)		W3-1	1	11
20/6/81	Seattle Sounders (A)		L0-1		11
24/6/81	California Surf (A)		L0-7		11
27/6/81	Los Angeles Aztecs (H)		L1-2	1	11
1/7/81	Vancouver Whitecaps (H)		L1-5		11
4/7/81	Fort Lauderdale Strikers (A)		L1-4		11
8/7/81	Tampa Bay Rowdies (A)		L2-4	1	11
11/7/81	Jacksonville Tea Men (A)		L3-4	1	11
15/7/81	Montreal Manic (A)		L0-4		11
22/7/81	Fort Lauderdale Strikers (H)		W3-2	2	11
25/7/81	Los Angeles Aztecs (A)		L0-3		11
1/8/81	Portland Timbers (H)		L1-2	1	11
5/8/81	San Diego Sockers (A)		L0-3		11
15/8/81	San Diego Sockers (H)		L2-3	1	11
19/8/81	Vancouver Whitecaps (A)		L1-3		11

Bournemouth 82/83

Date	Opponent	Comp	Score	Goals	Number
26/3/83	Newport County (H)	Div 3	L0-1		7
9/4/83	Chesterfield (H)	Div 3	W2-1		7
16/4/83	Southend (A)	Div 3	D0-0		7
23/4/83	Lincoln (H)	Div 3	W1-0		7
7/5/83	Wigan Athletic (H)	Div 3	D2-2		7

Brisbane Lions 1983

Date	Opponent	Comp	Score	Goals	Number
3/7/83	Sydney Olympic (H)	NSLA	W2-1		7
8/7/83	St George B'pest* (H)	NSLA	L0-3		7
10/7/83	Marconi (A)	NSLA	D1-1		7
17/7/83	Adelaide City** (H)	NSLA	L0-4		7

Tobermore United 1984

Date	Opponent	Comp	Score	Goals	Number
9/2/84	Ballymena Utd (H)	BIC		L0-7	7

Northern Ireland - Youth International

Date	Opponent	Comp	Score	Goals	Number
11/5/62	England (A)		D1-1		10
18/5/62	Wales (A)		D1-1	1	10

Northern Ireland - Full International

Date	Opponent	Comp	Score	Goals	Number
15/4/64	Wales (A)	HI	W3-2		7
29/4/64	Uruguay (H)	F	W3-0		7
3/10/64	England (H)	HI	L3-4		7
14/10/64	Switzerland (H)	WCQ	W1-0		7
14/11/64	Switzerland (A)	WCQ	L1-2	1	7
25/11/64	Scotland (A)	HI	L2-3		7
17/3/65	Holland (H)	WCQ	W2-1		11
7/4/65	Holland (A)	WCQ	D0-0		7
7/5/65	Albania (H)	WCQ	W4-1	1	11
2/10/65	Scotland (H)	HI	W3-2		11
10/11/65	England (A)	HI	L1-2		11
24/11/65	Albania (A)	WCQ	D1-1		11
22/10/66	England (H)	ENCQ	L0-2		11
21/10/67	Scotland (H)	HI	W1-0		11
23/10/68	Turkey (H)	WCQ	W4-1	1	11
3/5/69	England (H)	HI	L1-3		11
6/5/69	Scotland (A)	HI	D1-1		7
10/5/69	Wales (H)	HI	D0-0		7
10/9/69	USSR (H)	WCQ	D0-0		11
18/4/70	Scotland (H)	HI	L0-1		11
21/4/70	England (A)	HI	L1-3	1	8
25/4/70	Wales (A)	HI	L0-1		8
11/11/70	Spain (A)	ENCQ	L0-3		8
3/2/71	Cyprus (A)	ENCQ	W3-0	1	11
21/4/71	Cyprus (H)	ENCQ	W5-0	3	11
15/5/71	England (H)	HI	L0-1		11
18/5/71	Scotland (A)	HI	W1-0		11
22/5/71	Wales (H)	HI	W1-0		11
22/9/71	USSR (A)	ENCQ	L0-1		11
16/2/72	Spain (N)	ENCQ	D1-1		11
18/10/72	Bulgaria (A)	WCQ	L0-3		11

14/11/73	Portugal (A)	WCQ	D1-1	11
13/10/76	Holland (A)	WCQ	D2-2	7
10/11/76	Belgium (A)	WCQ	L0-2	7
27/4/77	West Germany (A)	F	L0-5	7
21/9/77	Iceland (H)	WCQ	W2-0	10
12/10/77	Holland (H)	WCQ	L0-1	10

Competitions reference legend
FAC = English FA Cup
LC = English League Cup
CS = Charity Shield
IC FC = Inter Cities Fairs Cup
EC = European Cup
IC = Intercontinental Cup
WC = Watney Cup
BLI = Bass League of Ireland
ASC = Anglo-Scottish Cup
BIC = Bass Irish Cup
SPD = Scottish Premier Division
SFAC = Scottish FA Cup
SD1 = Scottish Division One
SLC = Scottish League Cup
NSLA = National Soccer League of Australia
HI = Home International
F = International Friendly
WCQ = World Cup Qualifier
ENCQ = European Nations Cup (European Championship) Qualifier

Bibliography

Blessed – The Autobiography (George Best – Random House)
George Best – Hard Tackles and Dirty Baths
(George Best – Random House)
The Best of Both Worlds (George Best – Corgi)
A Strange Kind of Glory (Eamon Dunphy – Aurum Press)
After The Ball – My Autobiography
(Nobby Stiles – Hodder & Stoughton)
Matt... United... And Me (Jimmy Murphy – Souvenir Press)
Sir Matt Busby: The Man Who Made a Football Club
(Patrick Barclay – Ebury Press)
Our George – A Family Memoir of George Best
(Barbara Best/Lindy McDowell – Pan)
Soccer at the Top: My Life in Football (Matt Busby – Sphere)
Docherty: Living Legend of Football (Brian Clarke – Mandarin)
Manchester United Football Book series
(David Meek – Stanley Paul)
My Manchester United (Bobby Charlton – Headline)
After The Ball (Nobby Stiles – Hodder)
Manchester United Man And Babe
(Wilf McGuinness – Know The Score)